THE INVENTION OF ROBER

THE INVENTION
OF ROBERT BRESSON

The Auteur and His Market

Colin Burnett

Indiana University Press

Bloomington and Indianapolis

This book is a publication of

Indiana University Press
Office of Scholarly Publishing
Herman B Wells Library 350
1320 East 10th Street
Bloomington, Indiana 47405 USA

iupress.indiana.edu

Manufactured in the United States of America

Cataloging information is available from the Library of Congress.

ISBN 978-0-253-02469-5 (cloth)
ISBN 978-0-253-02486-2 (paperback)
ISBN 978-0-253-02501-2 (ebook)

1 2 3 4 5 22 21 20 19 18 17

for Carol and Norman

To direct attention to the artist's market invites misunderstanding. There are those who resent any suggestion that the artist is not an absolute spirit pursuing his aesthetical way like a bird: they will read any proposition about the relation between artist and market as a coarse innuendo about artists following a style because it is profitable. . . .

But the artist need never become a creature of the market: he may choose which of the briefs he will take up, and he responds to some of its suggestions, ignores others, and sometimes turns yet others on their heads in a pointed way. Artists who get along in a market, and most of the ones we know about did so, manifest their brief and in it general social facts, as well as current ideas about art.

—Michael Baxandall,
The Limewood Sculptors of Renaissance Germany

Contents

Acknowledgments

I VIEW THIS BOOK as a testament to the power stubborn hunches often hold over the life of an academic. For roughly eighteen years, since I was an undergraduate student at Concordia University in Montréal, I've been riding a single hunch—that the cinema of Robert Bresson could be more effectively grounded in history. Many deserve thanks for helping me turn a hunch into a dissertation, and now a dissertation into a book.

In 1998, Edmund Egan, my professor of philosophical aesthetics, recommended Susan Sontag's "Spiritual Style in the Films of Robert Bresson." I read it—repeatedly. It was a defining experience. Two of her ideas set my mind abuzz (and continue to do so today): Bresson's is a reflective art that holds emotional payoffs in abeyance, and the tradition to which it belongs is poorly understood.

Concordia University is where the search for answers about this tradition first began to yield results. I am particularly grateful to my mentors there. Martin Lefebvre taught me the importance of methodological precision and lucidity, and of asking, why does this matter? John W. Locke generously committed to an independent study on Bresson's cinematographers when neither one of us was certain it would lead anywhere. Virginia Nixon introduced me to the work of Michael Baxandall, which proved to be pivotal years later. Peter Rist showed enthusiasm for my first paper on Bresson, and encouraged me to pursue an MA on the strength of it. Donato Totaro published my first piece on Bresson. And I had many long conversations about Bresson (and much else) with fellow MA students Michael Baker, Brian Crane, Santiago Hidalgo, Farbod Honarpisheh, Randolph Jordan, Chris Meir, and Adam Rosadiuk, and each left a lasting impression.

At the University of Wisconsin–Madison, my early findings grew into a dissertation project. Kristin Thompson and David Bordwell encouraged me to be creative as I expanded the range of my primary materials, shared their views on various art-historical approaches, and opened many doors. Lea Jacobs bolstered my commitment to close analysis. My dissertation committee—Jeff Smith, Ben Singer, Vance Kepley Jr., and Barbara Buenger—consistently pushed the project toward fresh avenues of film and art-historical research. I owe a special debt of gratitude to my advisor, Kelley Conway. Her extensive knowledge of France and of French film history and scholarship helped me make new connections and develop confidence as I dove deeper and deeper into the circumstantial matter. *Merci infiniment!*

My fellow Badgers endured my prattling on about Bresson for years. I hope they know how much I picked up from them—all passionate lovers of ideas and movies: Masha Belodubrovskya, Casey Coleman, Brandon Colvin, Kyle Conway, Kaitlyn Fyfe, Heather Heckman, Jonah Horwitz, Derek Johnson, Charlie Michael, Mark Minett, Sreya Mitra, John Powers, Matt Sienkiewicz, Josh Shepperd, Jake Smith, Katherine Spring, Dave Resha, and Brad Schauer.

My colleagues and students at Washington University in St. Louis, where I have been since 2011, created nothing short of ideal conditions for converting the dissertation into a book. Gaylyn Studlar, William Paul, Todd Decker, Jennifer Kapcynski, and Julia Walker read earlier versions of the manuscript and provided vital feedback. Robert Hegel, Diane Lewis, Philip Sewell, and Ignacio Sánchez Prado all generously shared their thoughts about the challenges of book publishing and much else. The final stages of research benefited from the intrepidity of Melissa Forbes, Eloisa Monteoliva, Carly Schulman, and Claudia Vaughn. And I would be remiss not to give special thanks to Rebecca Wanzo, a dear colleague and friend who at every phase of the revision process pressed me to think big—and then bigger—about the implications of my ideas and the reach of my findings. There's a Québécois expression: *je me souviens.*

Over the last decade, I've been lucky enough to benefit from feedback and encouragement from a number of colleagues in French film studies. Susan Hayward had kind words for my research way back at the 2005 Studies in French Cinema conference, and it was a considerable boost. Phil Powrie kindly walked a young MA student through some of the basics of scholarly publishing. James Quandt included an earlier version of chapter 1 in *Robert Bresson (Revised)*—a singular honor—and has allowed me to pick his brain about French cinema ever since. Dudley Andrew has shared numerous research materials over the years, and offered reassuring comment on an article that formed the basis of chapter 2. Richard Neupert read every word of the manuscript and reminded me at a crucial moment to think of the reader. And the two "anonymous" readers, Tim Palmer and Brian Price, provided sage advice that challenged me to clarify my intervention and—the best recommendation any author could hope for—to do what I do best.

I've taken several research trips to Paris over the years and been greeted with warmth and hospitality—despite my clunky *accent d'Québecker*. At the Bibliothèque du Film, archivist Valdo Kneubuhler and his patient team put up with my irritatingly frequent photocopy requests and assisted me in uncovering more than I could have imagined about the production history of Bresson's films. Many, many thanks are due to Jonathan Hourigan, who opened the most important door of them all, provided line-by-line commentary on my first scholarly article on Bresson, and continues to impress with his generosity and knowledge of all things Bresson. Sidney Jézéquel clarified for me the importance of his uncle,

Roger Leenhardt, to the postwar era, and provided important resources for and feedback on parts of chapter 2. And Mylène Bresson kindly hosted me for lunch on several occasions, countenanced my impassioned quibbling over the details of her husband's legacy, and helped me steer clear of error on several points.

Support from various Canadian institutions pushed things along here and there. I benefited from a Social Sciences and Humanities Research Council of Canada doctoral fellowship. Over the course of several summers, the archivists at the Cinémathèque Québécoise facilitated my discovery of several important texts. The Montréal-based Advanced Research Team on History and Epistemology of Moving Image Studies (ARTHEMIS) provided me a forum to present the book's argument at its 2010 conference. *Doublement merci à Martin!* And *La boîte noire*'s extensive catalogue of VHS tapes and DVDs allowed me to embark upon my initial *tours du France* on film. The day it closed marked the end of an era in Montréal film culture.

Writing a first book—especially one that veers off the beaten path of the conventional "director's study"—is much less a feat when you have the backing of a patient and rigorous editor like Raina Polivka of Indiana University Press. Raina and her impressive team—especially Janice Frisch!—made the last leg of this "hunch pursuit" as rewarding and smooth as I could have hoped.

Finally, thanks are due to my family. Lunches with my aunt Loraine reminded me to keep my feet on the ground *and* to go on dreaming large. Every day I am reminded that my brothers James and Sean do things so that I can go on being the impractical, hunch-driven, nose-buried-in-his-dusty-books academic. And my mother and father, Carol and Norman, to whom this book is dedicated: Your affection and guidance have been indispensable. Whenever I doubted this little gamble of following my hunches and making a career of them, I would think of your unstinting support, and the thought alone would set my nerves at ease and encourage me to go on taking risks.

THE INVENTION OF ROBERT BRESSON

Introduction

Why continue to study the auteur? Today, cinephiles and critics alike seem more interested in the dynamic exchanges between cinema and surrounding culture than in individual creators. Weary of celebrating the great masters, we probe the connections between film and other technologies, between meanings that emerge within media and carry across boundaries, between communities of viewers and producers, and between filmmaking and intellectual developments in philosophy, politics, and aesthetics. Why then return to a figure like the French auteur Robert Bresson (1901–1999), who distinguished himself through a creativity so private, secretive, and pure? When questions of connectivity, interactivity, hybridity, collective agency, negotiation, and various forms of cultural engagement and interface animate much of our discourse, what can the study of a director long admired for following his own aesthetic path add to the conversation?

This book contends that the auteur affords us the unique opportunity to explore the understudied connections between personal filmmaking and the cultures and practices that emerge near the fringes of the film market. It examines the auteur as a participant, albeit on unique terms, in an alternative cultural sphere invested in redefining cinema's central narrative tradition. It thus challenges the myth of the auteur as a singular genius whose style is the man himself, in the famous words of the Comte de Buffon, and calls into question traditional approaches to the auteur and their reliance on narratives of isolation.[1]

Traditional auteurists take it for granted that the auteur is a precious commodity whose very existence is owed to a natural predisposition to stand alone in opposition to prevailing production circumstances. Rooted in the famous *Cahiers du cinéma* mantra that the auteur is one who clears a distinctive path through a system rigged to deny distinctiveness, traditional auteurism concedes that auteur cinema is produced in a context of collaboration, but the value of this cinema rests in the attempt of a lone creator to express a unique personal vision that cannot be accounted for by the industrial and market conditions of negotiation and exchange imposed upon the creator.

Equally pervasive are isolation myths that protect particularly rare auteurs like Bresson from even the faintest hint of film-cultural influence. Aspects of their styles at times *resemble* other films, but their sources of inspiration are philosophers and poets rather than filmmakers. In 1957, the dramatist and filmmaker Jean Cocteau lent credence to this view by declaring that Bresson existed "apart from this terrible trade," creating works so personal and *sui generis* that they court widespread misunderstanding, except among those sensitive to non-filmic expressive traditions: "He expresses himself cinematically like a poet does with his pen. A massive obstruction separates his nobleness, his silence, his seriousness, his dreams from a world where all of this passes as indecision and idiosyncrasy."[2] Critic Amédée Ayfre, considered an authoritative voice in Bresson commentary, concurred: "Bresson, with an imperturbable disregard for the cinema around him, has only to be himself to gain quite naturally a place in the vanguard."[3] In the 1980s, another commentator, Michel Estève, wrote that Bresson created "an aesthetic system irreducible to any other [before it]."[4] Today, cinephiles and critics alike continue to celebrate auteurs like Bresson who appear to emerge without precedent or influence and produce genres unto themselves, best described by simply applying their names, to paraphrase one scholar.[5] Ultimately, only mysteries—the inscrutable complexities of philosophic and poetic inspiration—lie at the source of an art as delicate and personal as Bresson's. His small but impressive oeuvre (fourteen films made between 1934 and 1983) has little to teach us about the social and cultural forces that impinge upon the practice of filmmaking.

In Bresson's case, these assumptions could not be more mistaken. In what follows, I demonstrate that the origins of his style are best understood in light of the director's unique and timely engagement with an alternative film culture that represented a confluence of avant-garde, theoretical, literary, and cinephilic discourses and practices. Between the 1920s and 1980s, his art responded to the cultural market created within this alternative film culture, where ambitious ideas and cultivated forms of attention were exchanged in hopes of creating more stable cultural and institutional conditions for a narrative avant-garde within French cinema. In ways that commentators have yet to explore, the energetic efforts of patrons, producers, theorists, critics, and auteurs to alter the very foundations of film production and reception opened doors for Bresson, who fashioned one of the most influential and distinctive styles in the history of cinema from conceptual materials afforded by this market. To understand this meaningful trade in modes of art-making and support within Bresson's market and that of the "second cinema" of auteur films more broadly,[6] we must look past Cocteau's Romantic notion of the auteur and uncover the cultural dynamics it partially conceals.

The cultural market Bresson participated in was able to recast certain directors as visionaries or mavericks on par with the most revered of poets, musicians, painters, and novelists, in the process elevating cinema as a legitimate art in the minds of the cultural elite. Crucially, Bresson didn't resist the practices and discourses that stimulated this realignment. On the contrary, he adopted them as his own, even if the isolation myth has blinded us to that accommodation. This study therefore seeks answers to some basic questions never before posed about his cinema: How did Bresson participate in the exchange of aesthetic and intellectual ideas within alternative film culture? Did the market these cultures produced influence his art-making and vice versa? Would such an exchange reveal that his style is less personal, less *sui generis*, than previous assumed? Is it possible that, contrary to received wisdom, Bresson achieved his artistic individuality and forged the famously demanding *style bressonien* by accepting artistic challenges posed within the market? And what remains of the concept of authorial style if the auteur took his aesthetic bearings from prevailing preoccupations about art?

Although this book is devoted primarily to the cinema of Robert Bresson, I invite the reader to view it as an opportunity to rethink the role of auteur studies within the broader field of film and media criticism. A primer for newcomers to the Bresson style, this study also reconceives auteur cinema as an ideal means for exploring the deeper questions of how and why "individual" artists become implicated in communities of supportive viewers, critics, mentors, patrons, fellow travelers, and collaborators as they pursue their individuation—their own *becoming* as artists—through the medium of cinema.

The Bresson Mystery

Robert Bresson—a name that rings with mystery and paradox in contemporary film circles. For many, his cinema is so unique, personal, and inscrutable that it could not possibly have emerged from within the familiar terrain of film culture. Bresson's oeuvre is historically significant because it eschews the market-oriented climate of cinema in favor of the deepest wells of personal inspiration or artistic and intellectual traditions far removed from mere moviemaking. He is as noncinematic as an auteur of cinema gets.

Indeed, on first glance it appears that his body of work is so singular that any discussion of its origins can only lead back to the man himself. A true master, he is the innovator of a sparse and stringent style that exists without precedent. Unlike any filmmaker before him, he established cinema as a unique art form by demonstrating that it could escape its status as photographed theater. He expelled theatrical influences from his practice by training his actors, whom he called models, to defy convention by suppressing and delaying expressivity. His intimate, elliptical storytelling approach opposed conventional filmmaking by withholding access to a character's past, emotional reactions, and immediate motivations, choices that render his protagonists difficult to categorize, encouraging speculation about their spiritual or psychological mysteries. Furthermore, like no other filmmaker before him, he pared down his visuals by relying on the restrictive 50-millimeter lens, denying viewers the spectacle they normally associate with the movies and drawing attention to his idiosyncratic use of quiet, carefully mixed sound effects. Distinctively un- or even anticinematic, Bresson's films invite sympathetic reflection not excitement, sensitive cogitation not thrills.

What's more, his body of work appears to go off entirely on its own by rejecting popular cinema's preoccupation with straightforward plots and themes and creating narrative and visual experiences that pull us in irreconcilable directions. On the one hand, his cinema seems to solicit us to ponder divine presence and spiritual transcendence. His characters, through forces unseen, appear to achieve a state of grace (in the Christian sense), and his style, which strives for an anticinematic purity, seems to reach toward the ineffable. On the other, his films situate us in a world of material, even erotic, textures and relations. His protagonists are felt through their physical traumas, pleasurable pursuits, and entanglements with social forces, and his style, which strives for concreteness, seems to express an embodied experience and cue reflective thought about material realities. Conscious of the contradictory experiences elicited by his work, Bresson said of his 1956 film *Un condamné à mort s'est échappe, ou le vent souffle ou il veut*: "I was hoping to make a film about objects which would at the same time have a soul. That is to say, to reach the latter through the former."[7]

These and other formal and thematic peculiarities—inventing a cinema both material and spiritual—are thought to be uniquely Bressonian. He alone created them. And yet, other critics have argued that the distinctiveness of Bresson's cinema rests with its ambitious aesthetic and intellectual influences. Since Sacha Guitry's enthusiastic review of Bresson's first feature, *Les anges du péché* (1943), which he declared to be "much better than the movies,"[8] critics have taken it for granted that Bresson's anticinema owes little to traditions of film production and reception. By exploring his formidable philosophical, theological, or fine-arts sources, we can at least partially unlock the Bresson mystery; if properly situated in their noncinematic contexts, his films reinforce the dictum, as Michel Estève phrased it (misquoting Jean-Paul Sartre), that all artistic technique leads back to a metaphysics.[9] He calls film style to the service of ideas transposed from entirely different cultural spheres, like the writer who sets out to pen a "cinematic" novel or the comic-book artist who uses his medium to investigate Heidegger's concept of being. These artistic pathways are not merely unique in relation to the norm; they challenge accepted definitions of the medium and the distinctions between high and low culture. Bresson's art, by exploring philosophical or religious sources of inspiration that are foreign to a medium widely perceived as a form of spectacle entertainment, exposes the limited purview of the institutions of film production and reception. Tim Cawkwell crystallizes this view when he writes that Bresson's "influences were intellectual rather than cinematic and his style evolved in opposition to the common features of American and European cinema: the star system, big budgets and heavy sentiment."[10]

The "cinematic" Bresson thus awaits discovery.[11] In the meantime, it remains widely accepted that the unconventional nature of his films—their taxing austerity, their thoughtful investigations of the human spirit—rewards interpretations that move beyond filmic concepts and relationships. For many years, critics have speculated that Bresson's influences were predominantly religious in nature. Though he identified as a Christian atheist (yet another paradox!),[12] some like Henri Agel, who first proposed the idea in the 1950s,[13] have argued that Bresson embraced a Jansenist worldview, for like this seventeenth-century Catholic philosophy, his ascetic plots seem to express a commitment to divine predestination.[14] (Bresson dismissed this idea as "madness.")[15] Likewise, Amédée Ayfre and Susan Sontag see connections between Bresson's characters—isolated, uncommunicative, but often driven by an everyday project, a task, and eventually given to spontaneity—and various theological traditions, from Saint Augustine's association of freedom of action with grace, to the Christian philosopher Simone Weil's theory of grace as a movement of the soul that fills the emptiness of our disciplined lives.[16] Paul Schrader, for his part, proposes a "transcendentalist" approach that reads Bresson's work through aesthetic principles derived from medieval Scholasticism (an interest in mystery, the direct expression of ideas through form, and a synthesis of paradoxical elements) and Byzantine iconography (stripped down, flat surfaces and nonexpressive figures that serve as means to "an ineffable end").[17]

The "decinematization" of Robert Bresson has gained momentum in materialist circles as well. Recent interpretations reject the religious approach to his cinema in favor of an altogether different set of philosophical and aesthetic currents—again, largely from beyond the realm of cinema. Raymond Durgnat equates Bresson's emphasis on concrete objects—from *Pickpocket*'s (1959) many stolen watches, wallets, and purses, to *Un condamné à mort*'s spoons, which are used to chisel away at a door that allows the protagonist to escape his cell—to the New Novel of the 1950s and what James Quandt calls its descriptive *chosisme*.[18] Kent Jones seeks to return to "the aesthetic excitement and *sensual* impact of Bresson's art."[19]

"There is no spiritual or intellectual last stop" in his cinema; rather, his filmmaking draws on, and draws attention to, sensory impressions, to the sorts of encounters with the artist's perception that we "associate with spectatorship in the other arts," with the works of modernist painters like Henri Matisse and Paul Cézanne.[20] Erika Balsom and Ray Watkins enlarge on these ideas with completely different arguments. Balsom opposes the view that Bresson films withhold sensuous pleasures and reads his use of fragmentation as "*generative* of a kind of textual bliss and *jouissance* that is radically other to the spectacular pleasures of mainstream cinema."[21] Watkins argues that Bresson's main thematic preoccupations, like the automatism of the body, figural movement and status, and notions of presence and absence, are derived not from a particular painter or artistic movement but from "considering the philosophical concerns of postwar painting writ large."[22] Finally, nonreligious interpretations of Bresson ground his art in various modern philosophic currents, including ones that render this-worldly certain Christian ideas originally thought to provide a flight from the world. Brian Price situates his cinema at the intersection of several lines of radical thought, including Surrealist anticapitalism and contemporary secular reinterpretations of grace. Bresson's films aren't Christian in form or matter; rather, their style, storytelling, and themes evince a critique of Christianity that improves upon philosopher Alain Badiou's rereading of Saint Paul's concept of grace as a theory of chance, taken "as a model of resistance to law and the hardening of a social totality."[23]

These divergent reading practices have led some to associate Bresson with a "cinema of paradox," a label that suggests that these conflicting interpretations reflect the elusive quality of the director himself. Filmmaker Babette Mangolte writes that Bresson's films are "open to multiple interpretations," they are "complex. Robert Bresson, the filmmaker, remains a mystery."[24] While many promising theories have been proposed about the origins and aims of the Bresson style, no single cultural trend or tradition, it is thought, can account for an art that inspires such a diverse, even contradictory, interpretive culture.

* * *

There is a direct correlation then between the decinematization of Bresson—the construction of him as a figure whose alternative to conventional cinema owes little to cinematic contexts (the craft, métier, and business of filmmaking, and the discourses and artists associated with film)—and the mystification of the man and his art. Our sense of his elusiveness only seems to deepen when we turn to personal biography. Unlike other auteurs of his generation—Henri-Georges Clouzot, Roger Leenhardt, Jean Renoir, and others—Bresson's writings and interviews are enigmatic and evasive in addressing the sources of his art, and his life is shrouded in mystery. It is often said that we know far too little about him, what he thought, and how and why these films were made to decipher their true meaning or their place in history. Fragmentary, speculative, and conflicting, the contents of Bresson's biography and personal views provide little guidance to those in search of interpretations that rise above the exploratory, the provisional.

Famously secretive, Bresson was, like the Dadaist sculptor and painter Marcel Duchamp, suspicious of psychologism.[25] Duchamp created around his art a modernist "mystique of purity," as Renato Poggioli calls it, which aspired to "liberate art from any connection with psychological" reality, with his personal history.[26] In a 1967 interview, Bresson objected: "Must one look at the life of someone to judge his work? This is his work. And that is his life."[27] Perhaps for this reason he revealed little about his past.

Many critics have taken him up on this work-life split or denied that the biographical traces that have come down to us shed light on his style, thus contributing to the sense of mystery surrounding Bresson's art (even when this is not the intention). "Aside from conspicuous lineaments," writes Quandt, "there are few biographical details that help illuminate his art."[28] David Bordwell lends support to this position: "Bresson leaves few tracks. . . . We know almost nothing of his private life."[29] Because of the limited traces, Tony Pipolo proposes an approach called "aesthetic biography," for if we have no access to Bresson's life, the films—the characters, plots, etc.—must be read autobiographically, notwithstanding the auteur's opposition to psychologism.[30] Keith Reader is slightly more optimistic and emphasizes that numerous aspects of the filmmaker's biography are "uncontentious."[31] However, he concedes that "comparatively little is known of Bresson's life."[32]

The sorry situation of Bressonian biographical studies has only been compounded by the tendency on the part of critics to examine his personal and professional life (or what little we know of it) through the limited tool of periodization. It is now something of a cliché in Bresson commentary—although many auteurs have been studied this way—to interpret the director's life through its three or four chronological phases or acts. The assumption is that parsing events in this way sheds light on the development of his authorial vision.

But does it? Let us indulge this approach for a moment, if only to clarify its limitations. How might we periodize Bresson's career? What do we learn from this exercise in biographical sequencing? For some, it will offer suggestive patterns—that Bresson began here and ended there. But for those curious about the whys and wherefores, it will seem rather fruitless, creating order from a fragmentary and unsettled mixture of events and rumors (in other words, where no order in fact exists), and serving as yet another reminder that the turn to biography is futile in Bresson's case.

A four-phase schema of Bresson's life might look like this:

Early Life and Career, "Bresson before Bresson" (1901–1945)

The question of where Bresson came from has always been difficult to answer. We have but a few suggestive snippets of history to consider. He was born in 1901 in the region of Auvergne, although for some time, critics believed his date of birth was 1907 or 1911. Legal records suggest that Bresson may have belonged to a larger family that earned its keep in the business of asphalt (bitumen) mining near Puy-de-Dôme in the late nineteenth century.[33] One obituary confirms that his father was in the military, which frequently uprooted Bresson during his childhood.[34] He was educated in a rich suburb of Paris, at the prestigious Lycée Lakanal in Sceaux, a school with a strong literary lineage where Bresson matriculated in

Latin/Greek and philosophy.[35] In a 1983 interview, the director confesses that "by the age of seventeen [ca. 1918], I had read nothing and I have no idea how I was able to pass my exams. What I took from life was not ideas translated into words but sensations. For me, music and painting—their forms, colors—were truer than all of the great books. Novels at that stage struck me as farcical. Later, with quite the appetite, because I felt I needed it, I set upon Stendhal, upon Dickens, upon Dostoyevsky and at the same time upon Mallarmé, Apollinaire, Max Jacob and Valéry. Montaigne and Proust—their ideas, language—struck me tremendously."[36]

He appears to have begun his professional life in the late 1910s or 1920s. Some critics allege that during this time Bresson was employed as a male escort and model, but, thus far, no publicly verifiable evidence has been adduced to support the assertion.[37] In interviews, Bresson consistently claimed that his artistic life began as a painter, but he never exhibited his work, and no firsthand description of it has ever been published. The only firm fact we seem to have about the 1920s is a year, 1926, when he married for the first time to one Leidia van der Zee, a marriage that ended with her death.[38] (When Bresson was buried, it was next to her, in Droue-sur-Drouette.)

During the 1930s, he directed his first film, one thought to be lost until the late 1980s, the medium-length comedy *Les affaires publiques* (1934), but the rest of his time was apparently spent toiling away in the movie industry as he gained experience writing dialogue, adaptations, and original screenplays for popular films like *C'était un musician* (1933). It has long been claimed that in 1939 he served a one-year stint as a prisoner of war in a German camp, but we can now confirm that no military records attest to his service in 1939–1940.[39]

Under the extreme conditions of the Occupation, he finally became a feature-film director, completing two films, *Les anges du péché* and *Les dames du bois de Boulogne* (1945), the first from an original script and the second adapted from the Madame de la Pommeraye episode of Diderot's *Jacques le fataliste* (1796). According to some, neither film expressed the personal vision and style for which Bresson later became known.

The Mature Bresson of the "Prison Cycle" (1951–1962)

For many, it was only after the Liberation that Bresson discovered his mature, sparse style and devoted himself to the themes of isolation, imprisonment, and spiritual release—hence the "prison cycle" moniker given to the four films he directed during this era. With an adaptation of Georges Bernanos's novel *Journal d'un curé de campagne*, he also won his first awards, including the Grand Prize of the 1951 Venice Film Festival. The film's reputation (and Bresson's) only grew throughout the 1950s, becoming the subject of two of the era's most widely read critical essays, André Bazin's 1951 piece, "Le Journal d'un curé de campagne et la stylistique de Robert Bresson," and François Truffaut's notorious 1954 polemic, "Une certaine tendance du cinéma français."[40]

Inspired by the autobiography of military commander André Devigny, Bresson's next project was initially called *Aide-toi . . .* , but was renamed *Un condamné à mort s'est échappé, ou le vent souffle où il veut* to respect the title of the November 1954 *Figaro littéraire* story on which it was based.[41] The film, Bresson's first to feature an entire cast of nonprofessional actors (which, by the early 1970s, he preferred to call models), tells of the escape of a French soldier from a German prison in Lyon, 1943. For its accomplishments, the film garnered Bresson his highest honor to date, a best director award at the 1957 Cannes Film Festival.

On the heels of these successes, Bresson shot *Pickpocket* in 1959, based on an episode from Dostoyevsky's *Crime and Punishment* (1866), and *Le procès de Jeanne d'Arc* (1962), adapted from the original minutes of Joan of Arc's trial, which won the Special Jury prize at the 1962 Cannes Festival.

By now well known for his religious themes, Bresson was called to Rome in 1963 to direct an episode on the Book of Genesis in an omnibus film entitled *The Bible*.[42] Italian auteur Bernardo Bertolucci recalls the notorious incident when the film's producer, Dino de Laurentiis, who had hired a gaggle of animals for the episode, learned of Bresson's plan to depict the procession into Noah's Ark in an indirect manner—"*On ne verra que des traces sur le sable* (We will only see their footprints in the sand)," he told de Laurentiis. Bresson was immediately released.[43] His increasingly "suggestive" style, activating the viewer's imagination by showing very little onscreen, was officially at odds with commercial production norms.[44]

The Late Black-and-White Films (1966–1967)

With his next film, Bresson's artistic vision became somewhat bleaker and more "materialist" as he apparently turned away from the Divine. *Au hasard Balthazar*, his first original screenplay since *Les anges du péché*, tells the story of a donkey passed between sordid owners who abuse the creature, each symbolic of a cardinal sin.[45]

Adapted from the Georges Bernanos novel upon the request of the author's estate,[46] *Mouchette* (1967) was Bresson's last black-and-white project, and the first of several films to end with a suicide. It earned the Hommage unanime du jury prize at the 1967 Cannes Festival.

The "Pessimistic" Color Films (1969–1983)

At this stage, Bresson's vision became (for many critics) even more pessimistic. One commentator went so far as to speculate that he was headed for suicide.[47] Bresson scoffed at the suggestion, but conceded that his vision increasingly favored "lucidity."[48]

He adapted Dostoyevsky's *The Gentle Maiden* (1876) into his first color film, *Une femme douce* (1969), a decidedly sober depiction of contemporary marriage in which the protagonist, played by Dominique Sanda, leaps from the balcony of her Parisian apartment to her death. He returned to Dostoyevsky to make the comparatively innocent *Quatre nuits d'un rêveur* (1971). Drawn from *White Nights* (1884), the film won a British Film Institute Award, but it is now regarded as a minor work. Then, after twenty years of failed attempts, he completed *Lancelot du lac* (1974), taken from the anonymous narrative *La mort le roi Artu* (ca. 1225).[49] This relentlessly "this-worldly" film, about a spiritual crisis among the Knights of the Round Table, was screened at the year's Cannes Festival, where, as Keith Reader explains, Bresson won (and refused) the prestigious Prix internationale de la critique. Bresson proclaimed in an interview: "I don't want prestige, I want money and only the Palme d'or attracts money."[50]

Bresson's last two films, set in contemporary Paris, tend to be viewed as his bleakest. *Le diable probablement* (1977) dramatizes the disillusionment of young radicals in the post–May '68 context, and is Bresson's third film to end with the suicide of his protagonist.[51] It was greeted somewhat coldly. When it was excluded from the official selection at the 1977 Cannes Festival, Bresson reportedly pulled the film from its "fringe" event, the Director's Fortnight, proclaiming that he no longer wished to wade in Cannes' "polluted waters."[52] The film rebounded by winning the second-prize Silver Bear Award at the Twenty-seventh Berlin International Film Festival, but it did so only after the German director Rainer Werner Fassbinder and a British critic threatened to hold up the jury.[53]

Bresson's final film, *L'argent*, an adaptation of Tolstoy's 1911 novella *The Forged Coupon* released in May 1983, shows the tragic demise of a working-class protagonist who is falsely accused of counterfeiting and turns to crime and murder.[54] The project completed, Bresson shared the Grand prix du cinéma de création with filmmaker Andrei Tarkovsky at the 1983 Cannes Festival, an award presented by Orson Welles.

At the age of eighty-two, Bresson planned to make more films. In what appears to have been his final televised interview in 1983,[55] he indicated that he wished to return to "La genèse" (Genesis), the Bible project he had worked on in the 1960s. He also showed an interest in adapting J. M. G. Le Clézio's novella *La grande vie* (1982), a road story about two girls who save money to travel to Italy, but the film never came to fruition.

Robert Bresson passed away on December 18, 1999. He is survived by his second wife, Mylène Bresson, who worked on most of his films under her maiden name, van der Mersch.

* * *

Bresson critics have depended on biographical accounts of this sort for years, using them to arrange the auteur's career into manageable phases (four in this case) and developmental narratives (at least two)—a move to a mature, personal vision, and a waning of transcendence and religious themes in his films.

However, while appearing to lend a sense of order to his life, biographical periodizations simply reinforce how little we know. The problem rests not merely with the incomplete nature of Bresson's biography, a point often made in the critical literature, but with certain unexamined assumptions about biographical sequencing itself. Even if we fill in the gaps that remain about his life— and that is one of the aims of this book—setting his life's events into a linear biographical sequence, creating a chronicle of developments, will never provide us what we finally seek: sound historical explanations of those aspects of his art that are amenable *to* explanation. Did his experiences during the 1920s and 1930s shape his later art? Why did his style and themes ultimately change? What role did institutions, producers, awards, and critical assessments play in his career? None of these pressing questions are answered by compiling an inventory of arbitrarily periodized clusters of facts and rumors. On the contrary, a reliance on chronicles in Bresson commentary feeds the impression that his life and body of work ultimately rest beyond clarification, leaving commentators to play a role that might have been written by the director himself: one can only multiply the paradoxes, deepen the mystery.

In my view, enough information about Bresson's life is now available to allow us to reject this concession and move to restore to Bresson commentary its explanatory role, even if it is a modest or circumscribed one. What is lacking is an approach that not only allows us to interpret his cinema in light of cultural or intellectual history but provides us with the foundation for inferring causes for his aesthetic choices—causes derived from his immediate contexts. Developing such a framework will require us to set aside our assumptions about Bresson's individuality and apartness and to delve into the cultures of production and reception, into the social situations and connections that allowed him to produce and distribute his films, influenced his reputation and status in the film industry, and shed light on the market in which his films appeared. It will thus require us to entertain the possibility that neither the auteur nor his films are as elusive or mysterious as many contemporary critics allege. Moreover, the framework we seek will challenge the notion that one must appeal to nonfilmic theological or philosophical traditions to discover the sources of Bresson's cinema. This process will demand that we confront the assumption that far too little is known about his life and scrutinize available sources and firsthand testimony. In short, refining such an approach will urge us to shed the belief that critics can only add to the mystery and nowhere offer conceptually and historically sound theories about the cinematic origins of his style (where we interpret "the cinematic" in culturally specific ways).

A New Approach, a New Bresson

In order to lift rather than heighten the mystery surrounding Bresson, I propose that we view his biography and the cinematic contexts pertinent to his art in terms of a cultural marketplace.

As the quotation offered as my epigraph concedes, investigating the relationship between a major artist and his or her market is likely to stir controversy, especially for auteurs like Bresson whose highly unusual cinema has long encouraged cinephiles to retain a Romantic notion of art as a deeply personal form of expression that, by definition, eschews market-driven artistic choices. Thus, let us quickly address some major concerns readers might have with this somewhat unorthodox approach to Bresson.

A cultural marketplace is not an economic one and thus impinges on art-making in much less troubling ways than if one were to propose that Bresson simply chased the market in ways he found profitable. In this book, I do not recommend an approach that derives a purely commercial logic from his art and craft—although, admittedly, such a move would not be entirely inappropriate in Bresson's case. For instance, one of his films, *Les affaires publiques*, was at least partially produced to generate box-office revenue in order to finance his shift to feature filmmaking. However, by and large, Bresson's aesthetics are best understood by situating his choices—related to navigating the cultural terrain, finding institutional support to ensure continued performance, and even fine-grained artistic considerations like lighting and staging a scene—within a system of cultural rather than economic exchange, among his culture's prevailing thought about art and cinema. To posit that Bresson's films belonged to, and benefited from, a cultural market is not to claim that they were designed to fill the coffers of producers; it is simply to acknowledge that unique cinematic forms like his were forged from materials and relations tied to his culture's assumptions about cinema as an artistic medium and shaped not by intellectual and aesthetic trends far removed from the "base" of film production, but by conceptual and craft traditions that affected the working methods of French filmmakers.

This contextualized and ultimately social interpretation of the auteur's creativity and volition relies on Michel Foucault's useful concept of the author function, which argues that the author's cultural life is defined by "a series of specific and complex operations."[56] More than this, it draws on the work of social historian of art Michael Baxandall, who explains that when evoking the idea of the cultural marketplace, "there are those who will expect that the economic will play its full determining role, shaping in the last analysis everything from people's ways of working together and thus their consciousness (and thus the forms of their art), to the function of art and attitudes to artistic tradition."[57] A cultural market, by contrast, is more fluid and less deterministic. It is "one medium through which a society can translate . . . such preoccupations about art as it possesses into a brief the artist can understand."[58] In other words, this type of market functions to refashion a culture's paradigmatic interests in art into a series of tasks—into a brief that consists of a cluster of artistic problems and challenges that the artist is free to accept as they are posed or reinterpret in the process of art-making. The artistic briefs he takes up (and how) sheds light on the "uniqueness" of the artist in his time.

As Baxandall clarifies, in most societies "there is usually a plurality of markets embodying diverse briefs."[59] What this means for us is that, in reconstructing the role a specific cultural market or a set of cultural markets played in the development of an auteur's cinema, we can describe the social conditions that offer competing creative itineraries to the artist, who then intervenes in culture by reinterpreting these itineraries for his or her own creative ends. If we wish to explore how Surrealist anticapitalism or Jansenism shaped Bresson's practical artistic choice-making, how Popular Front socialism influenced Jean Renoir, or how trends in anticonsumerist satire affected Jacques Tati, we must focus on the often neglected cultural circumstances that presented the artist with these aesthetic or intellectual ideas, principles, and provocations. These art-world influences then enter into our explanatory account as raw materials; they do not on their own cause or determine the auteur's cinema. Rather, they function as a set of broad factors that become generative (of the art, of the auteur's personal style and thematic commitments, or of his or her reputation) only by virtue of the auteur's active engagement—response, appropriation, purification, rejection, etc.—with conceptual raw matter of this sort.

A cultural market turns on the circulation of wares of mind and of craft through specific modes of social exchange that make prevailing preoccupations about art available to the artist. The cultural marketplace critic seeks more than a loose inventory of aesthetic ideas and questions in the air that can be matched to features of an auteur's film. Instead, the critic has a two-pronged responsibility: he or she must demonstrate how these ideas are manifest in the auteur's film (as an artistic brief, or a set of practical creative problems or challenges) and how these ideas are evident in the languages and relations that organize the auteur's social life (and insert the auteur into what sociologist Bruno Latour calls an "actor-network").[60] If Bresson's use of culture involves the appropriation of Scholastic or Byzantine aesthetics, then the cultural marketplace critic will not just read these traditions through the films; for these aesthetic impulses to contain a level of explanatory force, the critic will demonstrate that they motivated or inspired the forms of exchange the auteur entered into as a social actor.

The mere suggestion that Bresson was a social actor, as remarkable as it might seem to those unfamiliar with the filmmaker's reputation, radically opposes received wisdom, which states that Bresson was not just secretive but a *recluse*, much like the fictional playwright Wilhelm Melchior in Olivier Assayas's *Sils Maria* (2014). We simply must confront this myth before turning to the spectrum of social relations explored in the cultural marketplace approach.

The image of Bresson as a recluse who removed himself from film culture remains a persistent one. Even our best critics pay lip service to it.[61] Perhaps its continued grip on our interpretations of Bresson stems from the support it lends to both the Romantic Cocteauian notion that he was a filmmaker apart and the belief that he drew inspiration only from nonfilmic intellectual and aesthetic traditions.

And yet, at least since the infamous footnote adorning his 1967 *Cahiers du cinéma* interview—where Bresson claims to have no knowledge about contemporary movie trends and the journal's editors offer the cheeky annotation, "Bresson goes to see all the films"[62]—critics have cast doubt on the recluse myth by uncovering his ties to various filmmakers and film cultures. In a groundbreaking 1996 article, David Ehrenstein unearthed the decade-long correspondence between Bresson and Hollywood director George Cukor, in which Bresson requested Cukor's assistance in casting Burt Lancaster for the lead role in his production of *Lancelot du lac* (because of his schedule, Lancaster could not accept).[63] Brian Price has shown that Bresson was not immune to the revolutionary fervor of May '68 and joined François Truffaut, Claude Lelouch, Alain Resnais, and Jean-Luc Godard, among others, in the upstart Committee for the Defense of the Cinémathèque to protest government meddling in the arts.[64] And James Quandt has confirmed that, in return for the appreciation he often expressed for Bresson's films, Bresson cofounded the Institut international Andreï Tarkovski in 1988 to promote his fellow auteur's films beyond Russian borders.[65]

In addition to suppressing this evidence, the recluse myth also depends on a narrow conception of what it means for an auteur to be socially bound. Supporters of the recluse narrative are likely to point out that Robert Bresson was never a society type; nor were his cultural interventions as consistently engaged (in the political sense) as some of his peers. Unlike Roger Vadim, for instance, who, as Vanessa Schwartz has written, used popular films like *Et dieu créa la femme* (1956) and his extensive media contacts to propel his wife, Brigitte Bardot, into megastardom,[66] Bresson was not an auteur who was drawn to the levers of celebrity. Unlike Jean-Luc Godard, moreover, Bresson never cofounded a film collective with a communal approach to filmmaking, like the Dziga Vertov group, and never used his films to intervene in debates about workers' rights and the efficacy of factory occupations. Unlike Bresson, we are told, Vadim and Godard were social actors in the truest sense; their activities as auteurs were frequently commercial, communal, or committed.

However, if we refine Baxandall's approach and conceive the social in relation to the spectrum of cultural practices that characterized Bresson's context, we can begin to challenge the recluse myth and reconstruct the forms of exchange that bound his filmmaking to the aesthetic and theortical "goods" traded in the cultural marketplace that surrounded French cinema between 1928 and 1983 (respectively, the dates of his first and last known works of art). Bresson participated in this cultural market through artistic partnerships, institution-building, alliances, competition, lexical and conceptual synchrony, and reciprocity—all of which informed the artistic briefs he worked through as he fashioned the distinctive *style bressonien*.

* * *

Hardly the recluse of legend, Bresson was, at significant moments in his professional life, active *within* film-production culture, not to mention numerous vanguard and cinephilic cultures. Bresson's activities within these diverse cultures did not consist of one-off engagements from which no conclusions can be drawn. A pattern emerges in which he practiced forms of interaction, cooperation, and address—some direct or intimate, others indirect or tacit—that put him in the position to explore and challenge prevailing assumptions about art and ultimately shaped his aesthetic outlook and artistic performance.

Let's sample the sorts of market relations that impinged on Bresson's art—ones that subsequent chapters will explore in greater detail:

Artistic Partnerships (or Direct Creative Collaboration)

If it is often thought that he forged his distinctive style in isolation—that it was somehow autopoietic or self-produced—Bresson's unique voice as an artist owes much to the direct ties he fostered early in his career with several prominent artists in the interwar Parisian art world. His collaborations with a group of Surrealists, vanguard musicians, and publicity artists, many close to the film scene, furnished him with the aesthetic raw materials to take a more experimental approach to publicity art in the early 1930s—in 1932, he worked with a mentor, Howard Hare "Pete" Powel, to produce a Surrealist advertisement for dental products—and to complete *Les affaires publiques*, a satirical comedy that promised (as he put it, somewhat hyperbolically) to "revolutionize French production."[67]

In ways that commentators have yet to address (perhaps because the early period of his career is often neglected), these same early artistic partnerships also rest at the origins of Bresson's mature visual style—the austere look of films like *Journal d'un curé de campagne*. The best evidence we have suggests that his commitment to stripping his images of visual and symbolic excess came not from Byzantine aesthetics but, it would appear, from his experience in interwar publicity art. Alongside his mentorship by Surrealists in the early 1930s, he worked for a reputable magazine, *L'illustration*, whose photography was overseen by Emmanuel Souguez, a vanguard photographer renowned for his minimalist and elegant style. The experience proved to be formative. The opportunity arose for Bresson to shift his publicity art to simpler, purer forms, now for women's perfumes and jewelry. When he became a feature filmmaker in the 1940s, he favored not his Surrealist tool kit but his minimalist one. Working with a different cultural resource now—a Souguez style refracted through the film-industry-acquired practices of collaborators like set designers René Renoux, Max Douy, Pierre Charbonnier, and cinematographers Philippe Agostini and Léonce-Henri Burel—he pursued the sparse aesthetics for which he became known.

Alternative Institution-Building

Particularly French conditions made speculative attempts to launch alternative institutions a common feature of the film industry during Bresson's career. As Colin Crisp has documented, by 1960 the compact geography of Paris and the proximity of the organs of production and reception promoted a "cultural ferment," "one of the most distinctive and beneficial features" of French cinema between 1920 and 1960.[68] Unlike Hollywood, the French system lacked a stable and relatively self-contained studio system of vertically integrated companies to promote the standardization of production, among other things. Instead, France promoted more fluidity and risk-taking. Unique even among European nations, France had a richer and more committed film press; a circuit for distributing unconventional cinema that dated back to the 1920s; a group of cinephilic, patronlike producers willing to take large risks on projects that did not guarantee a box-office return but that promised cultural prestige; and in the postwar era, a resurgent ciné-club culture, as well as a robust debate within cinephilic, production, and policymaking circles about government subventions to support risky auteur films. These exciting conditions made the industry receptive to influences from cultures desiring to promote greater autonomy for writer-directors.

At two key moments in his career, the partnerships Bresson formed to launch alternative institutions reflected this ethos and promoted his exploration of new creative itineraries suggested by his cultural surroundings. In the 1930s, he benefited from the Surrealist ferment—specifically, from the patronage of the Surrealist painter and poet Sir Roland Penrose—to launch his own independent production firm, Arc-Films, which financed *Les affaires publiques*. Penrose was one of the actors in Luis Buñuel's Surrealist film *L'age d'or* (1930), and *Les affaires publiques* promised to renew the cinematic avant-garde *L'age d'or* represented.

With this support, Bresson's first production drew on Surrealist storytelling strategies he had developed as a photographer just a few years earlier. He also worked with musician Jean Wiéner to create a musical score whose hybridity recalled the avant-garde style Wiéner innovated in the 1920s.

After the Liberation of 1944, Bresson was struggling as a feature filmmaker. *Les dames du bois de Boulogne* had been misunderstood by critics and audiences, and he was having difficulty finding producers to support his work. It was at this stage that he benefited from another ferment and joined in a second effort to relaunch the avant-garde in France. As Richard Neupert and Frédéric Gimello-Mesplomb have discussed, Bresson teamed with cinephiles like Jacques Doniol-Valcroze and André Bazin to found the ciné-club Objectif 49, which aimed to create a *nouvelle avant-garde* in postwar narrative filmmaking.[69] But far less appreciated is the importance of this club in presenting auteur cinema as a *cause-célèbre* in the era and associating pared-down narrative forms, often derived from literature, with the new cinematic vanguard. In this context Bresson accepted the role of copresident of the club (alongside Roger Leenhardt and Jean Cocteau) and took a commission to write and direct an adaptation of the austere first-person novel *Journal d'un curé de campagne*, which was received in cinephilic circles as a masterpiece of the new cinema. For Bresson, to be an auteur was to put pressure on the institutions of culture.

Alliances (or the Formation of Indirect or Broad Coalitions, Alignments, Affinities)

On a scale of intimacy, this dynamic entails a form of cultural exchange that is less direct than partnerships. Although auteurs like Bresson are often presented as individualists, they sometimes seek—through their rhetorical self-presentation in the press and their art-making—to establish intertextual connections between their art and the works and ideas of other artists and thinkers. This form of exchange serves to stimulate and feed the expectations of the market.

As Tim Palmer has argued, today these cultural practices are associated with the graduates of La fémis, one of France's national film schools, which encourages cinephilia and cineliteracy among its practitioners in training. Their films offer the viewer cinephilic flourishes—loving attempts to imitate and refine the styles of the masters.[70]

This affiliative impulse is hardly new. Beginning in the postwar era, Bresson connected his art to the work of essayists, philosophers, novelists, painters, musicians, and composers. A summation of ideas he had been developing as far back as 1946,[71] Bresson's long-awaited book on film practice, *Notes sur le cinématographe* (1975), related his artistic vision to classical and modernist sources, from Debussy, Racine, Pascal, and Cézanne, to El Greco, Purcell, Leonardo, Rousseau, Proust, Dostoyevsky, Montaigne, and Montesquieu.[72] Critics like Mirella

Jona Affron have made much of these nonfilmic alliances and the artistic briefs Bresson drew from them; for her, the unique problem Bresson imposed on himself and his actors in every production—"the actor's body must be bent through the repeated discipline of word and gesture prescribed by the 'ciné-matographe'; through automatism a new nature, that of the model, will replace the old, that of the actor"—was derived from Pascal's notion that the truth of faith commands the body only once it submits to religious habit (i.e., becomes an *automate, pace* Pascal).[73]

The cultural-marketplace critic can also draw inferences about the *cinematic* origins of Bresson's briefs. There are, for example, many concrete visual affinities between Bresson's works and the prevailing norms of his cinematic and artistic milieu. In the 1930s, he made art that took an interest in anthropomorphizing objects from material culture, thus showing affinities with his aesthetically distinct mentors and supporters in the era, from the painter and sculptor Max Ernst to Jean Aurenche, then a producer of publicity films. Furthermore, as he pushed his art toward greater and greater visual austerity in the 1940s and 1950s, his cinematographers functioned as repositories of tradition, drawing into his films artistic problems—related to the use of bare walls and depopulated compositions—that they had worked through, but never in such a refined way, on previous productions. If Bresson often suggested that his conception of cinema was aligned with nonfilmic sources, his films simultaneously presented themselves to the cultural market not as radical breaks from the cinema of the past but as keener and more sustained explorations of the potential contained within certain cinematic problems inherited from both independent and commercial production of earlier decades.

Competition

Critics have long positioned Bresson and his cinema as oppositional, but the implications of this have often been misunderstood: he acted combatively within film culture, not outside it.

In the midcentury cultural market, competition was a defining form of exchange among artists as well as professional and nonprofessional viewers (that is, cinephile critics and audience members). Both participants in and observers of film production intervened—with provocative films, polemics, heated interviews, and so on—to expose the limitations of the status quo and elevate this or that idea, principle, or tradition above others within alternative film culture.

Bresson declared in a 1957 interview: "I am against nothing, against no one, I follow my own path."[74] Cited in Jean Sémolué's monograph on Bresson, this statement shows the auteur attempting to claim a certain reputation, to lift himself and his oeuvre above the contentious debates that defined 1950s film culture, despite the fact that his cinema was very much marked by them. Consider how François Truffaut's notorious 1954 polemic, "Une certaine tendance du cinéma français," presented *Cahiers du cinéma*'s auteurist program as an oppositional one by using Bresson's films to mount an attack on the highly successful "quality" films of screenwriters Jean Aurenche and Pierre Bost and directors Jean Delannoy and Henri-Georges Clouzot. The fiery Truffaut declared: "I do not believe in the peaceful coexistence of the 'Tradition of Quality' and an 'auteur's cinema.'" This declaration of conflict between the two cinemas did not so much create as celebrate the space that auteurs like Bresson (whom Truffaut praises by name) had opened up for film directors. With a film like *Journal d'un curé de campagne*, which remained faithful to rather than distorted the intimate first-person storytelling approach and stirring themes of spiritual angst and isolation of the novel by Georges Bernanos, Bresson had taken on artistic briefs (suggested both by the novel and the reception cultures around failed attempts to adapt it) that placed his cinema at antipodes to the predictable products of these commercial-market-driven filmmakers. Bresson's artistic aims, in short, rejected the briefs opportunistically accepted by quality cinema (high production values, established stars, palatable third-person storytelling, and psychologically dark but cheaply provocative anticlerical tropes that had become clichés by the 1940s and 1950s).

The cultural-marketplace approach does not merely reveal that auteur cinema has often been interpreted as oppositional, however; it shows how cultural competition shaped Bresson's performance in substantive ways.

Bresson regularly engaged film culture by offering sharp criticisms of contemporary trends in film commentary, production, and distribution, especially those that sowed confusion about his films and aesthetic principles or presented barriers to an authentic auteur cinema. When it was released in New York in 1954, *Journal d'un curé de campagne* became the source of what the *New York Times* called "the Affaire *Priest*."[75] In his review, *Times* critic Bosley Crowther charged the film with being hopelessly obscure. "Sometimes it helps a little to be able to understand the motivations and maneuverings of the characters in a film," he wrote. "A few simple clues to their behavior do aid one to grasp what's going on. But these rather modest assistances are not provided—to this reviewer, at least—by the contents of Robert Bresson's 'Diary of a Country Priest.'"[76] Bresson responded with a letter that fiercely objected to the review on the grounds that it had failed to consider that his film was recut by the distributor (Fifth Avenue Cinema) in order to "improve" its pacing.[77] The blame for Crowther's confusion, Bresson contended, rested with a commercially minded distribution system that showed little regard for the integrity of the auteur's original vision.

Bresson was not shy about throwing his elbows at perceived rivals. In 1951–1952, he penned a script for *Lancelot*, based on the Arthurian legends, but just as it was set to enter preproduction, the producer backed out.[78] With *Lancelot* on hold, Bresson adapted another literary property, this one regarded as France's first psychological novel, *La princesse de Clèves* (1678) by Madame de la Fayette. No doubt sensing the need for an established name on the project (in order to stimulate the interest of producers), Bresson contacted the existentialist novelist and *résistancialiste* Albert Camus to write the dialogue.[79] Fortune didn't smile on the Bresson-Camus partnership. Jean Delannoy, a director with established commercial credentials, announced his interest in adapting the novel as well. Bresson once again took to the press, this time to stake a claim to *La princesse de Clèves*, and when Delannoy responded publicly, the exchange tipped off yet another *affaire* that pitted Bresson against the commercial status quo.[80] Bresson's peers mobilized around him and his cause. In an article published in February 1955, fellow auteur Marcel L'Herbier argued that the decision on the part of the state-owned production firm Union générale du cinéma (UGC) to hire Bresson to adapt the novel, only to renege on the deal in favor of the more popular *Chéri-Bibi* (1955), based on Gaston Leroux's widely read serial published in *Le matin* between 1913 and 1925, was nothing less than a blow to the entirety of French cinema. L'Herbier demanded the formation of a "Comédie française du cinéma" that supported commercially risky fare.[81] This alternative institution was never formed, and Bresson lost the battle to Delannoy (who completed an adaptation of *La princesse de Clèves* in 1961),[82] but the situation stimulated new alliances within the cultural market.

Art historian E. H. Gombrich describes the competitive aspect of art markets as "the logic of vanity fair."[83] This expression suggests that competitiveness consists merely of dramatic, even frivolous, displays of jockeying. However, Bresson's career reveals that being an oppositional force within a commercial art form entails more than polemics; it implicates the auteur's artistic choices—the briefs he or she adopts and rejects.

If Bresson drew the idea of visual elegance and sparseness from trends in 1930s high-end publicity photography, then, throughout the 1940s, 1950s and beyond, he turned his early isolated technical experiments in refined lighting and composition into a sophisticated aesthetic philosophy that critiqued the mainstream norms of film-production culture from virtually every angle. He sought, in other words, to reveal the virtues of a new visual language, which he dubbed *le cinématographe* (writing in motion). In his hands this language was steered toward a complex of artistic problems that opposed our common cultural assumptions about movies: movies are an art of melodramatic plotlines, elaborate camera movements, beautiful lighting schemes, florid color designs, emotive gestures and facial expressions by celebrity stars, wall-to-wall background scores that help us feel the action, and so forth and so on. Through an intricate counterbrief fashioned as a critique of popular norms, Bresson emerged as an artist best described in Svetlana Alper and Michael Baxandall's concept of the visual intellectual,[84] a figure who takes an activist role in living by and for fresh visual ideas and adopting an outspoken, engaged and even rebellious stance within his or her visual culture. In sum, Bresson's culturally engaged criticisms of contemporary trends—his rejection of cinema's conventions of visual spectacle and the "théâtre photographié" that made mainstream movies an actor's medium—shed light on the briefs he chose for his personal style.

Lexical and Conceptual Synchrony (or the Participation in Conceptual and Lexical Fields Characteristic of a Cultural Market)

Studies on Bresson tend to focus mainly on his canonical films. While the completed works remain the central focus of this study as well, this book also endeavors to expand our notion of the auteur's cultural performance by giving equal attention to his language acts, for the study of language allows us to observe how the pursuits of the auteur and interested onlookers—supporters, fellow travelers, etc.—intersected with and shaped one another.

Auteurs like Bresson achieve their status at least partially by writing critical, polemical, and theoretical texts for public consumption; giving interviews to the press; accepting invitations to speak at institutions of culture (like the Institut des hautes études cinématographiques [IDHEC], the national film school, where Bresson addressed its students in 1955);[85] and participating in festivals and ciné-club meetings. In each case, the auteur deploys language to express the major artistic focus of a film or his still-unfolding oeuvre. But this language is not an entirely personal one. He communicates his intentions in terms that are understood—that match the frames of reference of his perceived audience.

Beginning in the 1940s, Bresson spoke a language that reinforced, and was in turn reinforced by, the discourses of a community of cinephiles, authors, and critics committed in broad and fine ways to the auteur's cause. Influential journals associated with what Geneviève Sellier and Thomas Pillard call "la cinéphilie savante" (learned cinephilia),[86] like *L'écran français*, *Radio-cinéma-télévision*, *La revue du cinéma*, *Esprit*, *Téléciné*, *Cahiers du cinéma*, *Positif* and others, created what Antoine de Baecque calls a new way of looking[87]—another historian calls it a cinephilic "period eye,"[88] after Baxandall's study of Renaissance art and culture.[89] Film culture of Bresson's era placed a premium on specific areas of cinematic perception and experimentation, like faithful adaptation, first-person storytelling, realism, and rhythm. Cinephile critics carried the ideas in the public debates they waged into their discussion of auteurs' writings and interviews, and these patterns of language and thought even affected the festivals and ciné-clubs they organized in an effort to promote auteur cinema.

In ways that no Bresson critic has studied closely, as early as the 1940s, and through to the end of his career in the 1980s, his language was synchronous with the linguistic field that learned cinephilia cultivated. This synchrony in turn shaped the development of his artistic briefs—the creative challenges he undertook in his films.[90] By accepting his market's views about cinematic storytelling, adaptation, realism, and rhythm, he absorbed aspects of cultural thought into his personal identity as an auteur, into the problems he set out to solve. He fashioned a cultural lexicon into a private one.

In this way, Bresson's art didn't just *receive*; it *gave back*. His films challenged the cinephile's habits of interpreting and writing about films. Cinephiles writing about Bresson were encouraged to refine the arts of analysis and polemics; develop new approaches within the budding area of film theory; and draw into film-critical discourse recent literary, psychological, and philosophical thought. By considering the language of the market, we learn that Bresson and cinephiles were engaged in a productive (and subtle) give-and-take.

Reciprocity (within Partnerships and Alliances, through Strategic Competition, and Facilitated by Lexical and Conceptual Synchrony)

This is the social pillar on which these alternative film-cultural dynamics were built. Within communities near the margins of the film industry, through broad alliances and assisted by the linguistic and conceptual alignment with specific forces within alternative film culture, Bresson entered into a relationship of mutual influence, dependence, investment of all sorts, and action. Simply put, attention was sent one way, with the tacit understanding that it would eventually be returned. What forms of reciprocal attention did Bresson and alternative film culture ultimately exchange? What do these forms reveal about the cinematic contexts pertinent to Bresson's emergence as one of France's premier auteurs?

All film cultures to varying degrees see viewers circulate intellectual ideas, critical judgments, and analytical and ekphrastic descriptions around cinema, and filmmakers produce works that offer up new perceptual and narrative experiences. To study the markets that emerge within film culture is to view these ideas, judgments, descriptions, experiences, and solutions as aspects of a reciprocal trade in what Baxandall calls "mental goods."[91] Baxandall explains that in the relationship between artists and viewers, "the currency is much more diverse than just money: it includes such things as approval, intellectual nurture and, later, reassurance, provocation and irritation of stimulating kinds, the articulation of ideas, vernacular visual skills, friendship and—very important indeed—a history of one's activity and a heredity, as well as sometimes money acting both as a token of some of these and a means to continuing performance. And the good exchanged for these is not so much pictures as profitable and pleasurable experience of pictures."[92] Forms of reciprocal attention thereby become valued commodities whose "barter" expresses the variety of pleasures and rewards to be gained from participating in the market.

If properly documented, classified, and studied, the linguistic, historiographic, evaluative, conceptual, and perceptual goods exchanged one way and the other, between auteur and market, can form the basis for a causal history that productively links artist to culture, text to context. Mapping the currencies of attention within alternative film culture both illuminates the modes of community involvement upon which often-fragile alternative or oppositional cinemas depend (i.e., the types of support, provocation, and viewing skill viewers send in the direction of, or shore up for, the auteur) and provides an ample historical foundation to reinterpret the auteur's creative and rhetorical choices within film culture as decisions to select from and act upon (and to thereby directly or indirectly respond to) the forms of discourse and attention that viewing communities innovate.

The new Bresson discovered in this study was an auteur whose unique art was cultivated in a market where oppositional cinema was a struggle a director undertook not alone but in concert with small, informal, but innovative communities of supporters whose discourses and practices rewarded the pursuit of a distinctive voice and of vanguard narrative forms within industrialized culture.

What Lies Ahead

This book has two parts, each endeavoring to lift some of the mysteries surrounding Bresson's art by further examining his career in light of these cultural relations. Part I, "Alternative Institutions," addresses two critical moments in the filmmaker's professional life when intimate forms of cultural exchange permitted him to navigate alternative film culture and its institutions. Chapter 1, "Under the Aegis of Surrealism: How a Publicity Artist Became the Manager of an Independent Film Company," focuses on the partnerships, alliances, and institutions that Bresson created to surpass his modest beginnings as a fairly conventional publicity artist in the late 1920s. In a few short years, his ties within the art scene facilitated his shift to Surrealist photography and created conditions for him to manage his own independent film production company, which financed his debut film, *Les affaire publiques*. These relationships and experiences allowed him to accomplish something essential to any auteur: the opportunity to refine a distinct artistic voice and gain a foothold in Paris's creative industries in a period when the avant-garde was facing considerable headwinds.

Chapter 2, "The Rise of the Accursed: When Bresson was Copresident of an Avant-Garde Ciné-Club," argues that the Occupation represented a new beginning in the way he navigated the institutions of film culture. If in the 1930s he used his ties to strike out as an independent producer-director, in the 1940s, beginning with his collaboration with the influential novelist and dramaturge Jean Giraudoux, he shifted to a new strategy that involved both long- and short-term partnerships with established artists. This allowed him enter the feature-film industry. But when his second feature, 1945's *Les dames du bois de Boulogne*, proved to be a critical and commercial failure, Bresson's career was in peril. He decided that the best recourse was to join with fellow auteurs and cinephiles to defend auteur cinema as a new vanguard of *films maudit* as well as a true quality cinema in peril. Under these conditions, the name "auteur" materialized to describe not just personal filmmakers but *causes-célèbres* on whose behalf alternative film culture battled, particularly for institutional status.

Part II, "Vanguard Forms," consists of three chapters and marks a shift in emphasis in the book by focusing on relatively tacit or indirect forms of reciprocity with alternative film culture. Emphasis is placed on Bresson's visionary engagement with cultural raw materials—the aesthetic ideas, principles, and provocations alternative film culture put forward—to produce new creative forms that allowed him to emerge as one of French cinema's most distinctive auteurs. Chapter 3, "Purifying Cinema: The Provocations of Faithful Adaptation and First-Person Storytelling in "Ignace de Loyola" (1948) and *Journal d'un curé de campagne* (1951)," addresses the contact of creative agency that emerged between cinephiles interested in the film-literature question and those auteurs undertaking adaptations of first-person novels. This creative meeting point between criticism and filmmaking proved to be a necessary condition for Bresson's experiment with the adaptation of Georges Bernanos's novel *Journal d'un curé de campagne* as well as his discovery of a personal identity as an artist.

Chapter 4, "Theorizing the Image: Bresson's Challenge to the Realists—Sparse Set Design, Acting and Photography from *Les anges du péché* (1943) to *Une femme douce* (1969)," argues that Bresson also sought his self-realization as a film artist by taking on the role of visual intellectual within production culture. More precisely, he set his work in opposition to the existing regime of visual culture within mainstream cinema, one whose images were shaped by standards of hermeneutic expressiveness and pictorial excess, and he did so through his realist images—through properly visual ideas. In this, Bresson's art was culturally inscribed. Drawing on craft traditions and aesthetic ideas circulating in pre- and postwar film culture, he developed a visual style that positioned him at the vanguard of postwar realisms.

Chapter 5, "Vernacularizing Rhythm: Bresson and the Shift Toward Dionysian Temporalities—Plot Structure and Editing from *Journal d'un curé de campagne* (1951) to *L'argent* (1983)," demonstrates that Bresson forged his most personal contribution to the history of film style—an alternative postcinematic medium he dubbed *le cinématographe*—from the very conceptual materials film culture uniquely afforded the auteur: a cluster of midcentury psychological and philosophical theories that challenged the musicological notion of rhythm and thereby allowed it to enter the vernacular as a basic property of social, political, biological, and aesthetic experience. Bresson responded to available musical, panaesthetic, and vitalistic concepts of rhythm with a new storytelling approach that explored the temporalities of abstract visual patterning, remembrance, ritual, speech, erotic desire, and alienated modern life. With these experiments, he took part in an alternative film culture intrigued with the possibilities of cinematic rhythm. He also participated in a "drift" in French thought that saw "rhythm" imbued with the improvisational and spontaneous qualities of everyday language.

* * *

This book, in short, reconnects Bresson with film culture, revealing him as a social actor within various communities working just inside the margins of the film industry to create favorable conditions for a narrative avant-garde before and after the Second World War. It seeks to account for the distinctive Bresson style by revealing, for the first time, his participation in alternative institutions and appropriation of vanguard critical and theoretical discourses that refined his culture's understanding of unconventional stylistic and narrative forms. This active engagement with culture provided the groundwork for his innovations at the level of image craft, sound design, editing, and storytelling. At the source of the elusive *style bressonien* rests not a mystery, but a subtle form of exchange between an individual artist and the cultural market.

Notes

1. Traditional auteurism is a species of authorship criticism that argues that the role of the critic is to celebrate those director-auteurs who impose a unity on their body of work through a personal vision or worldview. More precisely, the auteur, as studied through *Cahiers du cinéma*'s *politique des auteurs* (auteur policy), has a distinctive stylistic "stamp" (particularly in his mise-en-scène), is committed to a consistent set of themes, truly "authors" the films (writes and directs), and stands as an improbable creative individualist.

Criticisms of the concept of the author/auteur are manifold. Groundbreaking texts that attack the traditional notion of the author (as a real, unified individual in history whose views decide "correct" interpretations of their works) include W. K. Wimsatt and Monroe Beardsley, "The Intentional Fallacy," in *The Verbal Icon: Studies in the Meaning of Poetry* (London: Methuen, 1970), 2–18; Roland Barthes, "The Death of the Author," in *Theories of Authorship*, ed. John Caughie (London: British Film Institute, 1981), 208–213; and Michel Foucault, "What is an Author?" in *The Foucault Reader*, ed. Paul Rabinow (New York: Pantheon, 1984), 101–120. For a useful commentary on some of the last two texts, see Seán Burke, *The Death and Return of the Author: Criticism and Subjectivity in Barthes, Foucault and Derrida* (Edinburgh: Edinburgh University Press, 1998). For a tidy overview of the theoretical underpinnings of the "death of the author" position, see Janet Wolff, *The Social Production of Art* (New York: New York University Press, 1981).

Film critics and scholars have offered numerous criticisms of their own—too numerous to list here. Two sources provide a sense of the range of objections that have been offered to this critical tradition. First, André Bazin argued that auteurism promotes a cult of personality of sorts by drawing critical attention away from the qualities of the films and toward the vision or persona behind them; André Bazin, "On the *politique des auteurs*," in *Cahiers du cinéma: The 1950s: Neo-Realism, Hollywood, the New Wave*, ed. Jim Hillier (Cambridge, MA: Harvard University Press, 1985), 248–259. Second, poststructuralist film scholars have denied the existence of individuals that are sufficiently unified to act as sole creators of their works and proposed that film authorship is ultimately a discursive construct; see Janet Staiger, "Authorship Approaches," in *Authorship and Film*, eds. David Gerstner and Janet Staiger (New York: Routledge, 2003), 27–57.

Film and media scholars nevertheless continue to view authorship as a useful critical, analytical, and historical tool. Two useful anthologies explore these aspects of media authorship in and beyond film: Torben Grodal, Bente Larsen, and Iben Thorving Laursen, *Visual Authorship: Creativity and Intentionality in Media* (Copenhagen, Museum Tusculanum Press, 2005); and Jonathan Gray and Derek Johnson, eds., *A Companion to Media Authorship* (Malden, MA: Wiley-Blackwell, 2013).

2. Cited in the epigraph of René Briot, *Robert Bresson* (Paris: Éditions Seghers, 1962).

3. Amédée Ayfre, "The Universe of Robert Bresson," in *Robert Bresson*, ed. James Quandt (Toronto: Cinematheque Ontario, 1998), 55.

4. Michel Estève, *Robert Bresson: La passion du cinématographe* (Paris: Editions Albatros, 1983), 9.

5. Lloyd Michaels, *Terrence Malick* (Urbana: University of Illinois Press, 2009), 6.

6. Fernando Solanas and Octavio Gettino offer a scathing critique of second or "author's cinema" in "Towards a Third Cinema," in *Movies and Methods: An Anthology*, vol. 1, ed. Bill Nichols (Berkeley: University of California Press, 1976), 51–52.

7. Cited in Ayfre, "The Universe of Robert Bresson," 43–44.

8. Sacha Guitry, "*Les anges du péché*," in *Le cinéma et moi* (Paris: Éditions Ramsay, 1977), 91.

9. Estève, *Robert Bresson*, 127.

10. Tim Cawkwell, *The Filmgoer's Guide to God* (London: Darton, Longman and Todd, 2004), 68–69.

11. In this book, I use the terms "filmic" and "cinematic" fairly interchangeably to refer to aspects of cultural discourse that circulate within film or film-related industries and/or the film or film-related cultures that insinuate themselves into film production in culturally specific ways. "Film-related" refers to those aspects of cultural production and practice that may not be common with the film industry at first but that, through the activities of "external" artists or viewers, directly influence craft practices within the film production sector. Nevertheless, I acknowledge that many theorists view filmic and cinematic as distinct concepts; see Christian Metz, *Language and Cinema*, trans. Donna Jean Umiker-Sebeok (The Hague: Mouton & Co. N.V., 1974), 47–49.

12. Raymond Durgnat, "The Negative Vision of Robert Bresson," in *Robert Bresson*, ed. James Quandt (Toronto: Cinematheque Ontario, 1998), 411.

13. René Prédal, "L'aventure intérieure," in *Robert Bresson*, ed. James Quandt (Toronto: Cinematheque Ontario, 1998), 104.

14. Durgnat, "The Negative Vision of Robert Bresson," 412.

15. Michel Ciment, "I Seek not Description but Vision: Robert Bresson on *L'Argent*," in *Robert Bresson*, ed. James Quandt (Toronto: Cinematheque Ontario, 1998), 501.

16. Ayfre, "The Universe of Robert Bresson," 55; Susan Sontag, "Spiritual Style in the Films of Robert Bresson," in *Against Interpretation and Other Essays* (New York: Anchor Books, 1990), 188.

17. Paul Schrader, *Transcendental Style in Film: Ozu, Bresson, Dreyer* (Berkeley: University of California Press, 1972), 86, 96, 98–99.

18. Cited in James Quandt, "Introduction," in *Robert Bresson (Revised)*, ed. James Quandt (Toronto: TIFF, 2012), 13.

19. Kent Jones, *L'Argent* (London: British Film Institute, 1999), 39; emphasis in source.

20. Ibid., 19–20.

21. Erika Balsom, "'One Single Mystery of Persons and Objects': The Erotics of Fragmentation in *Au hasard Balthazar*," *Canadian Journal of Film Studies* 19.1 (Spring 2010): 23.

22. Ray Watkins, "Robert Bresson's Modernist Canvas: The Gesture Toward Painting in *Au hasard Balthazar*," *Cinema Journal* 51.2 (Winter 2012): 25.

23. Brian Price, *Neither God nor Master: Robert Bresson and Radical Politics* (Minneapolis: University of Minnesota Press, 2011), 11–13.

24. Babette Mangolte, "Filmmakers on Bresson," in *Robert Bresson*, ed. James Quandt (Toronto: Cinematheque Ontario, 1998), 574.

25. See Robert Bresson, *Notes on the Cinematographer*, trans. Jonathan Griffin (Copenhagen: Green Integer, 1997), 82: "No psychology (of the kind that discovers only what it can explain)."

26. Cited in Martin Jay, "Modernism and the Specter of Psychologism," *Modernism/Modernity* 3.2 (1996): 96.

27. Quandt, "Introduction," 21.

28. Ibid.

29. Ibid.

30. Tony Pipolo, *Robert Bresson: A Passion for Film* (Oxford: Oxford University Press, 2010), 26–28.

31. Keith Reader, *Robert Bresson* (Manchester: Manchester University Press, 2000), 8.

32. Ibid., 8.

33. *Annales de la Société d'Agriculture: Histoire naturelle et arts utiles de Lyon*, quatrième serie, tome deuxième (Paris: Librairie de la société géologique de France, 1870), 235. This passage refers to two brothers, Marie and François Bresson, who claimed bitumen mines in Pont-du-Château, Puy-de-Dôme, where Robert was born to Léon and Marie-Elizabeth in a large manor house, presumably owned by the family. A photograph of the home is reproduced in Estève, *Robert Bresson*, 32.

34. Alan Riding, "Robert Bresson, Film Director, Dies at 98," *New York Times*, December 22, 1999, C27.

35. Denise Tual, *Au cœur du temps* (Paris: Carrère, 1987), 268. Jean Giraudoux, an acclaimed novelist and dramatist of the interwar period, matriculated at the same school, and perhaps because of this shared pedigree, he helped Bresson break into the feature-film industry during the German Occupation when he accepted to write dialogue for *Les anges du péché* (producers green-lighted the project as a result).

36. Cited in Estève, *Robert Bresson*, 139.

37. Jonathan Rosenbaum, "Defending Bresson," *Chicago Reader*, April 1, 2004, http://www.chicagoreader.com/chicago/defending-bresson/Content?oid=915048; see also Jonathan Rosenbaum, Review of Tony Pipolo's *Robert Bresson: A Passion for Film*, *Cineaste* 35.3 (Summer 2010): 59–60.

38. Riding, "Robert Bresson, Film Director, Dies at 98," C27.

39. Because he was born in Puy-de-Dôme, Bresson's military records would have been held at the Riom or Clermont-Ferrand offices of the Archives des forces armées. However, these

archives contain no documents confirming his service in 1921 (when he was first called to service) or 1939–1940.

40. André Bazin, "Le *Journal d'un curé de campagne* et la stylistique de Rober Bresson," *Cahiers du cinéma* 3 (June 1951): 7–21; François Truffaut, "Une certaine tendance du cinéma français," *Cahiers du cinéma* 31 (January 1954): 15–29.

41. Gallimard published a novelization of the film penned by Devigny: André Devigny, *Un condamné à mort* (Paris: Gallimard, 1956).

42. Reader, *Robert Bresson*, 69.

43. Bernardo Bertolucci, "Filmmakers on Bresson," in *Robert Bresson*, ed. James Quandt (Toronto: Cinematheque Ontario, 1998), 529; italics in source.

44. Production records reveal that Bresson had conducted casting tests for the role of Eve, and had asked his set designer (and longtime collaborator) Pierre Charbonnier to build miniatures of Noah's Ark and the Tower of Babel; see Pierre Charbonnier, and Philippe Arnaud, "La genèse: Documents de repérage," Fonds Pierre Charbonnier, CHARBONNIE3-B2, Bibliothèque du film, Paris, France.

45. The film has since become embroiled in speculation. It would appear that Bresson had been pitching *Au hasard Balthazar* to producers for five years and finally approached Anatole Dauman, the financier behind *Nuit et brouillard* (1955) and *Hiroshima mon amour* (1959), at the behest of Jeanine Bazin, critic André Bazin's widow; see Anatole Dauman, *Souvenirs-écran* (Paris: Éditions du Centre Pompidou, 1989), 119.

More scandalously, Anne Wiazemsky, the film's seventeen-year-old protagonist, reports in her controversial fictionalized account of the shoot, 2007's *Jeune fille*, that Bresson attempted to romance her on several occasions; see Anne Wiazemsky, *Jeune fille* (Paris: Gallimard, 2007), 75.

46. *Au hasard Bresson*, DVD, directed by Theodor Kotulla, Iduna Film Produktiongesellschaft, 1966.

47. Marvin Zeman, cited in Reader, *Robert Bresson*, 88.

48. This is discussed in Quandt, "Introduction," 14.

49. Kristin Thompson, "The Sheen of Armour, the Whinnies of Horses: Sparse Parametric Style in *Lancelot du lac*," in *Robert Bresson*, ed. James Quandt (Toronto: Cinematheque Ontario, 1998), 340.

The state-owned broadcasting company Office de radiodiffusion télévision française (ORTF), the actor-director Jean Yanne and "maverick" producer Jean-Pierre Rassam funded the project; see Reader, *Robert Bresson*, 116.

50. Cited in Reader, *Robert Bresson*, 116. The translation is Reader's.

51. To produce the film, he benefited from government subsidy apparently through the intervention of French officials. Although the decision for advanced financing through the 1959 *avance sur recettes* (advance on receipts) law usually falls to a committee that evaluates the artistic merits of a script, on this occasion, France's Minister of Culture, Michel Guy, granted the film a loan against the will of the committee. See Philippe Arnaud, *Robert Bresson* (Paris: Éditions Cahiers du cinéma, 1986), 187.

52. Reader, *Robert Bresson*, 133.

53. Ibid., 134.

54. *L'argent* benefited from *avance sur recettes* funds as well. Some have speculated unkindly that Bresson cast the daughter of the Minister of Culture Jack Lang as a quid pro quo, but this has never been confirmed. Ibid., 141.

55. *Entretien avec Christian Defaye*, *spéciale cinéma*, first broadcast in 1983 by TSR (Switzerland), *L'argent* New Yorker DVD.

56. Foucault, "What is an Author?" 113.

57. Baxandall, *The Limewood Sculptors of Renaissance Germany*, 95.

58. Ibid.

59. Ibid.

60. Bruno Latour, *Reassembling the Social: An Introduction to Actor-Network-Theory* (Oxford: Oxford University Press, 2005).

61. Kent Jones, "Robert Bresson," in *The Films of Robert Bresson*, ed. Bert Cardullo, (London: Anthem Press, 2009), 1.

62. Jean-Luc Godard and Michel Delahaye, "The Question," in *Robert Bresson*, ed. James Quandt (Toronto: Cinematheque Ontario, 1998), 483n1.

63. David Ehrenstein, "Bresson et Cukor, Histoire d'un correspondence," trans. Michelle Herpe-Voslinsky, *Positif* 430 (December 1996): 103. For the original letter from Lancaster, see Burt Lancaster, Letter to George Cukor, November 30, 1964, George Cukor Collection, File 709, Academy Film Archive, Fairbanks Center for Motion Picture Study, Beverly Hills, California.

64. Price, *Neither God nor Master*, 98.

65. Quandt, "Introduction," 17.

66. Vanessa Schwartz, *It's So French!: Hollywood, Paris, and the Making of Cosmopolitan Film Culture* (Chicago: University of Chicago Press, 2007), 79–82.

67. Cited in Henriette Janne, "À Épinay Cette Semaine . . . ," *Ciné-Magazine*, July 26, 1934.

68. Colin Crisp, *The Classic French Cinema, 1930–1960* (Bloomington: Indiana University Press, 1993), 149, 151.

69. Richard Neupert, *A History of the French New Wave Cinema*, 2nd ed. (Madison: University of Wisconsin Press, 2007), 26; Frédéric Gimello-Mesplomb, *Objectif 49: Cocteau et la nouvelle avant-garde* (Paris: Séguier, 2014), 51.

70. Tim Palmer, *Brutal Intimacy: Analyzing Contemporary French Cinema* (Middletown, CT: Wesleyan University Press, 2011), 195–216.

71. Jean Sémolué, *Bresson* (Paris: Flammarion, 1993), 21–22.

72. Bresson, *Notes on the Cinematographer*, 52, 128 (for Debussy); 72, 75, 121 (Racine); 84, 93 (Pascal); 86, 136 (Cézanne); 86 (El Greco); 115 (Purcell); 117 (Leonardo); 123 (Rousseau); 124 (Proust); 124 (Dostoyevsky); 131 (Montaigne); and 137 (Montesquieu).

73. Mirella Jona Affron, "Bresson and Pascal: Rhetorical Affinities," in *Robert Bresson*, ed. James Quandt (Toronto: Cinematheque Ontario, 1998), 176–177.

74. Cited in Sémolué, *Bresson*, 13.

75. Bosley Crowther, "On Editing Imports: French Film Man Vexed at a Usual Practice," *New York Times*, May 2, 1954, sect. 2, 1.

76. Bosley Crowther, "The Screen in Review: French Film, 'Diary of a Country Priest,' Opens," *New York Times*, April 6, 1954, sect. 2, 35.

77. Cited in Crowther, "On Editing Imports," sect. 2, 1. The vice-president of Fifth Avenue cinema subsequently justified recutting the film in a letter to the editor; Lillian Gerard, "A Trio of Footnotes on L'Affaire 'Priest:' Letter to the Editor," *New York Times*, May 9, 1954, X3.

78. Robert Bresson, Letter to Cukor from Bresson, June 29, 1953, George Cukor Collection, File 709, Fairbanks Center for Motion Picture Study, Academy of Motion Picture Arts and Sciences, Beverly Hills, California. Bresson refers to the project as "Lancelot."

79. Albert Camus, and René Char, "Albert Camus à René Char, 25 mai 1954," in *Correspondence, 1946–1959* (Paris: Gallimard, 2007), 121.

80. Arnaud, *Robert Bresson*, 177.

81. Marcel L'Herbier, "Chéri-Bibi contre la princesse de Clèves," *Combat*, February 14, 1955. In the same issue, the UGC president André Halley des Fontaines replied that *Chéri-Bibi* was

not chosen over Bresson's project; the former was rather a French-Italian coproduction and therefore an entirely separate consideration from "Princesse de Clèves." André Hayette des Fontaines, "Une réponse à Marcel L'Herbier," *Combat*, February 14, 1955.

82. Angie Van Steerthem, "Jean Cocteau collaborateur de Jean Delannoy pour *La princesse de Clèves*," in *Le revue lettres modernes: Jean Cocteau 5 (Les adaptations)*, ed. Serge Linares (Caen: Lettres modernes Minard, 2008), 111–129.

83. Ernst Gombrich, "The Logic of Vanity Fair," in *The Philosophy of Karl Popper*, ed. Paul A. Schlipp (La Salle, IL: Open Court, 1974), 927.

84. Svetlana Alpers and Michael Baxandall, *Tiepolo and the Pictorial Intelligence* (New Haven: Yale University Press, 1994), v.

85. Robert Bresson, "'Une mise-en-scène n'est pas un art:' Robert Bresson rencontre les étudiants de l'Institution des hautes études cinématographiques (décembre 1955)," *Cahiers du cinéma: Hommage Robert Bresson* (February 2000): 4.

86. Geneviève Sellier, "Editorial: Le cinéma populaire et ses usages dans la France d'après-guerre," *Studies in French Cinema* 15.1 (2015): 1; Thomas Pillard, "Cinéphilie populaire et usages sociaux du cinéma dans les années 1950: Le courrier des lecteurs du *Film complèt* (1949–1958)," *Studies in French Cinema* 15.1 (2015): 69.

87. Antoine de Baecque, *La cinéphilie: Invention d'un regard, histoire d'une culture, 1944–1968* (Paris: Librairie Arthème Fayard, 2003), 24–27.

88. Philippe Mary, *La nouvelle vague et le cinéma d'auteur: Socio-analyse d'une révolution artistique* (Paris: Éditions du seuil, 2006), 45.

89. For the original use of the concept of the period eye, see Michael Baxandall, *Painting and Experience in Fifteenth Century Italy: A Primer in the Social History of Pictorial Style* (London: Oxford University Press, 1972), 29–108. For a discussion of its impact on art history, see Allan Langsdale, "Aspects of Critical Reception and Intellectual History in Baxandall's Concept of the Period Eye," in *About Michael Baxandall*, ed. Adrian Rifkin (Oxford: Blackwell Publishers, 1999), 17–35. Sociologists of art have picked up on the concept in order to study the educational foundations of taste; see Jeremy Tanner, "Michael Baxandall and the Sociological Interpretation of Art," *Cultural Sociology* 4.2 (July 2010): 234–235.

90. Michael Baxandall inspired my focus on language. See Tanner, "Michael Baxandall and the Sociological Interpretation of Art," 237, for more on the art historian's interest in language; and Allan Langdale, "Interview with Michael Baxandall, February 3rd, 1994, Berkeley, California," *Journal of Art Historiography* 1 (December 2009): 1–3, for Baxandall's training under F. R. Leavis and the influence of Ludwig Wittgenstein in this regard.

91. Michael Baxandall, *Patterns of Intention: On the Historical Explanation of Pictures* (London: Yale University Press, 1985), 48.

92. Ibid.

PART I

Alternative Institutions

1 Under the Aegis of Surrealism:

How a Publicity Artist Became the Manager of an Independent Film Company

He spoke to me about his film. He began by declaring that the title is *Les Affaires publiques*, and that it is an extraordinary film, based on a premise never before seen in France [that] will revolutionize French production.

—critic Henriette Janne[1]

SUCH WAS ROBERT Bresson's ambition when he made his directorial debut, the *comique fou* short *Les affaires publiques* (1934).[2] Only in his midthirties, he set out to challenge an entire industry and launch a revolution in film practice. What factors put him in a position to do so?

For decades, commentators have had very little to say about Bresson's early art and film career. Some have even dismissed the period of the 1930s as irrelevant to his emergence as one of cinema's most revered auteurs. This chapter reveals otherwise.

In what follows, I uncover the social and institutional factors that permitted Bresson's entry into the world of filmmaking in the early 1930s. In ways that have yet to be fully appreciated by scholars, his first opportunities to pick up a movie camera came as a result of his ties to the Parisian avant-garde. This avant-garde, to a certain extent in decline, nevertheless remained a tight-knit group that allowed Bresson to come into contact with photographers, painters, sculptors, publicity artists, and patrons of the arts, who protected and nurtured his art, and ultimately afforded him something that is essential to any vanguard auteur: the opportunity to refine a distinctive artistic voice and thereby begin to gain a foothold in the cultural market.

This chapter and the next explore two contexts—the interwar and postwar avant-gardes—that are crucial to our reassessment of Bresson, backgrounds that make it vital to dispense with the convenient assumption that auteurs are mere individualists. Bresson did not discover his unique artistic commitments or establish himself within the cultural market through a strategy of extreme isolation and self-reliance, but through a combination of his own creativity and perseverance and intimate relationships with artistic fellow travelers, supporters, and patrons who sponsored and influenced both his art and the institutions needed to produce it. Bresson first showed an awareness of the importance of partnerships and alliances in the earliest phase of his professional life, as a publicity artist in the late 1920s and early 1930s, when he circulated in Surrealist circles. He then parlayed these experiences into a shift to filmmaking.

Many of our current misunderstandings about the sources of his cinema, dependent on the notion that he was a filmmaker apart with few connections to the cultures that directly or indirectly animated French film style, come from the fact that we have yet to appreciate this early phase, when Bresson relied upon the aesthetic, intellectual, and institutional resources provided by an interwar avant-garde that moved fluidly between media (painting, illustration, sculpture, photography, cinema, and fashion). Through an engagement with the avant-garde world around him—his work for the photography magazine *L'illustration* and in the publicity film business; his ties with Surrealists Max Ernst, Howard Hare "Pete" Powel, and Sir Roland Penrose; his partnership with the vanguard musician Jean Wiéner; and connections to the director René Clair—he was able to develop a personal style, launch and manage his own film production firm, Arc-Films, complete and promote a short film, and plan his first features. Bresson's ambition to launch a revolution in French cinema of the 1930s—an ambition that sheds light on the vanguard auteur he later became—has a social history, unrecorded and unacknowledged until now.

Faint Traces of a Motley Milieu

Only faint traces survive of the milieu Bresson circulated in when he made his first known works of art in the late 1920s and early 1930s. Firsthand accounts are admittedly scarce and difficult to substantiate. Nevertheless, these traces are worth recording, for they suggest a great deal about the mobility this milieu afforded figures like him within the cultural market. If Bresson gravitated toward Surrealists, he was also not really a part of the movement. Rather, he linked up with a loose network of vanguard artists who crossed "high" and "low" media, created a conduit between vanguard forms and creative industries, and stimulated interest in filmmaking of offbeat sorts. Bresson made the most of this fluid culture, moving on its fringes and dabbling, it would appear, wherever it benefited his artistic development.

While it may defy assumptions, one of his earliest creative partnerships was with film director, writer, and producer Jean Aurenche.[3] Today, in cinephilic circles, Aurenche is viewed as a pariah, a notorious *scénariste* best known for his collaborations with fellow *Tradition de la qualité* scribe Pierre Bost and with commercial directors like Claude Autant-Lara, for whom he penned *Le mariage de chiffon* (1942) and *L'auberge rouge* (1951), and René Clément, who worked with Aurenche on *Jeux interdits* (1952) and *Gervaise* (1956). In his 1954 *Cahiers du cinéma* polemic, "Une certaine tendance du cinéma français," François Truffaut all but sealed Aurenche's fate as a retrograde figure to be reviled by auteurists, symbolic of a commercial industry that saw little value in the films of visionary auteurs like Bresson.[4] But in Bresson's early professional history, an entirely different picture of Aurenche emerges. In the 1930s, he operated at the edges of a Parisian avant-garde that had been largely shut out of film production and distribution after "The *Âge d'or* Affair," when Luis Buñuel's 1930 Surrealist film (in which Aurenche played the part of a bandit) was censored, far-right groups associated with L'Action française trashed Studio 28, the Parisian theater where the film premiered, and exhibitors and financiers became reluctant to back avant-garde films as a result.[5] Forming an independent production company of his own in 1931, and relying on his connections (he was brother-in-law to the Surrealist painter Max Ernst and mixed socially with Cocteau, Jacques Prévert, and Jean Anouilh, not to mention two of Bresson's friends and future artistic collaborators, composer Jean Wiéner and painter Pierre Charbonnier), Aurenche sought on some level to revive the cinematic avant-garde in Paris and created new opportunities for young artists like Bresson.

Aurenche attributed many of the ties that he and other young artists had to the avant-garde to Cocteau, who provided them with opportunities to rub shoulders with their more celebrated peers, with painters, fashion designers, filmmakers, and musicians, throughout the 1920s. An eccentric and beloved filmmaker, poet, and playwright, Cocteau became a mentor to this generation, exposing them to the works of Apollinaire, Braque, Picasso, and the ceramic artist Josep Llorens Artigas, who also appeared in *L'âge d'or*. Of Cocteau, Aurenche wrote: "To educate us, he had us attend rehearsals of his plays. He introduced me to Picasso, and took me to visit him in his studio. There, I met musicians—[Georges] Auric and [Francis] Poulenc, who later composed scores for some of my films."[6] Cocteau had connections high in French society and the art world: "He introduced me to important people who liked to mingle with artists. . . . Chanel was a close friend, to whom he gave advice. . . . he created the artistic and intellectual climate that she needed. The truth is that Cocteau was a popularizer of genius. He introduced a small group of very rich and influential people . . . to painters, writers, musicians and filmmakers who, without him, would never have met."[7]

This context also shaped a generation's taste in film. Aurenche recalls that Cocteau "initiated me into the cinema. He brought a group of us to see movies, mainly American films, comedies, westerns. He also liked Russian films a great deal, the Eisensteins and the Pudovkins. I saw Expressionist films like *The Cabinet of Doctor Caligari*, *The Testament of Doctor Mabuse*, and *Nosferatu*." Though a prominent member of the French avant-garde, Cocteau found the "Impressionists" of the 1920s lacking: "He was unimpressed by Gance or the avant-garde. It was his opinion that, literarily speaking, Gance was little more than a serial novelist. Of L'Herbier, the less said the better. 'He picked up Oscar Wilde's pen without noticing that it was broken,' Cocteau said to me."[8]

The time Aurenche and other up-and-comers spent in Cocteau's company in the 1920s was effectively a crash course in art, literature, cinema, and making connections with patrons. One of the effects Cocteau had on the group was to inspire them with a passion for popular cinema, especially comedies. "In those days my ambition was to be a gagman for Keaton!" Aurenche confesses.[9]

This was a world Bresson surely knew on some level, although it is difficult to draw any definitive conclusions about his connections to the group. Perhaps Bresson's friendship with Cocteau, whose role as *dialoguiste* on *Les dames du bois de Boulogne* (1945) allowed the film to be made, reaches back to the 1920s. Additional facts suggest the tantalizing possibility of a Cocteau influence on the young Bresson: Bresson's personal taste for Keaton (whose "mathematical precision" and "elegance" he admired),[10] and his liking for other 1920s and early 1930s popular and comic fare, including Chaplin's *Gold Rush* (1925) and *City Lights* (1931) and for Eisenstein's *Battleship Potemkin* (1925).[11] A Cocteau link could also shed light on three aspects of Bresson's social and professional life in the 1930s—namely, his employment by Coco Chanel in the early 1930s; his collaboration with Jean Wiéner, who was a colleague of Poulenc and Auric, members of the *Groupe des Six* (or "les Six");[12] and his early interest, shared with Aurenche, in making comedies. Unfortunately, the threads linking these figures and ideas are rather thin.

Aurenche's recollections of the period have more direct relevance to Bresson in providing traces of his relationship with Max Ernst, the prominent Surrealist, and Coco Chanel, the icon of French fashion and design. Aurenche also had strong ties to the avant-garde through his sister Marie-Berthe. In 1927, Max Ernst— described by Aurenche as a "Surrealist, atheist, revolutionary and provocateur"[13]— married Aurenche's seventeen-year-old sibling. She soon befriended the father of Surrealism André Breton, the poet and screenwriter Jacques Prévert, and Cocteau himself, who recommended her as a model to Chanel. Ernst remained with Marie-Berthe until 1936–1937 when he began to court the British painter Leonora Carrington. His marriage to Marie-Berthe came to a de facto end in 1936 during a public confrontation[14] while Ernst was in London for the Surrealist International Exhibition organized by the British Surrealist poet and painter Roland Penrose.[15] Bresson, explains Aurenche, had close ties with this group:

> What few people know today is that Bresson began his professional life as a
> photographer. But not as a reporter of the *Paris-Match* variety, a kind of thug
> gish scrapper, oh no! Coco Chanel, to whom he was more or less related, built
> a whole studio for him and made him the photographer of her collections. She

did all of this without taking into consideration that Bresson was born a perfectionist. Alteration after alteration, reprint after reprint followed, months passed and Chanel, who was amused (and who, between us, had long since hired an experienced and efficient professional to reshoot her collection), told him: "It's obvious, I will never get a photo from you!" One fine day, Bresson proved otherwise with a series of masterpieces: absolutely beautiful photos of the show that had taken place eleven months before.

He was a good photographer. We spent a summer together, with Max Ernst, too, in one of Chanel's mansions near Lisieux. Bresson's wife was . . . just a moment . . . the sister of the wife of the son of Chanel.[16]

Bresson did indeed consider Ernst a friend.[17] And it was in 1926 that he married Leidia van der Zee, sister of Katharina, whose husband, André Palasse, was Chanel's nephew but was raised as her son after the death of his mother Julia-Berthe Chanel in 1913.[18] Through Leidia, Bresson had contact with the Chanel family until at least the late 1930s.[19]

* * *

If Bresson's relationship with Chanel gave him the opportunity to try his hand in fashion photography, it was Aurenche who facilitated Bresson's entry into filmmaking. While Bresson was working as a photographer, Aurenche launched a small production firm to make publicity films—advertising shorts to be shown in theaters during intermissions. His company secured contracts from wineries, furniture boutiques, and Gitanes cigarettes. His Gitanes ad featured a nearly forgotten Georges Méliès. While a number of the films were live-action, many were animation.[20]

Aurenche was taking advantage of a new advertising genre that emerged in France in the 1920s, simply called the *film d'entracte* (the intermission film).[21] The first screenings of these advertisements took place in March 1919 at the Max-Linder theater and the Omnia-Pathé. In the same year, the firm Publi-Ciné was formed, and five years later, Rapid-Publicité. These companies wrote scripts, produced, shot, and distributed the films. The business proved to be quite lucrative. And for young filmmakers, it was a context that allowed relative creative freedom.[22]

Between 1931 and 1934, Aurenche produced fifty such films, each lasting no more than ninety seconds, and developed something of a house style that combined comic effects and—crucially—a mixed cast that often included well-known avant-garde artists.[23] Bresson and other aspiring filmmakers were being trained in slapstick at the same time as they rubbed shoulders with the avant-garde. As Aurenche put it, the films were "tiny, crazy sketches" that built up to a punchline in "the form of a slogan."[24] They were impertinent, at times rather fantastic, and often employed object-oriented gags inspired by Keaton: "One had the impression that Buster Keaton said to himself, 'What can I do with a bucket . . . a typewriter . . . a submarine?' And these objects became poetic because they were used in uncommon ways."[25]

The poeticization of everyday consumer objects, as we will see, was a common trope in Surrealist art of the era. But remaining with Aurenche's ads, one of his first, for the modernist furniture boutique, Les Galeries Barbès, begins with an intertitle that reads: "At dawn, in Mexico, a man is about to be shot." A condemned man is shown with a cigar in mouth, blindfolded and bound to a chair. Artigas plays the captain of a Mexican firing squad, which includes Anouilh and Ernst. When the captain gives the order to fire, the soldiers revolt. In an over-the-top performance, Artigas blurts: "Why didn't you shoot?" Ernst steps toward the camera and declares: "We are not savages. We will not shoot a chair that comes from the Galeries Barbès!"[26]

While the politics of the piece are crude—it stirred controversy for caricaturing Mexican culture—it also shows how the *film d'entracte* mixed high and low, an avant-garde milieu with a pithy, legible aesthetic, established painters with up-and-coming filmmakers, and promotions of the latest high-end luxury items with gags inspired by popular cinema.[27] Consider for instance the importance of the film's location. With the permission of the *vicomtesse* Marie-Laure de Noailles, Aurenche and his crew gained access to the De Noailles Building on the Place des États-Unis in Paris, where members of the Parisian avant-garde were often lodged. This placed Aurenche and his young collaborators—Jacques B. Brunius, who edited the films and later performed in Jean Renoir's *Le crime de Monsieur Lange* (1936); and Paul Grimault, the condemned man in the Barbès ad who later directed some of the most revered films in French animation history, including the feature film *Le roi et l'oiseau* (1980)—in close proximity to some of the influential patrons of the interwar avant-garde. With her husband, the *vicomte* Arthur Anne-Marie Charles, she had financed two early sound avant-garde films, *L'âge d'or* and Cocteau's *Le sang d'un poête* (1930) and was famous for throwing extravagant parties whose guest lists read like a "who's who" of the art scene, including Picasso, Matisse, Giacometti and many others. Aurenche's firm, now a hub for young filmmakers, was doing for them what Cocteau had done for Aurenche: opening doors within the art world.

His firm was also gaining the attention of the film industry, stimulating interest in avant-garde filmmaking despite the apprehension of exhibitors in the wake of the *Âge d'or* Affair. It perhaps dismayed Aurenche and his young crews that, at first, exhibitors tended to treat these films with little regard. Aurenche didn't have the screen time for credits sequences, and the films were shown with the house lights on, although some were beginning to gain prestige. Perhaps the peak of his firm's output was Alexandre Alexéieff's 1934 *La belle au bois dormant* ad for Nicolas vineyards, a stop-motion puppet animation written by Aurenche himself and scored by Poulenc.[28] It was given a credit sequence and a substantial running time (ten minutes) and sold the Nicolas brand through a bizarre, Surrealist retelling of the story of *Beauty and the Beast*, including a delightful interlude where the slender prince, weaving his way through Beauty's castle, meets his own image behind a door that opens on both sides. With a reputable patron behind the film, exhibitors were willing to show it with the lights dimmed. But whether or not their films were garnering respect from exhibitors, young artists like Aurenche, Alexéieff, Grimault, Brunius, and Bresson were at least making movies that found an audience. The average Aurenche publicity film reached no less than 590,000 potential consumers across Paris and the outlying areas. Aurenche even struck a deal with Pathé-Natan, a vertically integrated movie company that owned the largest Parisian theater chain, to screen its ads from time to time.[29]

Aurenche's firm also taught these young artists about the division of labor on movie sets, and encouraged some, like Bresson, to gain experience with a camera. Grimault acted as the principal cinematographer for many of the advertisements, but Aurenche periodically recruited others as assistant directors or as cameramen, including Yves Allégret, who in time moved to directing, most notably for an adaptation of Jean-Paul Sartre's *Les orgueilleux* (1953); and Marcel Carné, who, by the end of the 1930s, was *metteur-en-scène* for such poetic realist classics as *Le quai des brumes* (1938) and *Le jour se lève* (1939). "At the time, they were starting out like me and were cheap," Aurenche commented.[30] "It was an excellent way to practice. Even Bresson came to work for me. . . . Bresson was a very refined cameraman [*opérateur*], but, as I said, I worked above all with Grimault."[31] Unfortunately for us, Aurenche never specified which films Bresson shot.

The Birth of a Visual Stylist: From Surrealism to Radiant Asceticism

Bresson's social milieu in the late 1920s and early 1930s created opportunities in photography and short filmmaking. But to what extent did his ties with the avant-garde and the world of publicity help him develop as a stylist? Let us reexamine this period then from a fresh angle. As an established auteur, Bresson, as we will see in subsequent chapters, became known for a distinctive visual style committed to sparse compositions, fragmented framing of the human figure, and the use of space beyond the frame. Since we have no reliable way of identifying which publicity films Bresson shot, we must look elsewhere for the origins of Bressonian aesthetics. Aurenche appears to have hired Bresson because of his keen visual sense. And this sense, as we will now learn, was nurtured by Surrealism—but a Surrealism of an unusual kind.

Before we proceed, we must briefly address a controversy recently stirred in Bresson studies over the filmmaker's relationship to the interwar avant-garde. Challenging the standard religious interpretation of Bresson's art whereby the filmmaker is seen as wrestling with questions about the Divine's role in life and innovating a style that is above all spiritual, film scholar Brian Price's 2011 book interprets the auteur as a radically political Surrealist.[32] He contends that we first see the "engaged, militant" side of Bresson in a 1932 Surrealist photograph, sometimes called *Lunar Landscape*,[33] a barbed critique of consumer culture: "Bresson's work has from the very beginning been engaged with questions of revolutionary practice and radical politics."[34] The photograph is taken as evidence of a "Surrealist sensibility" that was not as religiously austere or apolitical as commentators who focus solely on his canonical films allege.[35]

There is much to recommend in this new impulse in Bresson commentary. Indeed, until now, no study has attempted to take his Surrealism into consideration, and Price does just that in a way that raises some fundamental questions about Bresson's career: How do we square his mature, apparently spiritual style with his avant-garde photography? Did he simply abandon the Surrealist style and politics of his photography when he became a religious filmmaker? Or does the militancy of his earliest art encourage us to interpret his canonical films in a new light?

My answer is slightly different than Price's. Like Price, I believe that the 1930s photography is crucial to understanding the origins of the *style bressonien*. However, unlike Price, I would argue that any discussion of the early art cannot assume that Bresson appropriated Surrealism as an anticapitalist, militant intervention in visual culture. In fact, determining which version of Surrealism inspired him is not an easy affair. The Surrealist movement took multiple forms in the 1920s and 1930s, not all of which were anticonsumerist or anticapitalist.

To assess the nature of Bresson's Surrealism, we must take a greater measure of the relevant cultural history. As art historian E. H. Gombrich has argued, the analysis of an artwork's cultural function benefits from the consideration of "documented analogies."[36] By this he means that historical interpretations of art, like the effort to read *Lunar Landscape* as a product of interwar Surrealism, while incapable of proof or disproof, nevertheless accrue greater validity if measured against what is possible or likely in the context the artist occupied. If analogous artistic aims are discovered in a range of documented sources—in Bresson's case, in the other nine extant lithographs and photographs he produced between 1927 and 1932, as well as in the art of his peers—then our interpretation of Bresson's Surrealism is placed on firmer ground.

There can be no doubt that *Lunar Landscape* is a Surrealist artwork. An oddity of the photograph (one that Price also analyzes) is its use of hygiene products. The high-contrast composition shows approximately forty-five toothbrushes, with the brand name of Gibbs and the number 49 etched on their handles, lit from the top right to create strong highlights on bristles that shine against the empty black of outer space, each casting a long, dense shadow. Fanned out around an opening in the bottom center of the photograph, the brushes at a quick glance resemble bunches of underwater sea plants, reaching up toward the surface light, or even mineral formations of the kind discovered in deep subterranean caverns. From one perspective, they appear almost fossilized, ancient calcifications awaiting discovery. But cast your eye about and the brushes can also appear to move, even to the point of intermingling as they stroll in troupes along the grainy landscape at the edge of a moon crater. In the distance is a sphere that illuminates the moon's surface. Perhaps representing Earth or the Sun, the disk is in fact a container with the words *savon dentifrice*, or dental soap, faintly engraved on the upper edge.

The mystery surrounding the choice of hygiene products begins to clear when we consider that Gibbs specialized in these items precisely while Bresson was under the firm's employ. In 1906, Thomas et Gibbs, a French affiliate of the London-based company that specialized in perfume, soap, shaving, and brush products, opened headquarters in Paris and factories in the Parisian suburbs of Asnière and La Plaine-Saint-Denis.[37] The company sought to revamp its image in the 1920s and 1930s when it unveiled a stylish new Art Deco design for its logo and enlisted avant-garde artists to create advertisements. Bresson was among the artists hired, but his earliest works for the firm were of a decidedly "functional" nature, which is not to say that they were bereft of artistry.

Long thought to have been a painter who never exhibited his works—because Bresson held the view that "after Cézanne there was nothing more to do"[38]—he displays his skills with brush and oil in his earliest extant piece, a rather pretenseless lithograph for Gibbs published in 1927 or 1928 (figure 1.1). Although on the surface it is quite unlike the art for which Bresson became known, it nonetheless yields insight into his artistic development. Like many of his surviving photographs, the ad is printed in a large, 8½" × 14" format for a full-page magazine spread. Bresson shows his mastery of a printmaking process that involves drawing or painting on a flat surface (usually a stone) using an oil-based medium. He might have employed a wide range of media—crayons, chalks, paints, touches, inks, and the coarseness of his stone—to determine the look. Once the stone is finely painted, even carved, the image is etched onto the stone using a special acidic solution. Typically, the stone is then placed over a bed of ink and print paper and rolled through the press to produce the final picture.

Even an ephemeral piece like this tells a story about the origins of Bresson's style. The full-color advertisement bears his name (Gibbs artists signed their ads as early as the 1910s) and reveals an early penchant for simplified composition. It also creates a visual metaphor that relies on the suggestive use of space beyond the frame. In the bottom left is an assortment of Gibbs products—a razor blade, shaving cream in a tube, a shaving brush, and so on—and to create an image that restricts spatial depth, he allows a frosty bluish mirror captured at a slightly

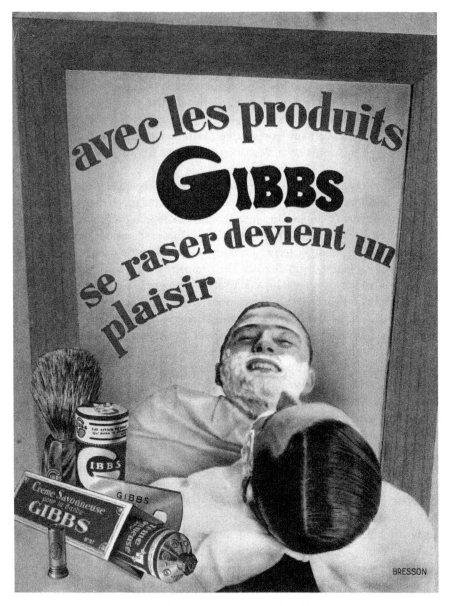

Fig. 1.1. Robert Bresson, advertisement for Gibbs [cosmetics], ca. 1927–1928. Lithograph, 26 x 35cm.

high angle to dominate the frame. Prominently displayed on the glass is the tag line "With Gibbs products, getting a shave is now a pleasure!" The name Gibbs features the Art Deco logo, and in the foreground right Bresson places a customer awaiting service, his face lathered with cream. The back of his head leans out toward the viewer and his reflection, with a full view of his grinning visage, occupies the center of the image. It's an odd and suggestive piece, to be sure, for the angle of the mirror and the two perspectives on the customer create a scene where the viewer stands in for an off-field barber looking down at his next job. The metaphor is clear: Gibbs products provide a shave as fine as any professional. Using techniques that gave him complete control over every detail of the image, Bresson produces a streamlined and even rather witty sales pitch whose "narrative" the viewer is invited to complete by imagining space beyond the frame. The Bressonian fragmentary aesthetic—an imagined whole suggested by visually represented parts—is already implied in his art of the late 1920s.

With the barbershop lithograph, we see that the proposition that Bresson staged a photographic revolt against Gibbs in *Lunar Landscape* is a little far-fetched. For although the piece as it appears in the Centre Pompidou's permanent collection has been stripped of the markers of its origins and purpose, it too was a commissioned a work for Gibbs, published in an October 1931 edition of *L'illustration*, a famous illustrated journal, which at the time claimed some 170,000 subscribers across France and the globe.[39] During the height of its success, the magazine's owner, René Baschet, hired Emmanuel Sougez, a modernist publicity photographer with close ties to the Surrealists Dora Maar and Man Ray, to run its photography wing. The glossy periodical soon emerged a trendsetter in high-end publicity art. The original *Lunar Landscape* is prominently displayed on its first page, in the *annonces* or advertisements section, thus confirming its cultural function (figure 1.2). The orb in the upper right of the original—the Sun or Earth as I have interpreted it—shows Gibbs's Art Deco mark. The distant celestial body is a tin of Gibbs dental soap. For reasons about which one could only speculate, the 1932 version of *Lunar Landscape* displayed at the Centre Pompidou (which Price analyzes) has been retouched to play down the Gibbs connection.

The alterations to the original photo are not merely of interest to the specialist. Other corrections to the 1931 original conceal traces of Bresson's early social bonds—that is, additional artistic partnerships that were crucial to his artistic development. Neither of the two signatories on the original appears in the 1932 version. The reader of *L'illustration*, however, learns that the Gibbs ad was created by "POWEL" and "BRESSON." Who is Powel, and why did Bresson receive credit as the work's second author?

Here we discover some of the deepest roots of Bresson's aesthetics—not in Surrealism, abstractly conceived, but in the collaboration he undertook with particular Surrealists. While working for Gibbs, Bresson was apparently taken on as

Fig. 1.2. Howard "Hare" Pete Powel and Robert Bresson, advertisement for Gibbs [cosmetics], 1931. Photograph, 28 x 39cm.

an apprentice by one Howard Hare "Pete" Powel, an American expat photographer and bon vivant who in the 1920s fled his affluent upbringing in Rhode Island for Paris and helped Bresson gain his footing in the avant-garde world. Powel and his wife, Gretchen, a Texas aristocrat, were close friends with Harry and Caresse Crosby, influential patrons of Salvador Dalí.[40] The Crosbys' Paris-based Black Sun Press, known for its limited editions of James Joyce, T. S. Eliot, and others in the 1920s, published a 1930 collection of the Powels' photography titled *New York 1929.*[41] The Powels and Crosbys were also close with Max Ernst, who perhaps introduced Bresson to the group. Ernst provided illustrations for the 1931 Black Sun republication of the Surrealist tale *Mr. Knife, Miss Fork*, the first chapter of René Crevel's *Babylone* (1927). The story, which initially appeared without illustration in 1929, follows a young bourgeois girl who copes with the effects of her father's infidelities and desertion of her family by retreating into a fantasy world where two runaway lovers represented as cutlery, Mr. Knife and Miss Fork, enjoy the delights of their affection.[42] For the book, Ernst produced nineteen *cliché-verre* prints—drawing and frottage on strips of tin transferred to photosensitive paper—which render the mental imagery belonging to a child whose dreams creatively anthropomorphize inanimate household objects and narrativize their relationships.

These Surrealist contexts reveal that Bresson was not averse to learning from his contemporaries, and together with his barbershop lithography they clarify *Lunar Landscape*'s function as a piece of Surrealist publicity art. Hardly a critique, the original Powel-Bresson advertisement, like Bresson's 1927–1928 lithograph, creates a minidrama that cleverly sells Gibbs's products. The setting and compositional arrangement implicate the visually attentive and imaginative consumer in a somewhat melancholy drama of separation with these items in the leading roles. The relationship between toothbrush and toothpaste is creatively considered through the moon's isolation from other bodies in the heavens. And with the camera positioned on the moon, as it were, the toothbrushes' predicament becomes the compositional and dramatic focal point. To some, the toothbrushes might seem doomed to a grim fate of inertness, frozen in time and unable to play the role of keeping teeth clean because the toothpaste they depend upon, shining down on the brushes from afar, is out of reach—a tragic separation that the consumer can rectify. But the brushes might also be yearning to move closer to the soap that hovers in the sky, projecting a warm light. The brushes take up a position, fanned out across the center in hopes that they can reunite with a celestial product that allows them to fulfill their *raison d'être*. Either way, the toothbrushes develop a character. They appear as figures separated on a cold and inhospitable landscape from the toothpaste they need to complete themselves. And by making an appeal to the consumer to unite them, just as one might unite companions kept apart by great distances, Powel and Bresson sell two of Gibbs's products as a related pair through the metaphor of bodies separated in outer space. The innovative duo has used the photographic assignment—to market these related wares—as a pretext for a Surrealist experiment, one that involves an absurd, schematic, but still rather tender drama between objects, not unlike that of *Mr. Knife, Miss Fork.*

It was hardly eccentric among Surrealists to use their work in the service of publicity in the early 1930s. In fact, Surrealism was in the midst of a commercial turn. The pertinent context for understanding this is not the movement's ideological aversion toward society and advertising's promotion of consumerist excess within it, but, as Georges Roque has shown, the Surrealist's fascination with advertising as a form of expression unique to modernity.[43] Françoise Denoyelle points out that in 1913, Guillaume Apollinaire, often credited with coining the term *surrealism*, described advertising as a "hymn to modernity."[44] Louis Aragon also praises publicity in his 1926 book, *Le paysan de Paris*, a landmark literary achievement of his Surrealist period devoted to mythologizing Paris as a cityscape. Numerous articles published between 1929 and 1935 in the influential journal *Arts et métiers graphiques*—which published texts by Cocteau, Valéry, and Apollinaire—praise advertising as the distinctive art form of modernity, as a vehicle for "contemporary lyricism,"[45] "commercial poetry,"[46] and as "the art of social expression of our time."[47]

Roque describes numerous Surrealist approaches to publicity. Among these is what we might call publicity as the poetry of objects. Initiated by Aragon, whom Bresson viewed as a friend,[48] this trend investigates the creative potential of publicity, experimenting with expressivity of modern objects.[49] The original *Lunar Landscape* photograph does just that. Roque explains that this approach "consists of diverting the creative potential of advertising and transforming it into poetry. According to Aragon, modernity is determined by a new attitude towards objects, whose efficacy has to do with the recent discovery of their new value of expression."[50] This encouraged "Aragon to suggest a strong parallel between modernity and 'surreality,' in so far as both have in common the discovery of a new use for 'modern objects'—that is, 'surpassing the one we knew, to such an extent that we forget it.'"[51]

*   *   *

If we assume that only Bresson's canonical films tell the story of his artistic development, then we neglect the auteur's many unexpected cultural links—his milieu, his partnerships, his apprenticeships, and so forth—and their role in the origins of his style. Perhaps this is why the early years of Bresson's career have remained so mysterious until now. Auteurism has encouraged us to take interest only in cinematic masterpieces that seem to confirm the purely self-derived quality of his art and his reputation as a staunch individualist.

After Bresson's early experiences with Surrealists, he took on new commissions. With this came opportunities to experiment with a wider variety of styles and media. His interest in the poetry of modern objects carried his second Surrealist photograph, an unsigned, and to the best of my knowledge unpublished, piece completed circa 1932. *Razor Blade Figure with Lasso*, as I call it, features a wire figure, perhaps handmade by Bresson, whose head and limbs are Gibbs razor blades.[52] The figure, standing on a rolling, gravelly plain against a black background, wields a lasso that ensnares a long strip of gray beard hair. If this is indeed another publicity ad for Gibbs, Bresson had once again used a poetry of objects to spin a fantasy promoting the company's wares.

At the same time, he drew on a style more akin to that of Emmanuel Sougez, the head of *L'illustration*'s photography department. Less florid and connotatively suggestive than that of the Surrealists, Sougez's photography consisted of elegantly simple compositions, especially still lifes. He was known for his "radiant asceticism."[53] Like Sougez's *Sardine* (1930), *Trois Poires* (1930), and *Repos* (ca. 1933), Bresson's two stills for the high-fashion house Lanvin, published in *L'illustration* in 1932, strip the image to the bare essentials.[54] Bresson was becoming a master of a luminous minimalism. As Souguez might, he used gracefully elongated female bodies and drapery whose waves and pleats captured a subtle range of grays.

Bresson's photography for Chanel—praised, as we saw earlier, by Jean Aurenche—pursues a radiant asceticism in a different medium. He expands his repertoire, driving his art toward pictorialism by printing soft images on creamy paper using a photogravure process, or what the French called heliogravure. In the same year that Pete Powel publishes four heliogravure works in *Arts et métiers graphiques*'s annual album *Photographie 1932* (a suggestive connection, to be sure), Bresson's diffuse and delicate images accentuate the beauty, and even otherworldly quality, of Chanel's wares.[55]

While none of the wares on display in Chanel's *Bijoux de diamants* exhibit were for sale, a handsome catalogue with a brief text by Chanel and photos by Bresson was sold to raise funds for local charities, like L'oeuvre de l'allaitement maternel, which supported maternal nursing.[56] In the catalogue, Chanel states that in a period of financial crisis (the Depression was beginning to have an impact on French society), "an instinctive desire for authenticity is reborn, one that restores to an amusing bauble its legitimate value."[57] Her jewelry designs for the show use bold crescent moon and star motifs, reviving what was, for her (and for many Surrealists, as we have documented), a genuine, modern fascination with magic and fantasy.

If the focus of Bresson's five photographs for the catalogue is the jewelry itself, the composition attests to his subtle mastery of visual media. He drapes Chanel's designs in an ethereal softness. The photos, again approximately 8½″ × 14″, show

Chanel's jewelry displayed on a mannequin's hairline, neckline, and wrists. In one photograph, the camera is placed at a high angle to a subject whose head is captured in three-quarter view against a soft, light gray background. The bottom frame-line trims the mannequin's face from the nose down—another early example of Bressonian compositional fragmentation. The lens, slightly wide-angle, mildly exaggerates the size of the figure's right eye and the diamond head-dress, whose silver or gold strips scale the forehead. In another photograph, a comet-like piece, culminating in a star of diamonds, reaches around the neck of a mannequin frontally positioned, with shoulders perpendicular to the camera axis. What is striking is the range of refined textures Bresson captures—the thin, dark eyelashes, the glistening diamonds, the soft shadows, and the tones of the mannequin's surface. The shadows are minimal—delicate and transparent. Bresson presents Chanel's works in a subtle play of halftones that, like the bold jewelry itself, combines elegance with a dreamy aura.

*   *   *

Bresson's brief foray in publicity does not merely explain mysterious episodes in an often mysterious career, it helps us understand the conditions that made his art recognizable in the art world. His earliest pieces reveal an interest in the meaning implied in, and the attention the artist can draw to, the space beyond the frame—that which is not rendered visually can complete and enhance that which is. Bresson's personal preoccupation with fragmentation and indirection (with suppressing parts of a larger story to create a fuller role and experience for the viewer) were later combined with a Surrealist impulse—namely, an anthropomorphism of household objects (apparently inspired by Max Ernst) during his collaboration with Pete Powel. These partnerships then gave Bresson the opportunity to break away from the overt symbolism of the Surrealist style and increasingly strip his pictures of excess. While working for *L'illustration*'s Emmanuel Sougez, himself a sparse stylist, and under the patronage of Coco Chanel, Bresson entered his most prolific phase as a photographer, producing over a half-dozen photos whose textures, increasingly ascetic, radiant and elliptical, anticipate the "mature" Bresson aesthetic. A consideration of partnerships and alliances led us directly to the roots of the Bresson style.

Arc-Films: The Wager on Independence

Just as Bresson had begun to master a simplified style in photography, new challenges beckoned in the shape of a permanent move to film production. Although we may never know why he abandoned still photography in 1933–1934, it seems clear that the attempt to strike out as an independent producer of auteur cinema was a risky one in these years. Nevertheless, he gambled that it was the time to do so, to move to a new medium and produce art that, for the first time in his professional career, did not publicize and aestheticize a commodity product, but projected his own aesthetic sensibility. This wager on independence followed Jean Aurenche's model of creating an independent production house and required, like his *Lunar Landscape* ad, the partnership of a Surrealist.

Bresson's first years as a writer-director were won through a combination of art-world affiliations and alliances. From various sources, he acquired the financing to launch a new firm, first called Vega but renamed Arc-Films, on May 18, 1934 (the same year Aurenche's publicity company closed its doors).[58] Through the patronage of the Surrealist Sir Roland Penrose, the firm was capitalized at 25,000 francs, one-fifth of which was contributed by Bresson through a personal advance from Penrose for his future work as "metteur-en-scène" for the company.[59] Directly sponsoring avant-garde projects was not unusual for Penrose. He had also financed Max Ernst's *Une semaine de bonté*, a collage novel, in 1933–1934, and it was Ernst who introduced Bresson to Penrose, who quickly became "firm friends."[60]

Bresson would not just write and direct movies for Arc-Films; he would take on the duties of producer. By 1934, with publicity and other experience in the film industry, he perhaps felt equipped for the job. At the time, he and Penrose were coming together on the Arc-Films project, he was working as *dialoguiste* for the popular musical comedy *C'était un musicien* (1933), a Franco-German film coproduced by Zelnick and Pathé-Natan's Bernard Natan for the Compagnie Cinématographique Continentale, starring Fernandel. Officially adopting the title of company manager, Robert Bresson set up Arc-Films at 108 rue Denfert-Rochereau in Paris, which he used as his residence until 1937.[61]

Unfortunately, the state of French cinema assured that launching a successful auteur-centered firm in these years would be a challenge.[62] Nevertheless, for a film director with auteurist aspirations, two aspects of the film scene would have seemed encouraging. First, prior to its collapse, Pathé-Natan, one of two fairly sturdy vertically integrated conglomerates in the film industry, appeared to be weathering the strains of the Depression. It was producing films at a pace of fifteen to twenty per annum and owned some of the best theaters in Paris. Having worked for Aurenche's publicity firm, Bresson would have recognized that a partnership with Pathé-Natan's theaters could guarantee a large audience even for offbeat, independent fare. Second, the artistic talent needed to produce films outside the mainstream was there to be tapped. The late 1920s, early 1930s avant-garde that had stirred controversy with films like *L'âge d'or*—painters and patrons like Max Ernst, Roland Penrose, the *vicomte* de Noailles—and nurtured young filmmakers (Jean Aurenche, Claude Heymann, Jacques Brunius, and so on) were still on the scene.

In his capacity as Arc-Films' writer-director-producer, Bresson immediately arranged financing, again through Penrose, for *Les affaires publiques*, working title *Le chancelier*.[63] The venture was a speculative one for Bresson and Penrose. It was Bresson's intention to produce a commercially successful *court métrage* to reimburse Penrose's not insubstantial investment and launch two other feature-length productions Bresson was already preparing at the time of the *Affaires publiques* shoot.[64] But creating a success—economic or critical—with a film at least partially rooted in the avant-garde was difficult in an environment where the art-cinema circuit, driven by theaters like Jean Tedesco's Vieux Colombier and Armand Tellier's Studio des Ursuline, was adjusting to flagging revenues by programming standard fare.[65] Moreover, the controversy over the banning of *L'âge d'or* shortly after its release potentially stigmatized other offbeat films as unsafe for more mainstream audiences in the minds of exhibitors and distributors concerned about the bottom line.[66] *Les affaires publiques* simply might not earn a return on investment. Cumulatively, these factors meant that the Bresson-Penrose gamble on a vanguard, auteur-centered production firm was perhaps three or four years too late to capitalize on transition-to-sound-era modernist film culture.

Propelled perhaps only by Bresson's drive to develop a distinct voice in the industry, Bresson and Penrose agreed that the firm should aspire to self-sufficiency through vertical integration. A business with production, distribution, and exhibition wings, however modest, could cut costs, guarantee multiple sources of revenue, and ensure a theatrical run for experimental Arc-Films releases. The initial contract drawn up between Bresson and Penrose states that the company would be involved in the "production, distribution and sale of *films cinématographiques*."[67] Arc-Films productions would premiere in the firm's own theater, Raspail 216, located a few blocks from the Denfert-Rochereau headquarters and partially owned and managed by the musician Jean Wiéner, whom we'll return to momentarily. Completed in 1932 by Polish-born architect Bruno Elkouken, the theater was housed in a studio building and used a Streamline Moderne or Art Moderne late Deco design shorn of ornament, with 278 white leather seats, a balcony, and sparse, pastel decorations.[68] The theater had opened on September 15, 1932, with a screening organized by Pathé-Natan that featured Carl Theodor Dreyer's *Vampyr* (1932) and two shorts, Harold Lloyd's *The Fox Hunt* (1921) and a documentary, all with musical accompaniment by the then-famous piano duo of Wiéner and Clément Doucet. The modernist, elite ciné-club-like would provide Arc-Films with the venue it needed to launch its "revolution," as Bresson called it.

Les affaires publiques: An Auteur Film Borne of Collaboration

Just what kind of progress did Robert Bresson make as a vanguard auteur? Some would suggest that *Les affaires publiques* lies outside the Bresson canon for two reasons. First, the method of production on the film seems distinctly nonauteurist.

While he wrote and directed the film, *Les affaires publiques* was a fairly modest comedy made "entre amis."[69] Second, as a casually produced popular genre film designed for the commercial market, Bresson's directorial debut does not evince the aesthetic preoccupations of the auteur's canonical works. He had either failed to impose his unique vision on the work or else he had yet to discover it.

Of course, this book is attempting to expand auteurism to examine the role that various social dynamics—like the auteur's artistic partnerships and alliances—played in Bresson's development as a unique voice. The fact that a given work depends on creative collaborators hardly disqualifies it from his history as an auteur. Under Penrose's patronage, then—his personal investment and protection—Bresson had no difficulty getting Arc-Films' first project underway. Between May and November 1934, Bresson received ten financial installments from Penrose to complete the *Les affaires publiques* production.[70] With a projected budget of 230,500 francs,[71] Bresson shot much of the film outdoors in the former Éclair back lot at Épinay, then owned by La société française des Films Sonores Tobis.[72] His cinematographer, Toporkoff, used cutting-edge technology well adapted to the environment, a Caméréclair Radio that Arc-Films rented from Enregistrements sonore Marcel Pétiot.[73] First introduced in 1933, the Caméréclair Radio was a lightweight camera that allowed synchronous sound recording onto a separate reel.[74] Unencumbered by "blimps" and other forms of soundproofing, this smaller technology, equipped to record sound a great distances, gave Bresson the freedom to shoot in a variety of natural locations.

The production completed, the task was to forge a relationship with the cultural press. No doubt aware from his years as a publicity artist that magazine culture had the power to shape public sentiment, Bresson, from the very beginning of his filmmaking career, used his interviews to clarify, pique interest in, and package his works as manifestations of his own unique aesthetic commitments. Through conversations with critics and reporters, he encouraged a fundamental aspect of auteurism: a new viewing practice. The auteur who wished to experiment with alternative styles, challenging and complex themes, and unorthodox storytelling forms could never trust that the works spoke entirely for themselves. He would have to prime the spectator to interpret them "correctly." Question-and-answer engagements with the cultural press provided Bresson a forum to express a series of generalizations, at times tantalizingly abstract or metaphorical, about his individuality in the industry, about his art or his inventive process, and to propose a rhetorical framework—call it an amplifying language—that expanded the reader's sense of the ambitions behind the art and encouraged appreciation for it as a demonstration of these broader commitments.

Bresson's skillful use of amplifying language is already apparent in his first interview in 1934 with Paul Gilson, a sympathetic interviewer who, as a poet and former member of the avant-garde group Les XX, believed that "poetry was everywhere, in the most banal entertainment [*spectacle*] as well as in cinema."[75]

Printed in the widely read *Pour Vous*, a glamorous fanzine with an Art Deco design that was edited by dramatist, novelist, and screenwriter Alexandre Arnoux, the interview addresses several of the aesthetic principles that drove the making of *Les affaires publiques*, and set Bresson apart as a filmmaker:

> Cinema interests me only at the point of creation. All the rest of it seems totally useless to me. It would be impossible for me to begin work on a film without having developed the screenplay myself—impossible to translate the work of a stranger. This would be like stopping someone who's passing by in order to wax his shoes. How many failures can be attributed to this lack of interest, the impression that directors have that they are enslaved? I therefore made a film 1,200 meters long, because that's how one has to begin one's career, where I wrote the screenplay, directed the actors—in short, took on every responsibility. In my estimation, mistakes that we make while directing come from a lack of precision. Instead, I got to know my film *Les affaires publiques* by heart before undertaking the project.[76]

The quality of his rhetoric is worth noting here. He states some of the goals behind the film as general commitments, not merely as solutions to particular production circumstances:

> I almost never worked in the studio. I contented myself with sets I found outdoors. I had no problem finding them, because all I needed was a wall, a tree and a sky. Otherwise put, this is not an *artistic* film; rather, poetry should come uniquely from a certain consistency of invention. In the same way, if I chose Béby [the clown] to play the Chancellor of Crogandie, it is because his bizarre character struck me, and I could not have conceived *Les affaires publiques* without him. Did I have to make them act—him and the other actors, like [Marcel] Dalio, [Gilles] Margaritis, André Servilanges? Because I place no importance on plot [*action*], it was simply a matter of getting them to react.[77]

Bresson's self-confidence even at this early phase of his career is rather striking, and if we parse his words, so too are his auteurist ambitions:

An Auteur avant la Lettre

Bresson expressly identifies himself as the work's auteur. He makes explicit that he would never direct a film based on someone else's script; he claims responsibility for multiple roles in the production; he claims the virtue of precision in the execution of his art; and he claims a consistency of invention (or a style) in his approach.

A Sparse Stylist

To clarify his personal aesthetic, Bresson commits his art to sparse means that renounce the artistic polish achieved in studio-made films. A filmmaker who needs only a wall, a tree, and a sky is not interested in using his camera to show lavish sets and costuming. Rather, Bresson's "poetry" resides in a consistent method—a limited amount of props and actors to achieve effects that conventions of studio design and performance deny.

A Director Opposed to Conventions of Performance

Bresson declares an aesthetic investment in innovating a performance style that rejects the convention of coaching actors to *act*, because he is concerned less with plot than with observing actors' reactions or behaviors. From the very start of his career, Bresson sought alternatives to the norms of film performance. Later in his career, he called his actors models, a point that will also be examined in later chapters.

An Experimental Filmmaker

Finally, Bresson begins to define his alternative to cinema—that is, to present cinema as a creative process first and foremost, rather than a method for creating polished masterpieces. With amplifying language of this kind, Bresson drew attention away from the final product and toward his unique process of making. This prefigures later statements in which he refers to his films as a means of discovery about the limits of cinema as a medium. As he puts it in a 1963 interview, "My films have been strivings, attempts."[78]

* * *

Through interviews with the press and the patronage of Penrose, Bresson began to reinvent himself within the cultural market as an *auteur de film*. And just as he had done with his Surrealist photography, he enlisted the talents of his peers to work aspects of vanguard culture into *Les affaire publiques*. Jean Wiéner, the composer who programmed for Raspail 216, worked closely with Bresson to transform *Les affaires publiques* into an eclectic film that fused popular comedy with a bold experiment in film scoring that carried the potential to stir controversy.[79]

By the time he wrote *Les affaires publiques*' eclectic score, Wiéner was already well known in France. Music historians Alain Lacombe and François Porcile situate him among the "serious" composers—Arthur Honegger, Darius Milhaud, and Georges Auric, all three members of the *Groupe des six*—who tried their hand at film music in the 1930s.[80] In Wiéner, Bresson found a collaborator whose importance to avant-garde culture propelled him to notoriety in artistic and literary circles—circles that Wiéner introduced to jazz. In 1921, he opened Gaya, a cabaret bar where he played piano for the African American banjo player and saxophonist Vance Lowry. When the bar expanded and moved close to the

Place de la Concorde in January 1922, it was renamed *Le boeuf sur le toit*, the title of a Surrealist ballet-pantomime that premiered in 1920 and was scored by Milhaud, written by Cocteau, and influenced by the rhythms of Brazilian samba. The phrase "faire le boeuf" soon entered the idiom as a common expression for having a jam session.[81] Ludovic Tournès writes that the venue became "the rendez-vous of choice for the artistic avant-garde and Parisian intellectuals—to such a degree that on one night, according to Wiéner, André Gide, Serge Diaghilev, Picasso, Mistinguett, Léon Volterra, Maurice Chevalier, Francis Picabia, Tristan Tzara, Georges Auric, Léon-Paul Fargue, Fernand Léger, Jean Cocteau and Maurice Ravel were in attendance all at once!"[82] In such elite circles, Wiéner was seen as a controversial "ennobler" of jazz.[83] He believed that jazz deserved a place next to more traditional forms and created his celebrated "concerts-salade" to shake up the music scene.[84] Critical to introducing African American music to the audiences of "legitimate" music concerts, the first *concert-salade* was staged on December 6, 1921. This appears to be the first time that jazz—usually associated with the music hall—entered a concert hall ordinarily reserved for classical forms.[85] The event placed Billy Arnold's orchestra next to a piano rendition of the *Rites of Spring*, played by Stravinsky himself, and Milhaud's own *Sonata pour piano et instruments à vent*. The composer Albert Roussel, shocked by the presence of a jazz band on stage, promptly left in protest. Others, like Roger Desormière, who in the Occupation lent his name to Wiéner's film scores,[86] heralded the concert as a triumph, with jazz orchestral compositions finally taking their place alongside chamber music.[87]

Throughout the 1920s, Wiéner often collaborated with the Belgian pianist Clément Doucet. They teamed up in January 1926 for a soirée at the Opéra and played a set that included W. C. Handy's *St. Louis Blues* and compositions by Gershwin in between pieces by Vivaldi, Bach, and Mozart. Both then were invited for a North American tour in 1931.[88] These circumstances of French music are significant to Bresson's debut film because these concerts established Wiéner's reputation for shocking eclecticism and daring juxtaposition of high and low forms—which Bresson creatively incorporated into the film's overall design. With its offbeat character, *Les affaires publiques* proved to be the ideal canvas for Wiéner's playful genre mixing, allowing him to develop his *concert-salade* aesthetic in film.

Set in the fictional country of Crogandie, Bresson's film, as it survives, depicts the country's Chancellor (played by the famous clown, Béby) taking part in three public ceremonies: the unveiling of a statue of the Chancellor, a firefighters' demonstration, and the launching of an ocean liner.[89] Wiéner's eclecticism sits comfortably alongside Bresson's earliest efforts to uncover sound's suggestive force, in this case by restricting music to diegetic sources. The film begins with a radio broadcast connecting a series of disparate spaces: an elderly couple's living room, the husband reading the newspaper, the wife sewing; a bearded man sitting up in bed; and a young woman in a field. In each case, the origin of the radio broadcast—a series of gramophones, except for another man shown in bed, who listens through a headset—is prominently positioned in the frame. We then cut to the film's first sound-related gag. In a medium shot, the Chancellor rides in a motorcade showered with confetti. He lifts his hat to salute an offscreen crowd that is heard cheering enthusiastically. A cut to a wider shot creates a comic "reveal": the Chancellor is in fact on a stroll through the countryside, and an assistant in the back of the car is dispensing the confetti. A gramophone manned by another assistant pipes in canned cheers. "That's enough," barks the Chancellor. A close-up shows the assistant quickly lifting the needle off the record and the crowd noise abruptly stops. In the first minute and a half of the film, the viewer is cued to attend to the presentation of sound and its sources.

Wiéner's theme for the Chancellor is first heard over the opening credits. Appropriate to the film's genre, it recalls the Three Stooges' "Three Blind Mice" cue, with its straightforward, jaunty melody, upbeat tempo, and thin, brassy orchestration. Throughout the film, each time the Chancellor appears and the theme is cued, the same four- (sometimes five-) man band is shown somewhere in the *mise-en-scène*. The perches from which they play—poking out of a bush during the firefighters' sequence, as if in a half-hearted attempt to hide them from view; awkwardly crammed onto a rowboat during the liner scene, again suggesting a dim-witted, and ultimately self-defeating, effort to position the players away from the public's attention—become a running sight gag. The cue itself is a fanfare in the most literal sense, acting as a diegetic leitmotif for the Chancellor and signaling his appearances on spectacular occasions, despite the fact that the gatherings tend to induce boredom in the crowd and the Chancellor alike.

The musical styles Wiéner uses throughout the film help structure its various segments, driving narrative action and becoming the source of comedy. What's more, Bresson does not call upon his actors to perform roles; rather, their gestures and expressions serve Wiéner's music. Not unlike his *concerts-salade*, disparate forms are pitched into the film's musical salad bowl and tossed about, at times even cued unexpectedly, and the characters are forced to react. Humorously trapping his characters in the repetitive formalities of ceremony, Bresson uses the Chancellor's Jazz-Age style theme to signal the start of each scene. Decorum demands that the band never be shown coming and going; it must always already be there, prepared to announce the Chancellor's arrival. But if the band serves as a symbol of the contrived order of head-of-state ceremony, it also contributes to its dissolution into chaos by interfering with the proceedings. During the firefighters' demonstration, the Chancellor prepares to set flame to a mock-up of a house (designed by another of Bresson's colleagues, the avant-garde painter and filmmaker Pierre Charbonnier).[90] As he bends over to do so, the band begins the Chancellor's theme, but the bulbous tuba player hits his note so hard that it blows the entire mock-up out of sight. Moments later, as order is being restored, ceremonial music is exposed as a useless frivolity. The firefighters, embarrassed, urgently struggle to push the house back into position, but, rather than assist in the effort, the band's lanky flutist—the shapes of the instrument and the musician again echo one another—skips about like a pied piper, playing the Chancellor's theme with a sense of whimsy that makes light entertainment of the firefighter's grueling labor. The characters are not fully developed; instead, Bresson conceives of them as devices. His actors react to musical-comedic circumstances rather than concern themselves with fleshed-out dramatic roles.

Relying on relatively short scenes and musical cues—they abruptly pop in and out—Bresson and Wiéner pack the film with a variety of comic scenarios enhanced by a pot pourri of musical genres. During the statue unveiling and the firefighter sequence, Bresson stages several music-hall performances. Prior to the presentation of the monument, six high-school girls, led by their principal, sing "Honor to the Chancellor."[91] Arranged in a chorus line, they burst into a dance number with jaunty brass accompaniment, kicking their legs out from their slit skirts. Ceremonial decorum once again gives way to comedy: At the end of their routine, they bend over, rear ends facing the Chancellor, and flip up their skirts to reveal their backsides. (This gesture takes on new meaning in Bresson's 1967 film, *Mouchette*: When the young protagonist's classmates greet her with this obscenity act, it serves to confirm her as a social outcast.)

The attraction woven into the firefighter scene perhaps best illustrates Wiéner's musical eclecticism. A trumpeter's fanfare announces the start of a number. Two firefighters leap out of the windows of the mock-up house, each time accompanied by a single, gentle note played by warmer brasses. The male firefighters, more or less paired off with some holding hands, begin to dance slowly to a minuet. After several measures, the music unexpectedly shifts tempo to a swing-style cue, which the men dance to in an improvisational Lindy-hop fashion, kicking their feet from side to side. The pace slows back to the minuet, and then speeds up when the swing music is cued again to end the dance. Bresson and Wièner disrupt musical decorum and gender roles through a blending of high and low styles and a comic reversal of the masculinity of the firefighters.

In *Les affaires publiques*, a variety of "high" and "low" cues—drawing on jazz and classic styles—have sway over objects and bodies. The object-oriented approach of Aurenche's publicity films and Bresson's Surrealist photography is woven into a new sound-image aesthetic, and extended to the human form; in Bresson's first foray into reaction-based performance, Wiéner's eclectic music motivates expression, gesture, and movement.

The Demise of Arc-Films

As planned, Arc-Films launched *Les affaires publiques* at a premiere event at Raspail 216.[92] The film received favorable reviews in two prominent publications, *Pour Vous* and the intellectual journal *Esprit*. A discourse was beginning to form around Bresson.[93] His innovations were not lost on reviewers. Paul Gilson notes that the film's comedy anthropomorphizes objects:

> From beginning to end, objects play a large role in failing to do what the actors want them to do. The statue of the head of state yawns, thus preventing the Chancellor of Crogandie from talking; the condemned house runs away when firefighters, who want to put the fire out at all costs, approach; the ocean liner that's being launched prefers to sink rather than to receive a baptism of champagne. . . . *Les affaires publiques* allows us to partake in this revolt of objects. One should congratulate Robert Bresson in his efforts: thanks to him, the much talked-about "way *things* go" finally finds a new path.[94]

Things appear to have been coming together for Bresson: certain members of the press were behind his work, he had a committed patron, he had secured a relative amount of creative freedom, his film pushed aesthetic boundaries, and he had presented the work as a substantive—even revolutionary—deviation from the norm, committed on some level to a sparse aesthetic. Why then do we not remember the Bresson of the 1930s as a major auteur?

In a word, his wager on independence in the 1930s faced insuperable setbacks. By 1936–1937, Arc-Films had fallen into receivership. *Les affaires publiques'* budget had swelled to 352,472 francs, leaving the firm in financial peril.[95] Raspail 216's debts were mounting, and to make ends meet, Bresson found himself working as a dialogue writer on feature-length comedies, *Courrier-Sud* (1936) and *Les jumeaux de Brighton* (1936), starring Raimu and Claude Simon, and then as an assistant director on the drama *La vierge folle* (1938). Reflecting on the demise of a venture he had pursued with such energy, he wrote to Penrose in February 1937: "I am very, very agitated, and beg your forgiveness."[96]

However, it would be reductive to simply point to the collapse of Arc-Films in 1937 as the sole reason for his failed wager. We must instead look for an explanation in terms of film culture and the dynamics it fostered and did not foster between the auteur and his supporters at this stage.

This chapter began with the proposition that during this era the dynamics of partnerships and alliances permitted Bresson to take up challenges that are of concern to any auteur: he had to refine an authorial voice and begin to position himself securely within the market. The *style bressonien* of the canonical films— *Journal d'un curé de campagne* (1951), *Un condamné à mort s'est échappé* (1956), and *Pickpocket* (1959)—used space beyond the frame and sparse images. These core aspects of Bresson's authorial voice were discovered during or cultivated through partnerships with Pete Powel, Emmanuel Sougez, and Coco Chanel. What's more, through the support of Jean Aurenche and Roland Penrose, Bresson was able to gain his first experience as a cinematographer and director. As a director, he relied on the talents of Jean Wiéner, and began to view sound as the source of some unique experiments, not the least of which were with cinematic bodies (here deployed for comic purposes). Finally, upon the completion of his debut film, he attracted the interest of the cultural press. Interviews and reviews from 1934 positioned him as an auteur who was determined to challenge cinematic convention.

In the end, we do not remember the Bresson of the 1930s as a major auteur because in spite of his progress on these fronts, he was too isolated and too marginal to bring about the cultural and institutional changes needed to establish a *cinéma d'auteur*. A single auteur cannot invent auteur cinema, and the failure of *Les affaires publiques* is evidence of this. Like perhaps no other film in his career, Bresson needed *Les affaires publiques* to be a commercial success. His position at the margins of the industry meant that had to generate his own financing to produce his first feature films. He thus needed at least one additional partner—a distributor—to recognize the virtues of his offbeat *court métrage*. For unlike New Wave auteurs of the late 1950s and 1960s, who could rely on intrepid producers like Pierre Braunberger and government subsidy to launch a feature-film project and relatively stable alternative exhibition sites like the ciné-club and the *cinéma art et essai* (art-house theater) to help such projects find an audience, a 1930s vanguard auteur like Bresson, who was just starting out in the industry, needed to appeal to the commercial market. His entire wager depended on it.

In retrospect, he tried to accomplish too much with his debut film. On the one hand, he wrote it in a popular genre that would, in principle, promise wide appeal. On the other, he wove into it vanguard cultural sources and oppositional aesthetic principles and pitched *Les affaires publiques* to intellectuals using lofty language that promised a revolutionary work. Pulled awkwardly in several directions at once, the film failed to find a distributor. And it was not for lack of trying. In early 1935, when *Les affaires publiques* was almost ready for wide release, Bresson arranged a meeting with René Clair, who was directing films for Pathé-Natan.[97] Presumably, he wanted to pique the interest of a mainstream director with avant-garde roots—Clair had directed the Dadaist film *Entr'Acte* in 1924—and build a relationship that would guarantee a large distribution for his films. Unfortunately, Bresson's timing appears to have been slightly off yet again, for Clair's power within the industry was waning. His last film, *Le dernier milliardaire* (1934)—whose similarities to *Les affaires publiques* could not have been lost on either director (both comedies are set in a fake kingdom)—was a commercial and critical failure. In early 1935, Clair left France for a two-year deal with a British company. Desperate, Bresson sold the rights to exhibit, rent, and sell *Les affaires publique* to a firm by the name of Films Pierre Mathieu, which assured Bresson that the film would be programmed.[98] It never was.

What Bresson needed during this difficult time, in order to recover from the Arc-Films disappointment and raise his prospects of directing a feature film, were alternative institutions that could provide his *court métrage* with an afterlife, as it were. These institutions—activist avant-garde or auteur-centered magazines, ciné-clubs, and festivals—would become a fixture of French cultural life again only after the Liberation of 1944. By that point, Bresson had directed his first features, the second of which, *Les dames du bois de Boulogne*, was also underappreciated and misunderstood, but now he could depend upon his affiliation with cinephiles to create an audience for his personal cinema.

Notes

1. Henriette Janne, "À Épinay Cette Semaine . . . ," *Ciné-Magazine*, July 26, 1934.

2. Bresson denied that his short film was a burlesque comedy, instead preferring the label "comique fou"; see Pierre Ajame, "Le cinéma selon Bresson," *Nouvelles littéraires*, May 26, 1966, 13.

3. Because few extant documents address Aurenche's specific claims about Bresson in the 1930s, it is difficult to verify each and every statement on its own. In such circumstances, the historian cannot rely on direct, corroborating evidence—the standard customarily applied to historical testimony—and must utilize other critical tools. Although it is admittedly less than ideal as a reliability test for specific claims, I have assessed the overall veracity of Aurenche's account by verifying the accuracy of his claims about a random sample of events and figures that do not pertain to Bresson. I have done so by checking all facts claimed against available firsthand testimony, scholarly histories, and pertinent audiovisual materials (i.e., films). As a result of these isolated tests, I have determined that Aurenche's memoir constitutes a relatively reliable anecdotal history, and the historian has no general reason to believe that Aurenche is distorting Bresson's early record. Naturally, historians will want to continue to scrutinize Aurenche's claims as new primary materials surface.

4. François Truffaut, "Une certaine tendance du cinéma français," *Cahiers du cinéma* 31 (January 1954): 15–29.

5. Paul Hammond, *L'âge d'or* (London: BFI Publishing, 1997), 58–70.

6. Jean Aurenche, *La suite à l'écran: Entretiens* (Arles: Institut Lumière/Actes Sud, 1993), 30.

7. Ibid.

8. Ibid., 30–31.

9. Ibid., 31.

10. Cited in Michel Estève, *Robert Bresson: La passion de la cinématographe* (Paris: Éditions Albatros, 1983), 120, n. 1.

11. Robert Bresson, "The Best Films of Our Life (suite et fin)," *Cahiers du cinéma* 12 (May 1952): 71.

12. Cocteau wrote the group's manifesto: Jean Cocteau, *Le coq et l'arlequin: Notes autour de la musique* (Paris: Éditions de la sirène, 1918).

13. Aurenche, *La suite à l'écran*, 33.

14. The rather colorful confrontation is recounted in Aurenche, *La suite à l'écran*, 36.

15. Penrose reminisces about the 1936 exhibition in Roland Penrose, *Scrap Book, 1900–1981* (London: Thames and Hudson, 1981), 60–67.

16. Aurenche, *La suite à l'écran*, 51.

17. Vincent Pinel, "*Les Affaires publiques*: Interview de Robert Bresson," in *Le cinématographe de Robert Bresson* (Tokyo: Tokyo International Foundation for Promotion of Screen Image Culture, 1999), 97.

18. Alan Riding, "Robert Bresson, Film Director, Dies at 98," *New York Times*, December 22, 1999, C27.

19. Bresson extends his best wishes on behalf of Leidia to Sir Roland Penrose in several 1937 letters; see Robert Bresson, Letter from Bresson to Penrose, February 25, 1937, Roland Penrose Archive, GMA A35/1/1/RPA 63/1/9, Dean Gallery, Scottish National Gallery of Modern Art, Edinburgh, Scotland.

20. Some of these were featured in a 2008 exhibit, *La pub s'anime! Les films d'animation publicitaire en France*, held at Les arts décoratifs in Paris. A DVD catalogue for the exhibit is available on Les arts décoratifs' website: http://www.lesartsdecoratifs.fr/ francais/publicite /editions-120/catalogues-d-exposition-121/le-film-d-animation-publicitaire.

21. I have not been able to confirm the name of Aurenche's firm.

22. By 1925, each ad cost approximately 1,950 old francs, which paid for the production of ten copies. They would then be sold to the advertiser for 51,588 old francs (which also included production and distribution services). See Amélie Gastaut, *Le film d'animation publicitaire en France, 1912–2007* (Paris: Chalet pointu, 2007).

23. Aurenche, *La suite à l'écran*, 50.

24. Ibid., 53.

25. Ibid., 60.

26. Ibid., 54.

27. For more on the controversy it stirred, see Aurenche, *La suite à l'écran*, 54.

28. Aurenche, *La suite à l'écran*, 55.

29. Ibid.

30. Ibid., 50.

31. Ibid., 51–52.

32. Brian Price, *Neither God Nor Master: Robert Bresson and Radical Politics* (Minneapolis, MN: University of Minnesota Press, 2011), 2.

33. The title *Lunar Landscape* comes from Agnès De Gouvion Saint-Cyr, Jean-Claude Lemagny, and Alain Sayag, *Art or Nature: Twentieth Century French Photography* (London: Trefoil Publications, 1988), 55.

34. Price, *Neither God Nor Master*, 2–3.

35. Ibid., 16.

36. E. H. Gombrich, "Michelangelo's Last Paintings," in *Reflections on the History of Art*, ed. Richard Woodfield (Berkeley and Los Angeles: University of California Press, 1987), 88.

37. Laboratoire de recherche historique Rhône-Alpes/Institut des sciences de l'homme, "Institutions: Thomas et Gibbs," Système d'information: patrons et patronat français, XIXe–XXe siècles, http://sippaf.ish-lyon.cnrs.fr/Database/Institutions_fr.php?ID=IN000007539 (September 29, 2009).

38. For the statement about Cézanne, see Tony Pipolo, *Robert Bresson: A Passion For Film* (New York and London: Oxford University Press, 2009), 27.

39. Jean-Noël Marchandiau, *L'illustration 1843–1944: Vie et mort d'un journal* (Toulouse: Editions Privat, 1987), 247.

40. Geoffrey Wolff, *Black Sun: The Brief Transit and Violent Eclipse of Harry Crosby* (New York: New York Review Books, 2003), 156.

41. Pete and Gretchen Powel, *New York, 1929* (Paris: Black Sun Press, 1930).

42. Hazel Donkin, *Surrealism, Photography and the Periodical Press: An Investigation into the Use of Photography in Surrealist Publications (1924–1969)* (PhD Diss., University of Northumbria at Newcastle, 2009), 189–192.

43. Georges Roque, "The Surrealist (Sub-)Version of Advertising," in *Surreal Things: Surrealism and Design*, ed. Ghislaine Wood (London: V&A Publications, 2007), 161–175.

44. Françoise Denoyelle, "Photographie et publicité, les promesses d'un art nouveau (1919–1939)," in *La photographie publicitaire en France: De Man Ray à Jean-Paul Goude* (Paris: Les arts décoratifs, 2006), 11.

45. Léon-Paul Fargue, "Salut à la publicité," *Arts et métiers graphiques* 45 (February 15, 1935): 6.

46. Pierre Mac Orlan, "Graphisme," *Arts et métiers graphiques* 11 (May 15, 1929): 650.

47. Ibid., 649.

48. Pinel, "Interview de Robert Bresson," 97.

49. Roque, "The Surrealist (Sub-)Version of Advertising," 162–163.

50. Ibid., 163.

51. Ibid.

52. The photograph is also part of the Centre Pompidou's permanent collection.

53. Noël Bourcier, "L'ascèse radieuse d'Emmanuel Sougez," *Photographie magazine* 49 (1993): 69–70.

54. The Lanvin photographs were signed "BRESSON" and published on April 23 and December 3, 1932.

55. *Photographie 1932*, sp. iss. of *Arts et métiers graphiques* (August 25, 1932), 9, 79, 89, 101.

56. Henry Gidel, *Coco Chanel: Biographie* (Paris: Flammarion, 2000), 254.

57. Coco Chanel, *Bijoux de diamants* (Paris: L'imprimerie Draeger, 1932).

58. Sewell and Branch, Paris, Letter to Roland Penrose, May 18, 1934, Roland Penrose Archive, GMA A35/1/1/RPA63/2, Dean Gallery, Scottish National Gallery of Modern Art, Edinburgh, Scotland.

59. Ibid.

60. Antony Penrose, *Roland Penrose: The Friendly Surrealist* (London and New York: Prestel, 2001), 67–68.

61. Robert Bresson to Roland Penrose, February 25, 1937, Roland Penrose Archive, GMA A35/1/1/RPA63/1, Dean Gallery, Scottish National Gallery of Modern Art, Edinburgh, Scotland.

62. During the conversion-to-sound period of 1929 to 1934, the film industry saw the rise of two vertically integrated conglomerates that promised to stabilize a production sector weakened by the collapse of the original Pathé Frères just prior to World War I. But this was at least partially an illusion. The first of these groups, Gaumont-Franco-Film-Aubert (GFFA), was in debt from the moment it was formed, a situation exacerbated by a banking crisis that forced GFFA to repay its debtors earlier than expected. GFFA closed its doors in July 1934. The other conglomerate, Pathé-Natan, went into liquidation in February 1936. See Colin Crisp, *The Classic French Cinema, 1930–1960* (Bloomington: Indiana University Press, 1993), 29, 31.

63. Éclair-Tirage, Paris, Report for Roland Penrose, January 7, 1935, Roland Penrose Archive, GMA A35/1/1/RPA63/4, Dean Gallery, Scottish National Gallery of Modern Art, Edinburgh, Scotland.

64. Janne, "À Épinay cette semaine . . ."

65. Crisp, *The Classic French Cinema*, 233.

66. Hammond, *L'âge d'or*, 60–70.

67. Sewell and Branch, Paris, to Roland Penrose, May 18, 1934. Roland Penrose Archive, GMA A35/1/1/RPA63, Dean Gallery, Scottish National Gallery of Modern Art, Edinburgh, Scotland.

68. Herbert Matthews, "Paris Views New Films and Theatres," *New York Times*, January 15, 1933, X4. See also Roberto Gargiani, *Paris: Architektur Zwischen Purismus Und Beaux-Arts, 1919–1939* (Wiesbaden, Germany: Vieweg+Teubner Verlag, 1992), 40–41.

69. Penrose, *The Friendly Surrealist*, 67–68.

70. Untitled Financial Statement, n.d., Roland Penrose Archive, GMA A35/1/1/RPA 63/3/4, Dean Gallery, Scottish National Gallery of Modern Art, Edinburgh, Scotland.

71. Ibid.

72. Janne, "À Épinay Cette Semaine . . ."; Donald Crafton, *The Talkies: American Cinema's Transition to Sound, 1926–1931* (Berkeley: University of California Press, 1997), 420.

73. Robert Bresson to Roland Penrose, undated letter, Roland Penrose Archive, GMA A35/1/1/RPA63/1/10, Dean Gallery, Scottish National Gallery of Modern Art, Edinburgh, Scotland.

74. Crisp, *Classic French Cinema*, 115–116.

75. Georges Charensol, *D'une rive à l'autre* (Paris: Mercure de France, 1973), 253.

76. Paul Gilson, "'Les Affaires publiques:' Film d'actualités imaginaires," *Pour vous*, August 30, 1934, 11.

77. Ibid. Gilles Margaritis was the film's chauffeur, and acted in Jean Vigo's *L'atalante* (1934) the same year. André Servilanges later performed in *La kermesse rouge* (1947) and *Chéri-Bibi* (1955).

78. Ibid., 1.

79. Perhaps due to widespread admiration for his canonical films, critics have tended to present Bresson as an auteur who rejected the traditional score in favor of what one critic called "meticulously orchestrated 'sound effects.'" See Donald Richie, "Bresson and Music," in *Robert Bresson*, ed. James Quandt (Toronto: Cinematheque Ontario, 1998), 299.

It should be said that Bresson viewed the score of his earliest film in a positive light: "The music is by Jean Wiener and I like it a lot. I find it very well suited to a film that takes place in an unreal, completely fabricated world"; see Pinel, "Interview de Robert Bresson," 97. Wiéner also scored parts of *Au hasard Balthazar* (1966), *Mouchette* (1967) and *Une femme douce* (1969).

80. Alain Lacombe, and François Procile, *Les musiques du cinéma français* (Paris: Bordas, 1995), 45.

81. Bernard Gendron, *Between Montmartre and the Mudd Club: Popular Music and the Avant-Garde* (Chicago: University of Chicago Press, 2002), 99. For more on jazz in the period, see Jeffrey H. Jackson, *Making Jazz French: Music and Modern Life in Interwar Paris* (Durham, NC: Duke University Press, 2003).

82. Ludovic Tournès, *New Orleans sur Seine: Histoire de jazz en France* (Paris: Fayard, 1999), 19.

83. Ibid.

84. Ibid.

85. Ibid., 19–20.

86. Desormière also conducted Wiener's first film score, for *L'âne de Buridan* (1932), and received a credit on *Les affaires publique* as a technical collaborator for Wiener's music.

87. Tournès, *New Orleans sur Seine*, 20.

88. Ibid., 20–21.

89. During postproduction, Bresson was tempted to cut the second segment due to the film's length and pacing. Originally 1,048 meters (or 3,438 feet) in length, he trimmed the film to

3,396 feet, or four reels, with an approximate running time of thirty-seven minutes and forty-four seconds (the version that survives is about twenty-three minutes long). See Éclair-Tirage, Paris, for Roland Penrose, January 7, 1935, Roland Penrose Archive, GMA A35/1/1/RPA63/4/3, Dean Gallery, Scottish National Gallery of Modern Art, Edinburgh, Scotland; Bonded Film Stores, London, to Roland Penrose, January 19, 1935, Roland Penrose Archive, GMA A35/1/1/RPA63/4/3, Dean Gallery, Scottish National Gallery of Modern Art, Edinburgh, Scotland.

In a letter, Bresson reassured Penrose that the final version would be shortened "by about one-third," that the "rapidity" of the other segments would allow him to retain the firefighter set piece, and that the film "will, in that form, pass muster with all audiences." See Robert Bresson to Roland Penrose, n.d., Roland Penrose Archive, GMA A35/1/1/RPA 63/1/10.

90. Charbonnier directed the Surrealist film *Ce soir à huit heures* (1930). See Estrella de la Torre Giménez, "Les essais cinématographiques de René Magritte," *Mélusine* 24, "Le cinéma des surrealists" (2004): 125.

91. William Johnson, *"Affaires publiques,"* in *Robert Bresson*, ed. James Quandt (Toronto: Cinematheque Ontario, 1998), 190. Johnson identifies the song as the Crogandian anthem, though I find no evidence for this title. For this reason, and because the song's lyrics celebrate the chancellor, I have named it the "Honor to the Chancellor" theme.

92. Penrose, *Roland Penrose: The Friendly Surrealist*, 67–68.

93. Roger Leenhardt, "À propos de films burlesques," *Esprit* 27 (December 1934): 494–499.

94. Gilson, "'Film d'actualités imaginaires," 11.

95. Sewell & Branch, Bilan au December 31, 1934, February 18, 1935, Roland Penrose Archive, GMA A35/1/1/RPA63, Dean Gallery, Scottish National Gallery of Modern Art, Edinburgh, Scotland.

96. Robert Bresson to Roland Penrose, February 18, 1937, Roland Penrose Archive, GMA A35/1/1/RPA 63/1/8, Dean Gallery, Scottish National Gallery of Modern Art, Edinburgh, Scotland.

97. Robert Bresson to Roland Penrose, n.d., Roland Penrose Archive, GMA A35/1/1/RPA 63/1/10, Dean Gallery, Scottish National Gallery of Modern Art, Edinburgh, Scotland.

98. Robert Bresson to Roland Penrose, February 18, 1937, Roland Penrose Archive, GMA A35/1/1/RPA 63/1/8.

2   The Rise of the Accursed:

When Bresson Was Copresident of an Avant-Garde Ciné-Club

> [*Films maudits*] are full of remarkable things, albeit unremarked, that continually move cinema forward, but that are savored at first only by a select few—these films that strengthen and nourish cinema as a whole.
>
> Robert Bresson[1]

WHEN ROBERT BRESSON spoke these words about the distinctiveness of *films maudits* (accursed films) in an April 1949 Radiodiffusion-Télévision Française broadcast, he did so as one of the copresidents of Objectif 49 (1948–1950), a ciné-club that represented the collective effort of a group of postwar auteurs and cinephiles to relaunch the avant-garde in French cinema. It was the eve of the club's second major event, the *Festival du film maudit* (July 28 through August 5, 1949), and Bresson's primary purpose was to discuss the festival's 16-millimeter-film competition, for which he would serve as a member of the jury: "The club 'Objectif 49' . . . believed that it would be appropriate to reward, alongside films thought of as commercial, those films to which cinema owes a great deal—I'd even say, everything. . . . Because cinema is immured in money and these 16mm films, which aren't under the surveillance of money, are made in conditions of great liberty and are capable of great audacity. . . . It's for this reason that this prize of one million [francs] that will be awarded to the best 16mm amateur film seems to me essential to the future of cinema."[2]

Why would Bresson, today viewed by many as one of cinema's great solitary artists, take such an activist role within the cultural market, teaming with cinephiles in support of the avant-garde?

The answer rests with the conditions Bresson faced as he transitioned to feature filmmaking in the 1940s. Like the 1930s, the decade of the Occupation and Liberation provides a pivotal background to the development of Bresson's aesthetics, when the auteur was discovering how to orient himself toward the cultural market and the market was doing the same with "accursed" avant-garde auteurs like himself.

By 1948, which is to say, ten years after the collapse of his independent production firm Arc-Films, Bresson had transitioned to feature filmmaking, but his career was flagging. His first feature, *Les anges du péché* (1943), was well received, but his second, *Les dames du bois de Boulogne* (1945), was generally greeted as a disappointment and nearly ruined its producer. Although this is difficult to imagine, for today he is so revered in international film culture, between 1945 and 1948 Bresson was something of a pariah director among reviewers, the author of a *film maudit*. Critics of *Les dames du bois de Boulogne* had "assassinated" him, he colorfully stated some years later: "It took me a long time to recover. Ploquin [the film's producer] locked the film away."[3]

It was at this stage that he joined Objectif 49, a community of intrepid auteurs and cinephile critics whose interventions in film culture and discourse were beginning to put pressure on the institutions of cinema. If Objectif 49 succeeded in shifting attention toward experimental narrative filmmaking that took financial risks to advance the art of cinema, auteurs like Robert Bresson could survive their intermittent "failures." These were the stakes.

Like the previous one, this chapter tells an institutional story, but the focus will not be on Bresson's background in a relatively established avant-garde, on his ties to its artists and patrons, and how they nurtured his creative endeavors. Instead, attention will be given to the postwar effort, spearheaded by Objectif 49, to reinvigorate French cinema, to shake the institutions of cinema to their foundations, and lend support to an avant-garde of *films maudits* whose contributions to film culture were being ignored by audiences, distributors, and producers alike.

Unfortunately, we know very little about Bresson's involvement in the club's day-to-day operations. Quite simply, no paper trail exists, no testimony survives, that allows us to tell this part of the institutional story. That being the case, this chapter will concentrate less on the role Bresson played within the club and more on the impact that the club and its members had on the rehabilitation of his reputation.

The club and its members interceded in the professional life of Robert Bresson, illuminating *Les dames du bois de Boulogne*'s significance within film culture, by strategically reinventing Bresson as a quality *and* as an avant-garde filmmaker. The reasons for this seemingly contradictory strategy stem from market conditions. The industry had already begun to develop an institutional discourse (based on notions of "quality") in order to promote the distinctiveness of French cinema on the international stage. Cinephiles affiliated with Objectif 49 appropriated the concept of quality as part of a call to action for better funding for *films maudits* like *Les dames du bois de Boulogne*, as well as an aesthetic label that helped to distinguish the aims of vanguard auteur cinema from those of the mainstream.

This, to a certain extent, defies conventional wisdom. François Truffaut famously used the term "quality"—the concept of a Tradition of Quality, to be more precise—as a negative label in his 1954 rebuke of contemporary trends, "Une certaine tendance du cinéma français."[4] But, as I intend to show, years before this, cinephiles deployed "quality" in the struggle over market support for vanguard auteurs.

Objectif 49 and its members appropriated another resurgent discourse—that of the avant-garde, a term then largely associated with abstract, "plotless" filmmaking—and linked it to the mission at the core of the club. It aspired to launch a *nouvelle* avant-garde culture, one that focused on rescuing *films maudits* from obscurity, not only by finding them distribution, but by encouraging the cultural market to rethink its assumptions about avant-garde cinema. Objectif 49's avant-garde was to be more than a fringe movement of filmmakers experimenting with nonnarrative forms; the club threw its support behind auteurs whose innovations in storytelling attempted to purify and simplify the aesthetics of cinema's central narrative tradition, which until now had served the desire for stylistic excess and spectacle entertainment. As a narrative avant-garde, it was, in principle at least, a popular avant-garde, consisting of auteurs who wove their stylistic and narrative explorations into plots driven by fresh approaches to character, plot, and theme that promised to attract a wider audience than experimental films of the 1920s.

What does this reveal about how Bresson oriented himself within the cultural market and how it oriented itself toward him? As we will see, the auteur's implication in the activities of Objectif 49, in a partnership that built a new alternative institution and relied on a language and set of ideas that unified the interests of cinephiles and auteurs, refashioned him within the market as a *cause célèbre*, the center of a battle for the cultural status that vanguard auteurs desperately lacked within the industry. Cinephiles affiliated with Objectif 49, like Alexandre Astruc, André Bazin, and Jacques Doniol-Valcroze, mounted a case for reforming the institutions of cinema so that they more adequately and consistently supported cinematic forms like Bresson's. And Bresson's *Les dames du bois de Boulogne* played an important role in this context as well. The film became an emblem, taken up in a series of interventionist and reformist discourses that sought to influence the means of funding, reception, distribution, and exhibition that the auteur depended upon to survive in midcentury France. Bresson and his film, in other words, became implicated in a collective institutional and rhetorical intervention dedicated to creating a new audience for auteurist experimentation with narrative form—an audience educated in and committed to the aesthetic ideas that had made these auteur films *maudits* (obscure, misunderstood by most, admired by few, and ultimately driven to nourish the *art* of cinema).

Institutional Struggles: Bresson's Early Feature Career

If the steps Bresson took in the 1930s—working on publicity films, forming his own production company, and accepting commissions as a screenwriter and *dialoguiste* on popular fiction films—were in some measure designed to gain him entry into the feature film industry, the professional challenges he faced once he got there left his career as a filmmaker equally precarious. The institutions of production and reception in 1940s France were ill-equipped to respond to Bresson's desire to reinvent cinema through a simplified aesthetic that subverted the industry's dependence on spectacle entertainment (Bresson's aesthetics will be addressed in more detail in the next three chapters). As a result, Bresson's cinema became touted in postwar film culture as a *cause célèbre*, a striking illustration of the failures of the French system.

Under the extreme conditions of the Occupation, Bresson was able to direct his first two feature films.[5] But his status as a viable "name," as an auteur worthy of consistent support within the industry, remained uncertain throughout the 1940s. His debut feature, 1943's *Les anges du péché*, inspired by a 1938 nonfiction source, *Les dominicaines des prisons*, recommended by the Dominican priest and film producer Raymond-Léopold Bruckberger,[6] received immediate praise from Roland Barthes, among others. And yet, Bresson's artistic vision was only intermittently acknowledged in reviews of the film.[7] Barthes didn't even name Bresson in his review, while another prominent critic credited Jean Giraudoux, who wrote the film's dialogue, for its authentic, almost documentary-like handling of convent life.[8] This lack of recognition must have frustrated the forty-two-year-old Bresson, for it was he who had initiated the project.

Critical neglect was the least of it. Like his entry into the industry in the mid-1930s, *Les anges du péché* was a precarious undertaking. As he had with *Les affaires publiques* (1934), he turned to partnerships with influential patrons and collaborators to produce the film. At first, Pathé, one of France's most reputable production companies, took interest in the project (apparently at the behest of filmmaker Christian Stengel, whose willingness to vouch for Bresson remains a source of mystery), but the firm judged the script too risky, with no commercial prospects.[9] Subsequently, Bresson approached Roland and Denise Tual, who managed the production company Synops, owned by the powerful publishing house Gallimard. The Tuals were in a position to gain the film favor in the industry, Roland Tual being a member of the consultation committee of the Comité d'organisation des industries cinématographique (COIC), the Vichy government's film regulatory body.[10] Moreover, the Tuals were artists, intellectuals, and patrons of the arts who would, at least in principle, be receptive to Bresson's daring project, especially given its literary connections via Jean Giraudoux. Briefly the French minister of information before the war (which placed him in charge of film production), Giraudoux was a respected and well-connected playwright and novelist whose name value would give the film clout in film and intellectual circles, as indeed it did upon its release, for as Barthes wrote, "The dialogue required of Giraudoux only his talent . . . and such talent is enormous."[11] With Giraudoux collaborating on the project, Synops could increase the film's visibility and take advantage of ancillary revenue streams. The Tuals secured the rights from Pathé,[12] Bresson's first feature-film production as director was finally afoot,[13] and the film's screenplay, attributed to Giraudoux, was published by Gallimard under the title *Le film de Béthanie* in 1944.[14]

Giraudoux was key to *Les anges du péché*, and Bresson was aware of it. Eager to bring him on board, Bresson ceded the higher salary for the film's script to the established author.[15] As Bresson later admitted, he owed his entry to feature filmmaking to Giraudoux: "Thanks to him, to his collaboration, I was able to get to the other side of the barbwire fence in which cinema encloses itself."[16]

With little in the way of critical recognition for his work on *Les anges du péché*, however, Bresson again relied upon strategic partnerships to launch his second Occupation-era feature, 1945's *Les dames du bois de Boulogne*. Adapted from the Madame de la Pommeraye episode of Diderot's *Jacques le fataliste* (1796), the film was produced by the newly formed Films Raoul Ploquin, whose owner had been the director of COIC until May 1942.[17] Early on, Bresson brought another culturally respected author onto the project, his friend Jean Cocteau, who wrote the film's dialogue, according to Bresson, in "less than one hour, sitting on the corner of a couch."[18] In addition, though they do not appear on the credits, Bresson enlisted two other established writers, the Surrealist playwright and poet Georges Neveux, and screenwriter Pierre Bost, for contributions to the dialogue and découpage.[19] But it was Cocteau's involvement that really excited the producer. Cocteau recalls: "Mr. Ploquin (the producer) was delighted: 'Fantastic! I'm going to get double my money: some Cocteau and some Bresson!'"[20]

Even with both their names as well as that of the rising star Maria Casarès on the marquee, *Les dames du bois de Boulogne* was a commercial failure from which Bresson almost did not recover. On the occasion of the film's revival in 1954, François Truffaut described just how misunderstood it had been among intellectual and popular audiences alike:

> Not ten years ago . . . our literature professor came into classroom and said, "Last night I saw the stupidest film in the world, *Les dames du bois de Boulogne*. . . ." The critics were not kinder. The public did not come, or if they did, it was only to smirk at one of Cocteau's lines. The producer, Raoul Ploquin, was ruined, and it took him seven years to recover.
>
> The Cinéma d'Essai has just put Bresson's film on the program as part of a retrospective, and I hear that the audience is greater than for any other film, that the audiences are quiet, and sometimes even applaud. To quote Cocteau, the movie "has won its case in the appeals court." After its spectacular commercial failure, *Les dames du bois de Boulogne* was shown in film clubs and almost all the critics made their amends. Today . . . Bresson is considered one of the three or four greatest French filmmakers.[21]

Despite the institutional challenges and commercial setbacks he faced during the mid-1940s, Bresson's 1945 film found an afterlife. His reputation rebounded.

According to Truffaut, a single institutional development had intervened. The postwar ciné-club had encouraged a widespread mea culpa and helped to establish Bresson as a culturally significant auteur. But to what ciné-clubs was Truffaut referring? And what conditions gave these clubs the power to rescue an auteur and his film from obscurity in 1940s and 1950s film culture?

A New Avant-Garde: The Intervention of Objectif 49

If several ciné-clubs were likely to have assisted in Bresson's recovery from the professional disappointments of the 1940s (namely, from the paltry cultural recognition he received for his unconventional narrative experiments), it was Objectif 49 that played the biggest role in turning Bresson's art into a *cause célèbre* and demanded that the entire market reconsider its negative reception of such "challenging" fiction films. They may have been "accursed" within culture at large but they were in fact leading a new avant-garde in world cinema.

Between September 1945, the date of *Les dames du bois de Boulogne*'s release, and September 1948, the end of that year's Venice Film Festival, something began to stir within French film culture. At first, there were only faint whispers within the cinephilic community, at least as far as the print record shows. Here and there, one finds traces of a growing interest in the return of avant-garde cinema. As new journals sprang into existence, their editors and critics weighed in on the possibilities of a postwar revival, of a *new* avant-garde.

Curiously, some determined that the very notion of the avant-garde was simply outmoded. An editorial published in a summer 1947 issue of *La revue du cinéma* documented the long history of the avant-garde spirit in French cinema and beyond, through German Expressionism, Delluc, Gance, Léger, Fischinger, Prévert, Cavalcanti, Painlevé, and Cocteau, and declared "The avant-garde is a thing of the past. The word should be filed away. AVANT-GARDE is a sign hung on a cinémathèque closet."[22]

Not long thereafter, *Revue du cinéma* refined its initial dismissal of this cultural project. Its editors now seemed convinced that a new avant-garde of sorts was afoot in a small group of postwar films that rejected cinema's attachment to narrative. But the prospects of this postwar vanguard were dim. In an issue of the journal that included Bazin's famous article on Hollywood director William Wyler,[23] Henri Langlois, the founder of the Cinémathèque française, wrote "L'avant-garde d'hier et d'aujourd'hui," a report on the 1948 Venice Biennale. For him, a film screened there, Hans Richter's *Dreams That Money Can Buy* (1947), was little more than a retrograde attempt to revive a 1920s-style avant-garde. After dismissing the "sad film" and "sad spectacle" of the Venice crowd applauding Richter's "avant-garde" film (the scare quotes are his), Langlois denounced such revivalist efforts as an attempt to appeal to an audience's "bad taste."[24] Langlois tore into the film by writing that if *Ballet mécanique* (1924), *Anemic Cinema*

(1926), *Un chien andalou* (1929), and *L'âge d'or* (1930) had also been screened at Venice—if, in other words, Richter's new film had been placed in its proper stylistic context—*Dreams That Money Can Buy* would have been exposed as "caricature and plagiarism."[25] However, he did not agree with the magazine's editors that the avant-garde ought to be relegated to the Cinémathèque's storage room. He instead attempted to pry the label loose from both narrative cinema and Richter's old-fashioned experimentalism.

Between November 12 and November 14, 1947, Langlois curated a Cinémathèque series also called "The Avant-Garde of Yesterday and Today." The lineup included films from an experimental lineage Langlois considered far more promising. The series looked beyond the 1920s to a long tradition of abstract, mostly animated, works: Émile Cohl's *Le retapeur de cervelle* (1911), Alexandre Alexéieff's *A Night on Bald Mountain* (1933), Oskar Fischinger's *Composition in Blue* (1935), recent films by Maya Deren and Norman McLaren, and Francis Lee's *1941* (1941) and *Le bijou* (1946).[26] Langlois' *Revue du cinéma* article framed the program as an exercise in art historiography on an international scale, excavating a forgotten trend and positioning Lee's works (in contrast to Deren's) as the heir to a tradition of rhythmic, abstract composition. Cohl and McLaren had "the gift of rhythm," he noted, and now Lee had "opened a new door for the cinema."[27] While McLaren was "sheer intelligence," Lee revealed the virtues of "sheer spontaneity."[28] Linking these recent experiments to an ultimate French source, Langlois perceived in Lee a rediscovery of Cohl: "What then is new in his work? Trying to follow music since 1929, the abstract film, born in the painter's studio, has rejoined Cohl and ballet. Francis Lee has returned it to painting."[29]

"Nouvelle avant-garde" swiftly became a term du jour. Yet it was more than a fad; it was a site of discursive and institutional competition. On the discursive front, Alexandre Astruc's "Naissance d'une nouvelle avant-garde: La caméra-stylo," published in a March 1948 issue of the cinephilic weekly *L'écran français*, declared the birth of a new avant-garde of an entirely different sort. Spurning Langlois's avant-garde of painted abstraction, he associated this new trend with narrative auteur cinema, and with this piece, the reconstruction of Bresson, the recognition of him as a *cause célèbre*, was under way. With cinema "becoming a means of expression," Astruc wrote, "the distinction between author and director no longer makes any sense. . . . Direction is no longer a means of illustrating or presenting a scene, but a true form of writing. . . . There is always an avant-garde when something new takes place."[30] Crucially, coming to terms with this required confronting the scandalous lack of recognition for Bresson's Occupation-era cinema. *This* new avant-garde comprised films that "criticism has ignored. . . . It is not just a coincidence that films from Renoir's *La règle du jeu*, to those of Orson Welles, to *Les dames du bois de Boulogne*, all of which sketch the contours of a new future, have eluded the attention of critics, who in any case were bound to be eluded by them."[31]

Mere months after Astruc's piece was printed, several cinephiles and auteurs joined forces to launch an intervention in the form of a new ciné-club. The club would focus its mission on a range of institutions that were failing the most promising talent in vanguard auteur cinema.[32] Jean-Charles Tacchella, then a reviewer for *L'écran français*, recalls that it all came together during the 1948 Venice festival, where he gathered with Jean Cocteau and several other *nouvelle critique* reviewers, future cofounder of *Cahiers du cinéma* Jacques Doniol-Valcroze, and André Bazin, then best known as a critic for the daily *Parisien libéré*, to diagnose the poor state of cinema's institutions: "We would talk with Cocteau about the position of French cinema in 1948, corseted as it was by administrative and trade union regulations. It lacked an avant-garde—perhaps we should create one."[33] If most contemporary ciné-clubs screened films from the past, what was needed was a club that showcased the vanguard auteurs *of today*. The club's aim would be bold and concrete: "To help get films released, particularly those that had not found a distributor, and to enable films that had not done well first time round to be presented to the public a second time. . . . This was the start of the adventure of Objectif 49."[34]

Almost immediately after the 1948 Venice Festival, Doniol-Valcroze convinced numerous players to throw material and moral support behind Objectif 49's new avant-garde initiative. The first to join its ranks were the young filmmaker Léonard Keigel, *Revue du cinéma* critic Jacques Bourgeois and aspiring film director Grisha Dabat, who became the club's first general secretary. They were followed by Jean-George Auriol, *Revue du cinéma*'s influential founder, critic and film director Pierre Kast, and of course Astruc, who wrote regularly for *Combat*.

Crucial to Objectif 49's institutional intervention was Léonid Keigel, Léonard's stepfather and owner of the Broadway, a first-run theater located at 34 Champs-Elysées. Keigel, also a distributor and the primary financier behind the postwar revival of *Revue du cinéma* (which had ceased publication in 1932), made room for Objectif 49 screenings in his programming schedule.[35] A wide range of contemporary films were subsequently rereleased at the Broadway, the Studio des Champs-Elysées, and the Musée de l'homme (among other major venues), including Bresson's *Les anges du péché*, Roger Leenhardt's *Les dernières vacances* (1948), André Malraux's *Espoir* (1939–44), and Jean Grémillon's *Lumières d'été* (1943), all screened at one-night events between January and July 1949 (where over thirty films were shown).[36] These screenings allowed the club to encourage the reevaluation of numerous French films that soon found their place in the canon of auteur cinema.

Objectif 49's intervention truly developed momentum with the *Festival du film maudit*. Often labeled Cocteau's brainchild, the festival would be a celebration of the new avant-garde, held between July 28 and August 5, 1949.[37] The organizers, Cocteau among them, planned the event at an office furnished by publishing giant Gallimard, at 5 rue Sébastien-Bottin in Paris. Recognizing the need for external support for an event of this scope, Cocteau invited the Marquis Pierre d'Arcangue, a colleague who lived near Biarritz, to become the primary patron of the event. D'Arcangue, then the head of events and festivals for the city, agreed to finance the club's activities and facilitated the festival's use of Biarritz's exquisite Art Deco casino as the prime exhibition site.[38]

With the club gaining traction, its members offered Robert Bresson and another revered figure in French film culture, the critic and filmmaker Roger Leenhardt, the honorary titles of copresident, alongside Cocteau. They both accepted and worked to increase the event's visibility in the lead-up to the festival. As we now know, it was at this stage that Bresson took to the press to promote the festival's 16-millimeter film award and discuss the unique qualities of the *film maudit*—of which the disappointing reception to *Les dames du bois de Boulogne* made him an expert.[39] Leenhardt, for his part, contributed to the club's institutional stability by securing the support of the Centre nationale de la cinématographie (CNC), France's government regulatory body for the film industry, with which he had ties.[40] The participation of the CNC, charged as of its founding in 1946 with developing a noncommercial distribution sector, would at least help to ease some challenges related to locating prints and acquiring rights to screen them.

Historians like Frédéric Gimello-Mesplomb have documented the evolution of this eight-day festival and other Objectif 49 events and begun to shed light on the club's influence on postwar film culture.[41] Despite its brief history, Objectif 49 left a mark on cinephilia and on the careers of numerous postwar auteurs in several ways. It did so, first, by codifying a range of cinephilic practices. Films like Bresson's were finally treated to critical discussion that illuminated their subtle stylistic and narrative experiments. During the *Festival du film maudit*, for instance, Bazin organized regular public discussions, from 3:00 p.m. to 4:00 p.m. at the casino, where the previous day's screenings would be analyzed and debated.[42] He wrote: "The most important aspect of the festival will not have been on the screen but in the theater."[43] These experiences proved to be formative for younger critics like Jacques Rivette, François Truffaut, Éric Rohmer, Jean Douchet, and Charles Bitsch, who were lodged at the dormitory of the Biarritz Lycée during the festival. The club even took these practices abroad. During a fifteen-day event held in Austria in January 1950, Doniol-Valcroze, Bazin, and Bourgeois screened twenty films, by Bresson, Cocteau, Eisenstein, Chaplin, and Von Sternberg, and held "passionate discussions" with students from Austria, Hungary, Germany, and Czechoslovakia.[44] Just as importantly, the club drew the attention of the industry. Not only was Jean Rouch one of the "great revelations" of the *Festival du film maudit*—his ethnographic film *La circoncision* (1949) won the 16-millimeter prize Bresson had promoted—but the festival became the site where Rouch met his future producer, Pierre Braunberger.[45] Finally, the *Festival du film maudit* contributed to the development of a third kind of exhibition site in France, the *cinéma art et essai* (art-house theater), a crucial venue for films like Bresson's over the years, by demonstrating the cultural and economic viability of a for-profit ciné-club whose very mandate was to support quality cinema that challenged convention.[46]

* * *

Much more so than any other ciné-club, Objectif 49, while short-lived (several events it staged in 1950 marked the end of its official existence),[47] succeeded in making concrete reforms to cinema's institutions. Just as importantly, it sought to intervene in the language of the cultural market by introducing new ideas into film aesthetics. On the one hand, it proposed the idea of a hidden avant-garde in Hollywood cinema. Its inaugural event, the *Festival du film noir américain* held on a single night, November 20, 1948, was, as Dudley Andrew argues, the "first concerted effort by French intellectuals to come to terms" with the advances being made in the art of cinema within (and despite) the Hollywood "machine."[48] On the other, Objectif 49 also mobilized around such distinctive "noncommercial" stylists as Bresson and Leenhardt. Quite astutely, the club's members defended these vanguard auteurs through three ideas that worked to elevate their films as part of a culturally valuable trend—one that audiences ought to appreciate and producers and distributors ought to make available to this newly appreciative audience.

A Popular Avant-Garde

The new avant-garde of Bresson and Leenhardt accepted some of the basic aesthetic qualities that made cinema a popular art—namely, its dependence on narrative. This is what made Objectif 49's avant-garde one that could, in principle, draw on the pleasures of mass audiences. André Bazin led the way on this front by strategically associating the avant-garde with new directions in cinematic storytelling that did not ignore the commercial market. Within a few weeks of Objectif 49's founding, the journal *L'écran français* published Bazin's "Défense de l'avant-garde," described by Tacchella as the club's manifesto.[49] As he would again and again on this issue ("Défense de l'avant-garde" was the first of four articles he devoted to the subject between 1948 and 1952),[50] Bazin distinguished the mass art of cinema from the "dead end" intellectualism of 1920s and 1930s experimental filmmakers like Luis Buñuel, Germaine Dulac, Fernand Léger, and Hans Richter. Their films, which conducted "aesthetic experiments founded on the restriction of their audience," were designed only for elites.[51] His logic was simple (one might even say simplistic): because cinema was an art that connected with the public, the narrow experiments of 1925–1930 were a failure. He insisted that film culture recognize the difference between the new avant-garde of Bresson (Bazin's 1948 piece names *Les dames du bois de Boulogne* as a neglected masterpiece) and the old avant-garde of Dulac and Richter: "One must know how to distinguish between innovations whose commercial failures were accidental and a matter of historical contingency from those that radically betray cinema's popular calling."[52]

Developing this populist message, Bazin attempted to assuage concerns about auteur cinema by reminding the public of the role of good criticism. (This position was not without its paradoxes. For instance, why would a popular avant-garde for a mass audience require a class of elite, learned critics? Bazin, writing as a spirited advocate, never paused to address such questions.) Criticism, he told *L'écran français*'s readership, was the handmaiden of the difficult film. It fulfilled a maieutic function and worked alongside the films of vanguard auteurs to facilitate the public's understanding of their cinematic experiments, ones that sought to challenge, but not necessarily alienate, the common filmgoer: "It belongs to the artist's genius and the work of criticism to discern good novelty from bad, the bold innovations to which the public will become habituated from those that are incompatible with the popular nature of cinema. . . . the 'avant-garde' of 1925–1930 was sullied by an aestheticism whose retrospective silliness proves today that it could never have had a steady commune with public taste."[53] Figures like Bresson and Leenhardt were addressing the tensions involved in undertaking innovation in an art whose power allowed it to touch the popular imagination through storytelling, and the task before the institution of film criticism, which had, as Astruc pointed out in his "Naissance d'une nouvelle avant-garde" essay just a few months earlier, failed in its duties to translate the subtleties of their purposeful narrative experiments to the reader.

An Avant-Garde of Narrative Deaestheticization

The club's members, building on previous trends in film criticism and French aesthetics, set out to render Objectif 49's stylistic revolution, as some called it, more palatable, more easily graspable for audiences by associating some of the films it screened and auteurs it sponsored with a new rigorous, pared-down storytelling form. Jean Cocteau was among those who recognized the need to classify vanguard auteur films in this fashion. "Boldness," he wrote in the handsome catalogue published for the *Festival du film maudit*, now "presents itself under the auspices of simplicity."[54] Cocteau's praise for the aesthetics of simplicity embraced by Objectif 49's auteurs mirrored what he wrote of French music after World War I. "[Erik] Satie teaches what, in our age, is the greatest audacity, simplicity," he stated in 1918's *Le coq et l'arlequin: Notes autour de la musique.*[55] That he later praised the *nouvelle avant-garde* of postwar cinema using almost identical language is quite revealing. He clearly believed that the broad aesthetic impulse that had defined French music after the First World War was now inspiring the vanguard of narrative filmmaking after the Second. Like Satie, auteurs like Bresson, whose *Les dames du bois de Boulogne* was screened at the *Festival du film maudit*, were auguring a new era of purified technique, sparse narrative, and rigorous refinement of earlier styles.

Cocteau was not alone in associating Objectif 49's vanguard with rigor and deaestheticization. Also screened at the festival was Dudley Nichols' *Mourning Becomes Electra* (1947), which, as Bazin enthusiastically proclaimed, confronted audiences with "the *film maudit* par excellence" by virtue of "the austerity of its subject as much as the uncompromising rigor of its *mise-en-scène*."[56]

In their defense of this trend, Bazin and Cocteau, as I have argued elsewhere, were drawing on the aesthetic ideas of copresidents Robert Bresson and Roger Leenhardt.[57] As we will see in subsequent chapters, Bresson overtly positioned his 1940s cinema as a search for greater simplicity at the level of style and storytelling. He stated in a 1946 interview: "In cinema, there is a prejudice against simplicity. Every time someone breaks with that prejudice, the effect is deeply moving."[58] Leenhardt, for his part, consistently urged French filmmakers, engaged in aesthetic play for its own sake, to reclaim the power of understatement in their storytelling and image craft throughout the postwar era. In "Continuité du cinéma français," published in 1945, he wrote that the conditions of *les années noires* "drove our cinema down a dangerous path, at the end of which one finds academicism and aestheticism."[59] As he would later argue in a piece titled "Le cinéma et les arts plastiques," "feature-length fiction films discover their highest calling" when they eschew "visual formalism (where they imitate painting without its force). . . . The image onscreen must remain subordinate to its meaning, at the same time as inspiration constrains itself by following a visual rigor that achieves a style."[60]

Leenhardt even at times criticized *Bresson* for his lack of simplicity! During an October 1945 radio review of Bresson's *Les dames du bois de Boulogne*, Leenhardt argued that, for all its promise, the film brought to light the limitations of conspicuous formal restraint for its own sake:

> This classic film, performed with only four characters, in an absolutely pared down décor, Bresson directed it, as is his habit, with the most precise rigor. Served once again by Agostini's admirable photography, he has made an elegant, precise and cold work. This high level of ambition deserves to be applauded, but we must acknowledge the fact that this lack of real world application makes the story unconvincing, and despite its style, gives *Les dames du bois de Boulogne* a desiccant gratuitousness.[61]

With this modern adaptation of Diderot's *Jacques le fataliste*, Bresson had taken a step toward elegant but lifeless minimalism, toward a style that betrays cinema's calling to discover life as lived, to inconspicuously peer out at characters and observe the nuances of psychology and routine that only the camera can capture. Simple forms, in Leenhardt's view, served a legitimate artistic purpose; chic formalisms drew attention to technique and thus offered empty delights.

To summarize, alongside its efforts to reform film distribution and exhibition, Objectif 49 was a club that sought to base its intervention in film culture on the defense of antiaesthetic principles devised by these auteurs, and it seems likely that this keen regard for trends in unconventional filmmaking is what ultimately encouraged Bresson to take on the role, however ceremonial, of copresident.

An Avant-Garde of Films Maudits

As we have seen, the club's new avant-garde also consisted of *films maudits*. According to Bresson, Cocteau coined the term after the idea of the *poète maudit* (among others, Villon, Baudelaire, Rimbaud, Artaud).[62] The introduction of this concept into cultural discourse allowed the club to stimulate a broad conversation about the auteur as *cause célèbre*, about the creative and institutional headwinds faced by auteurs working within the French system. Together with Cocteau's encomium to the aesthetics of simplicity, the *Festival du film maudit* catalogue included several manifesto-like essays that list, with eloquent precision, the forms of malediction—of accursedness—that auteur cinema tended to invite in contemporary film culture. Filmmaker Jean Grémillon's "La malédiction du style" urged that the task before "a film's auteur is now exceptionally complicated.... In a way that is inevitable ... those responsible for the concrete means of production choose subjects according to a sum of empirical and uncertain ideas about their potential profitability."[63] He invoked the name of the festival itself: "A 'film maudit' is therefore first and foremost one that cannot get made. We know the titles, from 'Force des ténèbres' to a French 'Joan of Arc' to a 'Country Priest.'"[64] Lamenting Bresson's still unproduced adaptation of Bernanos's novel, *Journal d'un curé de campagne*, one that would require testing the limits of convention, Grémillon denounced the commercial market that intervened between the public and the auteur: "There exists only a distribution apparatus with supreme power to forge a set of illusory norms. The search for style is very nearly invincible to these norms and in this, too, we see quite clearly why it is *maudit*. Distribution idealizes those objects that are appropriately neutral, always the same and different, in terms of form as well as content. In short, the opposite of style."[65]

Roger Leenhardt's "La malédiction de l'intelligence" furthered the idea of the auteur film as *cause célèbre* through a polemic against audiences who viewed intelligence and ambiguity as inimical to the popular art of cinema. After crediting Bresson's *Les anges du péché* for initiating the search for intelligence in French filmmaking, he advocated difficulty over intelligibility in cinematic storytelling: "Intelligence is ambiguity. And it is this that the public, demanding a direct approach and genres devoid of nuance, refuses to allow onscreen."[66] Intelligent cinema presented a unique vision, in his view, which the auteur achieved by eschewing the legibility of popular genres: "Today, we demand of our great novelists what our forefathers demanded of great philosophers: a '*Weltanschauung*.' Tomorrow, will we not ask the *auteur de film* for his 'vision of the world'?"[67]

The novelist Raymond Queneau's "Les dix malédictions du cinéma"—a list of punchy one-liners written in a parallel structure ("Maudits soit/soient . . ."/ "Accursed is/are . . .")—relied on apocalyptic hyberbole to target the commercial aspirations of the film industry: "In our times, the Antichrist has appeared in the guise of the Great Producer who owns a large pool and multiple telephones."[68] He adopted the voice of this reviled figure: "Accursed is the avant-garde that demolishes my beautiful business without considering the cost."[69]

Bazin's essay in the catalogue, with the simple title "Avant-garde nouvelle," focused on the market risks taken by vanguard auteurs: "The avant-garde for 'Objectif 49' consists of those films that are in advance of the cinema. We correctly say of the CINEMA, which is to say the production of a popular industry in which it would be out of the question to dispute the fundamental law that involves seeking in one way or another the assent of the public."[70] For Bazin, this avant-garde was riskier than that of the 1920s because it expressly depended on the attention of a wide audience and on producer support: "This avant-garde is no less accursed than the other . . . it is more so, for to the extent that it does not seek, in principle, to be incomprehensible and endeavors to include itself in the normal conditions of cinema, it runs the severest of risks: the misunderstanding of the public and the immediate withdrawal of confidence from producers."[71]

"The Patron Saint of this avant-garde," he mused, "is and will always be Erich Von Stroheim,"[72] the Austrian director whose the lost masterpiece, *Greed* (1924), a ten-hour-long experiment in tragic storytelling and deep-focus cinematography, was misunderstood by Hollywood producers and chopped down to a two-and-a-half-hour version that ultimately failed at the box office.

* * *

André Bazin emerged in the immediate postwar era as an invaluable advocate for auteur cinema, much as Apollinaire had been for Cubist painters between 1906 and 1910.[73] He was fulfilling a role that many art critics before him had fulfilled, projecting to the public great enthusiasm for the artists he embraced.

The midcentury cultural market was, however, a highly competitive one. Bazin and his allies had to contend with some equally well-positioned and vocal rivals who used *their* rhetorical interventions to question the effectiveness of Objectif 49's cause. Some who wrote for *L'écran français*, for instance, which was by now turning increasingly toward a harder Communist editorial position, rejected the very idea of a "formalist" avant-garde, arguing that a continuation of the 1920s exploration of the medium's stylistic language was both unwanted and unneeded. Spearheading this alternative to Objectif 49, Socialist filmmaker Louis Daquin and Communist critic Georges Sadoul believed that the only way to ensure the rebirth of French cinema, to move beyond the aestheticism of the Occupation era, and to reconnect accursed auteur cinema with the larger film-going public, was to promote an overtly political or working-class, as opposed to aesthetic, revolution in film.

Members of these formalist and political camps sparred in speech and in print, the most prominent instance being a 1949 clash sponsored by *L'écran français*.[74] An advertisement in a February 1949 issue of the journal announced the "big debate" between André Bazin, described as a "philologist" of film style on this occasion, and Georges Sadoul, introduced as an expert in film history (figure 2.1).

Fig. 2.1. Debate advertisement published in *L'écran français*, February 22, 1949.

A passionate one, the exchange held court from 9:00 p.m. to just before midnight. Bazin acknowledged that he was "75% in agreement" with Sadoul about the popular or social purpose of vanguard filmmaking.[75] The area of agreement between the two camps quickly contracted, however, as the balance of the debate focused on the main issue that divided postwar cinephiles, at least as far as the new avant-garde was concerned: the problem of form versus content. Sadoul presented the aesthetic avant-garde as a thing of the past. The first avant-garde of the 1920s had, in Sadoul's words, allowed cinema to take "full consciousness of itself as an art and not a simple attraction," while the second, during the conversion to sound, saw filmmakers "[revise] the grammar" of the art form.[76] But, "today, the problem of form is more or less settled," a report of the debate stated, paraphrasing Sadoul.[77] For this reason, "the avant-garde can no longer be found in 'form; it is found in content,'" the historian argued.[78] Vanguard filmmakers, he believed, were now in a position to use their art to stand with the proletariat through its radical subject matter.

The room splintered into opposing camps, as did views about how to support the *cause célèbre* auteur. Roger Leenhardt and Alexandre Astruc were present in support of Objectif 49. Siding with Sadoul was Louis Daquin, himself an auteur increasingly spurned by the industry. He attended the event to reinforce a position he later elaborated in some detail in a March 1949 *L'écran francais* polemic. Under the mischievous title "Remarques déplacées . . . ," Daquin launched a full-on assault on Objectif 49, particularly the writings of its critics over the last twenty months.[79] Citing a conversation with Sadoul about previous "aestheticist" trends in film history, the director of *Le point du jour* argued that the time for aestheticism had passed and denounced the desire of Astruc and others for a "formal revolution."[80] He believed that the "elitist" connoisseurship fostered by the Objectif 49 movement left a number of social and film-industrial problems unsolved. Particularly egregious was the club's formalism—its penchant for celebrating a film's storytelling and *mise-en-scène* style—for it failed to consider how the new avant-garde could threaten the capitalist tenets of the film industry. In the end, Objectif 49 abandoned the very filmmakers it sponsored to the vicissitudes of the commercial market. His fiery assault reveals the stakes of auteur cinema's battle for status within postwar film culture:

> I am convinced that in all creative work there is an interaction between form and content. The analysis [of the relationship between form and content] is even more complex than our PhDs imagine. They find in the artwork the role of the creative genius and individual and social factors, the harmonious combination of which gives the artistic creation its positive, real value, without any link to the imaginary and suspicious values that derive from an aestheticism or a formalism destined to disguise the emptiness and sterilization of those few works tolerated even today by a bourgeoisie attempting in vain to slow its

decadent decline and from a capitalism committed to destroy all that strives for the advent of a free and happy humanity.

"Objectif 49!" Speaking of which, here you have the first crystallization! A ciné-club of elites having as its goal "to restore the avant-garde idea to the spirit of new criticism."

I regret to say that you don't have the right to make declarations of that kind. It's charlatanism and your position is even more dishonest because your authority and your truth appeases only a few hundred snobs when cinema exists only by dint of hundreds of millions of viewers worldwide.[81]

Daquin's polemic highlighted the real-world consequences of Objectif 49's "formalist" conception of the avant-garde. Taking aim at the American directors admired by Objectif 49, he asked: "Will the methods of Wyler or Hitchcock revolutionize cinema? What does this question contribute, dear sirs, at a moment when our best directors are reduced to unemployment or to sporadic activity?"[82] The critics of Objectif 49, he believed, "don't notice that while they're debating 'forms and styles' the real problems of cinematic creation in a capitalist regime are evaded and they don't take into account that, unconsciously, they form a barrier to the great public awakening that some understandably dread."[83] As he saw it, French cinema had reached its vanguard apogee in 1936, with the sharp political thematics of the *Front populaire*. Appealing to national pride, he presented an alternative to Objectif 49's canon, one that replaced Bresson with the major auteurs of the 1920s and 1930s: "It's precisely through subject matter that Feyder, Clair, Renoir, Duvivier, Carné, Vigo and Grémillon mark their era, principally drawing their inspiration from our national heritage."[84]

Daquin cut straight to the heart of the matter: "Explain to me why Grémillon couldn't shoot *Le printemps de la liberté*, why the naïve Leenhardt or the tenacious Bresson, who are members of your club, can't manage to get their projects made."[85]

* * *

From a certain perspective, Daquin had a point. There is little evidence to suggest that Bresson's involvement in the club, or its support for his films, led directly to new funding opportunities with producers. Nevertheless, in ways that Daquin obviously failed to recognize, Objectif 49 succeeded in playing a significant role in the professional life of Robert Bresson. How?

As an institutional-reformist and rhetorical intervention in postwar film culture, the club ensured that Bresson's Occupation films, *Les dames du bois de Boulogne* in particular, were set in a new context, associated with a movement, however loosely defined or short-lived it was (the club fell apart in 1950). The Objectif 49 movement created an energetic critical environment in which audiences, distributors, and producers became witnesses to the rehabilitation of Bresson's reputation, through what I will simply refer to as showing, role-playing, and classifying. First, the club showed his films at one-night events in Paris, the *Festival du film maudit,* and to students abroad. The club also gave Bresson new cultural roles to play, as an ambassador of *films maudits* (in this capacity, he adopted the club's new language) and as a juror for the festival's 16-millimeter film competition. Although Bresson ultimately skipped the event, these roles placed him and his work in the public eye. Finally, and perhaps most importantly, the club situated his vanguard cinema in a now-recognizable new type of filmmaking. If his films were unique, they were also part of a trend of intelligent, experimental narrative cinema that relied on sober forms and thereby invited several types of malediction from the commercial market. If during the 1930s Bresson was largely left to his own devices to stimulate interest in his unconventional cinema, now he was part of a burgeoning cultural market whose discourses functioned alongside his own to foster a sense of familiarity with his work, through new ways of looking at and appreciating them.

The Objectif 49 project also benefited Bresson's reputation after the club's demise. Some of its members determined that if Objectif 49's influence on the language of cinema—on the words and concepts it used to reform film culture—were going to endure, it would have to create a discursive home where auteurs and cinephiles could pursue this exchange in the long term. Immediately after the club folded, Objectif 49's inner circle embarked upon a project that would remain focused on cinema and thus avoid the challenges of extravagant festivals. With the demise of Auriol's *Revue du cinéma* in October 1949, and *L'écran français* beginning to lose its readership because it shifted to a stauncher Communist Party line (to the frustration of many cinephiles), the marketplace presented an opening. This is Roger Leenhardt: "With the same team, I tried to give 'Objectif 49' a serious and more enduring sequel by founding a journal. . . . It was time to create a journal that . . . gave over most of its space to screenplays and reviews (or essays) on films—in short, a journal centered on cinema."[86] Accompanied by André Bazin and Jacques Doniol-Valcroze, he pitched the idea to Paul Flamand, editor of the Éditions du Seuil publishing house.[87] Flamand reportedly saw promise in the idea, but he had recently launched two new journals, and turned the project down. Nevertheless, the seeds for *Cahiers du cinéma* had been planted, and with the financial support once again of Léonide Keigel, its first issue was eventually published in April 1951.

The legacy of *Cahiers du cinéma* is well documented. In their impressive studies of the journal, Richard Neupert and Antoine de Baecque point out that it championed diverse views and approaches on world cinema.[88] But its troop of writers—Claude Chabrol, Jean-Luc Godard, Joseph-Marie Lo Duca, Maurice "Éric Rohmer" Shérer, Jacques Rivette, and François Truffaut, who became known as "young Turks" for their spirited, often vitriolic criticism—also united around the *politique des auteurs* whereby European, Asian, and Hollywood masters, from Alfred Hitchcock to Robert Bresson, were elevated as auteurs through close analyses that revealed their distinctive thematic commitments and *mise-en-scène* styles. The journal became a locus of cinephilic culture where the discourses supporting unconventional cinema found continued life (albeit in slightly different form).

Though Objectif 49 did not survive for more than a few years, some of the rhetorical strategies its members had devised continued to benefit the auteurs it had constructed as *causes célèbres* well after 1950. Objectif 49 alumni and the critics they influenced saw diminishing returns in staging a cultural intervention through the concepts of avant-garde cinema and the *film maudit*. They instead set their sights on the concept of quality, for in appropriating it, they could come to the defense of auteurs like Bresson from a fresh institutional angle.

A Cinéma de Qualité Moderne: The Intervention after Objectif 49

There is by now an almost unshakable legend among French film aficionados that the cinephile critics writing for *Cahiers du cinéma* in the 1950s were staunch opponents of quality filmmaking of all kinds, on moral and aesthetics grounds. When François Truffaut appropriated Jean-Pierre Barrot's concept of the "tradition de la qualité," a label the cultural director of the Fédération française des ciné-clubs first used in a seminal collection of essays published in 1953, *Sept ans du cinéma français*,[89] the feisty Truffaut, so the legend goes, rallied *Cahiers* critics and its readership against a group of commercial screenwriters and directors who had sent French cinema into a moral and artistic nosedive. Truffaut's *Cahiers* polemic, "Une certaine tendance du cinéma français" (1954), lambasted the Tradition of Quality for adapting literary works and creating films that were politically, ethically, and artistically retrograde, focusing on character interiority and self-obsession in a debauched and formulaic manner.[90] Perhaps most offensive of all for an auteurist critic like Truffaut, the *tradition de la qualité* was a cinema of screenwriters, like Pierre Bost and Jean Aurenche, who had won praise from the foreign press, come to represent France at international festivals, and accumulated numerous awards. Truffaut considered these figures guilty of shameful opportunism. Not only had their psychological realism—the "anguished interiority" of the characters, as one historian puts it—cheapened the more venerable poetic realist expressiveness of French cinema of the 1930s,[91] but these *scénaristes* were suspiciously uncommitted. Bost and Aurenche bounced from subject to subject and never directed their own films. Likewise, the directors they often teamed with—Jean Delannoy, Claude Autant-Lara, and René Clément—rarely contributed to their own scripts, outsourcing much of the vision behind the film to Bost and Aurenche. True auteurs like Robert Bresson, Jacques Tati, Jean

Cocteau, and Jean Renoir—not as recognized at festivals or among producers by definition (at least, from Truffaut's point of view)—composed their own dialogue and wrote and directed their own stories, showing a personal commitment to the characters and plots they brought to the screen. Truffaut cast contemporary French cinema as a war against quality: "I cannot see any possibility of a friendly coexistence between the Tradition of Quality and a *cinéma d'auteur*."[92]

This moral and aesthetic attack on the Tradition of Quality gained support among Truffaut's *Cahiers* brethren. André Bazin, apparently showing appreciation for his young colleague's fiery intervention, wrote his own rebuke of France's quality *scénaristes*, "De la carolinisation de la France," published in *Esprit* the same year. Bazin denounced the vulgarity of quality cinema, rejecting what he called "the disgraceful, impoverished, and laborious pornography," the "cinematic eroticism" of much of French filmmaking, pointing out that "vulgarity and smutty references" were "the rule in current film production."[93] Nudity and salacious subject matter were permitted because of the "alibi of talent" that taste in quality had fostered: "Quality is implicitly defined here as an external value to the subject matter supplied by the *scénariste* or the *metteur en scène*. An obviously ridiculous proposition, but one that is allowed by a public that makes judgments according to appearances and reputations."[94] Like Truffaut, he confronted quality in generic terms—"A new genre has emerged, 'quality,' founded on . . . the lowliest" of generic traits[95] and targeted those who viewed highly successful films like *La symphonie pastorale* (1946) and *Caroline chérie* (1951) as components of a formula for critical and commercial success:

Symphonie pastorale + talented *scénaristes-dialoguistes* + *metteurs en scènes idem* = "quality" French cinema

or

Caroline + talented *scénariste* + *metteur en scènes idem* = "quality" French cinema[96]

Bazin was concerned that tastemakers, producers, and audiences were identifying talent by the reputations of production personnel rather than the films they made. According to this impoverished critical logic, the Christian-Jaque of *Fanfan la tulipe* (1952) was identical to that of *Lucrèce Borgia* (1953).[97] (His much-cited 1957 *Cahiers du cinéma* essay, "De la politique des auteurs," expressed a similar concern. This "aesthetic cult of personality" was a harbinger of "impressionistic relativism," he wrote.)[98]

The legend of *Cahiers'* opposition to quality cinema is therefore not without its historical basis. Yet this legend ultimately conceals the fact that, during this era, *Cahiers* critics also associated the new cinema of Bresson, Leenhardt, and other vanguard auteurs with a more authentic, more modern quality filmmaking.

I therefore invite students of the period to distinguish between the *tradition de la qualité* that Truffaut and Bazin criticized and the *cinéma de qualité moderne* that they supported for reasons that overlapped with the support Objectif 49 gave to *films maudits*; modern quality cinema lacked institutional and cultural legitimacy.

Perhaps surprisingly, this new approach on the part of former Objectif 49 members found partners even among the Communist-Socialist editors of *L'écran français*—the notion of legitimate quality unified cinephiles of all stripes. In October 1950, just as Objectif 49 was collapsing, *L'écran français* published "Encourageons la qualité," an editorial that backed a recent manifesto by the Comité de défense du cinéma français (CDCF). Founded by director Claude Autant-Lara and the French Communist Party, the CDCF had produced a document demanding institutional recognition for quality cinema.[99] For *L'écran français*, "quality" referred to ambitious auteur films that surpassed the "mediocrity" of commercial production, but that found little support from producers.[100] Alongside Bresson, the magazine's editors drew attention to numerous *causes célèbres*: Daquin, who directed *Le point du jour* (1949) but remained unemployed for fourteen months before returning with *Maître après Dieu* (1951); Jean Grémillon, who had been one of the auteurs elevated by Objectif 49, but who had made only one feature between 1944 and 1950, *Pattes blanches* (1948); Georges Rouquier, who, likewise, had completed only one movie, *Farrebique, ou les quatre saisons* (1945), before the new decade set in; Pierre Prévert, whose last film was *Voyage surprise* (1947); and Marcel Carné, who had faced sporadic employment between 1946 and 1949. Several well-positioned figures in the industry lent their names to this effort to "encourage quality." The editorial cites Marcel L'Herbier, the president of the IDHEC, France's national film school, who had a vested interest in the future of his young charges. (L'Herbier, it should be said, had been fighting for special subventions whose sole purpose would be to stimulate quality, as opposed to purely commercial, cinema since the late 1930s.)[101] The CDCF/*Écran français* initiative also found an important ally in Robert Dorfmann, the head of Corona, one of the most successful distribution firms in the immediate postwar period and producer of the critically acclaimed *La justice est faite* (1950). Dorfmann told *L'écran français* that a recent government measure that taxed exhibitors to support producers whose previous productions were box office successes—the so-called Temporary Automatic Aid Fund of 1948, instituted after a massive influx of American films after the Liberation nearly suffocated indigenous production— was fundamentally flawed: "To encourage the quality of French cinema, we have to modify the conditions of allocation of the aid fund, giving a wage that is preferential to quality."[102] Drawing on a sense of public duty, he demanded that the industry and the government respond to the cultural need for quality films that appealed to a broad audience, a principle reminiscent of Objectif 49's notion of a popular avant-garde.

Former members of Objectif 49 took notice and spread out across the cultural terrain, using various organs of cinephilic and cultural discourse to continue this push for support for "quality" auteur cinema. The strategy gave some of Objectif 49's methods a new lease on life, for in appropriating the concept of quality, former Objectif 49 members continued their institutional intervention—in this case, by calling for a special financial-aid law that subsidized a *cinéma de qualité* that took risks. They also found new ways to rhetorically position cinephilic criticism as vital to the health of auteur cinema and the industry as a whole. In a 1951 polemic, "La difficile définition de la qualité," André Bazin joined Dorfmann and *L'écran français*'s editors in deriding the 1948 law as "une prime à la mediocrité" (a prize for mediocrity) and recommended that a portion of this government aid be responsive to the cultural market through "an assembly of disinterested critics rendering decisions on the aesthetic quality of a film" and mandated to allot the funds.[103] Three films that had difficulty finding an audience upon their initial release represented the "risks of quality," as Bazin put it.[104] Jean Renoir's commentary on bourgeois decadence and experiment with deep-focus cinematography, *La règle du jeu* (1939), Marcel Carné's poetic realist masterpiece in flashback storytelling and expressive lighting, *Le jour se lève* (1939), and Bresson's sparse *Les dames du bois de Boulogne*—each represented the kinds of experimental risk-taking that policy should promote.

One of Objectif 49's cofounders (and of *Cahiers du cinéma* after it), Jacques Doniol-Valcroze, supported Bazin's intervention. His 1954 *Cahiers* piece, "Problèmes et prospects du cinéma français," reported on a press conference given by Jacques Flaud, the director general of the CNC. Citing Flaud, he isolated two main problems with the current state of French cinema: the censorship of scripts, which led to "a deplorable sterilization of films at the screenwriting stage," and the fact that most of the funds allocated go to productions that took no risks, using experienced directors, stars, and spectacular effects in the "historio-Châtelet genre," a reference to the extravagant plays of the Théâtre du Châtelet.[105] The result was "the disappearance of purely French film with a medium-sized budget and that, in the distant and recent past was the one that revealed new talent, where research was conducted, and where, bit by bit, the elements that made our cinema what it no longer is were developed: one of the premier in the world."[106] Appealing to Bazin's "quality," Doniol-Valcroze believed that the concept must be rescued from the idea of financial success. "We need to find a formula that will allow the imperative of quality to intervene. But how?" he asked.[107]

François Truffaut, with his inimitable, brash style, attempted to answer this question, and, in the process, drive home Bazin's and Doniol-Valcroze's call for new standards of "quality," in a 1955 essay published in the cultural weekly *Arts* with the telling title, "Une crise d'ambition du cinéma français."[108] For him, the problems rested not with the system of funding but, rather, within the cultural market, within the exchange of language and ideas in the critical community. Critics, he pointed out in a manner reminiscent of Bazin's 1948 Objectif 49 manifesto, needed to lead the way and illuminate the distinction between true aesthetic ambition and lack thereof in French production. His piece is effectively a hierarchy of directors—a precursor to Andrew Sarris's book *American Cinema* (1968)[109]—under the headings "Ambitious," "Semi-ambitious," "Commercial, but decent," and "Deliberately commercial." Of the seventeen truly ambitious filmmakers, like Objectif 49 alums Robert Bresson, Roger Leenhardt, and Jean Grémillon, as well as Claude Autant-Lara, Jean Renoir, Jacques Tati, René Clément, and Max Ophüls, he wrote: "Here is the real 'qualité française.' Here are seventeen filmmakers who can say of themselves: 'I am currently shooting the best French film of the year.'"[110] They were aspiring to be the best for reasons that had united Objectif 49 and its members at least since Astruc's "caméra-stylo" essay in 1948: Bresson, Leenhardt, and the rest were "complete auteurs" who wrote and directed their films. He emphasized the crucial cultural shift: "I've said it before: the time of the *metteur-en-scène* has passed and the times of auteurs has arrived."

* * *

By the mid-1950s, the French government began to heed the call for support for quality alternative cinema. On August 6, 1953, it instituted a new fund to be awarded to quality short films. This *Prime à la qualité*, or Quality Reward, was decided in a thirteen-person commission composed of three government representatives, three critics, three directors of short films, three producers of short films, and the director of the CNC. From a certain perspective, the new measure was fairly conservative. With only ten percent of the original aid fund used to foster quality, it could finance only eighty short films per year.[111] Nevertheless, in government statements issued between 1953 and 1959, quality materialized as an important principle guiding decisions about financial aid for culturally significant, noncommercial filmmaking. Policymakers cast a wide net by defining a quality film, as follows in the August 1953 law: "A competition with a monetary prize of ten million francs could be allocated for French films that serve the cause of French cinema or open new perspectives on the art of cinema or popularize the big themes and problems of the French Union."[112]

Measures of this kind represented a new institutional mindset about cinema. No longer was cinema viewed as a commercial commodity alone. From this point forward, the French state acknowledged the medium's cultural and artistic value in its legislative decisions. What's more, as "culture" officially became a concern at the CNC, which regulated this new fund, "quality" came to symbolize an alternative to commercial cinema. The Quality Reward law was modified in 1955 to fund feature films. Further developments were to come. In 1959, the state added to the Automatic Aid (1948) and Quality Reward (1953, 1955) measures an *Avance sur recettes* law, which stipulated that "a system of selective aid" would be "based on a commission's determination of the artistic quality of films."[113] This gave first to producers and then, as of 1963, to auteurs directly, a low-interest government loan in advance of a production to be repaid through box-office returns. As Richard Neupert has demonstrated, this stimulated the entry into the industry of a wealth of new producers and writer-directors and helped spark a new movement, the *nouvelle vague*, which skewed heavily toward unconventional narrative and stylistic experimentation.[114] More time-tested auteurs like Robert Bresson, who had weathered the early tumultuous years of vanguard auteur cinema, benefited as well. In 1962, he received an advance from the government to produce *Le procès de Jeanne d'Arc*. He then received support for virtually all of his films after 1965 (with the exception of 1969's *Une femme douce*): 1966's *Au hasard Balthazar*, 1967's *Mouchette*, 1971's *Quatre nuits d'un rêveur*, 1974's *Lancelot du lac*, 1977's *Le diable probablement*, and his final film, 1983's *L'argent*.[115] The French market was finally able to ensure the survival of two cinemas: an indigenous commercial cinema supported by the Automatic Aid law and, encouraged by cultural institutions like cinephilic journals, the *art et essai* theater, and the government's *Prime à la qualité* and *Avance sur recette* measures, a risky auteur cinema that explored alternatives to commercial convention.[116]

Bresson and the Avant-Garde Old and New

For decades, it has been common for film critics to give Bresson's film and art career of the 1930s and 1940s short shrift. Paul Schrader, for instance, writing in 1972, simply determines that, before completing 1951's *Journal d'un curé de campagne*, Bresson "served no lengthy apprenticeship" and completed novice films that presented a "vision" not yet mature or, in the case of *Les dames du bois de Boulogne*, that told a story in "which Bresson found himself somewhat at odds with his material."[117] However, if we focus our analysis less on "masterpieces" and vague notions of maturity of vision, these decades of apprenticeship and institutional and cultural (self)orientation prove to be more significant than earlier critics seem to have been aware.

In the last two chapters, two backgrounds have been proposed as an aid to understanding the development of Bresson's professional life. We first concentrated on the 1920s and 1930s and discovered that Bresson benefited from an apprenticeship with Surrealists. His publicity art became more ambitious, more experimental on a formal level, and after a brief stint working on *films d'entracte*, he found a patron within the Surrealist community who facilitated his shift to short-film producing and directing. This gamble on independence—on becoming a producer of self-financed comedies that challenged convention—proved unsuccessful, for by the end of the 1930s, he had yet to direct a feature film. In this chapter, we have seen that Bresson's strategy during the Occupation period—collaborating with established literary figures like Jean Giraudoux and Jean Cocteau in order to offset the creative and financial risks he wished to take—allowed him to transition into feature filmmaking but ultimately left his career in a shaky position when his second feature, *Les dames du bois de Boulogne*, was a commercial and critical flop. Already aware of some of the benefits of implicating himself in the culture of the avant-garde, Bresson elected to form a partnership with the *nouvelle avant-garde* of Objectif 49.

What did his affiliation with Objectif 49 accomplish? It is safe to say that in the postwar years Bresson discovered in the avant-garde club a partner equipped to intervene in the fate of auteur cinema. Its members rewrote the accepted narrative on *Les dames du bois de Boulogne* by granting it an afterlife or, to employ Jean Cocteau's analogy, by helping it win its case in appeals court. Cinephilic discourses, at times directed at policymakers and at times aimed at promoting alternatives in French exhibition, elevated Bresson as a *cause célèbre*. His film became a symbol of the glorious risks of vanguard narrative filmmaking, a movie to lobby for in print, a neglected masterpiece that showed how broken the state's funding apparatus was, on one hand, and how aesthetically blind the institutions of reception and exhibition had been, on the other. Objectif 49's members successfully reinterpreted his oeuvre and placed it at the center of questions of reform and revivalism raised in "quality" and "new avant-garde" contexts.

It will be up to future researchers to refine the story of Bresson's professional life, both in the periods considered in the previous two chapters and in subsequent decades. There are two reasons for my leaving this question behind at this stage. First, as yet, Bresson's personal archive has not been opened to the public. If historians are one day granted access to it, it will surely provide a fuller picture of his daily activities, his cultural ties, and the choices he made in his approach to the cultural market. As I briefly stated in the book's introduction, we can confirm with the few traces in our possession that Bresson continued to navigate the market by seeking the patronage of intrepid, independent financiers, like Alain Poiré, "one of innumerable crazy students of cinema," as he called himself,[118] for 1956's *Un condamné à mort s'est échappé*; Anatole Dauman, who produced films associated with the vanguard *nouveau roman* literary movement, *Hiroshima mon amour* (1959) and *L'année dernière à Marienbad* (1961), for *Au hasard Balthazar*; Albina du Boisrouvray, who also made Orson Welles' *Immortal Story* (1968) and Marguerite Duras' *Jaune la soleil* (1972), for *Quatre nuits d'un rêveur*; and Jean-Pierre Rassam, the "maverick" producer,[119] who funded *Lancelot du lac*. Beyond this, with few resources to go on, there is not much of an institutional story to tell.

Second, I wish to move to the second phase of my argument about Bresson's relationship to the cultural market. Given the significance of new institutions and partnerships to Bresson's career, a more sustained engagement with his aesthetics in light of surrounding culture is, I think, in order.

To anticipate, then, in the next three chapters, I wish to explore his approach to the problems of filmmaking in relation to the cultural market's assumptions about the medium and those creative issues considered fundamental to it. As we will see, while he was able to maintain a number of his 1930s aesthetic commitments, his rhetorical performances and new film style engaged the postwar market through some of the very concepts that shaped its passion for vanguard cinema: faithful adaptation, first-person storytelling, realist style, and rhythmic conceptions of sound and image.

Notes

1. Robert Bresson, "Le festival du film maudit," in *Bresson par Bresson*, ed. Mylène Bresson (Paris: Flammarion, 2013), 43.

2. Ibid., 44.

3. Pierre Ajame, "Le cinéma selon Bresson," *Les nouvelle littéraires*, May 26, 1966, 13.

4. François Truffaut, "Une certaine tendance du cinéma français," *Cahiers du cinéma* 31 (January 1954): 15–29.

5. See Evelyn Ehrlich, *Cinema of Paradox: French Filmmaking Under the Occupation* (New York: Columbia University Press, 1985), 113–133, for a discussion of the period's new personnel.

6. M. H. Lelong, *Les dominicaines des prisons* (Paris: Éditions du cerf, 1938).

7. Roland Barthes, *"Les anges du péché,"* in *Oeuvres complètes*, tome I (Paris: Éditions du Seuil, 1993), 37–39.

8. François Vinneuil, "Giraudoux au couvent," *Je suis partout*, July 9, 1943, 7.

9. Denise Tual, *Au cœur du temps* (Paris: Carrère, 1987), 267.

10. Ehrlich, *Cinema of Paradox*, 118. See also Denise Tual, *Le temps dévoré* (Paris: Payard, 1980), 206.

11. Roland Barthes, "Robert Bresson's Film: *Les anges du péché,*" in Robert Bresson, ed. James Quandt (Toronto: Cinematheque Ontario, 1998), 213.

12. Tual, *Au cœur du temps*, 268.

13. Bresson worked closely with the Tuals in the preproduction phase. Roland Tual, for instance, assisted Bresson with the film's casting. Some of the screen tests survive in the CNC archive, under the title, "Essais d'acteur: Francine Bessy: Béthanie."

14. Jean Giraudoux, *Le film de Béthanie* (Paris: Gallimard, 1944).

15. Pierre Chéret, "Devis détaillé du film 'Béthanie,'" February 16, 1943, Fonds Crédit National, CN81-B51, Bibliothèque du film, Paris. Bresson's fee of 100,000 francs for his role as author of the film's script is half that earned by Giraudoux: 206,000 for the dialogue and découpage.

16. Ajame, "Le cinéma selon Bresson," 13.

17. Colin Crisp, *The Classic French Cinema, 1930–1960* (Bloomington: Indiana University Press, 1993), 51.

18. Ajame, "Le cinéma selon Bresson," 13. Cocteau earned 235,000 francs, while Bresson as primary author and director earned 550,000 francs; see Pierre Chéret, "Devis détaillé du film 'Opinion publique,'" May 9, 1944, Fonds Crédit National, CN110, Bibliothèque du film, Paris.

19. Chéret, "Devis détaillé du film 'Opinion publique.'" They earned 30,000 and 45,000 francs apiece.

20. Paul Guth, *Autour des dames du bois de Boulogne* (Paris: Juillard, 1945), 12.

21. François Truffaut, *"Les dames du bois de Boulogne,"* in *The Films in My Life* (New York: Simon & Schuster, 1978), 188.

22. "Editorial (à propos d'une avant-garde nouvelle)," *La revue du cinéma* 7 (Summer 1947): 3–11.

23. André Bazin, "William Wyler, the Jansenist of Mise-en-Scène," in *What is Cinema?*, trans. Timothy Barnard (Montréal: Caboose, 2009), 45–72.

24. Henri Langlois, "L'avant-garde d'hier et d'aujourd'hui," *La revue du cinéma* 11 (March 1948): 43.

25. Ibid., 44.

26. Ibid., 44, n. 1.

27. Ibid., 45.

28. Ibid., 47.

29. Ibid.

30. Alexandre Astruc, "Naissance d'une nouvelle avant-garde: La caméra-stylo," in *Du stylo à la caméra . . . et de la caméra au stylo: Écrits (1942–1984)* (Paris: L'Archipel, 1992), 324, 325, 327.

31. Ibid.

32. Roger Leenhardt, *Les yeux ouverts: Entretiens avec Jacques Lacouture* (Paris: Éditions du seuil, 1979), 142, 163.

33. Jean Charles Tacchella, "When Jean Cocteau Was President of a Cine-Club: Objectif 49 and the Festival of *Film maudit*," in *Cocteau*, ed. Dominique Païni (London: Paul Holberton, 2003), 83.

34. Ibid., 83–84.

35. Ibid., 84. For more on Keigel's importance in the period, see Frédéric Gimello-Mesplomb, *Objectif 49 et la nouvelle avant-garde* (Paris: Séguier, 2014), 50.

36. Tacchella, "When Jean Cocteau Was President of a Cine-Club," 84, n.1, 85. For a full Objectif 49 filmography, see Appendices I–III in Gimello-Mesplomb, *Objectif 49*, 213–224.

37. Leenhardt, *Les yeux ouverts*, 163.

38. Armand Gourmelen, "Le 'Festival du Film Maudit' et le 'Rendez-Vous de Biarritz' (Biarritz, 1949 et 1950)," *1895* 29 (December 1999): 111; Gimello-Mesplomb, *Objectif 49*, 80.

39. Bresson, "Le festival du film maudit," 43.

40. Sidney Jézéquel (Leenhardt's nephew), e-mail message to author, June 13, 2013.

41. For a detailed institutional and reception study of the Festival of *film maudit*, see Gimello-Mesplomb, *Objectif 49*, 75–133.

42. Gourmelen, "Le 'Festival du Film Maudit,'" 112–114.

43. Cited in Gourmelen, "Le 'Festival du Film Maudit,'" 119.

44. Jacques Doniol-Valcroze, "Les yeux ouverts," *Gazette du cinéma* 5 (November 1950): 3.

45. Tacchella, "When Jean Cocteau Was President of a Cine-Club," 98; Gourmelen, "Le 'Festival du Film Maudit,'" 118.

46. Gimello-Mesplomb, *Objectif 49*, 157.

47. Colin Burnett, "Under the Auspices of Simplicity: Roger Leenhardt's New Realism and the Aesthetic History of Objectif 49," *Film History* 27.2 (2015): 62–65.

48. Dudley Andrew, *André Bazin* (New York: Oxford University Press, 1978), 141. See also Gimello-Mesplomb, *Objectif 49*, 64–71, for an extensive account of the event and its implications.

49. Jean Charles Tacchella, "When Jean Cocteau Was President of a Cine-Club: Objectif 49 and the Festival of *Film maudit*," in *Cocteau*, ed. Dominique Païni (London: Paul Holberton, 2003), 84.

50. André Bazin, "Défense de l'avant-garde," *L'écran français*, December 21, 1948, 1; André Bazin, "Avant-garde nouvelle," in the *Festival du film maudit* Catalogue (Paris: Éditions Mazarine, 1949); André Bazin, "À la recherché d'une nouvelle avant-garde," in *Almanach du théâtre et du cinéma* (Paris: Éditions de Flore, 1950), 146–152; and André Bazin, "L'avant-garde nouvelle," *Cahiers du cinéma* 10 (March 1952): 16–17.

51. Bazin, "Défense de l'avant-garde," 1.

52. Ibid.

53. Ibid.

54. Jean Cocteau, "Il importe de nous expliquer sur le sens exact du terme 'maudit' . . . ," *Festival du film maudit* Catalogue (Paris: Éditions Mazarine, 1949).

55. Jean Cocteau, *Cock and Harlequin: Notes Concerning Music*, trans. Rollo H. Meyers (London: The Egoist Press, 1921), 20.

56. André Bazin, "Le Festival du Film Maudit s'est terminé cette nuit," *Parisien libéré*, August 6, 1949, 2.

57. Burnett, "Under the Auspices of Simplicity," 43–50.

58. Jean Queval, "Dialogue avec Robert Bresson," *L'écran français*, November 12, 1946, 12, emphasis in source.

59. Roger Leenhardt, "Continuité du cinéma français," in *Chroniques du cinéma* (Paris: Cahiers du cinéma, 1986), 135.

60. Roger Leenhardt, "Le cinéma et les arts plastiques," in *Chroniques du cinéma* (Paris: Cahiers du cinéma, 1986), 208.

61. Roger Leenhardt, "Le film qu'il faut voir: *Les dames du bois de Boulogne*," in *Chroniques du cinéma* (Paris: Cahiers du cinéma, 1986), 126.

62. Bresson, "Le festival du film maudit," 43.

63. Jean Grémillon, "La malédiction du style," in the *Festival du film maudit* Catalogue (Paris: Éditions Mazarine, 1949).

64. Ibid.

65. Ibid.

66. Roger Leenhardt, "La malédiction de l'intelligence," in the *Festival du film maudit* Catalogue (Paris: Éditions Mazarine, 1949).

67. Ibid.

68. Raymond Queneau, "Les dix malédictions du cinéma," in the *Festival du film maudit* Catalogue (Paris: Éditions Mazarine, 1949).

69. Ibid.

70. Bazin, "Avant-garde nouvelle," original emphases.

71. Ibid.

72. Ibid.

73. For more on Apollinaire, see Michael Baxandall, *Patterns of Intention: On the Historical Explanation of Pictures* (London: Yale University Press, 1985), 57. Bazin played a slightly more expansive role in film culture, for unlike Apollinaire, he was a fine critic of actual works.

74. For more on this event, see François Albera, *L'avant-garde au cinéma* (Paris: Armand Colin Cinéma, 2005), 117–121.

75. François Timmory, "Le débat Sadoul-Bazin-plus-public, sur 'l'avant-garde au cinéma,' est devenu 'La bataille de la forme et du fond,'" *L'écran français*, March 15, 1949, 2.

76. Ibid.

77. Ibid.

78. Ibid.

79. Louis Daquin, "Remarques déplacées," *L'écran français*, March 8, 1949, 3.

80. Ibid.

81. Ibid.

82. Ibid.

83. Ibid.

84. Ibid.

85. Ibid.

86. Leenhardt, *Les yeux ouverts*, 166.

87. Ibid.

88. Richard Neupert, *A History of the French New Wave Cinema* (Madison, WI: University of Wisconsin Press, 2006), 28–33; Antoine de Baecque, *Les cahiers du cinéma: Histoire d'une revue, tome I: À l'assaut du cinéma, 1951–1959* (Paris: Éditions Cahiers du cinéma, 1991).

89. Jean-Pierre Barrot, "Une tradition de la qualité," in *Sept ans du cinéma français*, ed. Henri Agel, Jean-Pierre Barrot, and Jacques Doniol-Valcroze (Paris: Éditions du cerf, 1953), 26–37.

90. Ibid., 23.

91. Crisp, *The Classic French Cinema*, 365.

92. Truffaut, "Une certaine tendance," 26.

93. André Bazin, "De la carolinisation de la France," *Esprit* 22 (1954): 302, 303, 304.

94. Ibid., 303–304.

95. Ibid., 304.

96. Ibid., 303

97. Ibid., 304.

98. André Bazin, "De la politique des auteurs," *Cahiers du cinéma* 70 (April 1957): 11.

99. Pierre Bloch-Delahaie, "Encourageons la qualité: Un aspect important de la Défense du cinéma français," *L'écran français*, October 16, 1950, 6, 23.

100. Ibid., 24.

101. Paul Leglise, *Histoire de la politique du cinéma français, tome I: Le cinéma et la IIIe république* (Paris: Librairie générale de droit et de jurisprudence, 1970), 176.

102. Ibid., 6.

103. André Bazin, "La difficile définition de la qualité," *Radio-télévision-cinéma*, April 8, 1951, 6.

104. Ibid.

105. Jacques Doniol-Valcroze, "Problèmes et prospects du cinéma français," *Cahiers du cinéma* 41 (December 1954): 49.

106. Ibid.

107. Ibid., 50.

108. François Truffaut, "Une crise d'ambition du cinéma français," *Arts*, March 30, 1955, 5.

109. Andrew Sarris, *American Cinema: Directors and Directions, 1929–1968* (New York: E. P. Dutton & Co., 1968).

110. Truffaut, "Une crise d'ambition du cinéma français," 5.

111. Frédéric Gimello-Mesplomb, "The Economy of 1950s Popular French Cinema," *Studies in French Cinema* 6.2 (2006): 147.

112. Cited in Doniol-Valcroze, "Problèmes et prospects du cinéma français," 50.

113. Centre nationale du cinéma et de l'image animé, *45 ans d'avances sur recettes* (Paris: CNC, 2004).

114. Neupert, *A History of the French New Wave Cinema*, 38–39.

115. Centre nationale du cinéma et de l'image animé, *45 ans d'avances sur recettes*.

116. Frédéric Gimello-Mesplomb, "Le prix à la qualité: L'état et le cinéma français (1960–1965)," *Politix* 61 (2003): 101. When the state passed a law on March 11, 1957, officially recognizing the status of author for works of an audio-visual nature, France had in place measures that, in theory, recognized and supported the *cinéma d'auteur*.

117. Paul Schrader, *Transcendental Style in Film: Ozu, Bresson, Dreyer* (Berkeley: University of California Press, 1972), 59.

118. Alain Poiré, *200 films au soleil* (Paris: Édition Ramsay, 1988), 9.

119. Keith Reader, *Robert Bresson* (Manchester: Manchester University Press, 200), 116.

PART II

VANGUARD FORMS

3 Purifying Cinema:

The Provocations of Faithful Adaptation and First-Person Storytelling in "Ignace de Loyola" (1948) and Journal d'un curé de campagne (1951)

> Let me begin by acknowledging the heroic effort of Robert Bresson, who intended to make *the* film of "perfect fidelity." But this paralyzing fidelity prevents Bresson from communicating with more than an infinitesimal number of spectators. Maybe he wanted it that way, and maybe he would not be willing to admit that this makes a film flawed. Yet, it is a flaw. . . . The search for "quality" means nothing if it is carried out at the expense of most viewers, if it turns its back on the public.
>
> —critic Roger Boussinot[1]

RELEASED ON FEBRUARY 7, 1951, Robert Bresson's adaptation of Georges Bernanos's 1936 novel *Journal d'un curé de campagne* is now regarded as one of the classics of world cinema. But it initially garnered a mixed response. Roger Boussinot's provocative *L'écran français* review, titled "Un film qui suscitera peu de vocations," dismissed the director for being behind the times, his interest in faithful adaptation one that would attract few followers. French cinema had left the idea of quality, "formalist" filmmaking for the select few behind it: "Recall that four or five years ago much ink and a torrent of saliva flowed in the newspaper columns of experts and in ciné-clubs over the question of whether a film could do anything but betray the book it was adapting. Over the last several years, the birth of a French realism . . . has quite rightly reduced interest in discussions of this kind."[2] Responding to debates waged among specialized critics and cinephiles a half decade earlier, Bresson's highbrow adaptation struck Boussinot as evidence that, despite being one of France's finest directors, Bresson had become seduced by academic pursuits.

The claim that Bresson's film was made strictly for a few detached elites, with no connections to broader viewing culture, is, to say the least, hasty (*Journal d'un curé de campagne*, as I intend to show, tapped into a widespread interest in adaptation and the relationships between film and literature). Nevertheless, it must be acknowledged that, as we saw in the previous chapter, Bresson's cinema tended to find its most enthusiastic supporters not among the cinephiles who argued in the pages of leftist journals like *L'écran français* that auteurs ought to produce socially engaged films, but among those intellectuals affiliated with Objectif 49, a ciné-club that tied the *nouvelle avant-garde* to an aesthetic rejuvenation of cinema via ambitious formal experimentation. For critics like Jacques Doniol-Valcroze, who was a founding member of the club and its offshoot, the journal *Cahiers du cinéma*, Bresson was one of the select few whose innovations in faithful adaptation addressed some rather refined artistic problems contained in the points of intersection between cinema and other media like theater and literature. In a 1953 essay, "De l'avant-garde," Doniol-Valcroze wrote of Jean Cocteau, another major voice of the Objectif 49 movement: "*Les parents terribles* [1948], a film that is doubly avant-garde: it solves an old problem in a new way, and notwithstanding the theatrical structure it faithfully adheres to, Cocteau has somehow surrounded his work with a cinematic fringe that has very little to do with the theater."[3] Doniol-Valcroze was, in effect, drawing attention to what he perceived to be an intermedial or formally hybrid avant-garde. One of the pleasures of films like *Les parents terribles* was that they presented long-awaited problem-solutions: "The dramaturge has given control over to the cinéaste, who has been faithful to him in terms of content but who has left him out of the form to create a film-through-the-keyhole—an idea incompatible with three-wall sets and closer to the novel or private diary than to the dramatic arts."[4] In the same essay, he likewise declared Bresson's translation of Bernanos "a cinematic original without equal."[5] Bresson was hardly old-fashioned. Even as critics like Boussinot rejected the idea of formal experimentation, others recognized films like *Journal d'un curé de campagne* and *Les parents terribles* for the exciting ways they erased the old lines that separated artistic media.

Boussinot dismissed *Journal d'un curé de campagne* precisely for this reason: its innovations excited the formalist passions of the "snobs," as some preferred to view them, of Objectif 49 and *Cahiers du cinéma*. However, if truth be told, Boussinot was ignoring developments in film culture at large. This chapter tells the story of how creative problems related to intermediality—to the relationship, in this case, between a book and a film and, more broadly, between literature and cinema—developed into a widespread concern in the postwar era. Interest in "perfect fidelity" was the norm in cinephilic culture, and this had an effect on the artistic development and career of Robert Bresson. How?

Journal d'un curé de campagne was celebrated in many quarters, not only helping Bresson recover from one of the longest periods of inactivity in his career but solidifying his status as a vanguard auteur. It presented the cultural market with an artistic solution it had long been awaiting: a faithful rendering of Bernanos that demonstrated cinema's ability to adhere to the "purity" of novelistic first-person storytelling. As I will argue, the stakes surrounding a successful adaptation of Bernanos's novel were high in the late 1940s and early 1950s. The challenges for this project were, to a certain extent, generic. Bresson had to confront the expectations facing all literary adaptations—or literary films—in the period. Film adaptations were thriving, but few showed that cinema could rise to the level of sophistication of the novel or the well-written stage play. Any film that appeared to be literary—either because of its narrative techniques or its efforts to adapt an esteemed property—was held to close scrutiny, meticulously compared to current literature in general or the original source in particular. It was in some measure as a response to these cultural tendencies that Bresson stated the following about his approach to *Journal d'un curé de campagne*: "I long ago developed the conviction that in certain works (those in which the writer inserts himself entirely, and Bernanos's book is in this category), what best reveals the author, and reveals his very substance, more than just his thoughts and his various personal experiences, is the particular way—his way—of combining and integrating them. . . . Or if you prefer, it is the solutions he arrived at (often unconsciously) to the problems that follow from all compositional work. (Should I admit to you that these compositional problems fascinate me?) So, for me, the one doing the adaptation, what matters is fidelity to the spirit by (or through) a respect for the construction and the proportions themselves of the book."[6]

However, as I have already suggested, when he took the commission to adapt the Bernanos text, Bresson had to be aware of an additional challenge, beyond just the pressure to deliver a faithful rendering of the source. Like the novels of Marcel Proust, *Journal d'un curé de campagne* was considered to be "unfilmable." The story was a spiritual one, to a certain extent sparsely told, and entirely in the first person, and in the years after the Liberation, it was thought that few films had been able to successfully navigate the challenges of intimate storytelling and of the cinematic "I." Bresson had been working through these problems on a project he eventually abandoned, "Ignace de Loyola" (1948). A failed adaptation that altered the novel and swapped first- for third-person narration might have placed Bresson not in the pantheon of *nouvelle avant-garde* auteurs but alongside Jean Aurenche and Pierre Bost, two screenwriters whose reputations suffered when François Truffaut famously accused them, in his era-defining polemic "Une certaine tendance du cinéma français," of betraying the novels they had adapted (Bernanos's among them). With his career floundering (the "Ignace" project never came to fruition, and he hadn't directed a film since 1945), and perhaps sensing the need to return with a statement, *Journal d'un curé de campagne* was a risk that Bresson was willing to take.

It is precisely what the artistic and career risks—the problems and challenges before Bresson—entailed that concerns us here. In the adaptation of *Journal d'un curé de campagne*, Bresson, I will argue, accepted certain problems as his culture posed them. But a skeptic might object: in presenting the dynamic between

Bresson and his culture this way, are we not claiming that Bresson was ultimately a passive figure, subordinating his will to that of the market, in the making of his own film? Or, to put it vulgarly, are we not suggesting that Bresson simply made his film "to order," accepting these challenges because he saw in the adaptation of Bernanos's novel an opportunity to advance his career? These questions raise important considerations that cannot be dismissed outright simply by virtue of Bresson's reputation today.

These concerns, while legitimate, can be dispensed with rather quickly by pointing out that not all artistic problems a filmmaker—even a revered auteur like Bresson—confronts are entirely of his own making. By setting out to solve the problem of faithfully adapting Bernanos, he was plucking from tradition, as it came down through cinephilic discourse, those aesthetic questions worthy of the attention of a serious fiction filmmaker who wished to advance the art of adaptation. Rather than positioning Bresson as passive, we are positing that he actively moved to turn his culture's concern about the *Journal d'un curé de campagne* project in particular, cinema's legitimacy vis-à-vis the established literary arts more broadly, and the set of creative restrictions, opportunities, and trajectories in film adaptation sketched by filmmakers, cinephile critics, and theorists throughout the period into a predicament where he could demonstrate his talent as a filmmaker who commanded both literary and cinematic technique.

By now, the implications of this relay of interests involving Bresson and his culture for our reconsideration of the auteur as a social actor in midcentury France should be clear. Both the making of *Journal d'un curé de campagne* and its reputation as a *nouvelle avant-garde* film (*pace* Doniol-Valcroze) were the result of a synchrony of concerns and practices—a coalescing of auteur and cinephile around a set of ideas about adaptation that created the terms for cultural reciprocity between them. In this way, this chapter sets the stage for the next two, which address similar synchronies in the realms of realism and cinematic rhythm. Bresson, in attempting a faithful adaptation of this first-person novel, participated in a form of reciprocal exchange in which he took interest in how elements of his culture attended to adaptations and the culture took an interest in the ways he attended to the subtleties of adaptation. If *Journal d'un curé de campagne* had only one auteur, its impact as one of the most successful adaptations of the era can best be appreciated by drawing out the "cultural goods" traded between Bresson and the cultural market through its creation.

Questions of Intermediality: The Temptation of Purity and the Sonic First Person

The postwar cultural market had a way of focusing on basic aesthetic questions, like cinema's relationship to social and perceptual reality (our concern in the next chapter) and whether film could become a truly rhythmic form like music (our concern in chapter five). It also drew attention to what we now call interme-diality (more precisely, medial transposition): what does film adaptation reveal about the similarities and differences between film and literature?[7] Is cinema a sufficiently complex or serious medium to address, through adaptation and other creative strategies, the depth and breadth of theme, character, and narrative form available to the novel and more established dramaturgical forms?

Let us take our initial bearings on these questions by considering several key texts that, quite usefully for us, assess contemporary developments in literary and adaptation theory and practice. In a 1958 issue of *La revue des lettres modernes* devoted to cinema and the novel, literary critic Georges-Albert Astre argues that the arts of cinema and the novel are "fated to depend on one another for a long time to come—adaptations remain a major source for production, novelists are finding inspiration in the techniques of the cinema and the latter, in turn, is redis-covering the enduring virtues of literary storytelling."[8] For Astre, the intersection between the two art forms remains a central concern, not only because novel-ists-turned-filmmakers like Alain Robbe-Grillet were collapsing the distinctions between cinema and the novel in their own work but because "the problems of adaptation" had maintained their "extreme importance" throughout the 1950s.[9]

Numerous pieces in the issue of *La revue des lettres modernes* take stock of the problems—evaluative, theoretical, historiographic, artistic—raised by the cross-pollinating tendencies among French novelists and filmmakers of the 1940s and 1950s. One of the most revelatory is an essay by Colette Audry, a prominent literary critic and screenwriter best known for her writing on Jean-Paul Sartre and her screenplay for René Clément's resistance classic *La bataille du rail* (1946). She examines the "camera" in Alain Robbe-Grillet's novels, bringing the lan-guage of film technique to bear on literature. We see here something of a literary inversion of Alexandre Astruc's *caméra-stylo*. Whereas Astruc's auteur wields a pen, Audry's novelist can now tell a story through a camera lens: "While Robert Montgomery makes a character of his camera, Robbe-Grillet for his part makes his characters into a camera. The former humanizes his camera lens; the latter makes the human character a lens [*objective*] in the fullest sense of the term."[10] Lens and gaze unite: "The gaze that the protagonist casts on the pier in *The Voy-eur* or the husband on his wife's back in *Jealousy* is a gaze without a background, on the surface of an eyelid. It's a dehumanized, desensitized, in a word objective gaze, of a single glass lens, of a pure *objectif*."[11]

Audry upholds a view first espoused in a classic of postwar literary criti-cism, Claude-Édmonde Magny's *L'âge du roman américain* (1948)[12]—namely, the arts of the novel and cinema have a common history: novelists and filmmakers share a set of "related problems."[13] Principal among these is an issue already men-tioned, that of the purification in cinematic and literary storytelling. According to Audry, when the French began to read American novelists in the late 1930s—Dos Passos, Hemingway, Faulkner, followed by Caldwell and Steinbeck—a debate arose about the limits of the narrator's voice in the novel.[14] At stake was the relative truth or authenticity of certain narrative devices. French authors wondered about how to render their characters more true to reality, whether psychological analysis of characters was passé, and whether the omniscience of the storyteller should be reined in. Some like Sartre, Audry writes, were skeptical about "whether the ubiquity of the novelist who knows all, at all moments, about all his characters, now positioning himself at the heart of their consciences, now acting as a spectator and describing individuals from the outside, wasn't an illegitimate approach, of dubious aesthetic value, about to become less and less convincing."[15] Those who were expressing these doubts concurred with Sartre, who "posed the problem"[16] in his famous February 1939 *Nouvelle revue française* essay, "François Mauriac and Freedom."[17]

A study of *La fin de la nuit* (1935), written by the Catholic novelist François Mauriac, Sartre's essay associates the values of modesty and philosophical authenticity with literary works restricted to a single character perspective. The novel's protagonist, Thérèse Desqueyroux, "struggles against her destiny."[18] But Mauriac's storytelling follows a "see-sawing" structure, oscillating between "Thérèse-subject" and "Thérèse-object" often in the same sentence. In an unseemly manner, Mauriac requires of the reader a "constant duplicity": "I have insights into her which she does not have. Or else, seated in the center of her consciousness, I help her lie to herself, and, at the same time, I judge and condemn her, I put myself inside her, as *another person*."[19] Mauriac, Sartre provocatively remarks, "has chosen divine omniscience and omnipresence. But novels are written *by* men and *for* men. . . . God is not an artist. Neither is M. Mauriac."[20]

According to Audry, this opposition to excess—to an author/narrator moving from first- to third-person storytelling, from subjective to objective perspectives on characters and events, from descriptions of behavior to judgments on them—was ultimately derived from a distinctly modern, even *American*, passion for aesthetic purity: "The novelty of the American novel . . . consisted in how it recounted events and described its characters exactly as they appeared to a central character, and to him alone. What the reader lost in terms of information, on character motivation and the hidden workings of actions and events, it regained and more in the form of an infinitely more vivid sense of the fullness and opacity of reality."[21] She firms up the intermedial link: "This form of exposition in the novel is a cinematic form, for the camera, even after the arrival of the talkie, shows what it sees more than what it can probe in the soul."[22] But the conditions of modern American life and the "vogue of behaviorism" were just as responsible as the influence of cinema on the renewal of literary technique,[23] and filmmakers were eventually faced with an artistic problem-situation long known to avant-garde novelists: "If it is true that the camera observes beings from the outside, does it also have the right to be everywhere at once? Is its ubiquity easier to justify than that of the novelist? Is it time for the camera to take its turn in adopting a well-defined lookout post? This was a period where *cinéastes* wanted to see the camera *become one* with the main character."[24] Audry dates this phenomenon loosely, relying on two examples culled from Magny: Orson Welles's ill-fated adaptation of Joseph Conrad's *Heart of Darkness* in 1940, and Robert Montgomery's adaptation of Raymond Chandler's *Lady in the Lake* in 1947. The significance of this moment in the history of art is clear: "What matters is that the problem was posed in cinema just as it was in the novel—in other words, the two narrative arts at this moment in their development succumbed to the temptation of purity that poetry had experienced with Mallarmé and painting with the non-figurative."[25]

A temptation toward aesthetic purification, Audry stresses, led to a number of creative innovations in cinematic storytelling. Filmmakers experimented with a form of restricted storytelling where the viewer "followed the story through the eyes of a single character," where other characters are "objectivized" only through external descriptions.[26] Filmmakers rejected the "indifferent eye" excoriated by Sartre, encouraging the viewer to identify with the coherent and complex world of a single character point of view.[27]

* * *

In the late 1940s, years before Audry's important essay on Robbe-Grillet, several prominent cinephiles were already debating the purifying potential of first-person storytelling. Consider the back-to-back articles published in the influential *La revue du cinéma*, a "*Cahiers* before *Cahiers*" that resumed publication in 1946. In a January 1947 issue that drew attention for a translation of Gregg Toland's 1941 *Theater Arts Monthly* piece on the cinematography of *Citizen Kane* (1941),[28] Jacques Doniol-Valcroze examines the historical and theoretical implications of first-person cinema, presenting the recent birth of a cinematic *je* as a fulfillment of cinema's innate potential. For him, Robert Montgomery's *Lady in the Lake* is "a real event" in the history of world cinema.[29] The reason is simple: it "obviously posed multiple technical problems, first and foremost that of the camera," and, in the process, had rediscovered cinema's "first vision." Drawing on the myth of spectators ducking below their seats at the sight of *L'arrivée du train à La Ciotat* (1895)—a response he credits to the fact that "they confounded their own vision with that of the camera lens"—he argues that film style subsequently changed course.[30] There emerged a "second vision" and with it a spectator best understood as an "homme de la salle obscure" (a man in the dark room), whose perspective is "omniscient" and "to a certain extent depersonalized," "plunged objectively into *stories* he did not experience and does not live himself."[31] Cinema's original spectator, by contrast, took himself to be "the source of the shot," accepting the experience in movies as his own. The Lumière camera did not move about or shift perspectives, and for Doniol-Valcroze, this immobile, personalized view was an object of nostalgia for filmmakers. The "initial adventure of the cinematic 'I'" was cut short and went underground, as it were, becoming a device among many used to tell stories.[32] The "first person" in *Roman d'un tricheur* (1936), *Dr. Jekyll and Mr. Hyde* (1941), *Murder, My Sweet* (1944), and *The Lost Weekend* (1945) constituted little more than "subjective morsels . . . always motivated by dreams, drunkenness and hallucination."[33]

Doniol-Valcroze does not mince words when he states that *L'arrivée du train à La Ciotat* prompted a "natural reaction" among viewers.[34] After this original experience, cinema was immediately overtaken by the sheer artifice of convention, but the problem is not the shift to a cinema of narrative integration. As we saw in the previous chapter, cinephiles like Doniol-Valcroze were searching for a new avant-garde within storytelling, believing that the nonnarrative vanguard of the 1920s had run its course. We see this in Doniol-Valcroze's assessment of Dziga Vertov. The title of his piece invokes Vertov directly—"Naissance du véritable ciné-œil"—but he quarrels with Vertov's "indifferent and remarkably stupid" camera eye.[35] Although it seeks to capture reality directly, Vertov's cinema-eye is unnatural and "impersonal" relative to Montgomery's, which achieves its naturalness through special effects that give the viewer the "impression of being the actor, too."[36] By means of a curious dialectic between the artificial and the natural, Montgomery can "render a world that is closest to our most intimate sensations and reactions."[37]

Titled "'Les 'films à la première personne' et l'illusion de réalité au cinéma," Jean-Pierre Chartier's essay, appearing alongside Doniol-Valcroze's, accepts that first-person storytelling allows for greater narrative purity and authenticity but rejects *Lady in the Lake* as a model, arguing that Montgomery's style restricts viewer perception and imagination. "It has often been written that the cinema, made of images of things," Chartier begins, "shouldn't aspire to the analysis of souls and that only the novel could penetrate deep down into the interior of characters."[38] A film like *Our Town* (1940) shows the folly of this assumption, for it is "enriched by a technique that seemed until recently the purview of the novel"— namely, "the story told through first-person perspective."[39] *Our Town* presents not only an alternative to the story "told by an omniscient author who has the capacity for ubiquity,"[40] but moves beyond *Lady in the Lake*. If Montgomery's experiments were limited to the visual first person ("la prise de vue de la première personne"),[41] *Our Town* builds upon Welles's Mercury Theatre's radio show "First Person Singular" and invents the sonic first person ("la première personne sonore").

Brief Encounter (1945) builds on this tradition of oral storytelling and acoustic subjectivity. Its relay of sparse image and first-person sound constitutes a revolutionary step forward in cinema, for with it, cinema surpasses the art of the novel: "Without doubt, this 'interior monologue' is much more elaborate than those often used in the American novel: midway between oral story and written thoughts, it approximates the stories we create for ourselves from our own thoughts. . . . to my knowledge, it is the first film to employ from beginning to end the technique of offscreen voice-over to give direct access to the thoughts of the main character."[42]

Why do these cinematic innovations ultimately trump those of the novel? Chartier theorizes that the cinematic "I" expressed through voice-over alters the spectator's point of view by granting the story "the tone and authenticity of a reportage."[43] The use of the first-person singular in this manner "brings the written story closer to the oral story," like Welles's radio programs, and transforms the viewer into a witness who has privileged access to the experience—that is, increases the "credibility" of the narration "because the author can address the reader as an eye witness who can say, 'I was there.'"[44] Just as Doniol-Valcroze analyzed first-person storytelling as a greater source for genuinely personal sensations and feelings than Vertov's nonnarrative cinema-eye, Chartier argues that stories truly told (through sonic first person) from a single point of view prompt the spectator to read the character's intimate thoughts and feelings as his or her own: "The reader or the listener, if the story is well told, thus puts himself in the place of the one recounting it, attributing to himself [the storyteller's] events and actions and grants to the story the same credibility he does to his own memories."[45] Narrative films were restoring cinema's first vision.

If Chartier questions the significance of *Lady in the Lake* in the development of film style, it is for good reason: he believes that the illusion of reality that cinema creates does not come from "the implacable precision of the camera" but from the "art of découpage and montage."[46] A film that limits itself to a single visual point of view, rather than increasing the "credibility" and "realism" of what is on display, instead works against "the play of attention" the viewer experiences in his or her "normal vision." Ordinarily, attention can be "focused or enlarged" and "situates itself at different distances and even completes itself not through images seen but ones imagined that are nonetheless an aspect of perception."[47] This phenomenological explanation of what we now call continuity techniques, based on a reading of Henri Bergson, persuades Chartier that filmmakers should pursue an acoustic solution to the problem of incorporating the first-person effects innovated in literature. While a visual first-person cinema, in limiting itself to a single vantage point, goes against the grain of the ordinary perceptual experiences that continuity editing techniques accommodate, a sonic first person builds upon these experiences by offering a whole new possibility: cinema told *in the past tense*. Again taking his bearings with a film-mind analogy at once literary and Bergsonian, he theorizes that if most films tell their stories in the present, the story told in sonic first person "creates the FEELING of the past and grants each image the character of a memory"[48]—a memory of one's own.

This kind of cinema reinforces a theory that Chartier attributes to Roger Leenhardt (but which was addressed more comprehensively by Claude-Édmonde Magny in 1948)—namely, that cinema is essentially a medium of ellipses.[49] Here we observe another aspect of the purifying impulse that postwar cinephiles read into first-person storytelling. Memory, as a cognitive model for film style, is selective and therefore incomplete; filmmakers rely upon ellipses as a stand-in for this mental faculty. Chartier explains:

> In order for a film's sequence of events to create the illusion of continuous duration, the moments in the action to be filmed would be precisely those retained in the memory of the protagonist. The filmmaker [*cinéaste*] would use ellipses for the rest. These ellipses of down beat moments in the action are not a necessary convention dictated by the impossibility of making a film that conforms exactly to reality; they correspond with psychological reality. The ellipses we find in films are the exact equivalent of the psychological reality of a story of the sort characters would remember. Once again, we discover that the illusion of reality created by cinema (here, in the temporal domain) does not originate with cinema's capacity (technological) to reproduce movement and thus the "time of things," but of a choice (artistic) that recreates the duration as it is lived by an individual consciousness.[50]

For Chartier, the sonic first person reveals the Bergsonian duration at the heart of cinema as an artistic, rather than simply technical, medium. What is more, it recommends a purifying process whereby filmmakers who adhere closely to the spectator's perceptual experience of the world and thus trim away those plot developments that are not be retained in the memory of the character from whose point of view the story is told.

An Auteur's Temptation, Too: A Brief History of the Bressonian First Person

The temptation of purity in first-person storytelling was, as the writings of Colette Audry, Jacques Doniol-Valcroze, and Jean-Pierre Chartier demonstrate, a widespread concern, as much among cinephiles as the literati. But to what degree does this temptation factor into Bresson's filmmaking?

His first two features, *Les anges du péché* (1943) and *Les dames du bois de Boulogne* (1945), were relatively conventional in their reliance on a fairly unrestricted narration in which the viewer's emotional responses and understanding of plot developments are not consistently aligned with a single character. However, rather abruptly, Bresson shifted his attention to the problems of first-person storytelling, and by the end of the 1950s, he had a reputation for films that explored the *première personne sonore*. As Claude Mauriac, the son of novelist François Mauriac, wrote in 1957's *Petite littérature du cinéma*, a book whose title captured the intermediality of postwar film culture: "From the very beginning of *Un condamné à mort s'est échappé* [1956], we have the impression, while listening to the text's recitation by a monochord but deeply moving offscreen voice, of listening to words already heard. . . . These words do not bring us back to the *Figaro littéraire* story where we once read them and from which Bresson took them, but to the last film by the auteur, *Journal d'un curé de campagne* [1951], where it was quite another voice that delivered a different, equally neutral, text. In this we see the instantaneously recognizable style of Robert Bresson."[51]

Opportunities presented by the market—namely, commissions—gave Bresson the platform for his initial forays into first-person filmmaking in the late 1940s. The first came from the Italian firm Universalia, owned and operated by Salvo D'Angelo, producer of early Italian neorealist films like *La porta del cielo* (1945), *Germanio anno zero* (1946), and *La terra trema* (1948).[52] D'Angelo commissioned Diego Fabbri, the Catholic playwright, to write a script based on the life of Ignatius of Loyola, one of the leaders of the Counter-Reformation. In the spring of 1947, representatives of Universalia went to France to meet with a number of literary figures and major film personnel to collaborate on the project, including the novelists Georges Bernanos, Julien Green, and François Mauriac, and the directors Jacques Becker, René Clair,[53] Marcel Carné, and Robert Bresson.

The film was never produced,[54] but documents that survive—mainly, letters and treatments of the film reportedly written after Fabbri consulted Green and Bresson[55]—suggest that, over the course of the production, Bresson began, like many of his cinephilic contemporaries, to view first-person storytelling as a purifying impulse within film style. Fabbri writes that the original idea was to make the film in a "double style," one for "modern" parts of the film and one for "historical" parts[56]—a hybrid form, partially representing modern-day Jesuit experiences and partially set in the tenth century during Ignatius's lifetime. Bresson criticized this elaborate approach. According to Fabbri, this double style "contradicted the personal taste of the director Bresson," who wanted "a single style for the entire story."[57] It would be more precise to say that Bresson was invested in "Ignace de Loyola" to the degree that it focused on a single character's point of view. In a 1951 interview for *Opéra*, he explained: "The script I wrote two years ago on Saint Ignatius, one that I will no doubt make into a film one day . . . approached Ignatius of Loyola internally. Also (as much as possible) I retained of him only the 'spiritual.'"[58] Mylène Bresson, Bresson's widow, confirms that his efforts on "Ignace de Loyola" proved essential to his preparations for his next film, *Journal d'un curé de campagne*.[59]

It was with *Journal d'un curé de campagne*, another commission, that Bresson picked up on novelistic traditions and used the *première personne sonore* to purify film style, experiment with the ellipsis, and create a cinematic time with

Bergsonian overtones. For one critic writing in *Opéra*, a revue published between 1943 and 1952 that included novelists Roger Nimier and François Mauriac among its editorial board members, Bresson's postwar films drove a revival of a literary tradition devoted to the psychological perspective of characters. Bresson, this critic wrote, "returns to the tradition of great analysts represented in literature by temperaments as diverse as those of Mme. de La Fayette, Racine, Benjamin Constant, Marcel Proust and Valéry Larbaud."[60] Among the most famous devices in Proust's seven-volume *À la recherche du temps perdu* (1913–1927) are the involuntary memories that sensory stimuli like touch, smell, and sight trigger in the narrator, Marcel, thus framing the various plots through the narrator's (and novelist's) subjective perceptions. Constant, a nineteenth-century Swiss-born French nobleman and writer, published only one novel, *Adolphe* (1816), told through the mental states of the son of a government minister, in this manner, avoiding the objective description of action. Perhaps most revealing, if only because it proved prescient, was the critic's association of Bresson with Mme. de La Fayette, author of *La princesse de Clèves* (1678). Considered by most literary historians to be the first *roman d'analyse*, this literary masterpiece grants access to the introspective insights of its protagonist, Mademoiselle de Chartres, a young heiress during the reign of Henri II, a veiled reference to Louis XIV. In 1953 Bresson began work on an adaptation, never completed, of *La princesse de Clèves*, for which he invited the existentialist novelist Albert Camus to write dialogue. In 1954, the project was abandoned when Camus, who had not received a contract from a producer, had a falling-out with Bresson.[61]

Undaunted by this failure, Bresson used his next film, *Un condamné à mort s'est échappé, ou le vent souffle où il veut* (1956), to further pursue his experiments in subjective storytelling. The voice-over commentary of the Resistance fighter Fontaine, as David Bordwell and Kristin Thompson explain, is nonsimultaneous, occurring at a time later than the images.[62] Based on a 1954 *Figaro littéraire* story by André Devigny, the commentary therefore emphasizes the patterns of memory; some lines of commentary emphasize that the story is a recollection of past events. We see this when Fontaine states of another character: "Terry was an exception; he was allowed to see his daughter. I learned this later."[63] In his 1956 review of the film for *France observateur*, André Bazin notes that this restricted understanding of events purifies the visual track, denying us "a view of the entire gallery onto which the cells open or that of the window of [Fontaine]'s cell in relation to the prison courtyard."[64]

"Nor will we ever get a clear sense of where the prison guards are located," he observes: "We see them so infrequently that we might even believe that they are absent. What's more, the very rare long shots do not, with respect to the layout of places and characters, clarify more than the close-ups."[65] Bresson carries the sonic first person to the point where it motivates the restriction of visual expressivity (a point to which I return in the next chapter).

However, for some critics, it was with the subjective narration of *Pickpocket* (1959), a Dostoyevskian study of a lonely thief in contemporary Paris, structured by the personal diary entries of the protagonist Michel, that Bresson truly explored the potential of Chartier's sonic first person.[66] The film relied on a cinematic time as it was lived by an individual consciousness, as David Bordwell explains: "We are confined almost completely to his range of knowledge at the moment when the story events occurred. Indeed, the diegetic recounting in the notebook does not as a rule fill in prior information or anticipate events. And the device of the written record enables Michel to explain his feelings and thoughts. . . . Ellipses are also subjectively motivated by the recounting."[67] In one of the most famous ellipses in French film history, Bresson shows Michel leaving Paris. He purchases a ticket and makes his way to the platform to board a train. We cut to a diary entry written in the past tense where he recounts the two years he spent carousing in England. We then cut to a shot of Michel returning to Paris. Bresson has completely elided the England episode, restricting what he shows of this plot element to the character's recollection of it. As Chartier might claim, this elliptical storytelling is filtered through the memory of the film's main character and thus reveals the cinematic time as a refraction of personal experience.

Critics making sense of the film's style took their bearings in the grammar developed by theorists to uncover the links between recent films and the modern novel. In a *Figaro littéraire* review, Claude Mauriac shows once again that he was one of the most perceptive critics of Bresson's literary leanings: "Bresson uses *Journal d'un curé de campagne*'s mode of narration: written confession, translated into restrained images, with brief recurrences of the handwritten page. But here and there it consists of a confession like no other in its purity: intended for oneself, so much so that anything that records the inessential in great detail is justifiably omitted."[68] Michel Estève observes in one of the earliest monographs on Bresson that by the end of the 1950s, voice-over formed a central pillar of the director's artistic conception of space and time.[69] Generalizing about the plot structures of *Journal d'un curé de campagne*, *Un condamné à mort s'est échappé* and *Pickpocket*, he draws out the Bergsonian implications: "The personal journal allows the protagonist to go beyond the level of [recording] simple sensations, to break the continuity of objective chronological time, which is external to the inner 'me,' and to reach interior duration, in the Bergsonian sense of the term. . . . *Journal*, *Un condamné* and *Pickpocket* are unified in this double subjective perception of space and time: each of these films, in a way, consists of images, dialogue and silences that unfold in the flow of the protagonist's conscience."[70] *Pickpocket*'s storytelling style warrants a comparison with Albert Camus's *L'étranger* (1942), which proceeds by way of an "impressionism" where the hero "experiences only sensory impressions" and develops an affinity not for people but for "objects" (in the case of *Pickpocket*, personal belongings that Michel steals).[71] Both Michel and Camus's main character, Meursault, are "strangers" to the world.[72]

Adapting *Journal d'un curé de campagne*: The Challenges of Fidelity

This preliminary sketch of the Bressonian first person puts us in a position to draw closer to a particular case—to examine *Journal d'un curé de campagne* and the culturally inspired motives behind the fine-grained decisions of Bresson's adaptation. Perhaps more than any other Bresson film, it addresses two paradigmatic concerns of cultural market: purifying single-character narration and faithful literary adaptation. His success in doing so, as we will see, allows him to put his personal stamp on a vanguard artistic endeavor throughout the 1950s— one that tills the fertile soil in the connections between literature and cinema— and secures his reputation in the canon of cinema's masters.

In the mid-1940s through the late 1950s, questions regarding the links between cinema and literature were most often viewed in light of cinematic adaptation. There is no need to puzzle over this: cinema had been overtaken by an adaptation craze. Denis Marion, contributing to a collection of essays assessing the year in film and theater, 1949's *Almanach du théâtre et du cinéma*, prefaces his piece on adaptations by remarking, "It is a fact that more than half of films, foreign as much as French, are adapted from a preexisting literary work."[73] Bazin confirms this intuition in his classic 1952 essay "Pour un cinéma impur (Défense de l'adaptation)," where he records that for films of the last ten years, "it is readily apparent that one of the dominant phenomena of cinema's evolution . . . is its ever more frequent recourse to our literary and theatrical heritage."[74] One year later, in an article playfully titled "L'amour de la rhétorique ou l'enfers de l'adaptation," the critic Henri Agel notes of French cinema that "the years since the Liberation have not shown any discernible fluctuation in the already quasi-ageless attraction for the novel."[75]

A curious trend in cinephilic writing that grappled with this explosion of adaptations and the connections between the novel and cinema—one that is pertinent to our understanding of Bresson's reputation in the postwar cultural market—was the dependence upon three-part taxonomies for classifying and evaluating the performances of adapters. Adaptation types always seemed to come in threes.[76] Before the release of *Journal d'un curé de campagne*, cinephilia was abuzz over the possibilities of fidelity, as Roger Boussinot stated in the review with which we began.[77] Representative of this trend, Georges Charensol's 1946 book *Renaissance du cinéma français* took stock of developments by describing three categories of adaptation in a descending order of value:

"équivalent plastique"
   (formal equivalency)

"illustration dans le marge du livre"
   (visual illustration in the margins)

"déformation systématique/trahison consciente"
   (systematic distortion/conscious betrayal)[78]

For Charensol, only one film truly achieved formal equivalency: *Espoir*, adapted by the author himself, André Malraux. Here was a film whose "syncopated rhythm," whose "elliptical composition . . . irresistibly evokes the books of its author. . . . Like the writer, the filmmaker presents successive scenes that have between them nothing less than spiritual links."[79] The film was not identical to the source text in every respect—"The film naturally has less scope," especially in its handling of the Spanish Civil War—but at significant moments it nonetheless approximated its formal parameters.[80]

Most filmmakers, Charensol believed, opted for the second and third approaches, denying respectable works the respect they deserved. This included Bresson's *Les dames du bois de Boulogne*, cited as an instance of distortion, despite its moments of brilliance. Charensol contrasted the essence of the original story with Bresson's "modernizing" interpretation: "Of what does it consist? A Diderot story taken from *Jacques le fataliste*. A cold debauchery, an intellectualism stripped of any reference to average humanity. To render the ordeal riskier still, the story was transposed to our age, deprived of the luxurious décors and costuming of the period of Courtly Love."[81] Bresson's modernizations were mocked: "Imagine what would become of *Les liaisons dangereuses* if the Marquise de Merteuil made use of the telephone to weave her plots or if Valmont drove around in an American automobile."[82] Like many of his learned contemporaries, Charensol hoped for an "interior" cinema that approximated the novel, but not through the "superadded ornaments" of isolated expressive effects that were found in movies like *Les visiteurs du soir* (Carné, 1942).[83] He recommended that if Bresson were to continue to adapt character studies like Diderot's he would need to expunge externalizing distractions from his work: "If one day Robert Bresson wants to find inspiration in the Mérimée of *La double méprise*, or in the Stendhal of *Lamiel*, or in the Joyce of *Ulysses*, or in the Proust of *Sodome et Gomorrhe*, how would he manage to bring to the screen these unflinching studies of the human heart?"[84] Charensol could detect in the Bresson of 1945 aspects of the first-person filmmaker that he became by 1951, but in order to achieve this feat, Bresson had to purify his storytelling.

He also had to fine-tune his approach to adaptation. The standard applied to *Les dames du bois de Boulogne* was that of fidelity. The film's story of the vengeance taken by a jealous woman on her former lover was criticized by some critics because, as André Bazin put it, "Bresson took liberties with the plot and retained only the situation and, if you will, a certain eighteenth-century flavour."[85] Bazin explained further: "The film has been reproached . . . for the way the characters are psychologically out of synch with the sociology of the plot. . . . in Diderot, the social customs of the day justify the choice and effectiveness of the revenge depicted," but "in the film, this vengeance is depicted abstractly, leaving the modern-day viewer unable to understand its underlying causes."[86] Bresson had taken a risk by engaging in a "subtle play of interference and counterpoint between fidelity and betrayal."[87] Writing some years later, François Truffaut agreed: "The adaptation is at once very faithful and very unfaithful."[88]

*   *   *

As the standard applied to all adaptations, faithfulness was the question dominating the attention of cinephiles as Bresson's *Journal d'un curé de campagne* went into production. The popular Catholic weekly, *Radio-cinéma-télévision* (now *Télérama*), followed the adaptation with great anticipation. A January 1950 news brief read, "There is once again serious talk of making a film of the 'Curé de Campagne' of Bernanos."[89] Another from March 1950 pondered the tempting possibility of a faithful translation: "Robert Bresson will shoot 'Le Journal d'un curé de campagne' by Georges Bernanos. Will he have the courage to give film audiences the intensity of the great Catholic author's language?"[90] *Gazette du cinéma*, a short-lived publication originally associated with the famous Ciné-club du quartier latin that often featured articles by prominent cinephiles like Éric Rohmer (Maurice Shérer) and Jacques Rivette, among others, also reported on the expectations cinephiles had built up for the film: "Those who wish to avoid conflating art with technique, style with process, who in order to admire [cinema] listen only to their hearts and their taste, expect of Bresson not only his best film but a work of art that is at least as important to the history of cinema as Bernanos's great novel was to our literature."[91]

Aware of the anticipation that was bound to follow his every move on a high-profile adaptation of this kind, Bresson did not take the commission lightly. Fidelity became for Bresson a personal dilemma with implications for the way he conceived of himself as an auteur. In a 1951 *Opéra* interview, he spoke candidly about his deliberations: "I took several weeks to decide whether I would adapt Bernanos's book. I had an infinite number of concerns . . . of all kinds, with regards to the book. . . . Among these concerns was that of betraying the novel."[92] He eventually came to the somewhat paradoxical view that faithful adaptation would allow him to reaffirm his own voice: "All of a sudden, my fidelity to myself seemed to be ensured by a fidelity to Bernanos. I made a mold (my mold). And I filled it with everything that would fit from the substance of the book, including those conscious and unconscious thoughts and experiences that are the author's own, which are more important than the events."[93] Ever partial to fine arts metaphors, Bresson understood the challenges of adapting the novel through imagery borrowed from sculpture. In order to answer the task of fidelity yet retain his creative agency as the adapter and director, he viewed his role as a process of mold making. The mold he cast allowed him to capture the spirit of the novel and retain its personal, Bernanosian qualities.

As Bazin reported at the time, Bresson's "commitment to fidelity since he began his adaptation" evinced a "desire to follow the book sentence by sentence."[94] But there is a further layer to consider here. If we situate Bresson's adaptation of Bernanos in a context of cultural reciprocity, additional levels of significance emerge. On one level, Bresson was challenging his culture to bring its aesthetic criteria to bear on his film. He was essentially announcing to the cultural market that his film, once complete, would reward its attention to the challenges of faithful adaptation. But, on another level, he was testing cultural assumptions about what faithful adaptation entailed by stipulating that near-perfect fidelity of film to novel should be appreciated for the way the adapter has respected the *original source's construction*. In April 1950, Pierre Leprohon, writing from the film's set in Pas-de-Calais, where Bernanos was born, interviewed Bresson about his approach to adapting Bernanos: "Avoid simplifying. . . . Find the substance. Respect the structure. The structure has the value of an idea."[95] In a public discussion of the film after its release, he elaborated on this point: "I long ago developed the conviction that in certain works (those in which the writer inserts himself entirely, and Bernanos's book is in this category), what best reveals the author, and reveals his very substance, more than just his thoughts and his various personal experiences, is the particular way—his way—of combining and integrating them. . . . Or if you prefer, it is the solutions he arrived at (often unconsciously) to the problems that follow from all compositional work. (Should I admit to you that these compositional problems fascinate me?) So, for me, the one doing the adaptation, what matters is fidelity to the spirit by (or through) a respect for the construction and the proportions themselves of the book."[96]

Bresson was performing a subtle maneuver here. If he was willing to announce his acceptance of a broad artistic problem as his culture posed it, he was also going to perform his faithful rendering of the text on his own terms, as a creative act of translating the novel's structure—the kind of first-person plot design he had been pondering since "Ignace de Loyola"—as though the structure alone were the essence of Bernanos's literary artistry.

* * *

Bresson's adherence to fidelity during the film's production was not just a response to generic interest in faithful adaptation; it showed sensitivity toward the concerns shared by many over the adaptation of this particular property.

After the Liberation, there were several attempts, spanning half a decade, to bring *Journal d'un curé de campagne* to the screen. What's more, Bernanos made public many of the factors that led to their failures, including ones related to the betrayal of its structure, its first-person narrational strategy. As a result, by the late 1940s, two major cultural currents—propelled by a cinephilia taken with the prospects of single-character narration and adaptation as fidelity (or formal equivalency) and a celebrated novelist who felt slighted by an industry that had shown little regard for his masterpiece—converged. Bresson's genius was in recognizing the nature of the public challenge facing the project, in which the values tied to first-person storytelling encountered the values of faithful adaptation.

In 1945, Bernanos began to show interest in adapting the novel himself. As the editor of his collected letters, Albert Béguin put it, Bernanos "was tempted by the cinema" after the Liberation.[97] He elected to take on a collaborator, the Dominican priest and film producer Père Raymond Léopold Bruckberger, who had worked with Bresson on *Les anges du péché*. Dudley Andrew reports that Bernanos and Bruckberger were composing an original script for a film to be called *Dialogue des Carmélites* when Bruckberger proposed that they adapt *Journal d'un curé de campagne* as well.[98] But the Bernanos-Bruckberger collaboration, despite their friendship, quickly became a tense one. Bernanos began a November 1945 letter to actor Jean-Louis Barrault who was being considered for the lead role, by sharing his perplexity with respect to Bruckberger's actions: "I am just as confused as you are over the intentions of Père Bruckberger, whom I rarely see. I know that there is a vague interest of bringing either 'Journal' or a novel that will soon be out, *Monsieur Ouine* [1946], to the screen. What I can tell you at the moment is that my confidence in you is equal to that which you have in me."[99] Subsequently, Barrault, whom the novelist praised as "the greatest among French film artists,"[100] wrote that Bruckberger had visited to pitch an adaptation of *Journal d'un curé de campagne* and offer him the role as the curé d'Ambricourt.[101] Bruckberger apparently believed that if the film was going to interest investors, it needed a bankable name like Barrault, the lead in Marcel Carné's popular *Les enfants du paradis* (1945), on the marquee. What's more, Bernanos was discovering that his own novel was posing more than a few challenges to the adaptation process; he wrote to a friend in December 1945: "This film seems difficult to me to carry out. If I could make a little bit of time I think I might succeed in adapting the novel for the screen by modifying the book."[102]

At this stage, with Bruckberger pursuing his own interpretation of the project and Bernanos seemingly uncertain about how to translate its characters and first-person approach to the screen, it was time to consider other options, and events were set in motion that culminated in one of the most notorious failures in the history of film adaptation. In September 1946, Pierre Gérin approached Bernanos with an offer to take over the production.[103] Described by Dudley Andrew as an "ambitious young producer,"[104] Gérin, the director general of the IDHEC (France's state film school) from 1942 to 1946 and now the head of the independent firm Les Productions Cinématographiques (LPC),[105] was well positioned to shepherd the film to completion. Just eight days later, he sent a letter to Bernanos confirming that Jean Aurenche, a publicity filmmaker in the 1930s but now a celebrated adapter of novels by Eugène Dabit (*Hôtel du nord*, 1938), Sibylle Riqueti de Mirabeau (a.k.a., "Gyp") (*Le mariage de Chiffon*, 1942), and Michel Davet (*Douce*, 1943), had accepted an offer to turn *Journal d'un curé de campagne* into a film for them.[106] By March 1947, the contract with Gérin was signed,[107] but trouble began to stir when the script by Aurenche fell well short of Bernanos's expectations (for reasons we will return to in a moment). Aurenche was deemed unfit for the task and "finally liquidated" (Bernanos's phrase) in December of that year.[108] Attempting to salvage the project, Gérin proposed that Bruckberger pen the script and Bernanos the dialogue.

As Bresson had with Diderot in *Les dames du bois de Boulogne*, Bruckberger's script modernized the story of the country priest. Andrew explains: "Bruckberger could not keep himself from rewriting the novel in the atmosphere of the Occupation, for he had been the chief chaplain of the Maquis, entering Paris at de Gaulle's elbow. While the tone of sordid collaboration in the parish which he invented doubtless clarified and tightened the curé's anxiety, this moral specificity couldn't have been more false to the 'general' condition of spiritual loneliness which Bernanos had so forcefully created in 1934 by setting the curé's tribulations in the pastoral indifference of a quiet village."[109] Bernanos was put off yet again. Albert Béguin stated some time later that Bruckberger set the story of the priest during the time of the collaboration and resistance in order to clarify the "obscure" relations between the novel's characters, due in some measure to the story's first-person structure, which "purified" the plot of details that exceeded the priest's understanding.[110] With Bernanos dismayed by the industry's failure to treat his novel faithfully or to find the appropriate way to alter it for the cinema, all parties were ready to abandon the project by April 1948.[111]

Soon, the wide literary and filmgoing public became privy to some of these failures. As film aficionados know, Jean Aurenche's failure was famously trumpeted in Truffaut's "Une certaine tendance du cinéma français," but as Dudley Andrew clarifies, Truffaut added little to Bernanos's own denunciation of the Aurenche script.[112] In a 2,200-word letter published in a November 1948 edition of *Samedi-soir* (with the massive weekly circulation of 650,000, it was the biggest newspaper in France at the time), Bernanos poured scorn on the infidelities of Aurenche.[113] "I have seen the spirit of my novel cruelly distorted," he wrote.[114] Bernanos would have remained content with a low-profile approach to the matter had Aurenche not questioned Bernanos weeks earlier in the very same publication.

Aurenche's decision to go public with Bernanos's rejection of his script, which encouraged the novelist to respond in print, almost certainly had an influence on Bresson's approach. For Bresson, the high-profile dismissal of the Aurenche effort became an opportunity with a clear set of guidelines. Although it has largely gone unnoticed by historians, Bernanos's *Samedi-soir* rebuke began with an apology. His public reply, he wrote, was regrettably forced upon him by the unfortunate and inaccurate account by the screenwriter of a meeting between the two in Tunisia in an October issue of the same newspaper. Moreover, Bernanos felt the need to respond because of the outpouring of support from *Samedi-soir* readers who had expressed their "disapproval" over the decision to bring the novel to the screen. Wishing to reassure his readers that he had "always reserved the right to intervene in the event that the spirit of the book was being distorted," Bernanos decided to explain his decision publicly.[115]

Bernanos's explanation brings together the various cultural strands we've been discussing—the challenges of first-person narration and the problems related to fidelity—into a single thread. Aurenche's script betrays the spirit of the novel by altering its structure and tone, especially the first and final acts. The exposition begins not with the priest (therefore displacing the character from whose perspective the story is ostensibly told) but rather with Chantal, the estranged daughter of the village's count and countess. The narration is shifted to the third person, and Chantal becomes in Aurenche's hands a blasphemer whose impertinence caricatures the acts of heartfelt defiance and the complex emotions she grapples with given her father's shameful promiscuity and her mother's solipsistic grief for her lost son. Bernanos explains, quoting the script directly: "At the beginning of the script, on the occasion of a birthday celebration for their daughter Chantal, the lord and lady of my little fictional village are kneeling at the altar. . . . Chantal 'takes her missal from the prayer-stool, half opens it and spits into its pages the host which she had kept in her mouth.' A little later still, having handed the host to a priest poised to accept it, the little girl remarks coldly: 'You've swallowed what I swallowed. Doesn't this disgust you?'"[116]

Additionally, Aurenche's revisions fundamentally alter the novel's final scene. Its "final words," Bernanos explains, "are provided by a certain Arsène, brought back incidentally throughout the book, but in no context that would make him particularly important. Standing before the tomb of my protagonist, this wretched man declares, with the solemnity of a fool: 'When one is dead, all is dead, all is dead . . .' The film of *Journal d'un curé de campagne* ends with these pessimistic words."[117]

These alterations violate the restrictions Bernanos had placed on himself as a storyteller by depicting through third-person narration events not recorded in the priest's diary. Bernanos is quite strict about this in his writing, and Aurenche's relative immodesty is interpreted as a great offense. In the novel, the only words not written by the priest himself consist of notes by an unnamed fictional editor, especially during episodes where the priest experiences deep spiritual self-doubt and resorts to crossing out entries or tearing out pages.[118] In addition, the novel ends with a letter written by another character, Louis Dufréty.

Addressed to the priest's close friend, the curé de Torcy, it describes the priest's final moments. Lying in bed after suffering a hemorrhage from his stomach cancer, the priest reaches for Dufréty:

> A few minutes later he put his hand over mine, and his eyes entreated me to draw closer to him. He then uttered these words almost in my ear. And I am quite sure that I have recorded them accurately, for his voice, though halting, was strangely distinct.
> "Does it matter? Grace is . . . everywhere."
> I think he died just then.[119]

Other translations offer a more familiar rendering of the priest's last words: "What does it matter? All is grace."[120] The contrast between the script and the original is striking. With regards to structure, Bernanos adheres to the very last to a storytelling mode that involves recounting only those events that the priest himself—or in this one case, another character—recorded in print. Aurenche disregards this "purifying" narrative self-discipline in favor of a relatively sensationalistic—and in the context of the postwar cultural market, immodest—alternative.

* * *

Bresson accepted the commission from producer Gérin after Bernanos's death in July 1948. He was almost certainly aware of the force that Bernanos's *Samedi-soir* letter exerted on public opinion.[121] What's more, he appears to have known the letter well, using it to justify for himself and the public his own faithful approach to the novel, even to the point of adopting the author's own words and ideas. In the letter, Bernanos explained his conception of a true novelist and the responsibility owed to the novelist by the filmmaker adapting his work: "I believe that a real novelist, I mean one who is really committed to his book—or where the majority of its situations and characters are derived from that core of subconscious experiences . . .—would never have the ridiculous pretention of controlling the filmmaker the way a writer controls a translator, for instance."[122] As we saw earlier, Bresson picked up on these tropes (leaving out the Freudian overtones—he was no admirer of psychology) and elected to go the path suggested by Bernanos himself: complete fidelity to the novel's spirit and structure and to the personal experiences that the author cherished so dearly.

These commitments helped Bresson's cause when Gérin rejected his first draft. Gérin judged that its fidelity to the novelist resulted in a story with (in Bresson's words) "no dramatic interest."[123] By then, however, the notion of a by-the-letter adaptation of *Journal d'un curé de campagne* had developed interest and momentum, as had Bresson. Confident in his approach, he turned to Bernanos's literary executor Albert Béguin, as well as a religious expert, to throw their support behind his script.[124] "I was immediately impressed by Bresson's concern for fidelity, but I admit that I was not totally convinced prior to seeing the premiere," Béguin wrote in 1951.[125] He expressed his reservations to Bresson: "Wouldn't an overly literal reproduction of written dialogue become an obstacle to verisimilitude, exposing the characters' responses to one another and the writer's stylization as unmotivated contrivances?"[126] But, "Bresson was so confident in his dismissal of my objections that I stopped dwelling on them, and for fear of disrupting his work as a director, I remained silent about another concern of mine: the dialogue he reproduced was at once so dense that it seemed to carry the weight of the entire film, and thus might have led to what is pejoratively called a 'literary' film, and at the same time so fragmentary that its removal from a Bernanosian context would result in a loss of all its connotative substance."[127] The *littérateur* eventually acknowledged his error in judgment: "I therefore thought that Bresson was inadequate as a man of cinema and would fail to replace speech with images. I was wrong."[128] With Béguin and then the Bernanos estate backing Bresson's version, Gérin became a hindrance, and although he was reticent about relinquishing the rights, the producer ceded the project to Bresson and Union générale cinématographique (UGC).[129]

Bresson was in the clear, as it were, to perform his experiment and completed the film in 1949–1950. The task called for him to cede some creative authority to Bernanos but also to address obstacles from the medium itself. Because the artistic and exhibition conventions of cinema prevented a literal word-by-word transcription (the distribution system of postwar France would not support a ten-hour project that translated every scene and character from a 250-page novel), Bresson had to condense scenes and omit characters.

By virtue of Bernanos's *Samedi-soir* remarks, the choices of scenes to cut and condense and of characters to omit might have been ones so delicate as to be crippling. After all, Bernanos's rejoinder to Aurenche might have made audiences overly sensitive to conspicuous omissions from the novel's dramatis personae. But given trends in the cultural market, Bresson could trust that cinephiles would not take his promise of a word-by-word adaptation too literally. The relatively loose standard of formal equivalency, the fact that Bernanos placed an emphasis on the first-person structure of his novel, and the inclination among critics to examine prized adaptations like *Espoir* for the way specific (but not all) scenes matched up with the source text ensured a degree of flexibility.

The Aftermath of *Journal d'un curé de campagne*: How Bresson Was Recognized as an Auteur

When the film was released, a wide range of critics not only showed an appreciation of the mechanics of Bresson's achievement but recognized that the film was somehow *his*, despite the fact that, from a certain perspective, he was less of an "author" of the 1951 film than he had been for *Les dames du bois de Boulogne*, where he truly transformed the original source. This peculiarity of the postwar cultural market reveals the extent to which, first, faithful adaptation and first-person storytelling were valued and, second, Bresson positioned himself to engage in a form of reciprocal exchange through these values, not only with the "elites" associated with ciné-clubs like Objectif 49 but with a broader community of viewers.

The word "fidelity" is conspicuous in virtually every major positive appraisal of the film, thus revealing how culturally ingrained this grammar for appreciating a film's rendering of a text had become. But as no mere word-by-word transcription, *Journal d'un curé de campagne* also tested the assumptions of literary and cinephilic tastemakers. The obvious discrepancies between the film and the text posed a new and unexpected challenge. Bresson's film was both faithful in ways that satisfied and something more.

In the disagreement between the source and the adaptation, the film presented keen viewers with cues to identify a pattern—a controlling agency—that could not be attributed to Bernanos. *Journal d'un curé de campagne* offered its adapter the challenges of first-person narration, but *how* this was accomplished in the medium of cinema was not derived from the novelist. Critics were witnessing the emergence of a new voice in the history of film style and rushed with excitement to classify its innovative, hybrid form of adaptation—part performance of the work of a celebrated literary author and part performance of the style of an emerging *auteur de film*.

For many observers, the film's austerity was a sign of two aspects of faithfulness, to the novel and to the transcendent. Jannick Arbois, critic for the ciné-club monthly *Téléciné*, summarized the efflorescence of praise for the film: "Specialists, critics and friends (religious and not) of Bernanos have generally praised Robert Bresson for the intellectual honesty, the intelligence, and the fidelity with which he adapted 'Journal d'un curé de campagne.'"[130] The angst over the production had become palpable: "The unfortunate experience of living through the adaptation of *The Power and the Glory* and . . . *La symphonie pastorale* justified everyone's anxiety. This undertaking was a challenge and everyone would have feared the worst if someone other than Bresson—the rigorist, the purist, and to borrow Leprohon's term, the Flaubert of French cinema—had tackled this novel."[131]

"By refusing to take the easy way out that other movies take and in choosing to approach this from the steepest incline," he maintained, "Bresson won the day. He showed no hesitation in making an austere, difficult film that eschewed fioritures."[132] During a roundtable discussion about the film in 1951 featuring Bresson himself, the actor Claude Laydu (who plays the priest), Albert Béguin, and Stanislas Fumet, a Catholic-socialist essayist and art critic who was a major champion of the avant-garde, Fumet focused on the film's "dépouillement" (asceticism or austerity), the source of which was Bresson's understanding of the theology behind both the novel's sparseness and the life of the protagonist: "Very often, God presents Himself through a form of dereliction, but what struck me as the most remarkable aspect of Bresson's film is that Bresson formally translated this bareness, this poverty and lack of provisions, that is the source of the drama of the novel and the film; what strikes me as very new and very bold in Bresson's film is this kind of cinematic classicism that he has invented. It seems to me that we find it in his other films where he is in constant search for asceticism."[133] The filmmaker garnered attention for having boiled the plot down to God and the priest and the simple life that connected them.

The sparseness of Bresson's images will be addressed in the next chapter. What concerns us here is the Bernanos-Bresson intermedial link. The choice of the term "dépouillé" is historically significant because it reveals that in this era of auteur-cinephile exchange, the boundaries between artistic media were collapsing to a certain extent. Artistic values and problems did not respect commonsense notions of medium specificity. When Bernanos's novel was originally published in 1936, its style also stimulated a discourse of *dépouillement*. Literary critics commented on the novel's austerity in two ways, in terms of its stylistic features and its lack of intrigue (the novel has a rather pared-down plotline with comparatively few events).[134] Critics devoted great energy to making sense of Bernanos's decision to eschew exterior action. One commentator praised the novel's "grandiose simplicity,"[135] while another critic found it amazing how with so few narrative facts, the novelist "has been able to give us a genuine novel in the form of an unceasing monologue where all the action is reduced to the recollection of memories or to secrets."[136] Stylistically speaking, critics commented on the way Bernanos's language is "dépouillé"—"Of this art without equal the world over," one wrote, "there is simplicity, plenitude."[137] Because of this simplicity, Bernanos had exhibited his "mastery of style."[138] For others, this "simple and pared down style" corresponded perfectly to the protagonist himself—a modest country priest.[139]

The phenomenon we observe here might be called lexical transference, in which the terms used to describe one artist are transferred to another. Bresson, already developing a sparse style of his own, becomes a stylistic heir to Bernanos. Just as importantly, Bresson uses his own medium to give Bernanos's austerity a new spin, translating the novelist's simplified prose style into a voice-over narration and innovating a series of austere visual correlates to Bernanos's rhetorical style.

Far more prominent in reviews of the film is the notion that its austerity stems from first-person storytelling. Given what we have seen of the culture's attitudes toward the film-literature relationship—Sartrean criticisms of the excesses of third-person narration imported into film theory; the Valcrozean search for the true cinematic "I"; the Chartierian distinction between *la première personne sonore* and *la prise de vue de la première personne*; and so on—this comes as no surprise. Claude Mauriac's *Figaro littéraire* review, titled "Le premier film de la vie intérieure," confirms that Bresson had given cinephiles just what they had been looking for—namely, a film that demonstrates that cinema can portray the inner world of a single character just as artfully as the novel. Separating himself from other reviewers, he notes that "most other critics attend only to spectacle," hence the "almost general ignorance of this work, one of the richest and most important in all of cinema."[140] As the title of the review proclaims, Bresson has undertaken a pioneering examination of the interior life by "sacrificing" that which gives cinemas its own unique "realm," the "external world." Mauriac credits Bresson's innovation to the "respect and fidelity without cinematic precedent" he showed to Bernanos's text, an accomplishment rooted in a distinctly "non-cinematic" and "simple method." Bresson's Bernaosian alternative spurned convention on four levels:

1. *The cinematography*—Bresson eschewed "all of the false beauty of *photogénie*" and instead sought "dépouillement."
2. *The staging of action*—Bresson avoided adding a single "gesture" that Bernanos had not described in the novel.
3. *The script*—His adaptation went "line-by-line" through the source text, "excluding anything in the film that is not in the novel" and including "in the film all that is in the novel." Bresson also reduced to a minimum the "tightening of lines" borrowed from the novel, maintaining their integrity.
4. *The première personne sonore*—With "the neutral tone, dull and relentless" of the priest's voice-over, Bresson created a genuine experience reminiscent of our "interior monologue."[142]

In Mauriac's judgment, the film had drawn on aesthetic qualities not customarily associated with cinema: modesty and humility. Bresson stood apart from contemporaries like Bost and Aurenche who, Maruriac reminds the reader, has not only rendered *Journal d'un cure de campagne* as an inaus+tere third-person plot, but had succumbed to the temptation of viewing themselves as "creators worthy of" (and thus on par with) the novelist in their lamentable adaptation of Radiguet's *Le diable au corps*. Bresson thus emerges in Mauriac's account as a committed, self-effacing facilitator. His was "the humble labor of a copyist with just as much genius as Bernanos but who shows no awareness of it."[143]

If Mauriac's interpretation of Bresson goes a bit far in comparing him to a copyist, other critics were reluctant to see all aspects of Bresson's art through the lens of faithful adaptation. Fidelity was simply too narrow a concern to account for the film's purifying visual and sonic effects. Although not a cinephile himself, Albert Béguin held sway in cinephilic quarters because of his proximity to

Bernanos. With one piece in particular, he led the way by legitimizing Bresson as an auteur in his own right. In "Bernanos au cinéma," published in a February 1951 issue of the influential Catholic journal *Esprit*, Béguin addressed the sensitive matter of attribution, of correctly ascribing aspects of the film to Bernanos and Bresson. His intimate knowledge of Bernanos and the adaptation's troubled history put him in a unique position to dislodge Bresson's association with mere transcription. As a Bernanos expert, Béguin possessed a fine scalpel for examining the original work of each artist layer by layer.

Although one might expect a literary critic who was also Bernanos's executor to subordinate the filmmaker's artistry to the novelist's, Béguin relied on Bernanos's own rationale that the novelist should not expect the filmmaker to adhere to his style alone: "I should add that going with a personal style, different from the novelist's, seems to me a right that the filmmaker should arrogate."[144] Béguin lauded Bresson for having taken on the "double peril" of the aesthetic and religious aspects of Bernanos's genius.[145] The risk he ran was in making a film that was "worse than a failure: an abusive annexation, dishonest, a fraud."[146] Instead, Bresson was "scrupulously prudent," which "multiplied the obstacles in his way." For if Bresson followed the story "step-by-step," kept "the personal diary character," and composed "the dialogue from sentences borrowed from the text itself," he did so by eschewing "the conventions of cinema."[147] "The result is clear," he declared, "for the first time—because neither *The Fugitive*, nor *Dieu a besoin des hommes*, nor even *Les anges du péché* by Bresson himself, had gone so far in discarding all pictorial, sociological or spectacular elements—for the first time, a film unfolds, from the first image to the last, in the austerity of a purely spiritual drama."[148]

"But between Bernanos and Bresson, the divergence of style is as big as one might imagine," he was quick to point out.[149] Béguin positioned Bernanos and Bresson at two extremes along a spectrum of austerity. One was invested in an art of spontaneity and impulse while the other gravitated to an art of restraint and composure. If Bernanos's style "conforms to a certain rhythm of inner life that is highly spontaneous," Bresson's style was one of "extreme rigor and aesthetic calculation."[150] Bresson pressed all aspects of his film, even the elements culled from the text, into the service of "purely cinematic means . . . the purest ones cinema has at its disposal: not by the expressionism of gesture and acting, which is almost always crude and of which Bresson has no use, but through the obsessive frequency of the same image (the face of the priest, his room, the alley of the château, etc.), the recurrent themes, their internal relation of proportion, of relative range, of speed or slowness—that is, those noble means that relate to composition and that become expressive only in reference to one another."[151] Bresson's art, unlike Bernanos's, compelled the viewer to appreciate it in terms of carefully controlled rhythms.

Bressonian rhythm is a subject to which we shall return in the final chapter. For the moment, one need only point out that Béguin perceived Bresson's agency as the creation of rhythms between "parallel and contrasted scenes," rhythms constructed from the bits of "faces" and "landscapes" and "fragments" of text "extracted from the book."[152] Despite this quasi-musical regulation of cues, at times, "the spirit of Bernanos seems to trump the caution of Bresson."[153] Moments of Bernanosian pathos flashed up, pushing through Bresson's careful control. This critic called attention to three instances when "the screen is suddenly submerged as if by a wave of emotion."[154] In the famous medallion scene, the priest and the countess wage a spiritual battle over the countess's soul that culminates with her resignation to a God of whom she had been wary for taking her son. Initially, the countess dismisses the priest's entreaties to pray. At the end of the scene, clutching a medallion containing a photograph of her son, she kneels in prayer. Later in the film, the priest, collapsed in exhaustion, finds himself in the care of the Séraphita, a schoolgirl who, earlier in the film, had treated him with scorn. And, finally, Béguin drew the reader's attention to a scene near the film's end when the priest has a touching conversation with the partner of his defrocked friend, Dufréty. She apologizes for their modest and filthy abode and, in a gentle tone, confesses that they are not married because she had wanted him to retain the option of returning to the priesthood. These intimate exchanges between characters were, for Béguin, signs that intermittently Bernanos's spirit warmed Bresson's calculated rhythms.

If some, like Mauriac, attended solely to the film's literary faithfulness, other cinephiles followed Béguin in mixing interest in fidelity with a fascination for attribution and Bresson's presence in the work alongside Bernanos. This balancing act proved to be a complex matter and encouraged cinephiles to adopt sophisticated tools and postures. In his 1959 monograph on Bresson—one of the first in any language—Jean Sémolué carefully examined the artistry *within* fidelity.[155] If Bernanos's text furnished Bresson with certain artistic motivations, Bresson had to reinterpret them by subtly filtering out parts of the novel. Also calling attention to the medallion scene, Sémolué speculated that "almost every aspect of the scene is carried out according to a mode described at one point by the writer."[156] The text provided clues for how to direct the scene. The countess "made this horrible statement without raising her voice."[157] For this critic, Bresson wisely removed everything from the original text that might compromise the relative austerity he was aiming for (the same austerity which, paradoxically, was inspired by Bernanos). Sémolué demonstrates this in a detailed comparison of excerpts from the text and the film (in this case, a conversation about the countess's daughter, Chantal, and the countess's own resignation to God). I cite this comparison as it appears in Sémolué (see table 3.1, note Bresson's omissions).[158] Whether the critic frantically scribbled the film's dialogue into a notepad during

Table 3.1. Jean Sémolué's comparison of novel and film versions of Journal d'un curé de campagne (*L'écran français*, March 8, 1949, 1).

NOVEL	FILM
Priest: I certainly fear she may be driven to extremes.	*Priest*: I fear she may be driven to extremes.
Countess: "To extremes"! How well you put it! I suppose you're suggesting she's going to kill herself. Why, it's the last thing she's ever think of. She's terrified of a sore throat; she's horribly afraid of death. In that alone she takes after her father.	*Countess*: It's the last thing she'd do. She's horribly afraid of death.
Priest: Madame, those are the very ones that kill themselves.	*Priest*: Madame, those are the very ones who kill themselves.
Countess: Really, you know—	*Countess*: Really, you know— someone must have taught you that. It can't simply be your experience.
Priest: Void fascinates those who daren't look into it. They throw themselves in, for fear of falling.	
Countess: Who taught you that? You must have seen it somewhere in a book. It can't simply be your experience.	
Countess: Resign myself? To what? Resign myself? What do you mean? Don't you think me resigned enough? If I hadn't been resigned, I'd be dead! Resigned! I've been too much so. It makes me ashamed. Oh! I've often envied weaker women who haven't the strength to toil up these hills. But we're such a tough lot! I should have killed my wretched body so that it shouldn't forget. Not all of us can manage to kill ourselves—	*Countess*: Resign myself? To what? Don't you think me resigned enough? If I hadn't been resigned, I'd be dead! Resigned! I've been too much so. I should have killed my wretched body so that it shouldn't forget.
Priest: That's not the resignation I mean, as you well know.	*Priest*: That's not the resignation I mean, as you well know.
Countess: Well then—what? I go to mass, to take my Easter. I might have given up going to church altogether—I did think of it one time. But I considered that sort of thing beneath me.	*Countess*: Well then—what? I go to mass. I might have given up going to church altogether—I did think of it one time.
Priest: Madame, no blasphemy you could utter would be as bad as what you've just said! Your words have all the callousness of hell in them. How dare you treat God in such a way?	*Priest*: How dare you treat God in such a way?

a screening, in anticipation of performing just such a comparison, or was given access to the screenplay by the filmmaker is not known to me. However he may have accomplished this level of analytical detail, in the end, Sémolué echoed conclusions drawn by Béguin almost a decade earlier.[159] The critic interpreted this elimination of inessential elements as evidence that Bresson consistently "disregarded all superficially dramatic energy and maintained the subject's deep tragic tension."[160] In the passages compared, Bresson removed those ideas and images that distracted from the drama by virtue of their explicit or florid nature. The excising of references to suicide (Chantal's and the countess's), "the Void," "weaker women," "blasphemy," and "hell" from the countess's callous words purifies the text of all the colorful excesses of the original and enriches its indirect quality, its intellectual and emotional suggestiveness.

If for Sémolué Bresson's presence was to be discovered in the work's "purifications" of Bernanosian language, some critics believed that the film's corrupting infidelities at the level of character and plot offered far more revealing answers to the conundrum of attribution. Writing in 1951, Jannick Arbois declared his suspicion of overly literary interpretations of Bresson's intentions. In his eleven-page analysis of the film—the most thorough one at the time—Arbois showed that a subtle and detailed consideration of Bresson's storytelling uncovered rifts between the film and the novel, and through this, an aspect of the Bresson style (namely, his exceedingly disciplined treatment of first-person narration) that was nowhere to be found in Bernanos.

Defiantly opposing the literary discourse that surrounded the film, Arbois launched his analysis with a "preliminary remark" on the relations between the film and the novel: "A film is a work of art, singular and concrete, which we must consider in and of itself and of which it is important to grasp what the auteur intended before we compare it with another."[161] Commenting on the responses given to the film by the literati, he boldly asserted: "In the case of *Journal d'un curé de campagne*, we have perhaps looked too often to Bernanos specialists who, elated at the sight of an honest adaptation ... have applauded the film with an enthusiasm grossly exaggerated by concerns that they have long suffered."[162] Arbois went on to make the case that the film was very much Bresson's by listing the scenes that he trimmed from the novel (but which were included in a longer, three-hour cut of the film that was never screened).[163] Under the section heading "The Film's Inadequacies Relative to the Novel," he documented how Bresson completely eliminated the novel's social and psychological elements, which according to Arbois, gave the impression that the priest simply "spends his time writing his memoirs and running to the manor to hear the confessions of the country lords."[164] Bresson excised those pages of descriptions of the "unsuccessful efforts of the priest to enter into pacts with his flock and to take charge of their community." Also "missing from Bresson's country priest is that painful past, that sad childhood, that sense of guilt and humility in the poor that makes them what they are, that explains his social awkwardness and his lack of influence on others."[165]

This is an astute observation. While other art films from the period delayed or dispersed exposition, *Journal d'un curé de campagne* did away with backstory almost entirely.[166] Bresson also downplayed the novel's social dimension. One of the most striking differences between Bernanos's priest and Bresson's was that the novelist's showed a deep commitment to alleviating poverty. In a reflection on the responsibilities of governments to the poor that lasts an entire diary page, Bernanos's priest wrote: "Willy-nilly the social order must henceforth share the natural burden of humanity, embark on the same divine adventure. In the past alike indifferent to good and evil, knowing only the laws of its own power, society has found a soul in Christianity, a soul to lose or to save."[167] Such progressive Catholic thought would almost seem out of place in Bresson's version, whose priest was simpler, less prone to punchy political discharges.

Arbois offered an explanation that reveals much about the period's cinephilic criticism. If Bernanos "seems less to describe a soul than to partake in its suffering," Bresson was an artist interested in cinema's ability to express inner states: "Bresson has been criticized for not expressing a particular joyful quality that the novel radiates, precisely the joy of God's presence, contained and almost suffocated until the instant where it is mysteriously released in the final words of the country priest: 'All is grace.'"[168] This was Bresson's most profound "betrayal" of the novel: "Nothing introduces them, nothing prepares us for them, nothing explains them. And I suspect that no place was made for any kind of grace in this film. Because it is not, like the novel, the work of a man seeking the truth, but the work of an artist seduced by the beauty of man's inner drama."[169]

Arbois used strong language in praise of the film and in criticizing it. Its complex relation with the source meant that he could not quite bring it on himself to rebuke the entire project. The complexities involved led Arbois to contemplate a basic question with respect to adaptation. Must we view the process of faithfully adapting a novel as "an admission of impotence"?[170] He borrowed these words from Henri Agel, who condemned Jean-Pierre Melville's *Le silence de la mer* on precisely these grounds. Or, Arbois inquired further, ought cinephiles to view fidelity as the use of the source text "to bolster a purely cinematic language" (a notion attributed to Béguin's writings on *Journal d'un curé de campagne*)?[171] Arbois's answer was once again revelatory. He tied this "original and purely cinematic work" to the postwar call for a truly first-person cinema: Bresson's style had "the effect of interiorizing the drama and of giving the spectator, perhaps for the first time in contemporary cinema, the impression of examining the internal drama of an individual soul."[172]

Conceiving Bresson's film as a challenge to the cinephilic sensibility also helps us understand the shift in tastemakers' assessments of adaptations in the wake of *Journal d'un curé de campagne*. Bresson's masterpiece was not alone in mounting this challenge, but it was uniquely effective in this regard. The tools critics and theorists had innovated were suddenly in need of refinement.

If, as we saw earlier, Charensol's triad of formal equivalency, visual illustration, and systematic distortion/conscious betrayal seemed adequate in 1946, and if only one film met the standard of formal equivalency at that time (Malraux's *Espoir*), by 1951, after more films had experimented with a wider range of original texts, critics sought new terms and greater clarity in their evaluative criteria. At stake was the development of a more nuanced conception of what the adapter aimed to achieve with the novel. Take for instance Henri Agel who, writing seven years after Charensol, adopted a different lexicon, one that focused less on how the adaptation was performed than on the yield of the final product, but the categories overlap (again, Agel presented them in descending order):

"renouvellement"
(renewal)

"transfiguration"
(profound change)

"dégradation"
(degradation)[173]

Of the first category, Agel explained: "We find an independent life and structure, distinct from the printed text and offering a whole just as good onscreen as it is in the book."[174] He admitted a dozen films to his pantheon. Accepting the judgment of predecessors like Charensol, Agel granted *Espoir* a position in the top category, only now Malraux's film shared this designation with Cocteau's *La belle et la bête*, Max Ophüls' *La ronde* (1950, from Schnitzler), Melville's *Le silence de la mer*, and Bresson's *Journal d'un curé de campagne*. "Almost all of the foregoing works," he added, "benefited from an intelligent and personal mise-en-scène, from which they approached a second incarnation generally as captivating as the book."[175] The critical emphasis was no longer, as it had been with Charensol, on how the adapter approximated the source—no longer a simple matter of keeping score of similarities and discrepancies—but rather on whether the filmmaker was able to make his agency known in the process by manifesting a style all his own.

Between 1946 and 1953, critics kept a keen eye out for virtuosic adaptation and developed a canon. The penchant for threefold categorization persisted, but one also observes a shift. Cinephile critics had become impatient with the idea of fidelity alone and began crafting entirely new concepts, or else started to probe the finer aspects of faithful intermedial relations. The summer 1958 issue of *La revue des lettres modernes* devoted to *Cinéma et roman* I cited —earlier is a prime instance. Writing in the second of the issue's four sections (on the creative problems associated), François Truffaut appeared almost irked by critical language. His contribution, "L'adaptation littéraire au cinéma," began with a dismissal: "In my view opposing by-the-letter fidelity to fidelity to spirit seems to falsify the issues at stake in the problem of adaptation, if such a problem exists."[176] As if to mock the proliferation of threefold classifications and overly complicated terms that describe them, he mischievously presented his own set of categories, suspicious in their simplicity (bear in mind that they describe the kinds of fidelity filmmakers seek):

> la même chose
> (the same thing)
>
> la même chose, en mieux
> (the same thing, only better)
>
> autre chose, de mieux
> (something else, only better)[177]

More importantly, the editors of the issue reprint what has become two authoritative articles on the subject by André Bazin, 1952's "Pour un cinéma impur," which I mentioned before, and a 1948 piece, "L'adaptation ou le cinéma comme digeste," to which I shall return. While these essays remain canonical in film studies, they should not overshadow Bazin's writing specifically devoted to Bresson's *Journal d'un curé de campagne*. For, indeed, this singular adaptation encouraged Bazin to develop some fresh ideas about intermediality that influenced many a critic during the 1950s.

As a case in point, Claude Gauter, a *Cinéma et roman* contributor who later became an expert on the films of novelist Georges Simenon, took his bearings on the question of film and literature by drawing on Bazin's 1951 article, "*Le Journal d'un cur de campagne* et la stylistique de Robert Bresson."[178] From Gauteur's standpoint, Bazin's three types of adaptation offered the most intelligent classification to date:

> "dialectique entre le cinéma et la littérature"
> (a dialectic between cinema and literature)
>
> "sympathie fondamentale du cinéaste pour le romancier"
> (fundamental sympathy of the filmmaker for the novelist)
>
> "traduction esthétique du roman dans un autre langage"
> (aesthetic translation of the novel into another language)

For Bazin, as for Gauteur, Bresson's adaptation was one of few films to attempt a dialectic between the two arts. That being the case, Bazin in particular felt that, to fully appreciate *Journal d'un curé de campagne*, one had to properly theorize Bresson's filmic and literary authorship.

Bazin's analysis of the unique intermedial exchange the film initiates was not without its own complexities. Bazin's article on *Journal d'un curé de campagne* described the film's dialectical relation between cinema and literature through yet another postwar category of adaptation strategies. He claimed, quite bizarrely, that in its faithfulness to the source text the film *multiplied* Bernanos's novel: "*Diary of a Country Priest . . .* is another thing altogether. In the final analysis, its dialectic of fidelity [*dialectique de la fidelité*] and creation boils down to the dialectic of film and literature. Here it is no longer a case of translating, as faithfully and intelligently as might be the case, and even less of being freely inspired by loving respect, to create a film that will be the novel's double."[179] Bazin's system of classification became more abstract: "The point, rather, is to construct on top of the novel, through cinema, a work in another state. Not a film which can be described as 'comparable' to the novel, or 'worthy' of it, but a new aesthetic existence, something like literature multiplied by cinema."[180] One might speculate that Catholic interest in the film's themes suggested to Bazin a Biblical image here. That Bazin would invoke the miracle of Christ's multiplication of loaves and fish (as described in Mark 6:41–44) seems plausible. He was well known for his creative allusions. But whether or not this was Bazin's aim, what this image means in terms of adaptation is by no means clear.

The answer is perhaps to be found in 1948's "L'adaptation ou le cinéma comme digeste." Here, Bazin tinkered with something like a Platonic conception of adaptation whereby the original idea of the work stood apart from its various incarnations. He crafted a pyramid metaphor to explain how a particularly skilled adaptation—not by a novelist of his own writing (like *Espoir*) but by an adapter of a text authored by another—added new facets to an existing work:

> It's possible to imagine that we are moving toward a reign of the adaptation in which the notion of the unity of the work of art, if not the very notion of the author himself, will be destroyed. If the film that was made of Steinbeck's *Of Mice and Men* had been successful (it could have been so, and far more easily than the adaptation of the same author's *Grapes of Wrath*), the (literary?) critic of the year 2050 would find not a novel out of which a play and a film had been "made," but rather a single work reflected through three art forms, an artistic pyramid with three sides, all equal in the eyes of the critic. The "work" would then be only an ideal point at the top of this figure, which itself is an ideal construct. The chronological precedence [*antériorité chronologique*] of one part over another would not be an aesthetic criterion [*critère esthétique*] any more than the chronological precedence of one twin over the other is a genealogical one. Malraux made his film *Man's Hope* before he wrote the novel of the same title, but he was carrying the work inside himself all along.[181]

Film critics like Bazin would not have long to wait. For just one year later, Bresson began work on his adaptation of *Journal d'un curé de campagne*, whose multiplication of the work (for this critic and others) surpassed the "chronological precedence" criterion. *Journal d'un curé de campagne* was identifiably Bernanos's novel *and* Bresson's film, each offering different sides of the same text. Like the multiplication analogy, this one suggested that the film and the novel somehow shared an identity embodied as separate material objects. Postwar critics had devised a theory not of coauthorship but of para-authorship—parallel creative patsh leading away from the same "source."

Whether we accept Bazin's analogies of pyramids or miracles, what is important is that *Journal d'un curé de campagne* assumed a film culture disposed to the new textual experiences of innovative film adaptation. Writing in 1952, Bazin acknowledged his culture's interest in a cinema that borrowed its experimental storytelling from the novel: "I am certain that *The Power and the Glory* and *Citizen Kane* would never have been conceived without James Joyce and John Dos Passos."[182] This was not a sign of cinema's artistic exhaustion; rather, "at the tip of the avant-garde in cinema today we see a growing number of films bold enough to take their inspiration from a literary style we might describe as ultra-cinematic."[183] One such avant-garde film was *Journal d'un curé de campagne*, which brought "hope to cinema."[184] Bresson's "adaptation achieves dizzying fidelity by means of a ceaselessly creative respect for its source," but true "fidelity to Bernanos's tone . . . required a kind of inversion of the book's violence. The real equivalents of Bernanos' hyperbole are Bresson's ellipses and understated *découpage*."[185]

One year later, Jacques Doniol-Valcroze described Bresson's oeuvre as the pinnacle of an *avant-garde interne*. Bresson had announced himself as "the originator of a new cinema, of a dialectical *mise-en-scène* of stunning rigor."[186] *Journal d'un curé de campagne* had rejected "all the virtuoso effects of cinema" by adopting a "spiritual and psychological economy that is the opposite to habitual approaches to adaptation and shooting a film."[187] Bresson revealed the contradiction at the core of the medium: "Cinema will not progress unless it accepts its own paradoxical nature: only by remaining as 'theatrical' as possible could Cocteau make the best cinema with *Les parents terribles*. It was in denying the screen its own spectacular function [*fonction spectaculaire*] that Bresson succeeded—like Chaplin—the most extraordinary spectacle: moving pictures that capture the inner life."[188] Doniol-Valcroze declared a new era: "In France today, the avant-garde does not consist of a few quasi-Surrealist experiments . . . but of *Journal d'un curé de campagne*."[189]

A New Auteur, A New Language

If we examine it in light of the postwar cultural market, the story of *Journal d'un curé de campagne*'s adaptation becomes one of reciprocal attention. Bernanos provided the filmmaker with a novel as well as a set of broadly drawn principles for adapting it. Members of the literary and cinephilic press provided Bresson with intellectual and perceptual raw materials to work with—interests in fidelity as formal equivalency and in purity and austerity in the guise of first-person storytelling. Bresson reciprocated with a film that not only provided a stimulating test of his audience's literacy and its tools for appreciating an adapter's subtle editorial decisions, but a new challenge to the categories cinephiles had created. It took some discussion in the critical press to work out whether an adapter could also be an auteur, and in this way, Bresson seems to have caught cinephiles off guard with a work that manifests two highly personal styles.

In this, Bresson was both ahead of his times and very much tuned into them. In their own ways, Gérin and Béguin found Bresson's first drafts of the script too unconventional and too risky—too bereft of narrative intrigue and too literary in its dialogue. In a visionary way, Bresson borrowed both strategies from Bernanos. His film actively invited a cultivated audience to compare it to the novel line by line and to appreciate his experiment in the sonic first person. But if Bresson wanted to display an art of elliptical creativity with respect to Bernanos's dialogue (omitting lines and words that were either too expressive or too overt), it was because he wanted to make a "mold" all his own. He envisioned a film composed of fragments from the Bernanos original that, once reorganized, resulted in a series of subtle relations through which expression and emotion emerged indirectly. He found his own answer to the temptation of purity that characterized literary and cinematic endeavors in the period.

In a cultural market context, auteurs do not act on their own. In Bresson's case, the cinephilic press played an important role as well, firming up expectations through a relatively refined language: a temptation of purity; a storytelling based on the sonic first person; the related concerns for ellipses and rhythm; faithful adaptation as formal equivalency; dialectical fidelity or multiplication; and the series of problems and solutions related to these "literary" interests in cinema. From our perspective, this language functions as a remnant of a social relation—an exchange of "mental goods" around the notion of intermediality—without which Bresson's successful forays into adaptation and entrance into the canon of auteurs would have been unthinkable.

Two of these aspects of the midcentury sensibility—taste for a pared-down cinema and for cinematic rhythm—deserve further attention. The next two chapters show how Bresson developed a style that furnished cinephiles with perceptual and intellectual challenges along these two axes and a rhetoric that framed his cinema as an antidote to spectacular entertainment and an investigation of the medium's rhythmic nature. In midcentury France, auteurs were made on such things.

Notes

1. Roger Boussinot, *"Journal d'un curé de campagne*: Un film qui suscitera peu de vocations," *L'écran français*, February 14, 1951, 8.
2. Ibid.
3. Jacques Doniol-Valcroze, "De l'avant-garde," in *Sept ans de cinéma français*, ed. Henri Agel, Jean-Pierre Barrot, and Jacques Doniol-Valcroze (Paris: Éditions du cerf, 1953), 10.
4. Ibid., 10.
5. Ibid., 14.
6. *Hommage à Georges Bernanos et débat sur le film "Journal d'un curé de campagne"* (Paris: Centre catholique des intellectuels français, 1951), 22.
7. Irina O. Rajewsky, "Intermediality, Intertextuality, and Remediation: A Literary Perspective on Intermediality," *Intermédialités* 6 (Autumn 2005): 51.
8. Georges-Albert Astre, "Avant-propos," *La revue des lettres modernes* 5.36–38 (Cinéma et roman) (Summer 1958): 131.
9. Ibid., 132.
10. Colette Audry, "La caméra d'Alain Robbe-Grillet," *La revue des lettres modernes* 5.36–38 (Cinéma et roman) (Summer 1958): 267.
11. Ibid.
12. Claude-Édmonde Magny, *L'âge du roman américain* (Paris: Éditions du Seuil, 1948).
13. Audry, "La caméra d'Alain Robbe-Grillet," 138.
14. Ibid., 265.
15. Ibid.
16. Ibid.
17. Jean-Paul Sartre, "François Mauriac and Freedom," in *Literary and Philosophical Essays*, trans. Annette Michelson (New York: Collier, 1962), 7–25.
18. Ibid., 9.
19. Ibid., 13.
20. Ibid., 25.
21. Audry, "La caméra d'Alain Robbe-Grillet," 138.
22. Ibid.
23. Ibid.
24. Ibid.
25. Ibid.
26. Ibid., 139.
27. Ibid.
28. Gregg Toland, "L'opérateur de prise de vue," *La revue du cinéma* 4 (January 1, 1947): 16–24.
29. Jacques Doniol-Valcroze, "Naissance du véritable ciné-œil," *La revue du cinéma* 4 (January 1, 1947): 25.
30. Ibid., 26.
31. Ibid., original emphasis.
32. Ibid., 28.
33. Ibid.
34. Ibid., 26.
35. Ibid., 28.
36. Ibid., 29.
37. Ibid., 30.
38. Jean-Pierre Chartier, "Les 'films à la premiére personne' et l'illusion de réalité au cinéma," *La revue du cinéma* 4 (January 1, 1947): 32.

39. Ibid.

40. Ibid.

41. Ibid., 33.

42. Ibid.

43. Ibid., 35.

44. Ibid.

45. Ibid.

46. Ibid., 36.

47. Ibid., 37.

48. Ibid., 38, emphasis in source.

49. Ibid., 39; see Roger Leenhardt, "Le rythme cinématographique," in *Chronique du cinéma* (Paris: Édition Cahiers du cinéma, 1986), 42. For the Magny, see *L'âge du roman américain*, 60, where the author states, "The novel, like cinema, is essentially an art of the ellipsis." The idea had long been a fixture of French literary thought. In his preface to Andreé Viollis' novel, *S.O.S. Indochine*, André Malraux writes that the recent "desire for truth" among novelists has manifested itself in the substitution of "an art that rested on the metaphor" for "an art that rests on the ellipsis"; André Malraux, "Préface," in *S.O.S. Indochine*, by Andreé Viollis (Paris: Gallimard, 1935), vi.

50. Chartier, "Les 'films à la premiére personne,'" 39–40.

51. Claude Mauriac, "Robert Bresson," in *Petite littérature du cinéma* (Paris: Éditions du cerf, 1957), 71.

52. Maria Carla Cassarini, *Ignazio di Loyola di Robert Bresson: cronoca di un film mai nato*, sp. iss. of *Ciemme: Ricerca e informazione sulla comunicazione di massa* 152–153 (September 2006): 43.

53. D'Angelo was a pioneer in postwar Franco-Italian coproductions, producing Clair's *La beauté du diable* (1950).

54. When Bresson left the project, Universalis continued to produce it, even casting Gérard Philipe in the role of Ignatius in 1952, but the project was never completed.

55. Cassarini, *Ignazio di Loyola di Robert Bresson*, 116 and 123–126 (Appendix, Documents 10–13).

56. Ibid., 126 (Appendix, Document 11).

57. Ibid.

58. "Conversation avec Robert Bresson," *Opéra*, February 14, 1951, 7.

59. Mylène Bresson, conversation with the author, June 2009.

60. "Conversation avec Robert Bresson," 7.

61. Camus colorfully wrote to the poet René Char: "For a month I worked on *La princesse de Clèves* and then Bresson was such a pain in the ass—he's a maniacal madman—that I had to quit;" cited in Oliver Todd, *Camus: A Life*, trans. Benjamin Ivry (New York: Knopf, 1997), 320. For the original letter, see Albert Camus, and René Char, *Correspondence, 1946–1959* (Paris: Gallimard, 2007), 121, n. 3.

The popular filmmaker Jean Delannoy had also suddenly renewed his interest in adapting the novel after a script Jean Cocteau originally wrote in the 1940s. For an account of the history of the Delannoy-Cocteau version of *La princesse de Clèves*, see Angie Van Steerthem, "Jean Cocteau collaborateur de Jean Delannoy pour *La princesse de Clèves*," *La revue des lettres modernes* (Jean Cocteau 5: Les adaptations) (2008), 111–129.

62. David Bordwell, and Kristin Thompson, "Functions of Film Sound: *A Man Escaped*," in *Film Art: An Introduction*, 5th ed. (New York: McGraw-Hill, 1997), 341.

63. Ibid., 342.

64. André Bazin, "*Un condamné à mort s'est échappé*," *France observateur*, November 15, 1956, 22.

65. Ibid.

66. *Pickpocket* is loosely based on episodes from Dostoyevsky's *Crime and Punishment* (1866); for a comparison between the film and the text, see Georges Sadoul, "Délits et châtiment," *Les lettres françaises*, December 24, 1959, 7.

67. David Bordwell, *Narration in the Fiction Film* (Madison, WI: University of Wisconsin Press, 1985), 291.

68. Cited in Michel Estève, *Robert Bresson* (Paris: Éditions Seghers, 1962), 193–194.

69. Ibid., 44.

70. Ibid., 48, 50.

71. Ibid., 46–47.

72. Ibid., 47.

73. Denis Marion, "Les adaptations," in *Almanach du théâtre et du cinéma*, ed. Jean Cocteau (Paris: Éditions du Flore, 1949), 132.

74. André Bazin, "For an Impure Cinema: In Defense of Adaptation," in *What is Cinema?*, trans. Timothy Barnard (Montréal: Caboose, 2009), 107.

75. Henri Agel, "L'amour de la rhétorique ou l'enfers de l'adaptation," in *Sept ans de cinéma français*, ed. Henri Agel, Jean-Pierre Barrot, and Jacques Doniol-Valcroze (Paris: Éditions du cerf, 1953), 87.

76. Georges Charensol, *Renaissance du cinéma français* (Paris: Éditions du sagittaire, 1946), 39; Agel, "L'amour de la rhétorique ou l'enfers de l'adaptation," 87; André Bazin, "*Diary of a Country Priest* and the Robert Bresson Style," in *What is Cinema?*, trans. Timothy Barnard (Montréal: Caboose, 2009), 157; and François Truffaut, "L'adaptation littéraire au cinéma," *La revue des lettres modernes* 5.36–38 (Cinéma et roman) (Summer 1958): 243.

77. Boussinot, "*Journal d'un curé de campagne*: Un film qui suscitera peu de vocations."

78. Charensol, *Renaissance du cinéma français*, 39.

79. Ibid., 81–82.

80. Ibid., 82.

81. Ibid., 76.

82. Ibid.

83. Ibid., 78.

84. Ibid., 79.

85. Bazin, "*Diary of a Country Priest* and the Robert Bresson Style," 143.

86. Ibid., 144.

87. Ibid.

88. Cited in Estève, *Robert Bresson*, 15.

89. "En deux mots," *Radio-cinéma-télévision*, January 29, 1950, 6.

90. Argus, "Le secrèt de Polichinelle," *Radio-cinéma-télévision*, (March 19, 1950), 4.

91. Jean Douchet, "Pour moi le cinéma est mouvement intérieur," *Gazette du cinéma* 2 (June 1950): 1.

92. "Conversation avec Robert Bresson," 7.

93. Ibid.

94. Bazin, "*Diary of a Country Priest* and the Robert Bresson Style," 140.

95. Pierre Leprohon, "Dans un château d'Artois, d'après l'oeuvre de Bernanos, Robert Bresson tourne Le Journal . . . ," *Radio-cinéma-télévision*, (April 9, 1950), 8.

96. *Hommage à Georges Bernanos et débat sur le film "Journal d'un curé de campagne"* (Paris: Centre catholique des intellectuels français, 1951), 22.

97. Georges Bernanos, *Correspondences inédites, tome II (1934–1948)*, ed. Albert Béguin (Paris: Librarie Plon, 1971), 731, n. 1.

98. Dudley Andrew, "Desperation and Meditation: Bresson's *Diary of a Country Priest* (1951)," in *Modern European Filmmakers and the Art of Adaptation*, ed. Andrew Horton and Joan Magretta (New York: Frederick Ungar Publishing Co., 1981), 22. *Dialogue des Carmélites* was finally produced in 1960, directed by Philippe Agostini.

99. Georges Bernanos, "À Jean-Louis Barrault" (November 1945), in *Correspondences inédites, tome II (1934–1948)*, ed. Albert Béguin (Paris: Librarie Plon, 1971), letter 749.

100. Ibid.

101. Bernanos, *Correspondences inédites, tome II (1934–1948)*, 580, n.1.

102. Georges Bernanos, "À Guy Hattu" (December 1945), in *Correspondences inédites, tome II (1934–1948)*, ed. Albert Béguin (Paris: Librarie Plon, 1971), letter 752.

103. Bernanos, *Correspondences inédites, tome II (1934–1948)*, 695, n. 1.

104. Andrew, "Desperation and Meditation," 23.

105. Bernanos states that he had been contacted by the production firm responsible for *La symphonie pastorale*; see Georges Bernanos, "À Yves Bernanos" (November 18–19, 1945), in *Correspondences inédites, tome II (1934–1948)*, ed. Albert Béguin (Paris: Librarie Plon, 1971), letter 846.

106. Bernanos, *Correspondences inédites, tome II (1934–1948)*, 695, n.1.

107. Georges Bernanos, "À Luc Estang" (March 12, 1947), in *Correspondences inédites, tome II (1934–1948)*, ed. Albert Béguin (Paris: Librarie Plon, 1971), letter 853.

108. Georges Bernanos, "À Henri Jacques" (December 23, 1947), in *Correspondences inédites, tome II (1934–1948)*, ed. Albert Béguin (Paris: Librarie Plon, 1971), letter 874.

109. Andrew, "Desperation and Meditation," 22–23. The novel was published in 1936, although some critics believe that it was first redacted in 1934; see Joseph Jurt, *La réception de la littérature par la critique journalistique: Lectures de Bernanos, 1926–1936* (Paris: Éditions Jean-Michel Place, 1980), 230.

110. Albert Béguin, "L'adaptation du 'Journal d'un curé de campagne,'" *Glanes: Cahiers de l'amitié franco-néerlandaise* 18 (May–June 1951): 24.

111. Bernanos, *Correspondences inédites, tome II (1934–1948)*, 739, n.2. It should be noted that Bernanos sent a letter to Barrault indicating that if the film is ever produced he would be given the title role; see Georges Bernanos, "À Jean-Louis Barrault" (January 26, 1946), in *Correspondences inédites, tome II (1934–1948)*, ed. Albert Béguin (Paris: Librarie Plon, 1971), letter 768.

112. Andrew, "Desperation and Meditation," 22. Curiously, although Truffaut mentions Aurenche *and* his longtime collaborator Pierre Bost, Bernanos names only Aurenche in public and private letters on the subject. Whether Bost was actually involved on the project remains for me an open question.

113. "The Press: Where is the Tra-La-Lo?," *Time*, February 9, 1948, http://www.time.com/ime/magazine/article/0,9171,856016,00.html (December 2009).

114. Georges Bernanos, "Lettre à « Samedi-Soir »," in *Correspondences inédites, tome II (1934–1948)*, ed. Albert Béguin (Paris: Librarie Plon, 1971), 732.

115. Ibid.

116. Ibid., 733.

117. Ibid.

118. Georges Bernanos, *Diary of a Country Priest*, trans. Pamela Morris (London: Fontana Books, 1965), 126, where the fictional editor writes (in italics): "*N. B.—These last words, scribbled in the margins, have been scratched out.*" The original novel also contains no chapters. See also page 93, where the fictional editor notes (again, in italics): "*N. B.—The next few pages of the exercise-book in which this diary is written have been torn out. A few words still left in the margin have been carefully erased.*"

119. Ibid., 253.

120. Cf. Andrew, "Desperation and Meditation," 21.

121. Albert Béguin reports that the letter was reprinted in *Le bulletin* in 1951; see Bernanos, *Correspondences inédites, tome II (1934–1948)*, 731, n.1.

122. Bernanos, "Lettre à « Samedi-Soir »," 732.

123. Pierre Ajame, "Le cinéma selon Bresson," *Nouvelles littéraires*, May 26, 1966, 13.

124. Janick Arbois, Analysis of *Journal d'un curé de campagne*, *Téléciné* 25 (1951).

125. Béguin, "L'adaptation du 'Journal d'un curé de campagne,'" 26–27.

126. Ibid.

127. Ibid.

128. Ibid.

129. Ibid., 24.

130. Arbois, Analysis of *Journal d'un curé de campagne*.

131. Ibid. Arbois is referring to *The Fugitive* (Ford, 1947), an adaptation of Graham Greene's story, *The Power and the Glory* (1940).

132. Ibid.

133. "Débat sur 'Le Journal d'un curé de campagne," 30.

134. Jurt, *La réception de la littérature par la critique journalistique*, 230.

135. Ibid., 273.

136. Ibid.

137. Ibid., 280.

138. Ibid.

139. Ibid.

140. Claude Mauriac, "Le premier film de la vie intérieure: *Journal d'un curé de campagne*," *Le figaro littéraire*, February 10, 1951, 10.

141. Ibid.

142. Ibid.

143. Ibid.

144. Albert Béguin, "Bernanos au cinéma," *Esprit* (February 1951): 248.

145. Ibid.

146. Ibid., 249.

147. Ibid.

148. Ibid.

149. Ibid., 250.

150. Ibid.

151. Ibid.

152. Ibid.

153. Ibid., 251.

154. Ibid.

155. Jean Sémolué, *Bresson* (Paris: Éditions universitaires, 1959), 113.

156. Ibid.

157. Cited in Sémolué, *Bresson*, 113; Bernanos, *Diary of a Country Priest*, 135.

158. Sémolué, *Bresson*, 113–114. My translations are based on the Pamela Morris translations I have been citing throughout this chapter; see Bernanos, *Diary of a Country Priest*, 134–135 and 143.

159. Ibid., 115.

160. Ibid., 112.

161. Arbois, Janick, Analysis of *Journal d'un curé de campagne*.

162. Ibid.

163. Ibid. This version does not appear to have survived.

164. Ibid.

165. Ibid.

166. András Bálint Kovács, *Screening Modernism: European Art Cinema, 1950–1980* (Chicago: University of Chicago Press, 2007), 37, 61.

167. Bernanos, *Diary of a Country Priest*, 42–43.

168. Ibid., 11.

169. Ibid.

170. Ibid., 9.

171. Ibid.

172. Ibid., 9–10.

173. Agel, "L'amour de la rhétorique ou l'enfers de l'adaptation," 87.

174. Ibid., 88.

175. Ibid.

176. Truffaut, "L'adaptation littéraire au cinéma," 243.

177. Ibid.

178. Bazin, "*Diary of a Country Priest* and the Robert Bresson Style," 139.

179. Ibid., 157.

180. Ibid.

181. André Bazin, "Adaptation, or the Cinema as Digest," in *Bazin at Work: Major Essays and Reviews from the Forties & Fifties*, ed. Bert Cardullo (New York: Routledge, 1997), 49–50.

182. Bazin, "For an Impure Cinema," 120.

183. Ibid.

184. Ibid., 123.

185. Ibid., 125.

186. Doniol-Valcroze, "De l'avant-garde," 14.

187. Ibid., 15.

188. Ibid., 16.

189. Ibid., 8.

4 Theorizing the Image:

Bresson's Challenge to the Realists—Sparse Set Design, Acting, and Photography from Les anges du péché *(1943) to* Une femme douce *(1969)*

> Georges Sadoul: In terms of aesthetics, do you believe that one must obey rules, elaborate theories?
>
> Robert Bresson: Some view me as a theoretician. It is perfectly true that, given the complexity of film, I view it as profitable to reflect on one I've just completed in order to try to understand why I was successful with one thing and failed with another.
>
> If these reflections give birth to theories, it is because they help me feel free—I feel free precisely because these theories exist.
>
> —Interview, March 1963[1]

ROBERT BRESSON MIGHT have made an avant-garde career of his achievements in adaptation alone. A decade after he revolutionized the art with his faithful rendering of Georges Bernanos's *Journal d'un curé de campagne* (1951), he turned the original minutes of Joan of Arc's trial into an uncompromising, historically truthful drama, *Le procès de Jeanne d'Arc* (1962). He returned to Bernanos's vision of contemporary rural life with the critically acclaimed *Mouchette* (1967), this time taking more liberties with the novel's structure and tone. Abandoning the idea of fidelity entirely, he then experimented with adaptation as a form of modernization, transforming stories from Dostoyevsky (*Une femme douce*, 1969; *Quatre nuits d'un rêveur*, 1971), the tales of King Arthur and the Knights of the Round Table (*Lancelot du lac*, 1974) and Tolstoy (*L'argent*, 1983) by playing down the historical specificities of the original sources and granting them a more contemporary feel, in terms of dialogue, themes, locations, costuming, and overall structure. Throughout his career, Bresson experimented with adaptation—literary and historical, faithful and modern—from virtually every angle available to him.

Bresson was determined to reshape the art form, and our understanding of it, in more ambitious ways as well. Between films, he took to theorizing about his craft in a manner that not only set the terms for his creative freedom from cinematic convention but questioned some basic assumptions of contemporary thought about cinema as well. One such theory was his idea that the film image must be denuded, deaestheticized, and rendered almost uncommunicative—an idea that both affirmed and challenged the tenets of cinematic realism, a paradigmatic concept of postwar film culture. Take, as an initial example, Bresson's 1963 interview with one of the period's foremost advocates of realist cinema, Georges Sadoul, who invited the auteur to situate his style within this trend:

> G. S.: I am persuaded that the art of cinema and all the arts, to live and renew themselves, borrow their substance from reality. . . . Do you believe that your films, perceived by some as existing outside of time and of life, draw their substance from reality?
> R. B.: What I do resembles what a gardener or horticulturalist does: transplanting, growing from cuttings. I take cuttings of reality, and I plant them in a film.[2]

Now twenty years into his feature filmmaking career, Bresson believed that the photographic process of reproducing "cuttings" of reality alone did not guarantee realism. For a film to truly sprout life, the excesses of the film image had to be tamed. He shifted metaphors to explain: "If you want the electricity to pass, you must strip the wires."[3] As he stated more prosaically some years later, "What I disapprove of is photographing with that extraordinary instrument—the camera—things that are not real. Sets and actors are not real."[4] Bresson didn't distance himself from realism. Instead, challenging certain assumptions about realism, he philosophized about his visual artistic practice in a manner that rendered the sparse craft and the eschewal of the theatrical conventions of elaborate scenery and professional performances essential to the rediscovery of cinema's fundamental connection to reality. As he had with adaptation, he placed himself at the vanguard by reinventing cinematic realism as a concept that served his interests as a filmmaker.

How Bresson invented a realism of his own is the subject of this chapter. This will require us to look beyond his verbal statements on the matter, which were few and far between and, as this small sample demonstrates, tended to be brief and suggestive rather than exploratory. Assessing Bresson's place in the period's realist thought means coming to terms with the fact that much of his theorizing—his thinking through of the possibilities and limitations, the basic technical properties and perceptual effects, of an image that approximated certain aspects of empirical perception—occurred directly in visual form.

Bresson's response to the possibility of cinema's intimate connection with reality demonstrates his properly visual intelligence, to adapt an expression from art historians Svetlana Alpers and Michael Baxandall.[5] Many of his major contributions to the midcentury realism consisted of visual experiments—interventions in the realm not of verbalized argument but of perceptual concepts. We saw in chapter 1 that as a nimble image-maker in the 1920s and 1930s, Bresson used a variety of visual media to test the compositional possibilities and narrative implications of light and shade, color and tone, depth and line. As a feature filmmaker, he undertook his inquiry into realism through similar media, seeking out in visual form that zone of creative image-making that escaped cinematic and other types of artifice (symbolic expressiveness, visual excess, theatrical convention, the star persona, etc.).

What was the ultimate aim of his visual inquiry—of his *essai visuel*, as he might have called it?[6] If we consider his public statements and look closely at the evolution of his realist style throughout the 1940s, 1950s, and 1960s, we learn that Bresson sought nothing less than the end or the supersession of the "cinematic" image—to develop a visual style that used set design, acting, and photography[7] to liberate the eye of the restless quest for titillation promoted in modern image culture. Through artistic experimentation, he came to understand the anticinematic image as one not only free of codes of aesthetic beauty but that aspired to capture preverbal sensations and, thus, quiet the hermeneutic impulse to read the image as an affective, political, or philosophic statement in the literal sense. "Our senses tell us more than our intelligence," he told Charles Thomas Samuels in an interview in 1970.[8]

These ideas, honed through a combination of artistic invention and verbal theorization, were both unique and culturally inscribed. Like the cinephile-theorists of his time, Bresson's motivation for developing a realist image remained consistently oppositional. André Bazin and Georges Sadoul, to cite only two of the period's most prominent thinkers, stood with Bresson in decrying those films that failed to make the most of the photographic properties and reliance on real-life bodies that guaranteed the medium's direct access to the world of phenomenal or social experience. However, unlike these critics, Bresson set out to critique the visual with the visual.[9] Working with sets, camera lenses, human figures, and lighting units, his opposition took the form of the untapped perceptual potential of stark monochromy, simplified geometry, muted color, uncommunicative light, denuded space, and minimally expressive movement and gesture from his actors (who were eventually replaced with "models")—all strategies that negated the artifice of cinematic convention by negating its visual appeals.

His realist theorizations were culturally inscribed in a different sense as well. Not only was his concept of the realist image part of a cultural movement to rethink cinema's relationship with reality (one spearheaded by both auteurs and cinephiles), but to light a scene or design a set in a manner that transformed the arts of lighting and design according to entirely new anticinematic principles, the auteur depended upon various midcentury production cultures, on the craft practices, traditions, and skills of his creative personnel. Working closely with him to solve a variety of innovative "realist" problems, Bresson's cinematographers and production designers contributed directly to the theories he came to view as crucial to the productive elasticity of his visual thinking—to the freedom from convention that only theory (and theory-driven practice) could ensure.

Two Perspectives: The Realisms of Georges Sadoul and André Bazin

As Laurent Bertrand Dorléac writes in his authoritative study of *les années noires*, "from the start of the Occupation, the German presence on the art scene fostered a system of widespread self-censorship."[10] After the Liberation of 1944, French artists suddenly experienced fewer (self-imposed) constraints and various "new realisms" were unleashed, each seeking, on their own terms, to respond to postwar everyday life and reject the established conventions of art. Alain Robbe-Grillet's *nouveau roman* of the 1950s focused on objective descriptions, the "thingness of things," and elusive meaning in ways that opened up the art of the novel to everyday experience.[11] The sparse, object-oriented décors and Cocteauesque "plus vrai que le vrai" in Roger Blin's stage adaptations of Samuel Beckett in the 1950s and 1960s challenged the artifices of theatrical production. Jean Tinguely also simplified his forms, famously repurposing *objets quotidiens* in sculptures like *Baluba* (1961–1962).[12] Perhaps most ambitious of all was the painting of André Fougeron, who in such works as *Les parisiennes au marché* (1948) used thick palette-knife strokes and social-realist themes to promote the radicalization of the fine arts.

In film culture, realist styles and theories of style also took their position at the vanguard. Filmmakers, theorists, and critics alike relied on notions of realism to stimulate a new understanding of the medium's special connection with the world "out there" and critique French cinema's march toward an aestheticized, academic style during the Occupation.[13] Auteurs as distinctive as Jacques Becker, Louis Daquin, Roger Leenhardt, Max Ophüls, Jean Renoir, Alain Resnais, and Robert Bresson—many of whom began their realist projects before the Liberation—pursued their pared-down styles and everyday, at times even socialist, characters and themes with renewed vigor, impelling cinephiles to stretch "realism" into new conceptual domains.

What did it mean for a style or for a medium to be realist in this context? From a certain perspective, this question is almost unanswerable. "Realisms" of all kinds proliferated in the language of cinephiles and in the visual and storytelling forms of auteurs. What's more, alongside these realisms, various naturalisms and verisms took hold as well. Nevertheless, we can take a measure of the complexity of this category of filmmaking—of its rich polysemy—and, in the process, begin to contextualize the significance of Bresson's realism by briefly exploring the writings of two of the most influential thinkers of 1940s and 1950s,

Georges Sadoul and André Bazin, who documented (and stimulated) this explosion of realisms. The cultural market, as we will see, encouraged extending the concept into fresh areas of thought.

From his regular column in *Les lettres françaises*, a weekly journal backed by the French Communist Party (PCF), Sadoul distinguished between three postwar realist and pseudorealist modes—realism proper, descriptive naturalism, and verism—according to their representations of social relations, especially those of working-class life. Like his close friend, the filmmaker Louis Daquin and the critics of the cinephilic monthly *Positif* who followed in his footsteps in the 1950s,[14] Sadoul, committed to reviving the engaged cinema of the Popular Front,[15] believed that realism should explore social reality in an effort to expose the exploitation of workers and peasants. Realist cinema ought to reveal how the exploited can become conscious of their condition and dramatize the terms of worker emancipation. He evidently held realist cinema to high standards, and although he often decried the "commercialization" of realism and was disappointed with realist filmmakers, his language carefully mapped their progressive styles and themes.[16] Genuinely realist or not, major auteurs practiced at least three potentially progressive modes:

Realism Proper

This mode utilized a sparse approach to visual style and storytelling as a means to depict original social content and sharp critique. In "Une nouvelle avant-garde," a review of Daquin's *Le point du jour* (1949), Sadoul remarked on the film's realist affinities with Vittorio De Sica's *Ladri di biciclette* (1948).[17] If both made use of a "pared down dramaturgy," Daquin's film deserved a special place in postwar realism for offering a truly authentic and insightful representation of a working-class milieu until now bungled by Anglo-American filmmakers. Neither *How Green Was My Valley* (1939) nor *The Stars Look Down* (1940) depicted the lives of miners in such a straightforward way; the latter's exteriors, for instance, "had something authentic about them, but not the script, and the mines felt too much like a studio."[18]

"In *Le point du jour*," by contrast, "the men and their lives are what's essential. Shot almost exclusively outside the studio, this film is not a documentary. The protagonists, performed by excellent actors, live lives that are novelesque, and the tableau of their long days is more than the dull cinematography that simply captures life in a manner opposed to true realism: here, the real world is elaborated, transposed."[19] This required an evolution of form and content. *Le point du jour* showed that "true changes in the social milieu demand a transformation of subject matter, of how actors perform, of style, of the dramatic conception, of the *découpage*, of the cinematography. With this, Daquin's experiment joins Italian productions and places itself at the avant-garde of contemporary cinema—because the avant-garde is not the manufacturing of ingenious embroideries on well-known themes, comfortably wearing out borrowed formulas, but a job where one risks getting one's 'face smashed in'"—a reference to the daring, rough-and-tumble conditions of the production.[20] Sadoul's realist avant-garde wasn't for the faint of heart. It was an aggressive socialist cinema whose rejection of aesthetic norms was motivated by an equally forceful interrogation of political realities.

Verism

Verist cinema took realist technical choices as ends in themselves, detached from both socially progressive subject matter and political critique. He reserved this category mainly for American and Italian styles that merely mimicked realism's look. In a September 1948 article titled "Le néo-réalisme américain?" he stressed the terminological error: "Among the most well intentioned critics the word *realism* is employed in every sense imaginable. Recently, it has been applied indiscriminately to the entire Italian school—for which the word *verism* would have been more appropriate."[21] If Sadoul had his druthers, the movement would have been labeled 'Italian neo-verism,' for the authentic realism of some Italian filmmakers had to be distinguished from their many copycats: "Today, some want to use it to designate a new trend in American cinema that for the most part uses exteriors, employs a pared down style of cinematography, demands restraint from actors and decorators, and that tells 'true stories.'"[22] But he urged, "Do not confound the *objectivity* of the style employed with true realism."[23] His review of *The Street With No Name* (1948), about an FBI agent who infiltrates a gang in the fictional Center City, tallied the elements designed "to impose on the viewer the impression that the film was really shot 'on the fly'" but ultimately chided the script for failing to make the characters seem more than "schemas brought to life."[24] He concluded: "The authenticity of the characters in De Sica, Rossellini or Visconti naturally does not come from their 'open-air' quality, but from their straightforward humanity, from their social character. One does not make artificial characters and an inane plot true by inserting them into an authentic décor. *The Street With No Name* makes that abundantly clear."[25]

Descriptive Naturalism

Sadoul situated descriptive naturalist cinema somewhere between realism and verism. A filmmaker belonging to this stylistic class used pared-down techniques like nonprofessional actors, location shooting, and deep-focus cinematography as well as social content, but offered no discernible critique of the status quo. Sadoul coined the term in a review of the French film *Tabusse* (1949), which focused on a village "anarchist"—a Don Quixote who refused to uphold his social obligations and believed that a farmer's daughter had upset the social order and fallen in love with him. In the final analysis, the film was "incomplete" and "flawed" because it merely described the social relations within the village and offered no "constructive" critique of society through this fictionalized depiction.[26]

Sadoul, one of cinema's most influential critics, encouraged cinephiles to interpret the latest productions from three of the top film-producing countries across the globe—France, the United States, and Italy—through realist criteria. What of Bresson's style? Some reviewers adopted this Sadoulian distinction and approached Bresson's pared-down films as straightforward displays of the possibilities of naturalism.[27] Sadoul, for his part, felt disarmed by the paradoxes of the *style bressonien*. "I found *Pickpocket* [1959] disconcerting," he confessed in his review. "And for ten days the film has haunted me."[28] On the one hand, "one might compare [Bresson] (he has never denounced the metaphor) to a great pianist, who is willing to repeat Mozart or Chopin a thousand times in order to then give the public an interpretation bereft of virtuosity or fanfares, flowing like the crystalline waters of a spring, with the *natural* fruits of ten thousand repetitions, retakes and deletions."[29] And yet on the other, the film was also set in an oddly "abstract" Paris; Bresson "refused to show it as a documentary."[30] The tensions between naturalism and abstraction in *Pickpocket* resulted in a form—at once moving and Brechtian in its detached representation of the modern cityscape—that left the critic in a reflective state: "'Distanciation,' in this curious Bresson, is never indifference, coldness or (this particularly) contempt. Sincerity reigns. Human warmth passes through the walls of seeming indifference."[31] Bresson's films accessed a profound sentiment through an intelligent visual style that, in itself, avoided sentimentality.

*　*　*

The flaw in Sadoul's interpretation of the Bresson style as a paradoxical, Brechtian-humanist naturalism is that it shortchanged the genuinely realist work a filmmaker could pursue at the level of the image alone. Another corner of the cultural market was influenced not by Sadoul's social-content-driven approach to realism but by Bresson's Objectif 49 colleague André Bazin, who was far more attuned to realism as an aesthetic inscribed in the filmstrip itself. In "L'ontologie de l'image photographique," originally published in 1945 and reprinted (with substantial revision) in the 1958 collection *Qu'est-ce que le cinéma?* Bazin argued that cinema's realism was innate and stemmed from the basic fact that film stock created an imprint of the objects in reality it records. These objects reflected light waves, and when captured on the filmstrip's photosensitive material, the waves effectively created a mold of the objects themselves (in the form of a visual image). As Daniel Morgan writes in his fine essay on Bazinian realism, Bazin believed "that an object in a photograph is ontologically identical to the object in the world (however murky this idea may be)."[32] The implications for the history of film style are clear: "A film, if it is to be realist, must construct a style that counts as an acknowledgement of the reality conveyed through its photographic base."[33] A realist filmmaker used the unique visual materials of the medium to refer to, play up, or explore reality's physical attributes (be they the dimensions of space or time, or aspects of texture and movement), turning the principle at the core of photographic reproduction into a robust aesthetic.

The photographic realism prescribed in Bazin's ontological theory did not prevent him from recognizing the "spectrum of realisms" that accessed the full potential of the film image.[34] Tailored to the rich experimentation of postwar auteur cinema, his language remained strategically flexible and polysemic; it was receptive to the wide range of solutions within this stylistic trend. Years after "L'ontologie," Bazin wrote in an essay on Jean Renoir that "the word 'realism' as it is commonly used does not have an absolute and clear meaning, so much as it indicates toward the faithful rendering of reality on film. Given the fact that this movement toward the real can take a thousand different routes, the apologia for 'realism' *per se*, strictly speaking, means nothing at all. The movement is valuable only insofar as it brings increased meaning (itself an abstraction) to what is created."[35] Different auteurs did so along different stylistic axes. Bazin's writings theorized at least four distinct realist styles, two derived from film's ontological-photographic relationship with physical reality and two that emphasized a different sort of imprint on the film strip, that of sound waves.

High Visual Artifice

In "Le réalisme cinématographique et l'école italienne de la libération," Bazin argued that Orson Welles's films achieved realism by way of an "overabundance of artifice" primarily on the visual track, from the "exceptional control" of depth of field, lighting, film stock, and the bodies of theater actors (as well as depth of sound).[36] This control allowed Welles to move beyond conventional *découpage* that used analytical editing to select what the viewer will attend to in a scene and in the process impose upon it specific meanings. But Welles's realism came at a cost: the loss of "the inimitable qualities of an authentic document."[37]

Raw Visual Document

The "Réalisme cinématographique et l'école italienne de la libération" essay also acknowledged a visual realism of a different sort. Georges Rouquier's *Farrebique* (1945) presented itself as an "authentic document" at the surface level.[38] Like Welles, Rouquier offered an "objective" perspective on scenes, unfettered by moral judgments or meanings artificially imposed by technique. But, different from Welles, he relied on natural settings and lighting, outdoor scenes and non-professional actors. These, too, came with a trade-off: the raw document never achieved "technical perfection."[39]

Sonic Fidelity

Bazin's essay "Le cas Pagnol" defended the idea of sonic realism. He conceded that, from a visual standpoint, Marcel Pagnol often created "theatricalized cinema . . . an example of what should not be done in the adaptation of theater to the screen."[40] The visual properties of his films weren't realist at all; but their faithfulness of sound asserted cinema's capacity to preserve the real textures of voice, in this case, of the Provençal accent: "This accent is not just a picturesque addition to Pagnol's films; it's not there merely to inject a note of local color into the proceedings. It unites with the script, and thus with the characters, to create the essential nature of a Pagnol film. . . . The accent is the true substance of their language and is consequently the heart of its realism. Pagnol's cinema is quite the contrary of theatrical, then: it immerses itself, through the intermediary of language, in the realistic specificity of film. . . . In short, he is one of the greatest authors of *talking* cinema."[41]

A Dialectic of Sonic Artifice (a Spoken Text) and Visual Restraint

We see this realism in Bresson's *Journal d'un curé de campagne*, which created a dialectic of two realisms, one abstract and the other culled from reality. Bazin wrote in "Le *Journal d'un curé de campagne* et le stylistique de Robert Bresson" that the film's soundtrack was dominated by a "post-synchronized monotone recitation" of the Georges Bernanos text that Bresson adapted, but—and here Bazin pushed realism to a whole new meaning—"this text . . . is itself a second reality, a raw aesthetic fact."[42] This abstract realist element collided with the photographic reality of the film's restrained images: the soundtrack's "realism is its [monotone] style, when the style of the image is above all its reality and the style of the film, precisely, the clash of the two."[43] The film's contribution to the history of style rested in the difficulty of having "two realisms on the go."[44]

Considered together, these auteurs—Welles, Rouquier, Pagnol, Bresson—made maximal use of the recording properties of the filmstrip to create a spectrum of visual and sonic realisms. An additional thread ran through many of these auteurist styles: the power of cinema to achieve objective or neutral images and sounds that minimized conceptual meddling with the viewer's understanding of the film. In a 1949 review of Roberto Rossellini's *Germanio anno zero* (1948), Bazin explained: "Rossellini . . . knows how to get us interested in an action while leaving it in an objective context. Our emotion is thus rid of all sentimentality, for it has been filtered by force through our intelligence. . . . Isn't this, then, a sound definition of realism in art: to force the mind to draw its own conclusions about people and events, instead of manipulating it into accepting someone else's conclusions?"[45] For Bazin, realist styles used the image not to control or arrest a film's meaning—to make of a film a complete statement by the auteur—but to leave some meaning-making up to the viewer.

* * *

To develop an image devoid of artifice and predigested meaning—this notion of what pared-down filmmaking entailed, much more so than Sadoul's concept of descriptive naturalism, came closest to capturing the true spirit of Bressonian realism. It should be said, however, that Bresson was not unsympathetic to the oppositional impulse of Sadoul's language. Bresson's realist image-craft was an engaged one, albeit on the auteur's own unique terms.

Louis Malle, who was hired as an assistant on Bresson's *Un condamné à mort s'est échappé* (1956) for his experience in documentary film, perhaps understood this dimension of Bressonian realism best. As he explained in a December 1959 essay, Bresson's style relied on images and sounds so sparse, stripped even of the conventions of realism itself, that it was in effect a form of violent intervention: "He starts by strangling realism by the throat, that touchstone of cinema which, quite often, is still only an instrument of reproduction."[46] Cinema's instrumentalization in the service of the mechanical reproduction of reality had to be met with force. Bresson is "revolutionary" because his version of realism ripped these bits of reality from the cinematic conventions that corrupted them in mainstream film practice: "That which [Bresson] omits or rejects is, obviously, the picturesque, the gratuitous detail, even, and especially, if it 'looks real.' Just as a soundscape is reduced to all its essential components, so will a voice, a gesture, be stripped away of all flourishes, all suspicious embellishments."[47]

Distinctive among the period's many realisms, verisms, and naturalisms, Bresson's style opposed conventional thought about realism through an anticinematic image that made even other realist modes seem suspiciously artificial or removed from direct phenomenal experience by comparison—either too controlled by political messages that determined the viewer's response (Daquin's socialist realism) or composed through an overabundance of florid technique that drew the viewer's attention to visual style (Welles's realism of high artifice).

Bresson's Anticinematic Image, An Evolution

If much critical attention has been given to Bresson's realist sound design, the nature of his visual intervention in midcentury thought about realism remains understudied. As was just documented, some Bresson contemporaries like Louis Malle, rare though they were, understood Bressonian realism, inscribed in the image itself, as oppositional. The implications of this for how we understand the Bresson style, however, have yet to be fully understood. First, we now have reason to reject the already suspect notion that the Bressonian anti-image was simply an extension of Bresson himself, as if the Comte de Buffon's adage that "the style is the man himself" and its corollary—that the critic need only get to know the artist's personality to appreciate the origins and contours of the style—were the only recourse for those seeking explanations for the auteur's sparse visuals. This position can safely be put to rest because in accepting Bresson's visual style as oppositional we accept that it was formed as a response to dominant film aesthetics. To be visually oppositional entails registering an acute sense of shifting cultural norms in one's image practice; as norms shift, so too does one's oppositional style.

This brings us to a second implication, namely that Bresson's anticinematic realism *evolved*. To study Bressonian realism is to acknowledge that he did not, despite his reputation, arrive on the scene with a fully formed aesthetic system, but worked over the course of decades to refine a form of cultural intervention with distinct verbal and visual components and create his own spectrum of realisms—a diversity of creative ideas that promised to liberate his art from cinematic convention and challenge his culture's assumptions about realism itself. Perhaps more so than any other French auteur, his flexible concept of realism extended the idea into fresh areas of creative thought.

From his interviews and writings—let's begin with these—we learn that Bresson evolved five creative concepts that allowed him to negate the influence of cinematic artifice on visual style:

No Bursts of Stylization on the Visual Track

Initially, Bresson's theorization of the end of the cinematic image was quite broad and took the form of a periodic defense of a cinema *sans éclat* (without moments of ostentation). In a 1946 interview, published after completing *Les anges du péché* (1943) and *Les dames du bois de Boulogne* (1945), he aligned his cinema with an aesthetics of simplicity that stood against the status quo: "In cinema, there is a prejudice against simplicity. Every time someone breaks with that prejudice, the effect is deeply moving."[48] He believed that techniques that dazzled the viewer's eye ignored those more effective, ultimately minimal, means by which a film created its subtle, affective play of relations, which was for Bresson the true art of cinema: "A film is above all else *relations, because the subtlety* [of cinema]—*it's in the relations that one must find it.* Relations between actors, between actors and the objects and décor that surrounds them, between the action and the rhythm of images, etc."[49] In 1951, after the release of *Journal d'un curé de campagne*, he modified his defense of simplicity somewhat. If individual images were going to create relational effects, they must develop "an exchange value."[50] This could not be achieved, so he thought, so long as individual images stood apart from the rest. Images must instead have "something in common"—they must be flattened out and rendered uniform so that they "participate *together* in a kind of *union.*"[51] Bursts of style that denied this play of relations, while typical of conventional cinema, ultimately denied the art form its subtle force.

No Distracting Color Designs

Also in 1946, he expressed concern over cinema's recent turn to color to seduce audiences. Highly skeptical, Bresson argued that the seductions of cinematic color were innately antithetical to cinema's potential as a dramatic form: "The problem of color isn't a problem of color. It is something else entirely. It matters little whether a film's color is good or bad. One can always find a good way of using a bad tool, *on the condition that one realizes that it is a bad tool.* This is what distinguishes a good craftsman from the bad ones: the good craftsman *knows how to choose* his tools, and *often chooses the bad ones.* But this isn't the problem. The problem lies in color's power to charm; its *dispersive, distracting* power prevents its use in drama and tragedy at the moment."[52] Bresson spent the next two decades devising a less distracting, noncinematic polychromatic alternative (a point to which we will return when we consider his visual practice in greater detail).

No Photographed Theater

By the mid-1950s, Bresson presented his image-craft as a principled alternative to the photographed theater of popular cinema. In 1957, after completing his second postwar work, the prison-break film *Un condamné à mort s'est échappé,* he took to the press to criticize the current state of the commercial industry, which presented too many barriers to artistic liberty: "The obstacles we encounter are insurmountable. We are less and less free (capital, routine, stars). The current formula (of screenwriters, adapters, dialogue writers and directors at odds with one another) blocks all the routes."[53] The problem, according to Bresson, was that cinema had become a commodity, a mere tool for creating and recording the performance of the star for posterity—"a means of *reproduction* (photographed theater) rather than a means of *expression.*"[54] The commercial cinema of filmed theater prevented the auteur from transforming cinema into a unique form of personal communication.

He was just as critical of the use of realism in a theatrical manner—of what Bazin called the realism of high artifice. A realist style like that of Orson Welles's *Citizen Kane* relied on ornate décors and costumes that drew attention to the image *as* an image, that afforded the pleasures of theater-derived craft. Bresson wished to replace this ersatz realism with a more transparent form: "My hope is that my sets and costumes will go unnoticed. . . . For me, realism is not an end, but a means."[55]

No Actors, No Stars

Both Robert Bresson and Henri-Georges Clouzot were, as Colin Crisp has written, among several postwar auteurs who reconceived the actor as a visual element.[56] For Bresson the question of how the director should employ the actor—his or her body, star image, and creative volition—was ultimately one with pressing realist implications. By the late 1940s, he resolved that stardom and established codes of performance should be cast out of filmmaking, for, as he had discovered in his first two features, they were in fact potent impediments to sparse realism. And yet, from a creative standpoint, the concept of the *modèle* became such a potent aspect of his long-term artistic brief—the source of artistic challenges that freed him to envision a distinctly realist medium and allowed him to extract from his process the kinds of artifice and mimicry encouraged in the crafts of theater and film production—that he was willing to endure the commercial and professional risks.

From a certain perspective, Bresson's rejection of stars and trained actors had a negative effect on his career. This stance led to pressure from actors' unions and rebuffs from producers.[57] And yet, from a creative standpoint, the concept of the *modèle* became such a potent aspect of his long-term artistic brief—the source of artistic challenges that freed him to envision a distinctly realist medium, that allowed him to extract from his artistic process the kinds of visual artifice and mimicry encouraged in the crafts of theater and film production—that he was willing to endure the commercial and professional risks.

One of Bresson's most distinctive contributions to the history of film style, the concept of the *modèle* had two sides to it, I would argue. As he explained in his 138-page compilation of filmmaking aphorisms, *Notes sur le cinématographe* (1975) (some of which were written between 1950 and 1958), the aim was to call upon bodies to simply "be":

> No actors.
> (No directing of actors.) No parts.
> (No learning of parts.) No staging.
> But the use of working models, taken from life.
> BEING (models) instead of SEEMING (actors).[58]

With no notion of their own images as performers or of the craft of acting, the *modèle* freed the auteur to access elements of real life:

> Your models, pitched into the action of your film, will get used to gestures they have repeated twenty times. The words they have learned with their lips will find, without their minds taking part in this, the inflections and the lilt proper to their true natures. A way of recovering the automatism of real life. (The talent of one or several actors or stars no longer comes into it. What matters is how you approach your models and the unknown and virgin nature you manage to draw from them.)[59]

As he explained to the students of the IDHEC (the national film production school) in 1955, the way of the actor was the way of photographed theater: "The cinema we see until now isn't cinema, but, and without exception, photographed theater, where the means of expression are theatrical—that is, the means of actors, with impersonations, gestures. Cinema, if it wants to be cinema, has to absolutely abolish all theatrical expression, including the expression of actors. From the moment the expression is theatrical."[60]

On one level, then, the theory of the *modèle* proposed that the realist auteur use nonprofessionals and reject cinematic and theatrical acting conventions. In particular, the auteur must replace overt, modulating expression with simple, indirectly or minimally expressive movements by employing repetition (in the form of multiple takes, where the *modèle* performs the same basic movements over and over) to draw out these pared-down behaviors nonconsciously.

But this was no independent theory of acting. The concept of the *modèle* was the product of Bresson's visual thinking. It proposed that the human figure onscreen be viewed as a pictorial element first and foremost, one capable of impressing upon the viewer direct sensorial experiences that remained, to a degree, semantically "open." By reinterpreting the role of the actor in this fashion—as a source not of expression that determined the significance of the image onscreen but of automatic, naturalistic movement and vocal tones and rhythms whose meanings were relatively indeterminate—he could continue his search for a realist alternative to a medium that merely recorded the actor's performance.

No Images That Beckon the Viewer with Symbolic or Semantic Plentitude

Bresson's commitment to a concept of realism that urged the filmmaker toward simplicity and away from both the excesses and staged performances of conventional cinema evolved into a more theoretically ambitious one that sought to strip visual images even of semantic meaning. A realist image, as he writes in *Notes sur le cinématographe*, must "touch" the viewer directly—which is to say, precognitively:

> The real, when it has reached the mind, is already not real any more. Our too thoughtful, too intelligent eye.[61]

The realist filmmaker must thus erase awareness of the image:

> In this language of images, one must lose completely the notion of the image. The images must exclude the idea of images.[62]

The artistic brief before the truly realist, anticinematic filmmaker, then, entailed the search for a truer expression of the real, avoiding all forms of aestheticization and creating, to the extent that it is possible, presemantic, nonverbal visual units. These aims were once again expressed in the *Notes sur le cinématographe*:

> Retouch some real with some real.[63]

> Not beautiful photography, not beautiful images, but necessary images and photography.[64]

> Apply myself to insignificant (nonsignificant) images.[65]

Reflexive and critical, Bresson's realism was conscious of convention and consisted mostly of a series of negations. But, through these negations, there emerged a positive picture of an alternative cinema that was a subtle relational art and a unique form of expression, a cinema composed of unconventionally parsimonious perceptual moments that truly impressed themselves on the senses, rather than on the viewer's intelligence. By stripping away consciousness of and artifice within the image, he was imagining a new visual form that offered the purest of sensorial experiences onscreen.

Visual Experiments I: Bresson's Décor—Simplified Architecture, Monochromatic Palettes, Denuded Spaces

We develop only a partial appreciation of Bresson's intervention in midcentury thought if we focus on interviews and writings alone. In order to fully understand Bressonian realism, we must move beyond his verbal approximations—his five negative concepts—and reconstruct his precise visual experiments.

Several of Bresson's general principles—no bursts of stylization (instead, pursue visual simplicity and uniformity), no distracting or superfluous color designs, no photographed theater (no sets), and no images with striking aesthetic and hermeneutic qualities—were honed over the course of several decades of experimentation at the level of décor or set design. Like his verbal theorizing, Bresson's craft practice promoted the virtues of creation by negation. He adopted an artistic process of *dépouillement* (paring away), eliminating from his style those techniques that encouraged the viewer to interpret the image as a text (a direct stimulation of verbal associative thought) or a tableau (a direct display of beauty that rewarded aesthetic contemplation). More than this, he responded to specific production conditions and traditions and relied on the skills and expertise of his set designers to develop a series of anticinematic visual concepts or artistic briefs, related to simplified architecture, monochromatic palettes, and denuded spaces.

Shot during the difficult conditions of the Occupation,[66] Bresson's first productions were studio-bound and plagued by power outages and the difficulties of overnight shooting schedules, and yet he was able to challenge some of the most skilled set designers in the history of French cinema, like René Renoux, to create innovative design styles. As innovatively austere as they were, they also drew on the set designers' previous solutions. In his work for another auteur some years earlier, on Abel Gance's *Lucrèce Borgia* (1935)—an un-Bressonian film with rather ornate orgies and battle scenes—Renoux relied on the time-tested approach of using sets to create character and to invoke theme.[67] Framed by Niccolò Machiavelli's (Aimé Clariond) writing of *The Prince* (1532), the film follows Césare Borgia (Gabriel Gabrio), son of Pope Alexander VI (Roger Karl), and his carnal and political escapades. The framing story not only codes the film as a period piece, it reveals a strategy. In a single take, the camera arcs around to reveal Machiavelli sitting in a chapel, writing his masterpiece in front of Domenico Ghirlandaio's *The Birth of John the Baptist* (1486–1490), a fresco found in Santa Maria Novella in Florence. Subsequently, scenes are often set in front of canonical works of art. Later, a group of Lucrèce's (Edwige Feuillère) companions rush about preparing for one of the film's famous bath scenes. Shots are blocked so that the actors scramble excitedly in front of Sandro Botticelli's enigmatic *Primavera* (ca. 1482). Once again Renoux and Gance use a painting—this one famously depicting the origins of desire in a springtime setting—to situate the viewer contextually (figure 4.1). Botticelli's painting captures the themes of youthful exuberance, lust, and fertility.

Fig. 4.1. Sandro Botticelli's *Primavera* (ca. 1482) in *Lucrèce Borgia* (Gance, 1935).

Fig. 4.2. Austere set design in *Lucrèce Borgia*.

Lucrèce Borgia's set design also contrasts the flamboyant lives of some with the restraint of others. When a messenger with news of an assassination genuflects at the center of the frame, Pope Alexander, in white, rises from his desk (figure 4.2). Renoux places him in quarters that are fittingly austere: bare white walls (a common French solution in the period),[68] two rough-hewn altars, and few freestanding decorations (a single, basic candleholder stands on the left side of the frame), all below a spartan, rounded archway. These sets are conventionally cinematic in the way Bresson eventually criticized: they convey beauty and overt expressivity (character, theme, historical setting).

To discover the elegant simplicity Bresson was looking for eight years later for *Les anges du péché*, Renoux refines some of these solutions. Adapted from a chronicle of Dominican nuns and their intervention in the lives of delinquents, the film depicts the disciplined, routinized order in its efforts to rescue women from crime.[69] Early on, the wealthy Anne-Marie (Renée Faure) believes that she has found her calling by joining the convent. She soon finds herself visiting a prison and meets Thérèse (Jany Holt), a troubled young woman who, when released, kills the man responsible for her imprisonment. Anne-Marie invites her to take refuge in the convent, which disrupts the disciplined life there. Seeking

Fig. 4.3. Fra Angelico's *The Coronation of the Virgin* (1430–1432) in *Les anges du péché* (Bresson, 1943).

consolation, Anne-Marie attends the convent chapel to pray. As she enters the chapel, our eyes fix upon a prominent female figure in the mural that borders the archway (figure 4.3a). When Anne-Marie pauses at the altar, the figure in the mural maintains her prominence, now positioned next to her. Anne-Marie adopts a pose that echoes the painting (figure 4.3b). The postures are not identical. The figure in the mural has her eyes closed and arms crossed, holding a lamb, while Anne-Marie looks up and to the left, hands clasped in prayer. Anne-Marie's eye line links her to the figure on the wall.

The modifications Bresson and Renoux made to the painting show the degree to which they had intended for the two figures to be connected compositionally and conceptually—much like the Botticelli in *Lucrèce Borgia*. Fra Angelico's *The Coronation of the Virgin* (1430–1432), originally a painted retable, shows Mary, flanked by angels and saints, receiving her crown as queen of Heaven. In the Louvre since 1812, the work was commissioned by several Dominicans, who appear in the piece along with Saint Dominic, shown with a red star above his head. The figure whose posture Anne-Marie mimics even in the longer views (figure 4.3c) is Agnes, a popular early Christian virgin martyr whose name evokes the symbol she cradles (*agnus* is Latin for lamb). Renoux increased Agnes's prominence in the composition by enlarging her, placing her against a darker background and some drapery so that she comes forward, and by isolating her from the crowd of spectators at Mary's coronation, positioning her on the right side of the arched portico. This marked perhaps the first and last occasion Bresson used such overtly symbolic imagery—in this case, Anne-Marie became associated with a martyr whose innocence and angelic protection made her popular among believers. The imagery required visual and conceptual nimbleness; the auteur expected us to use our eyes smartly and decipher the meaning.

Unlike *Lucrèce Borgia*, which was austere only in isolated scenes, Bresson required a spare architecture to create a feeling of visual and tonal unity throughout the entire film. Encouraged to create a pared-down look in a variety of locales, Renoux's sets bring the film a pictorial simplicity that was conspicuously geometric—reliant upon strong vanishing points, recessive diagonals, and regular, unbroken forms.

Les anges du péché's preamble reveals the film's overall aesthetic purpose: "This film is inspired by the life of a French Dominican order founded in 1867 by Father Lataste. The authors have a responsibility to the plot they have created, but they have endeavored to express in images and details taken from reality the atmosphere that prevailed in these convents and the spirit behind their mission." Aspiring to documentary accuracy, Bresson and Renoux represent the discipline and aversion to ostentation of the Dominican order in a chapel sparse to the point of elegant minimalism: white walls, off-white pointed arches, and a black crucifix above a rudimentary altar (figure 4.4). Above that is a prominent rose window

Fig. 4.4. The elegantly geometrical chapel in *Les anges du péché*.

stripped of its ornate, rose-like qualities in favor of stacked glass cubes. Bresson accommodates the set with a slightly high-angle shot and an almost immobile linear arrangement of figures that create receding diagonals pointing toward the altar. To illustrate the order's consistency, Bresson and Renoux design the convent's foyer with identical pristine achromatic walls, shiny-clean floors, rounded arches, and dark square window frames. Outside the convent, the designs are just as sparse. When Anne-Marie leaves the prison where Thérèse is held at the beginning of the film, she navigates a corridor whose dull gray sides are punctuated only by a row of black doors and a dark border that runs along at waist level. Both elements contribute to a heavily linear composition by virtue of Bresson's just-off-center camera. When one of Anne-Marie's fellow sisters-in-training begs for forgiveness, she follows the Dominican technique of prostrating herself. The hallway in which she performs this act of renunciation, once again captured at an angle that emphasizes a strong vanishing point at the end of the hall, is purged of all furnishings, garnished only by cinematographer Philippe Agostini's rectangular–window frame effects lighting. And in a scene where Thérèse confronts her jailer, Bresson and Renoux extend the rule of restraint into the realm of the Parisian apartment, where a more planimetric composition (flatter because the

Fig. 4.5. The angular designs of a barren hall in *Les anges du péché.*

camera lens is almost perpendicular to the back wall) shows an overwrought character as she walks down a barren hall to murder the man she blames for her plight (figure 4.5).

The solutions Renoux arrived at for Bresson—minimal, geometric, with moments of subtle symbolism—were pared down even further two years later in *Les dames du bois de Boulogne.* Hélène (Maria Casarès), a socialite, takes revenge on her former lover by having him marry *une grue* (a prostitute), Agnès (Élina Labourdette), who is often shown in a raincoat, a costume used in 1930s French cinema to codify women characters as sexually promiscuous. For this project, the artistic brief as far as the set design is concerned was simple: maintain a simplified black-on-white color scheme. As production manager Robert Lavallée tells a reporter who was granted full access to the production, "Bresson wants soft, white walls. Over it, a nice piece of furniture, a large window showing that we're in a chic *quartier.* The décor will disappear behind the actors' performances."[70] Bresson inserts the 1930s white-wall technique into a new sparse aesthetic.

This severe monochromatic approach created a series of secondary problems for collaborators. The film's makeup artist, Boris Karabanoff, remarks: "Bresson wants characters in black in white décors. Tragic characters acting almost in front of a curtain. The cinematography risked being too harsh. It therefore called for thin makeup and soft lighting."[71] In terms of lighting, a stage manager comments: "Whites and blacks. . . . White dinner shirts and black coats against white walls, it's challenging."[72] Another member of the photography crew asserts: "Especially when the people are in the dark and the décor is lit!"[73]

The story unfolds in diverse spaces, and while under conventional circumstances the tone of the décor would shift to establish different atmospheres or characters (like *Lucrèce Borgia*), Bresson and his production designer, the legendary Max Douy, once again favor a relatively uniform approach. Locations as diverse as a low-rent apartment (where Agnès and her mother live, figure 4.6a), a high-end flat (where Jean and Hélène meet at her piano), an upscale home (where Jean and Agnès reside once they are married), and a dance hall (where Agnès performs at the beginning of the film, figure 4.6b) are all given the white-wall treatment. Bresson and Douy strip the walls of inessential decorations and adorn the sets with dark wood furnishings and other neutral objects.

Conceived as an intimate, anticinematic drama about the interior struggles of a few carefully drawn characters, *Les dames du bois de Boulogne* required a visual intervention in craft norms. "I wanted a film with three or four characters," Bresson told the reporter. "A study undertaken with great simplicity, with great scarcity."[74] He extrapolates: "One must leave cinema behind and let instinct take control, write and compress. Compression leads to extraordinary results."[75] Bresson's cowriter on the project, Jean Cocteau, remarks: "It's a film of tragic intimacy, in a tone light on floridness, which is unusual for cinema. A film of faces."[76] A uniform, monochromatic décor restrained the range of visual stimuli and focused attention on the character's visages, their internal reactions.

This visual idea often became a labor of love in practice, creating additional artistic challenges. In an early scene set in Hélène's bedroom, she declares her intentions to take revenge on Jean (figure 4.7). Bresson shaped the photography to the black-on-white brief: "A very diffused photography, atmospheric. Effects, but very soft effects. Go from pure white to pure black, through a very broad range of grays."[77] While directing this particular scene, the task he set for cinematographer Philippe Agostini seemed simple: "Show off her eyes."[78] This created new hurdles, however, when Bresson staged the scene with Casarès (Hélène) lying on the bed. Pillows were arranged "so that her suffering takes place in pure white," the reporter explains in his chronicle. The director sought to create a double visual emphasis on the character at this all-important phase of the drama: her black attire against white pillows combined with effects lighting to emphasize her eyes. Bresson and Agostini also wanted to motivate the lighting, to avoid florid expressive effects disconnected from the luminous textures of the space. Next to the character's bed is a window (on the left of the frame) that serves as the light's motivation. Agostini used a flag to insert a faint shadow between the light

Fig. 4.6. Bare white walls and dark wood furnishings in *Les dames du bois de Boulogne* (Bresson, 1945).

Fig. 4.7. "Black-on-white" lighting in *Les dames du bois de Boulogne.*

that falls on the upper bed frame (coming from offscreen left) and the light that falls on Casarès (coming from overhead), a configuration that amplifies the sort of window frame we see in this space. As Hélène declares her revenge, the key light emanating from offscreen left isolates the actress's eyes and forehead while a flag casts a shadow on her cheeks and mouth—again, the window motivates. The problem with Bresson's black-on-white aesthetic is that Agostini had to deal with the reflective properties of the white pillows. The reporter cites the cinematographer's response to Bresson's direction: "He complains about the excessive whiteness of the pillows: 'I can't throw any ambient light on them. It's not working at all, this window effect.'"[79] In the final shot, one cannot help but notice that this double visual emphasis of black costuming against white pillows and the illumination of the figure's eyes creates two 'hot spots,' with the white pillows flaring up behind the actor.

*   *   *

Les anges du péché and *Les dames du bois de Boulogne* demonstrate the degree to which Bresson's craft and those of his collaborators were shaped by his search for an aesthetic of simplicity, first through geometrically ordered compositions and "images and details taken from reality" (in the words of *Les anges du péché*'s preamble) and then via a stark monochromy that governed the set design, as well as lighting, costuming, and makeup.

The postwar context allowed Bresson's visual explorations in stark, anticinematic set design to take new directions. Designed by a close friend, the painter Pierre Charbonnier, who created the sets for his 1934 short *Les affaires publiques*, *Journal d'un curé de campagne*, Bresson's first film after the Liberation, went on location and allowed the auteur to enter a new phase of realist *dépouillement*. Shot entirely in the Northern Pas-de-Calais region, the film garnered attention from the widely read weekly *Radio-cinéma-télévision*, which reported in an April 1950 issue that Bresson's decision to shoot in a small village lent the film an aura of authenticity, for the novelist Georges Bernanos had grown up in this part of France, and the original novel was set there.[80] Bresson and Charbonnier responded to the rural setting rather as a land artist responds to a landscape, through site-specific improvisation utilizing organic media and the indigenous spaces of cultural life.

Undergoing a stylistic purification of his own in the postwar era, depicting in his paintings interiors emptied of human figures, populated only by mundane objects like chairs, mirrors, and lamps,[81] Charbonnier's previous experience using sparse means in rural locations made him an ideal collaborator for Bresson at this stage. In 1933, Charbonnier codirected with Jean Aurenche a short documentary, *Les pirates du Rhône*, which studied the peculiar predicament of Rhône river fishermen who can legally ply their trade only in designated areas. Dubbed a *film-enquête* (a film-investigation), this admirably simple documentary—Bazin's expression "authentic document" comes to mind—included some staged events exhibiting the techniques of fishermen. One could have shown the techniques in a single take, but Aurenche and Charbonnier broke the action into isolated gestures and used a no-frills approach that concentrates one's attention on the perceptual event. In one such event, a local fisherman, shot from a high angle against the flat, tranquil river, gathers a net in hand (figure 4.8a). The process and indigenous tools of the craft are put on display as he raises a pinch of net to his mouth and takes it between his teeth (figure 4.8b). We cut to low-angle shot as the figure casts the net toward the camera. Finally, we see the man from an extreme high angle that shows him in his boat in the middle of an empty stream. Charbonnier and Aurenche elect for simplified compositions inspired by the rural space. The action remains at the center of a depopulated frame so that the single motion captured does not compete with distracting stimuli. The acting, such as it is, is a function of streamlined takes cut together to create a barebones feeling of continuous time—a pre-Bressonian achievement by two of Bresson's artistic collaborators (Aurenche before the Occupation and Charbonnier after).

Fig. 4.8. Isolated gesture and the depopulated frame in *Les pirates du Rhône* (Aurenche and Charbonnier, 1935).

Bresson explored the potential of this kind of scenographic sparseness over the course of several films. From the preproduction phase, Bresson and Charbonnier envisioned *Journal d'un curé de campagne* as a stark show—like *Les pirates du Rhône*, the rural venue welcomed it. While the rule of scene-to-scene restraint reigned during the production (as it had for *Les anges du péché* and *Les dames du bois de Boulogne*), the film evinces new solutions mixed in with ones acquired on previous projects. The modest country priest of the film's title resides in simple quarters found in Pas-de-Calais, decorated by Charbonnier with a single bed with basic iron frame, a dark wood desk, a lamp, and a dormer window. The walls aren't white this time. Charbonnier lends character to the room using wallpaper that is faintly patterned and torn here and there. The priest's kitchen reveals further signs of modesty: a wood-burning stove, plaster walls, and more tattered wall dressing (figure 4.9a). Later in the film, a rural café the priest frequents while seeing a doctor about his failing health is almost interchangeable with his living space: pale plaster walls and a dark wood table. In a hallway outside an apartment rented by Louis Dufréty (Bernard Hubrenne), the priest's friend from seminary, cinematographer Léonce-Henri Burel lights the banister from above to bring out its tarnishes (figure 4.9b). The destitution of *Journal d'un curé de campagne*'s sets here combine with a solution Bresson preferred in *Les anges du péché* and *Les dames du bois de Boulogne*: Charbonnier uses a white wall in the background, which Burel lights to accentuate the priest's comparatively dark frock.

Despite these commonalities with his earlier works, *Journal d'un curé de campagne* represents a shift in Bresson's concept of realism. Now shooting on location, fruitful constraints are imposed upon him. He no longer has the luxury of the expansive spaces of studio sets. Working in the tighter confines of actual private and public spaces, his framings become closer, which in turn leads to a decreased emphasis on sets. Set design becomes almost subaesthetic or subcinematic relative to his previous films. Favoring the medium close-up and medium shot, *Journal d'un curé de campagne*'s framings are taken with a 50mm or normal lens, which, as cinematographer Burel explains, creates "very tight compositions without the slightest hint of a panoramic view."[82] Shooting outside the studio provides Bresson with a new means for achieving an increasingly austere, even rough look that moves away from the long-shot option of *Les anges du péché* and *Les dames du bois de Boulogne*, where figures are staged in large spaces whose emptiness, linear purity, and monochromatic patterns feel aestheticized by comparison. If *Les anges du péché*'s and *Les dames du bois de Boulogne*'s sets catch the eye with a chic minimalism, *Journal d'un curé de campagne*'s designs—more organic, naturalistic, captured with a lens that diminishes their significance—feel "undesigned." In the film, they simply *are*.

With *Un condamné à mort s'est échappé*, set during the Occupation, Bresson further pushes the concept of denuded décor. Gone are the overtly geometrical

Fig. 4.9. The raw modesty of the sets of *Journal d'un curé de campagne* (Bresson, 1951).

sets of *Les anges du péché* and the stark black-on-white aesthetic of *Les dames du bois de Boulogne*. A prison film, shot partially on location and focusing on the inner drama of a prisoner of war, Bresson uses the occasion to play with the gray scale and show that a feature film can almost completely do away with set design. Working again with Charbonnier, he now repurposes the textures of *Les pirates du Rhône*: tight, depopulated views with simple actions centered in the frame. One might even say that *Un condamné à mort*'s sets are so pared away as to defy commentary. Carrying less and less of the film's overall signifying force, Bresson provides very little to see or match to words.

We begin with another written prologue attesting to the film's authenticity. "This is a true story. I've told it as it happened, unadorned," the auteur explains. Prior to the escape, which begins seventy-five minutes into a ninety-minute film, Bresson's camera grants the viewer only restricted or partial views of sceno-graphic space. Operated by Jean Chiabaut—one of Bresson's most important col-laborators—the camera more often than not maintains a tight angle, especially when the film's protagonist, Fontaine (François Letterier), finds himself in two cells, one on the ground floor and one on the second floor of the prison.[83] The longest shot of the first cell shows gray walls, a single cot, a plaster doorframe, a corner shelf that Fontaine uses to climb up to the window, and a wooden door—to a certain extent, one's verbalizations must remain banal and list-like (figure 4.10). His second cell duplicates the first in its sparseness. When Fontaine looks out his barred window to scout the terrain or converse with a neighboring pris-oner, Bresson provides startlingly noncommunicative views—a flat composition with the camera just off the perpendicular axis (figure 4.11a) and a high-angle point-of-view shot of the courtyard below (figure 4.11b). A woman is shown walk-ing to the center of the frame; she pauses when a firing squad putting a pris-oner to death is heard offscreen and turns back. Bresson's compositions are by now so minimally communicative that pressure is placed on the combination of elements through editing—in this case, offscreen sound effects—to construct a sense of the film's diegetic space.

Concrete sound effects in fact play a crucial role in Bresson's *visual* thinking. Beginning with *Un condamné à mort*, he experiments with the power of offscreen sound in such a way that allows him to abandon intricate or complete onscreen sets. Bresson is able to pare his décor virtually to the bone. As Michel Chion has argued, the film's space becomes a series of concentric circles with Fontaine's cell at the center—an apt decision given that the story is told exclusively from the perspective of a character who is confined for much of the film.[84] Of the approxi-mately six distinct diegetic spaces depicted, five are often constructed through offscreen sound alone. We see Fontaine's cell through partial views. Just beyond are numerous adjacent cells that the camera barely accesses. Instead, Bresson provides hints of the life in them as Fontaine taps on the walls using Morse code

Fig. 4.10. Fontaine's (François Leterrier) sparse cell in *Un condamné à mort s'est échappé* (Bresson, 1956).

to communicate. One of his neighbors, whose cell we never see, apparently occupies his time by learning patriotic song lyrics. Beyond the cells are the hallways of the prison, bustling with sounds of officers marching and clacking their keys on iron railings, and the prison yard outside, which is apparently rife with activity, but what we immediately observe of that activity is quite limited. Bresson's sound replaces direct representations of these settings at the same time as it suggests how we might visualize them. Outside the prison are a train station and a street, it seems. Sounds of streetcars, children carousing, people gossiping, and car motors humming give us a sense of free life beyond the gates of the prison. And the station appears to be in a town, represented by the sound of a church bell. Again, the church is never shown, but the viewer (and Fontaine) knows it is there because the church clock chimes every hour.

In addition, the spaces we perceive—visually or aurally—bypass the cognitive or symbolic associations Bresson experimented with in *Les anges du péché*'s chapel sequence and leave us with more direct, impressionistic perceptual textures: gravelly prison yards, the unforgiving springs of Fontaine's bedframe, blood-soaked clothing, and corrugated granite walls. Deaestheticized, the denuded locales of *Un condamné à mort* spurn the delicate, the decorative.

Fig. 4.11. Minimally communicative compositions in *Un condamné à mort s'est échappé*.

Fig. 4.12. The restrictive handling of space in *Un condamné à mort s'est échappé*.

Bresson commits his art only to the stark essentials, stripping his compositions of distracting, beautifying superfluities. We are given only a low-angle shot of the top half of Fontaine's cell door rather than the geometric designs of *Les anges du péché*'s hallways (figure 4.12a). When Fontaine is taken to a hotel to hear his death sentence, the establishing shot of the location—revealing a depopulated entranceway reading "Hotel Terminus"—hardly establishes anything about the space at all. On those rare occasions when Fontaine is free to roam throughout the prison, tight framings restrict the range of visible spatial cues—either in the stairwell of the prison, in the communal washrooms (figure 4.12b), or in the courtyard when panning shots follow Fontaine as he surveys the prison grounds. No master shots allow us to gain a full appreciation of the sets, of Fontaine's surroundings. Since Bresson restricts most of the action to centered gestures in tight framings, there is no more need for intricate set design. There is nothing left to "read" here.

Visual Experiments II: Bresson's Acting and Photography—Minimally Expressive "Modeling," Uncommunicative Light, Unified Color

Bresson was a remarkably consistent filmmaker, but not in ways that some critics have argued.[85] He did not rely on the same creative concepts and solutions in film after film; instead, he remained committed to a process—a realist or anticinematic *dépouillement*. At the same moment he was working with his crew to revolutionize set design, Bresson took photography and performance through a similar process of realist purification and devised a new principle (no actors, no stars) while he simultaneously reinforced others (no bursts of style, no florid color designs, no symbolically or semantically rich imagery).

This also took time and required the expertise and flexibility of his collaborators. Pushing back against craft norms (actors trained to emote and cinematographers skilled in the art of modeling these actors with "polished," meaningful light), Bresson pared away expressive styles of illumination, often used to embellish the actor's evocative gestures and direct emotional expression and photogenic beauty, and eventually discovered a new cinematic body—the *modèle*—whose minimally communicative gestures and movements were matched with an opaque, "detached" lighting style and, later, uniform, polychromatic color schemes. Like his restrained, linear architecture, stark monochromatic sets, and denuded spaces, these alternative visual concepts or artistic briefs freed him from convention, from the use of the film image to create distracting *éclats* (moments of ostentation).

As we saw in chapter 1, Bresson's quest for a more restrained and behavioral (rather than expressive) acting style began with his first film, the comic short *Les affaires publiques*. Nine years later, Bresson, working with a full cast

Fig. 4.13. Classical, communicative lighting to make distinctions between characters in *Les anges du péché*.

of professional actors on *Les anges du péché*, renewed the quest for a concrete alternative. He did not encourage his actors to "become the part" but rather to focus their talents on the power of a few simplified actions as well as a motivated form of gestural restraint. One scene reveals the discipline of the Dominican order when a nun responds to the protagonist Anne-Marie's mother, who arrives at the convent early in the film to rescue her daughter, whom she believes to be ill-suited for convent life. Bresson shoots the scene in a legible shot/reverse shot schema. Anne-Marie's mother (right) expresses concern that her daughter—accustomed to purity and luxury—will never truly be happy working with the criminals welcomed into the order (figure 4.13a). The actress playing the mother, Yolande Laffon, uses an array of fluid gestures to communicate firmness of mind. Shrugging her shoulders to show her certainty that Anne-Marie will wish to leave and then enthusiastically punctuating her statements with frequent nodding and blinking and by waving about her fur-covered right hand, she glibly asserts: "I couldn't myself imagine being face-to-face with one of them [criminals]." We cut to the reverse angle for the reaction of a nun positioned on the left of the frame, Mère Dominique (figure 4.13b). Actress Paula Dehelly restricts her movements and gestures. "It's quite easy, Madame. I am one of them," she retorts. Controlling of her posture and avoiding abrupt motions of the head and neck, Dehelly simply lowers her gaze to show a hint of guilt about her past and perhaps to avoid locking eyes in a confrontational way with a woman who had unintentionally insulted her. Bresson here seeks authenticity by relying on a hybrid of stylized and restrained performance styles.

Cinematographer Philippe Agostini's light tells the story, too. Here, and in their next collaboration, *Les dames du bois de Boulogne*, he provides Bresson with what Fabrice Revault D'Allones calls "classical" solutions.[86] Best known for high-contrast cinematography and effects lighting that suggested the natural illumination of lamps, sunlight, and candles, Agostini's classical approach was sought out by several other auteurs as well. Marcel Carné hired him for the poetic realist classic, *Le jour se lève* (1939); Jean Grémillon for a film that premiered at an Objectif 49 event, *Les pattes blanches* (1949); and American director Jules Dassin for the dark crime thriller *Du rififi chez les hommes* (1955). He was master of a polished studio look that relied upon theatrical convention; like theater lighting, classical lighting in the cinema *signifies*. It makes light "speak," as Revault D'Allones puts it.[87] A form of illumination that guides attention as well as cognitive and affective response, classical choices differ markedly from a more natural approach, which tends toward meanings that are "ambiguous (opaque) or ambivalent (diverse)."[88]

Agostini's classical lighting for this *Les anges du péché* scene makes explicit the contrast between the modesty of the nuns and the exuberance of Anne-Marie's mother. In the first shot (figure 4.13a), the nuns, particularly their heads and shoulders, are lit rather flatly with an even illumination that reveals few folds

Fig. 4.14. Subtle affective illumination in *Les anges du péché*.

or pleats in their headdresses. Agostini avoids flashy halo effects and highlights on the nuns' headgear, and, as a result, they take on the character of undifferentiated monochromatic planes. In the second shot (figure 4.13b), Agostini uses a window-frame effect in the background to highlight the space behind them and lift the figures from the white wall. Much as he did in the bedroom scene from *Les dames du bois de Boulogne*, Agostini's window-frame shadows concentrate the viewer's attention on the actresses' faces. Anne-Marie's mother, by contrast, is lit for relief to show up her wares, especially in the first shot. A background light, casting a shadow from an object hanging offscreen right, creates a noticeable glare around her, as if her attire were glowing with affluence. Reinforcing this schema, a backlight creates a rim atop her ornate hat, accentuating its silky quality, and along her right side, bringing out the rich mink of her fur coat.

Although Bresson and Agostini mainly show the Dominican nuns with even illumination—a lighting strategy that renders their religious habits as flat planes that echo the smooth, clean surfaces of the convent itself—at critical moments in the film, Anne-Marie is handled differently from the other nuns by virtue of some subtle lighting touches that accentuate the distinctiveness of the character's self-sacrifice. In a moment of spiritual purification—of divestiture of those material goods and memories from her past life—Anne-Marie gathers some photos of her mother and prepares to set them aflame (figure 4.14). Agostini's soft lighting on the figure and walls remains relatively even. But he lowers the intensity of the lighting on the upper walls, which has two effects: it lifts the figure's upper body from the background and creates soft contrast with the brightest point of the frame, Anne-Marie's face. With a key light positioned offscreen left, Agostini makes the tear below the figure's right eye glisten ever so slightly, bringing the viewer closer to the character emotionally. Bresson and Agostini create the right conditions for such subtle play. In a film where actors playing nuns were weaned off of showy emotive gesticulations and where a relatively distant camera and flatter illumination are a norm, emotion is often revealed through light.

* * *

With *Journal d'un curé de campagne*, Bresson's approach to acting and photography shifted radically. To begin with, he adopted as his own the new vanguard approach of mixing trained with untrained performers (unlike *Les anges du péché* and *Les dames du bois de Boulogne*, which featured all-professional casts). In a classic of cinephilic criticism, 1948's "Le réalisme cinématographique et l'école italienne de la libération," André Bazin noted that many realist films followed this "rule of the amalgam" despite the risks they created for the filmmaker in the commercial market of postwar Europe.[89] Bazin lamented that producers all too often appealed to "the public's well-known preference for finding its favorite actors in their usual roles."[90] The realist film, by contrast, boldly upheld a "specific denial of the star element and an indiscriminate use of actors by trade and actors by chance."[91] The aesthetic benefits were clear: working alongside people plucked from the streets and encouraged to simply be themselves, stars like Anna Magnani, Pina in *Roma, città aperta* (1945), learned to approach their roles afresh by adopting a naturalism of the everyday and leaving their star personas behind. For all its aesthetic promise, however, Bazin determined that the rule of the amalgam was increasingly threatened by "the tyranny of the star."[92]

Even before he employed nonprofessionals, Bresson took steps to oppose this tyranny by attempting to wean his professional actors off the habit of dramatic expression, but this came at the cost of strife on his sets. Some of his actors, befuddled by his soft-spoken but unrelenting coaching and insistence on tedious repetition and retakes, designed to remove vocal inflection from a line of dialogue or render a glance or gesticulation unselfaware, interpreted his techniques negatively, as a form of aggression or abuse. During the making of *Les dames du bois de Boulogne*, Maria Casarès, in her second film role after appearing in Marcel Carné's massively successful *Les enfants du paradis* (1945), famously tussled with Bresson over the more overt, emotive touches she, as an experienced theater actor who had a firm sense of the limitations of cinema as an actor's medium (especially for women), wished to bring to the role of the affronted and vengeful Hélène. In her eyes, Bresson, whom she admired and respected as a person, became a "tyrant"; he set out to break her will, to turn her into a "robot."[93]

To be sure, the gender politics of Bresson's methods, interpreted in this case by a female performer as an effort to strip her not just of her own creative volition but of control over her voice and body, are troubling and cannot be ignored. As Geneviève Sellier has argued, the all-controlling male auteur was ascendant in the 1950s and 1960s and garnered praise precisely for his mastery of all aspects of production, including the female bodies he employed.[94]

And yet, we must also acknowledge that the concept of the *modèle* was designed to oppose a different power structure, one that stars like Casarès represented. From Bresson's perspective, figures like Casarès were part of a commercial system in which stars and producers were invested in using film style to enhance an actor's image, to draw on the cultural associations, social and gendered performances, and forms of pleasure projected by and onto the actor and that ultimately promoted a film's mass appeal and a strong box-office return. Effectively anticommercial, Bresson's idea of a realist image *sans* stars and glamorous photography opposed this mode of thinking from within the system, and this at a time when the vanguard auteur had difficulty gaining a foothold on the industry by virtue of its dependency on attractions, on big-name actors and stylistic razzle-dazzle. Under these circumstances, Bresson joined the ciné-club Objectif 49, which aimed to launch an alternative distribution system and a separate cultural market of *nouvelle avant-garde* films that challenged the status quo (issues raised in chapter 2).

Thus, if Bresson deserves some criticism for his at times problematic treatment of actors (or, at least, for his failure, early in his career, to properly explain these anticommercial intentions to the professionals under his employ), he nevertheless deserves credit for envisioning an alternative notion of the screen body that shook the power structures of stardom and commercialism at their very foundations. Today, these aspects of his cinema find support among feminist directors and actresses, like Babette Mangolte and Tilda Swinton, suggesting that the concept of the *modèle* is compatible with a feminist perspective—in Swinton's case, with alternative forms of femininity onscreen.[95]

In any case, by the time *Journal d'un curé de campagne* went into production, Bresson had resolved that the best way to limit the star's influence on the film's visual style was to employ none at all. Instead, he mixed relatively unknown professionals, former stage performers, and nonactors who had no interest in stardom. A relative unknown, the twenty-three-year old Belgian-born *suisse* Claude Laydu, the film's priest, although sometimes described as a nonprofessional,[96] worked for film-and-theater actor Jean-Louis Barrault's company in Brussels before being contracted by Bresson.[97] (Industry connections made this possible; it was Jacques Becker who recommended Laydu to Bresson.[98]) Likewise, Bresson cast Nicole Ladmiral, who had some film experience as a voice-over narrator for the documentary *Le sang des bêtes* (Franju, 1949), as the countess's daughter Chantal. Another trained actor, this time a well-regarded one, Marie-Monique Arkell, known in theatrical circles as Rachèle Berendt, played the film's countess. As a member of the Comédie Française, she starred in the inaugural production of Belgian playwright Fernand Crommelynck's *Chaut et froid* (1934), among other roles,[99] but she was decades removed from her last stage performance.[100] Cast next to these actors were many nonprofessionals, most notably Dr. Adrien Borel, a psychiatrist, who only accepted the role of the fatherly priest of Torcy on the condition that his name be removed from the credits.[101]

This hybrid casting strategy brought together professionals and nonprofessionals who had one thing in common: they had very little experience in front of a movie camera. This meant that the camera now served the auteur's eye alone— his realist artistic brief. But how was he going to photograph these actors?

During the production of *Journal d'un curé de campagne*, Bresson's thinking through of the possibilities of the sparse image truly began to distinguish itself by deviating from classical norms. The subtle modulating beauty of Philippe Agostini's photography commented too overtly on different scenes and different characters and, like the mixed performance styles of *Les anges du péché*, rendered individual images and moments too remarkable in themselves. Working toward an alternative to these still rather cinematic touches, Bresson sought to impose a uniform sparseness on the film as a whole.

As we have already seen, *Journal d'un curé de campagne* is based on a 1936 Georges Bernanos novel. As its title suggests, the priest recounts in diary form the events of his life. With few exceptions, plot developments in the novel are filtered through the private thoughts of the protagonist. We learn of his arrival at a new parish, his attempts to improve the lives of his parishioners, the advice shared with him by the priest of Torcy, his increasing isolation from the village's count and countess, his difficulties praying, and his terminal illness all through the point of view of the young curé.

The photographic concept emerged from a creative problem: how would the novel's first-person form be translated onto the screen without using the florid, variable techniques of conventional cinema? Bresson's aversion to showy compositional strategies meant that punctuating the film with ornately choreographed point-of-view tracking shots or overt dream or hallucination sequences as the priest's mental and physical health deteriorated was out of the question.

In his memoir, cinematographer Burel recalls how he and Bresson worked through the problem. During their initial encounter, the auteur invited him to a screening of a film that had won the Grand Prix Award at the Cannes Film

Festival in 1949, *The Third Man* (1949): "I arrived in Paris. Bresson . . . brought me to see a film, *The Third Man*, indicating to me: 'You see, this is the kind of thing I'd like to do.' The cinematography was extremely hard and contrasty. I shared my astonishment that he wanted this kind of cinematography for *Curé*: this violence, these harsh whites, didn't seem to suit the story."[102] After the screening, they "dined and spent the evening together discussing this. He told me that the idea was to develop a photography that was almost blurry, very diffused, very reserved, very flat, without contrast. I reminded him that this was the exact opposite of the film we had seen! Perhaps he had thought it over in the interim. . . . he's very resourceful!"[103]

Bresson's visual concept soon became clear to Burel. Bresson was challenging him to develop a photography that was both like and unlike *The Third Man*'s—a photography that avoided sharp contrasts while still maintaining a wide tonal range between the brightest highlights and darkest shadows in the frame. It was decided that they should conduct tests. But since Burel did not have his usual production team with him in Paris to perform the experiments Bresson requested, he worked with a camera operator and an assistant furnished by the studio they were renting. The peculiar events that transpired—that shaped the film's realist images—must be recounted in full:

> When Bresson asked me what kind of lens I was going to use, I said I was thinking of 50mm. It doesn't give you much depth, which he evidently didn't want anyway, and it concentrates the action. I also told him I would use relatively powerful diffusers in order to get the extreme contrasts he liked. Now, I had brought along my own diffusers which were made especially for me and which were in effect cylindrical lens additions. We shot various tests using 50 and 75mm lenses. But the man who was acting as my assistant wasn't used to these diffusers, and he must have changed them while changing lenses, getting them on back to front. When I saw the rushes, I was appalled; it wasn't diffused, it was out of focus. At which point Bresson came rushing up excitedly, saying, "That's it! You've got it, my dear Burel. That's exactly what I want for my film."[104]

A further layer of collaborative negotiation ensued. Burel: "I like diffused effects and I don't like high definition, but I wasn't going to make a film that was entirely out of focus. However, we lunched, we talked, we looked at those rushes over and over again. Finally, he said that perhaps we could compromise, meet each other halfway over what he wanted and what I refused to do."[105]

"Since Bresson was making demands on me, I also made demands on him." Burel continues:

> I told him I saw the film entirely without luminous contrasts, as something rather insubstantial or immaterial which I wanted to handle without any suggestion of shadows. All right, he said, but how? Since he had the budget to do it, and since there usually isn't much sun in the north anyway (the film was

shot entirely on location in Pas-de-Calais), I suggested that we should shoot without sun, doing the exact opposite of what everybody usually does and shooting indoors when the sun did come out. That way I thought we could give the film a texture, a style, an entirely new feel.[106]

Burel ultimately praised Bresson's unique visual concept: "His idea to make a film with heavy contrasts but also heavy diffusion (diffusion usually thwarts contrast—if you diffuse a lot, you need high contrast lighting or else the image will have no volume) was a good one. It made for a very special photography."[107]

The photography's effect is twofold. First, Burel's unique diffusers mute the contrasts but also weave into the film a visual tradition that tends to be associated with high artifice: pictorialism, a style Bresson briefly experimented with in his 1932 photography for Coco Chanel. A photographic aesthetic associated mainly with the late nineteenth century, pictorialism uses lens and lamp diffusion in the form of gauzes and scrims, as well as developing techniques, to soften and thereby aestheticize the photographic image. In film history, pictorialism makes its way into German and then Hollywood filmmaking as the "soft style" of 1920s cinematography.[108] Eventually, this approach becomes associated with glamorous close-up shots of female stars. Like his appropriation of the white-wall solution, Bresson discovers in pictorialism a means to develop a sparse look by making it a consistent element of the film's form—by using it to establish a shot-to-shot unity.

Second, the diffused-contrast effect provides a subtle glimpse into the protagonist's psychological state. If considered in isolation, the film's shots seem to contain potentially distracting, beautiful qualities. Bright background candles subtly shimmer behind the priest, light flowing into his apartment from a dormer window carefully "bleeds" onto the surrounding frame, and the contour lines of a twisting expressionist-style tree blur to envelop the character (figure 4.15a). Established as the film's strict photographic norm, Burel's 50mm lens, patented lens diffuser, light gauzes, and the decision to shoot the film in low lighting conditions, drape Claude Laydu's relatively expressionless face, downcast eyes, and slow-paced, naturalistic gestures—peeling potatoes, stirring morsels of bread into wine—in an ascetic luminosity, rendering the images of the story's suffering country priest rather ethereal and delicate (figure 4.15b).

This union or commonality among images ensures the erasure of discrete moments of overt symbolism in favor of an unvarying experience of indirect suggestion. The country priest, embroiled in a spiritual struggle with the outside world, has a rather restricted understanding of the circumstances around him. Delicate images capture his encounter visually; they limit spatial depth, render details opaque, and, thus, offer an understated perceptual surrogate for the inner life of a character unable to grasp the full implications of his spiritual journey.

Fig. 4.15. Expressive use of diffusion and contrast in *Journal d'un curé de campagne*.

As Fabrice Revault D'Allones puts it, the Bresson-Burel collaboration moved away from classical modeling toward modern solutions—toward "neutralized meanings" in which the photography shows an "'indifference' to the scene, to the action it bathes" by virtue of an overall look that remains consistent from scene to scene.[109]

Sensing that his images were still too expressive and aestheticized, Bresson and Burel pared the visual track down even further for *Un condamné à mort s'est échappé* five years later. In many ways, the film defined the Bresson visual concept for decades to come. He further neutralized the expressive value of individual shots by flattening the lighting even further, doing away with Burel's custom-made lens diffuser. Shot with the 50mm lens, the film eschewed the delicate highlights and effects favored by Agostini and the soft, rounded-edge approach of *Journal d'un curé de campagne* in favor of a starker bounce lighting technique that avoided high-contrast contours and silky outlines.[110]

Using a cast now composed exclusively of nonprofessionals, Bresson had designs on an increasingly deglamorized feel. It has often been claimed that Bresson cast his *modèles* over the telephone, by listening only to their voices.[111] In an aphorism from *Notes sur le cinématographe* on "the choice of models," he wrote: "His voice draws for me his mouth, his eyes, his face, makes for me his complete portrait, outer and inner, better than if he were in front of me. The best deciphering got by the ear alone."[112] And: "Telephone. His voice makes him visible."[113] But, once again, in practice Bresson often mixed convention with innovation. François Leterrier, who played Fontaine, the protagonist of *Un condamné à mort*, explains that he had to complete a screen test where he was directed to recite lines from *Les anges du péché* in the neutral tone of Claude Laydu.[114] The screen test was projected several days later for a small audience, Leterrier included.[115] It was only then that Bresson called the nonactor to tell him how pleased he was with the tests and to offer him the part.

Bresson was interested not just in his vocal tones and rhythms but in his look. Like Laydu and other Bressonian *modèles*, Leterrier has a long face, thin cheeks, and distinctive, large eyes—features not of a movie star but of a natural face that fit the role, in this case of an undernourished POW planning his escape from a Nazi prison in Lyon. Rather than light him with strong highlights to accentuate an expensive costume or high-class *coiffure*, Leterrier's ragged and bloodstained shirt and greasy shock are lit rather flatly, as we see in a crucial scene late in the film when Fontaine must decide whether to trust his young cellmate, Jost, to help him with the escape.

If lens diffusers had previously been adequate to create a neutral, even-keeled look, Burel now relied upon reflected light to deglamorize the figures and give shots a relatively constant quality both in relation to adjacent shots and in terms of the contrast within individual compositions. As I have written elsewhere, to create a more realist effect quite unlike the lighting solutions used in big-budget star vehicles, Burel and Bresson here decided to "live dangerously by filming almost without light," as they had with *Journal d'un curé de campagne*.[116] Only now, they aimed to create a photography style "without artifice or dramatic effect."[117] Burel opted for a solution uncommon for the period: "I think I was one of the first cameramen to use reflected instead of direct light."[118] The conditions chosen by Bresson for the shoot (some scenes were shot on location in the confined spaces of Montluc prison in Lyon) gave him the opportunity to use bounce light as the dominant method of illumination for much of the film. Burel explains: "I threw light on to a sort of large white shield, so that instead of falling directly on the actors, it was reflected on to them. It became an ambiance, an atmosphere, and though directed, came not from a particular point but from an extensive surface."[119] This solution suited other aspects of Bressonian realism: "It was easy enough really because Bresson works so much in close-up and because there were never more than three actors in shot. With a big set or a wider field, I could never have done it."[120]

The effect in the scene with Fontaine and Jost is that the compositions are bereft of dark, dense shadow play that, in conventional films with expressive lighting, communicate the inner workings of character psychology or the dramatic tenor of the scene. The lighting is now relatively detached from the drama. Leterrier is shot with what appears to be a two-point system (figure 4.16b) with a key light positioned above the figure from offscreen right and a fill emanating from the upper left. The light has been dispersed on a white shield (one of which seems to be reflected in Leterrier's eyes). The direction is discernible, but the shadow attached to the figure is soft and there are few highlights. When we cut to the reverse angle (figure 4.16a), we see that Charles Le Clainche (Jost) has received similar treatment, only his lighting is even more ambient. The directional nature of the soft light can be perceived in the delicate shadow he casts on the wall behind him. Both shots are captured with a tightly framed camera that sports a 50mm lens, and the backgrounds show no detail, communicating only the shallow nature of the cell's space. The photography, set design, and performance style—neutral gazes and monotone delivery that gain an expressive quality only in the context of surrounding shots and scenes—now work together to create a seamless antispectacle uniformity. Bresson's set of realist visual concepts had reached their apogee.

* * *

With bounce lighting, Burel provided Bresson with a solution that the director used to create relatively "neutral" images in later films. We see a similar technique being used on location in the 1967 production, *Mouchette*. A documentary

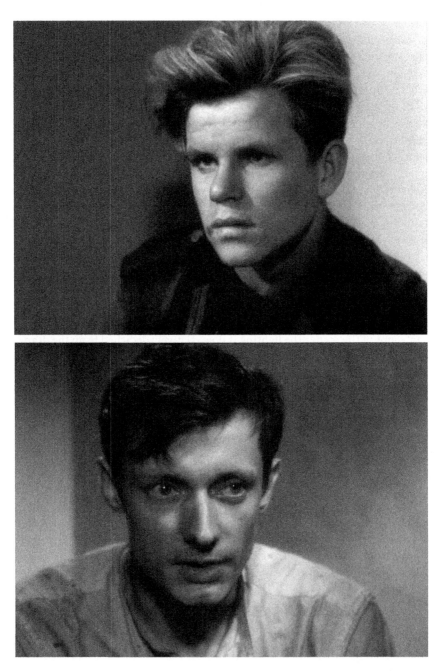

Fig. 4.16. The unclassical, ambient lighting schemes of *Un condamné à mort s'est échappé*.

filmed during the shoot shows that Bresson's next cinematographer, Ghislain Cloquet, had hung a row of lighting units along the ceiling of a sparsely decorated bedroom (figure 4.17).[121] Cloquet's lamps point upward toward the plafond in order to reflect the light and avoid "sourcy" effects on the *modèles* (positioned center right). A unit located above the bed points downward toward the *modèles*, but a white shield diffuses the beam. The final scene, set at night as the young Mouchette attends to her ailing mother and awaits her father and brother, has a relatively even illumination devoid of striking effects that comment on the action.

Bresson, as I have argued throughout this chapter, was a fluid, not a rigid, visual thinker. He at times subtly deviated from this sparse, uncommunicative style. When the New Wave arrived, films like *Le beau Serge* (1958), *Les 400 coups* (1959), and *À bout de souffle* (1960) were inspired by predecessors like Bresson whose cinema devoid of artifice had challenged the convention of beautiful and expressive studio-made images in narrative film. He had opened French filmmaking onto new vistas of pictorial restraint, even grittiness. Now, these young filmmakers took up the mantle and launched a new trend by moving film production into the streets of Paris. Intrigued by the possibilities, Bresson set his 1959 film

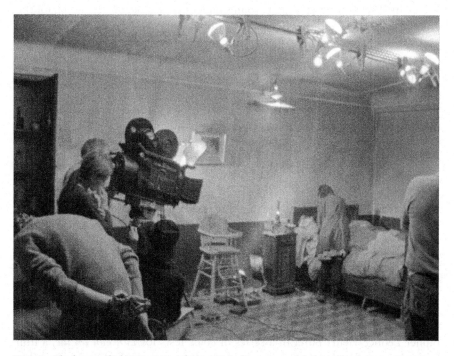

Fig. 4.17. The bounce lighting set-up of *Mouchette* (Bresson, 1967), from the documentary *Au hasard Bresson* (Kotulla, 1967).

Pickpocket in the French capital as well. Based on an episode from Dostoyevsky's *Crime and Punishment* (1866), the film shows Michel's (Martin LaSalle) desperate descent into thievery to support his dying mother. Kassagi, a real-life pickpocket hired as consultant on the film to ensure authenticity, trains him in the art of pickpocketing. But Michel's demise is inevitable. After his arrest, only the young woman, Jeanne (Marika Green), who had cared for his mother, visits him in jail.

With his performances now reduced to controlled, evocative postures, simplified gestures, and carefully timed glances (often downward), subtle variations in lighting serve an unlikely purpose in a mature Bresson film. In separate scenes with Michel, Jeanne and the setting behind her are treated fairly evenly by the light, whether in her modest apartment upon his return from abroad (figure 4.18a), where he promises to care for her and her child, or during a visitation once he is imprisoned (figure 4.18b). Jeanne's poses—the placement of her hands and her downcast gaze—carry the just-noticeable modulations in affective tone here, not extravagant displays of light and shadow. But in the film's climax, Bresson violates his own rule, it would seem. Moments before these two lonely souls share a touching caress and Michel utters the most famous line of the film— "Oh Jeanne, what a strange path has led me to you!"—the character's voice-over shares an observation that is more than slightly mystifying for the viewer, for the event is so fleeting and visually subtle as to leave us questioning our own eyes. "Something lit up her face," he declares in a matter-of-fact way, and for but a few moments of screen time, Jeanne glows as the space around her is delicately wrapped in shadow (figure 4.18c). Perhaps just this once, Bressonian uniformity gives way to expressive luminosity.

However, even in this case, as the Bressonian image accommodates projections of verbal paraphrase, of affective elation, its underlying visual concept— uncommunicative light—recommends that we take some distance from them.

* * *

In his late 1950s film practice, Bresson was clearly tempted by the possibilities of necessarily brief moments of expressive form, even though his verbal theorizing seemed opposed to it. He also became interested in representations of beauty, specifically through color. By the time he produced his first color film, 1969's *Une femme douce*, Bresson's visual thinking had evolved to consider whether displays of subtle polychromatic beauty could be rendered anticinematic as well.

Although, as we saw earlier, he was reticent about the aesthetic distractions inherent in color photography, in 1957 he enlisted the assistance of cinematographer Léonce-Henri Burel in a series of color tests for *Lancelot du lac*, a film he finally completed in 1974. The aim was to discover a method of shooting that replaced the "dancing" saturated hues of conventional cinema with a muted,

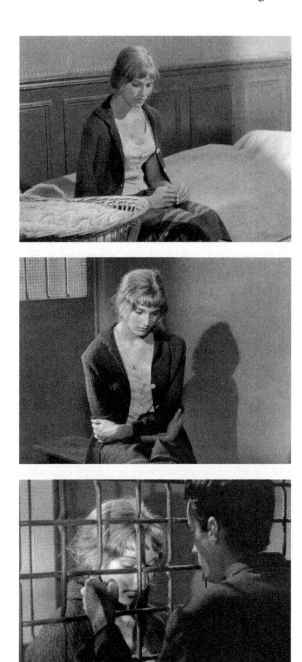

Fig. 4.18. Unexpressive, followed by expressive luminosity in *Pickpocket* (Bresson, 1959).

uniform, and intelligent alternative that allowed color to quietly impress itself on the spectator as he or she attended to the restrained acting of the *modèle*. We can glimpse the evolution of Bresson's thinking from the following letter from Burel (Bresson's side of the exchange has not survived): "The tests will produce the kind of photography you desire. That is, well defined figures with blurred backgrounds (with it being understood that the backgrounds will remain well defined in their hues and not in terms of contrast)." But, Burel warns, "we will have to do a number of delicate tests, some of which will be quite risky and which will surely disappoint, but which will permit us to discover a style that color films until now lack." In the tests, "we will look for graduated diffusion, seek out concerted relations between hues, and determine the color and density of smoke and gauzes designed to haze the backdrops," which suggests that Bresson's main concern was the distracting colors that appeared behind his *modèles*. Through these techniques, he remained convinced that "we can get away from the laundry blue, syrupy gooseberry and lifeless spinach acid green that so complacently degrade our screens."[122]

The same concept—of concerted or unified color that didn't "pop," that was aesthetically pleasing, but not distracting—helped Bresson think through a new challenge in the production *Une femme douce* over a decade later. His color films included young *modèles*—Dominique Sanda in *Une femme douce*, Isabelle Weingarten in *Quatre nuits d'un rêveur*, Humbert Balsan in *Lancelot du lac*—who displayed conspicuous facial and bodily beauty. How to render them uncinematic, unstarlike? He wagered that their beauty could be rendered realist, more natural through performances that were subdued, stripped of straightforward charisma, even at times opaque. At the same time, he concluded that color could be used to tie their beauty to the other perceptual textures of a film—to create the kind of simplified uniformity he had been committed to since his first verbal statements against cinematic convention in the 1940s and 1950s. He elected to create uniformity by deriving a color scheme from the *modèles'* skin tones: "Since the first rule of art is unity, color threatens you because its effects are too various. However, if you can control and unify the color, you can produce more powerful shots in it than are possible in black and white. In *Une Femme douce* I started with the color of Dominique Sanda's skin and harmonized everything to it."[123]

A Realist Auteur in a Realist Culture

Though often characterized as one of the fathers of cinematic minimalism,[124] it is more accurate historically to describe Bresson as Nicole Brenez has in her work on the period—as a realist auteur working in a realist film culture.[125] He was challenging the realist sensibility pervasive in midcentury France with aesthetic ideas and forms that seemed intent to distinguish not only between realist cinema and the theater-based artifice of popular film but between the still rather conspicuous, symbolically rich, and convention-laden realism of other vanguard auteurs from a truer, self-effacing realism that hid and even denied its own artistry.

And yet, despite these contextual ties, it is challenging to sort out the causal relationship between his filmmaking and surrounding culture. On the one hand, it would appear that Bresson was one of a handful of auteurs (Roger Leenhardt, Jean Renoir, and perhaps a few others) who, through their films, interviews, and writings, anticipated the postwar interest in the concept of realism. On the other, 1930s French film culture, from its larger studio productions (like *Lucrèce Borgia*'s white-walled sets) to its small independent films (*Les pirates du Rhône*'s sparse reenactments), seemed to have been inclined toward realism—visual simplicity, at any rate—years before Bresson made his first feature. The boundaries between Bresson's creative volition and those of certain segments of his culture are at times so blurry that a simple, linear chronology—x (Bresson) set y (his culture) into motion, or y determined x's style—is, if not impossible, certainly impractical at this juncture.

It seems fair to assert, however, that Bresson's verbal and visual practices became part of a cultural market—an exchange of ideas, a competition of forms— that was driven by the search (among filmmakers and cinephiles) for new simplified, realist styles and storytelling modes. Influential cinephiles like Georges Sadoul and André Bazin registered this exchange or competition in their writings, in the verisms, naturalisms, and various sonic, visual, and political realisms they chronicled in the performances of auteurs. These collective cultural practices also ensured that sparse styles and modes became associated with the postwar *nouvelle avant-garde*. For Sadoul, the socialist themes of Louis Daquin's *Le point du jour* represented the direction the new avant-garde needed to take in the post-Liberation moment. For those who became affiliated with Objectif 49, the postwar avant-garde promised to revolutionize narrative form and visual style. Prior to the formation of the club, one of its future copresidents, Roger Leenhardt, argued that innovation was needed as a result of a crisis of content and aestheticized style that had set in during the Occupation. As I have shown in a different context, Leenhardt revealed the promise of sparse narrative form and a visual realism of his own in his 1948 film *Les dernières vacances*, celebrated by Objectif 49 as a paragon of the *nouvelle avant-garde*. We have seen how Bresson, another of the club's copresidents, defended the virtues of an aesthetic of simplified realism throughout the 1940s and well into the 1950s and 1960s. It was in recognition of Leenhardt, Bresson, and other sparse realist auteurs that, on the occasion of the club's *Festival du film maudit* in 1949, Jean Cocteau, the third copresident, wrote in the catalogue for the event that in the new avant-garde, "boldness present[ed] itself under the auspices of simplicity."[126]

Despite these cultural affinities, two factors eventually distinguished Bresson's realism from that of his peers. First, the longevity of his theorization of and experimentation with realism far outstripped that of Daquin and Leenhardt, for instance, whose feature-film careers experienced considerable setbacks during the 1940s and 1950s, in part due to their unique approaches to realism. Daquin's radical socialism resulted in censorship, most famously for his adaptation of Guy de Maupassant's *Bel Ami* (1955).[127] When *Les dernières vacances*'s contributions to the history of realist style and pared-down storytelling were widely misunderstood by audiences, and his 1948 adaptation of an innovative story with no male characters, Federico García Lorca's three-act play *The House of Bernarda Alba* (1945), was scrapped after a legal dispute over rights to the property, Leenhardt abandoned feature filmmaking and his own search for a new realism almost entirely.[128]

This longevity allowed Bresson to refashion the stylistic and conceptual resources circulating within film culture (namely, its sense of what a film—realist or not—ought to look like) into a rich range of new visual concepts, which he worked through over the course of decades of film practice. As we have seen, his style was able to evolve and mature as a result of fresh artistic briefs (often negotiated using the skills and expertise of his creative personnel) at the levels of set design (geometricized architecture, high-contrast monochromy, stripped-down spaces on location), photography (uncommunicative and indirectly suggestive light, polychromatic images that create visual unity), and acting (minimal expressivity by his nonprofessional *modèles*). These briefs in turn fulfilled the requirements of a unique and developing set of anticinematic principles or theories (no stylization, no ostentatious color, no filmed theater, no professional performers, no images that call upon the viewer to interpret or decode them) that, in his view, liberated Bresson's craft from convention.

Second, Bresson's realism was unique, even in this context, because, as he stated, it was not an aesthetic end unto itself but a means to an end. On one level, Bresson's realism had a clear purpose, a cultural and oppositional one: to critique the (cinematic, pseudorealist) visual with the (sparse, truly realist) visual. However, as I have suggested throughout this chapter, Bressonian realism served another purpose as well, one that will preoccupy us moving forward. It was Bresson's belief that sparse realism allowed the individual image to take on meaning and purpose indirectly, in relation to other images and formal elements. Realism, for Bresson, prepared the way not only for the supersession or end of the cinematic image but for cinema's ultimate transformation into a nontheatrical, purely relational and rhythmic art.

Notes

1. George Sadoul, "Robert Bresson à Georges Sadoul: 'Si l'on veut que passé le courant électrique, il faut dénuder les fils . . . ," *Les lettres françaises*, March 7, 1963, 9.
2. Ibid.
3. Ibid.
4. Charles Thomas Samuels, "Robert Bresson," in *Encountering Directors* (New York: Capricorn Books, 1972), 58.
5. Svetlana Alpers and Michael Baxandall, *Tiepolo and the Pictorial Intelligence* (New Haven: Yale University Press, 1994), v.
6. Bresson preferred to think of his films as "essays" or attempts; see Sadoul, "Robert Bresson à Georges Sadoul," 1.
7. Throughout this chapter, I rely on the term "photography" rather than "cinematography" in order to keep clear the distinction between the way Bresson and his directors of photography lit and composed shots and Bresson's alternative to cinema, *le cinématographe*, which will be discussed in the next chapter.
8. Samuels, "Robert Bresson," 61.
9. I wish to situate Bresson in a long tradition of French artists who took an activist role in living *by* and *for* ideas and adopting an outspoken, engaged, and even rebellious stance within cultural life; see Bruce Robbins, "Introduction: The Grounding of Intellectuals," in *Intellectuals: Aesthetics, Politics and Academics*, ed. Bruce Robbins (Minneapolis: University of Minnesota Press, 1990), xi, xxiv. As Paul Johnson writes of this tradition, the intellectual will assert the right to reject the existing order and confidently "refashion[s] it from the bottom in accordance with principles of his own devising"; Paul Johnson, *The Intellectuals* (New York: Harper & Row, 1988), 2.
10. Laurent Bertrand Dorléac, *The Art of the Defeat: France, 1940–1944*, trans. Jane Marie Todd (Los Angeles: The Getty Research Institute, 2008), 295.
11. Margaret Key, *Truth from a Lie: Documentary, Detection, and Reflexivity in Abe Kobo's Realist Project* (Plymouth, UK: Lexington Books, 2011), 138.
12. David Bradby, *Le théâtre français contemporain, 1940–1980* (Lille: Presses universitaires de Lille, 1990), 249–251; Rosemary O'Neill, *Art and Visual Culture on the French Riviera, 1956–1971: The École de Nice* (Burlington, VT: Ashgate, 2012), 93–126.
13. Colin Burnett, "Under the Auspices of Simplicity: Roger Leenhardt's New Realism and the Aesthetic History of Objectif 49," *Film History* 27.2 (2015): 33–75.
14. For Daquin, see Raymond Barkan, "En faisant voire la vérité, le cinéma travaillera pour la paix . . ." (Interview with Louis Daquin), *Les lettres françaises*, August 26, 1948, 1, where Daquin states, prior to his visit to a United Nations congress in Warsaw, that it is indispensable "to create works marked by an honest social realism and democratic conceptions of life in society." For *Positif*, see "Réalismes," *Positif* 5 (December 1952): 1; Edoardo Bruno, "L'évolution de De Santis," *Positif* 5 (December 1952): 19; and Guy Jacob, "Température du néo-réalisme," *Positif* 5 (December 1952): 14–18. Sadoul has an article in this issue of *Positif* devoted to "realisms": Georges Sadoul, "Quelques aspects du cinéma soviétique," *Positif* 5 (December 1952): 2–10. *Positif* also addresses Bresson's realism (in favorable terms) in one entry of its multipart examination of Bresson: Bernard Chardère, "À propos de Bresson I: Les rouages de la réalité," *Positif* 4 (November 1952): 43–48.
15. Olivier Fortin, "Les élites culturelles et la diffusion du cinéma italien en France de 1945 aux années 1970," *Rives méditerranéennes* 32–33 (2009), http://rives.revues.org/2960.
16. Georges Sadoul, "Naturalisme descriptif," *Les lettres françaises*, October 13, 1949.

17. Georges Sadoul, "Une nouvelle avant-garde," *Les lettres françaises*, May 19, 1949.
18. Ibid.
19. Ibid.
20. Ibid.
21. Georges Sadoul, "Le néo-réalisme américain?," *Les lettres françaises*, September 30, 1948, emphasis in source.
22. Ibid.
23. Ibid., original emphasis.
24. Georges Sadoul, "Néo-réalisme américain: *La dernière rafale*," *Les lettres françaises*, August 18, 1949.
25. Ibid.
26. Sadoul, "Naturalisme descriptif."
27. Editor's preface to François Leterrier, "Philosophe de métier, vedette de fortune," *La nef*, December 1956, 47; Michel Estève, *Robert Bresson* (Paris: Éditions Seghers, 1962), 79–80.
28. Georges Sadoul, "Délit et châtiment," *Les lettres françaises*, December 24, 1959, 7.
29. Ibid., 7, original emphasis.
30. Ibid.
31. Ibid.
32. Ibid.
33. Daniel Morgan, "Rethinking Bazin: Ontology and Realist Aesthetics," *Critical Inquiry* 32 (Spring 2006): 471.
34. André Bazin, "Cinematic Realism and the Italian School of the Liberation," in *What is Cinema?*, trans. Timothy Barnard (Montréal: Caboose, 2009), 231–232.
35. André Bazin, *Jean Renoir*, trans. W. W. Halsey II and William H. Simon, ed. François Truffaut (New York: Simon and Schuster, 1973), 85.
36. Bazin, "Cinematic Realism," 231–232.
37. Ibid.
38. Ibid. See also André Bazin, "*Farrebique*, or the Paradox of Realism," in *Bazin At Work: Major Essays & Reviews from the Forties & Fifties*, ed. Bert Cardullo (New York Routledge, 1997), 103.
39. Bazin, "Cinematic Realism," 231–232.
40. André Bazin, "The Case of Marcel Pagnol," in *Bazin At Work: Major Essays & Reviews from the Forties & Fifties*, ed. Bert Cardullo (New York: Routledge, 1997), 53, 54.
41. Ibid., 54–55.
42. Ibid., 155.
43. Ibid.
44. Ibid., 154.
45. Bazin, "*Germany Year Zero*," 124.
46. Louis Malle, "With *Pickpocket* Bresson Has Found," in *Robert Bresson*, ed. James Quandt (Toronto: Cinematheque Ontario), 570–571. See also Philip French, Interview with Louis Malle, in *Robert Bresson*, ed. James Quandt (Toronto: Cinematheque Ontario, 1998), 570.
47. Ibid.
48. Jean Queval, "Dialogue avec Robert Bresson," *L'écran français*, November 12, 1946, 12, emphasis in source.
49. Ibid.
50. *Hommage à Georges Bernanos et débat sur le film "Journal d'un curé de campagne"* (Paris: Centre catholique des intellectuels français, 1951), 32.
51. Ibid., 32, original emphasis.
52. Ibid.
53. "Entretien avec Robert Bresson," *Unifrance film* 45 (December 1957): 1.

54. Ibid.

55. Ibid., 2.

56. Colin Crisp, *The Classic French Cinema, 1930–1960* (Bloomington: Indiana University Press, 1993), 312–313.

57. Robert Bresson, "'Une mise-en-scène n'est pas un art:' Robert Bresson rencontre les étudiants de l'Institution des hautes études cinématographiques (Décembre 1955)," *Cahiers du cinéma: Hommage Robert Bresson* (February 2000): 6. For a discussion of the actors union's opposition to directors who transform actors into mere "objects" in the mid-1950s, see Colin Crisp, *The Classic French Cinema, 1930–1960* (Bloomington: Indiana University Press, 1993), 312–313.

58. Robert Bresson, *Notes on the Cinematographer*, trans. Jonathan Griffin (Copenhagen: Green Integer, 1997), 14, original emphasis. Originally published as *Notes sur le cinématographe* (Paris: Gallimard, 1975).

59. Ibid., 69, original emphasis.

60. Bresson, "'Une mise-en-scène n'est pas un art,'" 4–5.

61. Bresson, *Notes on the Cinematographer*, 70–71.

62. Ibid., 88.

63. Ibid., 78–79.

64. Ibid., 92.

65. Ibid., 21.

66. Evelyn Ehrlich, *Cinema of Paradox: French Filmmaking Under the German Occupation* (New York: Columbia University Press, 1985), 97.

67. Léon Barsacq, *Le décor du film* (Paris: Éditions Seghers, 1970), 104, where the set designer points out that a film's décor should capture the psychology, the behavior of the characters who are supposed to inhabit it.

68. David Bordwell, "The Exchange: Narration and Style in *Les Anges du péché*," in *Robert Bresson (Revised)*, ed. James Quandt (Toronto: TIFF, 2012), 245.

69. Michel Lelong, *Les dominicaines des prisons (Béthanie)* (Paris: Éditions du cerf, 1938).

70. Paul Guth, *Autour des dames du bois de Boulogne: Journal d'un film* (Paris: Juillard, 1945), 35.

71. Ibid., 71.

72. Ibid., 60.

73. Ibid., 61.

74. Ibid., 106.

75. Ibid.

76. Ibid., 37.

77. Ibid., 28. Bresson had a different cinematographer, Armand Thirard, conduct tests for the film during the preproduction phase. He appears to have returned to Agostini out of dissatisfaction for Thirard's work; see Guth, *Autour des dames du bois de Boulogne*, 29–32.

78. Ibid., 121.

79. Ibid., 122–123.

80. Pierre Leprohon, "Dans un château d'Artois, d'après l'œuvre de Bernanos, Robert Bresson tourne Le Journal . . . ," *Radio-cinéma-télévision*, April 9, 1950, 8.

81. Pierre Gabaston, *Pickpocket de Robert Bresson* (Crisnée: Yellow Now, 1990), 119. Charbonnier's archives include dozens of pen and watercolor sketches in neutral tones (pale brows, grays, and blues) that were reminiscent of his paintings from the period. See Pierre Charbonnier, "Cuisine Ambricourt presbytère [sans date] [Maquette de décor]," Fonds Pierre Charbonnier, Dessins numérisés de costumes ou de décors, Bibliothèque du film, Paris, France; and Pierre Charbonnier, "Chambre presbytère Ambricourt [sans date] [Maquette de décor]," Fonds Pierre Charbonnier, Dessins numérisés de costumes ou de décors, Bibliothèque du film, Paris, France.

82. René Prédal and L. H. Burel, *Souvenirs de L. H. Burel* (Paris: Avant-scène, 1975), section B10.

83. See Leterrier, "Philosope de métier, vedette de fortune," 47–48.

84. Michel Chion, *Un art sonore, le cinéma: Histoire, esthétique, poétique* (Paris: Éditions Cahiers du cinéma, 2003), 288.

85. As Jonathan Rosenbaum has convincingly argued, it is quite common to "stereotype him in relation" to "his allegedly all-encompassing 'system'"; see Jonathan Rosenbaum, "Robert Bresson's *Affaires Publiques*," JonathanRosenbaum.net (July 18, 1999), http://www.jonathanrosenbaum.net/1999/07/robert-bressons-affaires-publiques-tk/ (July 29, 2015).

86. Fabrice Revault D'Allones, *La lumière au cinéma* (Paris: Éditions Cahiers du cinéma, 1991), 11–17.

87. Ibid., 14.

88. Ibid., 16.

89. André Bazin, "Cinematic Realism and the Italian School of the Liberation," in *What is Cinema?*, trans. Timothy Barnard (Montréal: Caboose, 2009), 224.

90. Ibid., 225.

91. Ibid.

92. Ibid.

93. "Maria Casarès sur 'Les dames du bois de Boulogne," *Gros plan*, Office national de radiodiffusion télévision française (Paris: ORTF, February 8, 1958), http://www.ina.fr/video/I00014702 (August 4, 2015).

94. Geneviève Sellier, *Masculine Singular: French New Wave Cinema*, trans. Kristin Ross (Durham: Duke University Press, 2008), 145–183.

95. Babette Mangolte, *Les modèles de Pickpocket*, 2003, Pickpocket Criterion DVD; Vera Von Kreustbruck, "Interview with Tilda Swinton: 'I am Probably a Woman,'" *The Wip* (March 20, 2009), http://thewip.net/2009/03/20/interview-with-actress-tilda-swinton-i-am-probably-a-woman/ (August 20, 2015).

96. Susan Sontag, "Spiritual Style in the Films of Robert Bresson," in *Against Interpretation* (New York, Anchor Books, 1990), 192; and Ronald Hayman, "Robert Bresson in Conversation with Ronald Hayman," *Transatlantic Review* 46–47 (Summer 1973), http://www.mastersofcinema.org/bresson/Words/TransAtlanticReview.html (April 12, 2008). Bresson himself makes this point in an interview: *Pour le plaisir*, "Un metteur en order: Robert Bresson," first broadcast on May 11, 1966, dir. Roger Stéphane, *Au hasard Balthazar* Criterion DVD.

97. Leprohon, "Dans un château d'Artois, d'après l'oeuvre de Bernanos, Robert Bresson tourne *Le Journal . . .*," 9. Laydu would land parts in a number of other movies, most notably *Nous sommes tous des assassins* (Cayette, 1952), *Interdit de séjour* (de Canonge, 1955), and *Dialogue des Carmélites* (Agostini and Bruckberger, 1960), the last based on a Georges Bernanos play. Laydu also wrote and provided voice-over for the children's show, *Bonne nuit les petits* (1962), which was later remade as *Nounours* (1995).

98. Jean-Guy Moreau, "Allô Bresson? J'ai un petit prêtre pour toi," *Radio-cinéma-télévision*, February 11, 1951.

99. See Alain Piette, and Bert Cardullo, *The Crommelynck Mystery: The Life and Work of a Belgian Playwright* (Selinsgrove, PA: Susquehanna University Press; London: Associated University Presses, 1997), 81.

100. Arkell had to quell Bresson's concerns by explaining to him that she hadn't performed for the theater in twenty years. Nevertheless, they quarreled on the set. Bresson: "I left the sequence with the countess . . . just as 'groggy' as if I had been in a boxing match"; Pierre Ajame, "Le cinéma selon Bresson," *Les nouvelle littéraires*, May 26, 1966, 13.

101. Georges Charensol, *D'une rive à l'autre* (Paris: Mercure de France, 1973), 245.

102. Prédal and Burel, *Souvenirs de L. H. Burel*, section B10, n.p.

103. Ibid. *The Third Man* (1949, Reed) was released in Paris on October 20, 1949. Shooting for *Journal d'un curé de campagne* began on March 6, 1950.

104. Rui Nogueira, "Burel & Bresson," in *Robert Bresson*, ed. James Quandt (Toronto: Cinematheque Ontario, 1998), 515. I have made slight changes to Nogueira's text based on my reading of a similar passage in Burel and Prédal, *Souvenirs de L .H. Burel*, section B10, n.p.

105. Ibid., 515–516.

106. Ibid.

107. Burel and Prédal, *Souvenirs de L. H. Burel*, section B10.

108. Kristin Thompson, "The Major Technological Developments of the 1920s," in *The Classical Hollywood Cinema: Film Style and Mode of Production to 1960* (New York: Columbia University Press, 1985), 287–293.

109. Revault D'Allones, *La lumière au cinéma*, 10.

110. It has often been said that Bresson shot everything using a 50mm lens. However, there are many notable exceptions: the shot of the shawl falling after the suicide of Dominique Sanda's character at the beginning of *Une femme douce* (1969) was shot with a telephoto lens; many of the shots in the joust sequence of *Lancelot du lac* (1974) were shot with a variable focal-length (or zoom) lens; and the opening shot of *Un condamné à mort s'est échappé* seems to have been taken with a longer lens as well because of the way the space between prison itself and the walls surrounding it is compressed.

111. Doug Tomlinson, "Performance in the Films of Robert Bresson: The Aesthetics of Denial," in *More Than a Method: Trends and Traditions in Contemporary Film Performance*, ed. Cynthia Baron, Diane Carson and Frank P. Tomasulo (Detroit: Wayne State University Press, 2004), 75, 92 n.7.

112. Bresson, *Notes on the Cinematographer*, 22.

113. Ibid., 120.

114. Leterrier, "Philosophe de métier, vedette de fortune," 47.

115. Ibid., 48.

116. Nogueira, "Burel & Bresson," 517.

117. Ibid.

118. Ibid., 518.

119. Ibid.

120. Ibid.

121. Theodor Kotulla's 1966 documentary, *Au hasard Bresson*, available on the *Au hasard Balthazar* Criterion DVD.

122. Léonce-Henri Burel, "Lettre de L. H. Burel à Robert Bresson (Préparation de Lancelot du lac), 26/6/57," in *Souvenirs de L. H. Burel* (Paris: Avant-scène, 1975), sec. F4, n.p.

123. Samuels, "Robert Bresson," 32.

124. András Bálint Kovács, *Screening Modernism: European Art Cinema, 1950–1980* (Chicago: University of Chicago Press, 2007), 141.

125. Nicole Brenez, "'For it Is the Critical Faculty that Invents New Forms,'" in *The French Cinema Book*, ed. Michael Witt and Michael Temple (London: British Film Institute, 2004), 230.

126. Jean Cocteau, "Il importe de nous expliquer sur le sens exact du terme 'maudit' . . . ," in *Festival du film maudit* Catalogue (Paris: Éditions Mazarine, 1949), n.p.

127. Susan Hayward, *French Costume Drama of the 1950s: Fashioning Politics in Film* (Bristol: Intellect, 2010), 327–346.

128. Burnett, "Under the Auspices of Simplicity," 66.

5 Vernacularizing Rhythm:
Bresson and the Shift Toward Dionysian Temporalities—Plot Structure and Editing from Journal d'un curé de campagne *(1951)* to L'argent *(1983)*

The omnipotence of rhythms.

—Robert Bresson[1]

MORE SO THAN any other area of film aesthetics, rhythm brings us to the core of Bresson's intervention in the midcentury cultural market. As we will see, he eventually perceived in the concept of rhythm the potential for an entirely new creative medium, one distinct from cinema, which he dubbed le cinématographe (writing in motion) in a manner that was, perhaps tellingly, reminiscent of the interwar period.[2] But what did the concept of rhythm entail for Bresson?

When Bresson entered the industry, filmmakers like René Clair, associated with the silent-era avant-garde (1919–1929), viewed rhythm as "an all purpose structural concept" that allowed them to carefully regulate the timing and duration of shots in order to give their scenes a conspicuous tempo.[3] Clair carried the idea into the conversion-to-sound era (1929–1934) with tight image-and-music coordination that offered sprightly explorations of pulsating sonorized movement in such films as À nous la liberté (1931).[4]

Clair and others from the interwar era were effectively accepting the musicologist's notion of rhythm, which involves creating from groups of abstract or nonrepresentational pulses or beats a discernible tempo or speed. In most folk music, jazz, and other very rhythmic forms, the pulse drives the listener's experience—makes us want to tap our feet or clap our hands. Musical rhythm breaks up or distinguishes these pulses in order to create emphasis. This is accomplished through the subdivision of tones, as well as through meter, the repetitive pattern of strong and weak tones. Strong notes, in the musicologist's jargon, are accented; important notes are stressed, with weak notes and intervals inserted in between—the *tick*-tock-*tick*-tock of a musical cue. Furthermore, the intervals between accents are given a set periodicity. For rhythm to exist, the duration between accents must be mathematically precise, consistent, and predictable.

Perhaps unfamiliar to an interwar avant-garde determined to transform cinema into a musical form, some very different notions of rhythm were available to French artists. As Laurent Guido has shown in his study of French concepts of rhythm between 1910 and 1930, it was already a fashion in Gallic art criticism of the early 1900s to comment on the rhythms not just of poetry and music but of atemporal artistic media like painting and architecture.[5] Well before the films of Clair, Jean Epstein, and Germane Dulac, rhythm was slipping through the musicologist's fingers, and a variety of theorists and artists formed something of an unacknowledged movement committed to creatively extending the concept into new realms of thought and practice. This rhythmic drift, as I call it, was pursued well after the 1930s and shaped discourse in art theory, psychology, and philosophy during the "long" postwar period of the mid-1940s through the mid-1980s.

Perhaps the most prominent theorist to promote this drift from music theory was Henri Meschonnic, author of the seminal *Critique du rythme* (1982),[6] who wrote quite provocatively that "rhythm is no longer, even if certain philistines haven't realised it, the alternation of the tick-tock on the cheek of the metronomic metrician."[7] For him, rhythm was an inherently unstable concept that addressed phenomena whose beats and pulses were irregular, embodied, intuitive—that is, *sans mesure* (beyond precise measure). Rhythm, in Meschonnic's view, created temporal relationships that destabilized regular time and fixed lexical meaning; no musicological concept could possibly grasp this.[8]

While distinctive, Meschonnic's efforts to wrest the concept of rhythm from its musicological roots belong, like those of Henri Lefebvre, Julia Kristeva, and Gilles Deleuze,[9] to a long line of French thought. In postwar France, "rhythm" seeped into the vernacular as a fundamental aspect of human perception and understanding, aesthetic or otherwise, and this, as I will argue, shaped and was shaped by critical and theoretical discourses within film culture.

Into this multifaceted discourse entered Bresson, whose postwar cinema extended the category of rhythm through the art of *le cinématographe*. As he began to establish himself as a feature filmmaker, a repertory of strict musical, panaesthetic, and vitalistic versions of "rhythm" flourished around him, enriching both cinephilic discourse and his own, and creating a new passion for auteur films that experiment with rhythm. This passion was not expressed in a desire to see cinema mimic music's mathematical precision alone, its oscillating system of metrically timed notes. The cultural market's overlapping but distinct ideas— that every art manifests its own unique form of rhythm (the panaesthetic version of rhythm) and that life itself has core rhythms that art can capture, analyze, and shape (the vitalistic version)—presented auteurs with new opportunities to take up the tenacious riddle, what is cinematic rhythm?

Because this aspect of his film practice has yet to be mapped, we have also yet to appreciate the precise nature of Bresson's intervention in midcentury film and intellectual culture. Tracing the diversity of "rhythms" circulating within his culture will provide us with the lexical and conceptual tools to return to Bresson's craft with a fresh perspective. If some of Bresson's films created stable "classical" experiences composed of carefully ordered durations and intervals (the metric style of *Journal d'un curé de campagne*), others offered unstable, ruptured, or embodied experiences (the vitalistic style of the post–May '68 film *Le diable, probablement*). The amazingly diverse range and complexity of Bresson's temporal experiments make of his *cinématographe* a deposit of a culture's own notions of time—a deposit that permits us to track the shift away from Apollonian toward increasingly Dionysian impulses within the French passion for rhythm.

The Postwar Rhythmic Drift

Partially inspired by the silent-era avant-garde,[10] postwar film culture saw a rhythmic revival. Vanguard filmmakers once again proclaimed rhythm a fundamental characteristic of the art of cinema. In 1952, Jean Cocteau wrote: "Editing is the most important work of the cineaste. It's his style, his form of writing. It is the way images are glued one to the other that gives a film its rhythm."[11] Jacques B. Brunius, the Surrealist critic, actor, and director, offered this theoretical appraisal in 1954: "Because surface and movement define three-dimensional space and duration, cinematic rhythm, very different from the whirring of music, consists of the photography of space-time, to which is adjoined the phono-photography of dialogue and sound. Endowed with these natural advantages, cinema more than any other art offers almost the perfect means to represent perceptible reality."[12] Apparently frustrated with contemporary discussions about rhythm, Jean Renoir, in a 1959 piece defending the arts of acting and staging, declared: "Rhythm is no longer produced through editing."[13] Young Turks of the French New Wave, like Éric Rohmer, compared the order and restraint of auteur cinema with the rhythms of poetry: "Just as one cannot conceive of a poet who is insensitive to rhythm, we consistently discover in all great cinematic work the presence of a certain geometric rigor, not superadded of course, like a pointless ornament, but absolutely consubstantial with [the work]."[14] Other auteurs whose film careers began in the 1950s spoke of the centrality of rhythm to their filmmaking in subsequent decades. In the 1980s, Agnès Varda coined the neologism "cinécriture" (ciné-writing) to describe her inventive process, where "the rhythm of filming and editing" has, like other elements of style, been "felt and considered in the way the writer chooses . . . chapters which advance the story or break its flow."[15] Jean-Luc Godard described his art as a "search for another rhythm," a discovery of "the rhythm through which cinema can represent life. . . . Today, with rhythm, everything remains the same. We give someone a kiss with the same rhythm that we get in the car or that we buy a loaf of bread."[16] Rhythm played actively on the creation of *France/Tour/Détour/Deux/Enfants* (1977), where he and Anne-Marie Miéville "did things in slow motion, changed rhythms, which I would call decompositions, making use of the combined techniques of cinema and television" to make new rhythmic discoveries.[17]

In the postwar era, rhythm was, as we can now see, reinvented as a broad term associated with notions of personal expression via rigorous control of shot relations, with a meticulous concern for the overall balance and pacing of a film, and with the suggestion of an invisible, even esoteric, quasi-geometric system that the discerning filmmaker derives from life and the cinephile decodes from a film. In this, the language of filmmakers was of a piece with midcentury French thought in the realms of poetics, aesthetics, and philosophy, which set out to explore rhythm as a concept both broader and more fundamental than that of the musicologist's carefully timed metric pulsation of notes. The proliferation of "rhythms" in this drift, as I am calling it, stemmed from a common Apollonian attitude or posture. By and large, aestheticians and philosophers of rhythm focused on hidden harmonies, underlying laws, the order of things, their rigorous restraint, symmetry, and geometry. However, there was also a great deal of variation—of creative extension—in the period's language.

Strict Musical Rhythms

Between 1930 and 1970, many critics and theorists relied on the authority of positivist philosopher and lexicographer Emile Littré, whose famous dictionary, affectionately known as "the Littré," defined rhythm as the regular, perceived intervals between long and short musical tones.[18] But even this fairly orthodox conception found some unorthodox applications. A distinguished figure of midcentury psychology, Paul Fraisse, who would have been known to postwar cinephiles through his affiliation with the Sorbonne's Institut de filmologie in the late 1940s,[19] published numerous groundbreaking and widely read studies on the psychology of time that expanded musical rhythm as a fundamental aspect of biological and cognitive processes. In his 1956 study, *Les structures rythmiques*,[20] and a work that built on it, *Psychologie du rythme* (1974), Fraisse explored the points of overlap between rhythm in human activity (like musical composition) and what he called biological rhythm, which he defined as "an oscillating system in which identical events are produced by intervals of time perceived as equal"[21]— the beat of the heart, the electrical pulses in the brain, the circadian cycles in the movement of leaves, and the regular need to urinate. Fraisse also took interest in spatial rhythm, in the psychological dynamic involved in imposing rhythm on visual experience. As we gaze at the Acropolis, for example, we perceive oscillating, repeated elements like columns and the gaps between them presented at even intervals. The visual encounter becomes rhythmic, he wrote, when we train our eyes to organize these stimuli into a pulse-like perceptual event (with the columns as the proverbial accents)—*column*-space-*column*-space-*column*-space-etc. But this, argued Fraisse, was merely a virtual rhythm, not rhythm that emerged from what he called "exteroceptive stimuli"[22]—cues that originate from sources outside the human body. Spatial rhythm was for Fraisse merely analogous with musical rhythm, but it still shed light on our penchant for rhythmically interpreting structures dependent on the principle of oscillation.

The influence of Fraisse's still fairly musical understanding of rhythm was felt most directly in film discourse in texts like Jean Mitry's extraordinary two-part *Esthétique et psychologie du cinéma* (1963–1965), which held that in cinema, rhythm existed only "in its most general sense: of time evolving in a succession of alternating and interrelated durations. It is 'order in movement,' to use the simplest Platonic definition, a form which allows the 'continuity' to develop and become organized in time."[23] Like Fraisse, Mitry was skeptical that nonmusical forms like cinema could create strict musical rhythms because, at least in the case of narrative cinema, elements of film form possessed representational qualities that drew attention away from "the beat." He channeled Fraisse:

> As Fraisse points out, "the less constrictive the sensory data, the greater the influence of the perceptual processes and even attitudes or personality of the perceiver." Now, the film image, with the signification and objective value of its content, is about as constricting as anything can be. There is, therefore, no similarity between film rhythm and musical rhythm involving relationships of proportion and recurring patterns. Though it is an organization of pure associations, a specific rhythm can only involve elements with no precise signification (or at least no clearly defined objective qualities) in the formation of these associations. Sound—and sound alone—responds perfectly to these requirements.[24]

Mitry concluded that rhythm must be viewed as a latent feature of the viewer's encounter with cinematic stimuli: "When rhythm involves concrete elements with meaning of their own, it becomes incapable of signifying 'by itself' and ends up *organizing significations*."[25] Like the Acropolis, a narrative film—burdened by its own signifying systems—simply cannot achieve "pure" musical rhythm.

Panaesthetic Rhythms

Evidently, the musical sense of rhythm was not abandoned in midcentury France. It survived on numerous cultural strata, in psychology and film theory. However, its claim of denotative authority was certainly challenged in analogous ways in film culture and a range of philosophical and intellectual discourses that upheld rhythm as a principle governing all of the major art forms. This challenge began earlier than the postwar era, when figures like mathematician and composer

Pius Servien published his classic *Les rythmes come introduction physique à l'esthétique (Nouvelles méthodes d'analyses et leur application notamment à la musique, aux rythmes du français et aux mètres doriens)* (1930), which explored the rhythms of French prose and poetry. In several works between 1919 and 1949, music critic René Dumesnil took this idea a step further, presenting rhythm as the principle of order or symmetry behind any work of art, not just poetic or musical composition.[26]

Despite its title, Dumesnil's major study on the subject, *Le rythme musical* (1949), denied that any serious examination of rhythm's role in aesthetics could limit itself to musicological distinctions and concluded that "the objection that seems to stand in the way of all general definitions of rhythm is that it is impossible to compare the diverse aesthetic categories—that is, the different forms by which Art manifests itself as Fine—because there is no common measure among them."[27] This posed no problem to the aesthetician who situated rhythm "in neither space nor time conceived as such, but in the creative genius of the artist who uses them as a frame for the symbols that find unity therein. His oeuvre, whether it is a pictorial, musical, literary—or even cinegraphic—translation of his emotion, draws from rhythm the order and proportion without which there is no work of art."[28] Dumesnil moved to establish rhythm as the essential characteristic of art itself, as the ordered, symmetrical expression of an author.

A contemporary of Dumesnil, Matila Ghyka, another mathematician, defended rhythm as a feature of all arts, both temporal and spatial. Spatial media didn't merely approximate or analogize musical rhythm; they acted on rhythmic laws all their own. This is the thrust of his *Essai sur le rythme*, first published in 1938 and reprinted in its eleventh edition in 1952.[29]

Surely the most common conception of rhythm in midcentury film culture—the belief that cinema possessed its own rhythms, sometimes similar to those of music and poetry and sometimes entirely distinct to film form and expression—was widely embraced among filmmakers, like those cited earlier (Cocteau, Renoir, Rohmer), as well as cinephiles and critics, like those writing for influential journals such as *Téléciné* (1947–1978), a publication distributed across the national ciné-club circuit. *Téléciné* tended to associate rhythm with the director's creation of order and symmetry within narrative time. For example, Henri Decoin's romantic thriller *La vérité sur bébé Donge* (1951) stood out for *Téléciné* critic Jeannine Marroncle not because it worked with the musicologist's carefully measured beats and nonrepresentational cues but by virtue of the oscillations it created between larger-scale "chunks" of plot. François Donge (Jean Gabin), a wealthy manufacturer and philanderer, is bedridden at the clinic of Doctor Jalabert (Jacques Castelot). His wife, Élisabeth (Danielle Darrieux), the "baby" of the film's title, had poisoned him. Marroncle wrote that "editing plays a significant role in the film. Scenes are often fragmented, giving the film a remarkable rhythm. Note in particular the scenes in François's hospital room, cut short by the 'atmosphere' of Jalabert's office. In this way the dramatic progression is skillfully developed." In other words, unlike Mitry, critics like Marroncle treated cinematic rhythm as a legitimate, distinctive expression of rhythm that depended not on the viewer's ability to tap his or her foot to it, but on the perception of meticulous control in the duration of scenes. The time of cinematic rhythm was to be measured not according to sixty or more beats per second, but in the length and coordination of large units of plot: "The duration of . . . scenes is minutely calculated. Thus the visits of Bébé [to François's hospital room] are very short . . . we could even say that they have very little 'presence.' In contrast, the moments where François, alone, is looking for his missing wife, last much longer."[30] The viewer becomes taken up in the film's rhythmic pendulum swing between these narrative threads. One scene shows François in bed, with Doctor Jalabert attending to him. Approximately one minute and thirty seconds later, Jalabert is called away just as the judge advising François arrives to consult him (call this segment A). One minute, twenty seconds later (after the completion of segment B), we cut to a very brief scene (segment C), almost exactly thirty seconds in length, with the Doctor, who has since taken a telephone call seeking expert advice about the severity of François's condition. We then cut back to François's hospital room, only to learn that a temporal ellipsis has taken place: the judge has left the room, and now sitting in front of François is Élisabeth. This segment (D), which ends when Elizabeth leaves François's room, lasts another one minute, thirty seconds. Finally, we cut to a final thirty-second segment (E) where the doctor completes his telephone conversation. Crosscutting and segmentation in the sequence create an alternation structure linking two lines of action at relatively regular intervals:

A (1:30)→B (1:20)→C (00:30)→D (1:30)→E (00:30)

For Marroncle, cinematic rhythm entailed the control of narrative durations.

But if the plot rhythms created by most filmmakers were intermittent, isolated, auteurs like Bresson, argued *Télécine* critic Janick Arbois, were taken with "the problem of composition" above all, expressing themselves *exclusively* through rhythms at the expense of "the habitual means used in cinema: the effects of *mise-en-scène* within a given shot, the value in itself of an actor's performance, links between shots through an elementary associationism."[31] For Arbois, Bresson was a uniquely "demanding artist" in an Apollonian sense: he possessed a "taste for perfection pushed to extreme meticulousness," especially in terms of "*la composition*" of *Journal d'un curé de campagne*. Sensing that the term would appear novel to his readers, he defined filmic composition as Marroncle would: "The repetition, alternation, or parallelisms of scenes, by the relation [*rapport*] of length between one scene and another."[32] *Journal d'un curé de campagne* develops a sustained rhythm through the many shots of the priest writing in his diary, which stood out for the "rhythm of their insertion," whence their "significance in the whole."[33] Bresson's art, in sum, was a new form of "writing on the screen" that allowed the auteur to consistently "express himself through shots of varying length and of varying angles."[34]

Taken as a whole, postwar film culture displayed a Dumesnilian flexibility in its understanding of rhythm. If *Téléciné* critics focused on plot rhythms, others perceived nonmusical rhythms elsewhere in a film's construction and in the viewing experience. Written by the president of the Union des cinéastes amateur du nord, Robert Bataille, the 1944 manual *Le savoir filmer*, endorsed by IDHEC president Marcel L'Herbier and a precursor to his popular *Grammaire ciné-graphique* (1947),[35] argued that the film auteur created rhythm at the level of the shot (through the speed of actor and camera movement), the sequence or scene (through varying shot durations), and the film as a whole (through a regulation of the viewer's attention and interest).[36] There were, Bataille claimed, four ways an auteur could ultimately manage the viewer's rising and falling attention: *teeth of a saw blade* interest is created with short passages that pique attention and short transitions that reduce it; *plateau* interest rises slowly but in fits and starts; *slope* interest also entails a slow rise but in a barely discernible manner; and *spike* interest is brusquely piqued and allowed to fall off just as sharply.[37] Jean Keim's *Un nouvel art: Le cinéma sonore* (1947), praised by contemporary reviewers as a standout among a wave of postwar books reevaluating film history,[38] worked through the "fusion of modes of expression" that French cinema had undergone in the 1930s when it borrowed heavily from music.[39] During editing, he argued, images and sounds were combined to follow continuous rhythms (a relatively stable flow in terms of duration and synchronization) or discontinuous rhythms, with alternations between "hard" and "soft" rhythm (created by varied durations between shots and sounds).[40] More ambitious filmmakers experimented with the "moving-image-sound" unit, Keim's cinematic version of the musical cue:

> The possible combinations are innumerable: a given rhythm can move faster, slower, can be interrupted, replaced by another, and recovered again; the changes made to rhythmic movement can affect either the entire moving-image-sound; or one of these elements alone; the themes created may not be complete in both components; they can include visual or sonic variations—subdivisions, collisions, returns; the melodies, stacked one on the other, can form a manifold of orchestrations of sound and light. Symmetry, opposition, balance, shock—the elements dance with one another; sometimes an element is swept back, modulating for the purposes of contrast or harmony.[41]

Finally, in 1946, the respected film-music composer Pierre Schaeffer wrote three widely cited essays for the influential film journal *La revue du cinéma* in which he proposed four localized forms of music-image rhythm. Among them are *synchrony* (when, as he puts it, "the rhythm of the music is tied very precisely to that of the image, or vice versa"[42]—he has in mind rhythmic effects like Mickey Mousing); and *syntony* (when image track and music work in different rhythms). Like Keim, Schaeffer believed that continuous (synchrony) and discontinuous rhythms (syntony) were possible in both musical and dynamic visual arrangements.[43]

Vitalistic Rhythms

Alongside these musical and panaesthetic discourses, rhythm became applied to broader and broader spheres of experience. As Michael Temple has shown, influential art historian Elie Faure wrote in *L'esprit des formes* (1927) about "cultural time" as a *grand rythme* "derive[d] from an alternation between the individual and the collective, between knowledge and faith, between periods of analysis and periods of synthesis."[44] Life itself was organized through discernible, though distinctly "non-metric," rhythms. The time of rhythm was now to be intuited in all things big and small, and its patterns were at times sub- or suprarational, unwieldy, pointing to the limits of musical metrics. Such vitalistic ideas about rhythm, indebted to the philosophy of Henri Bergson, entered the vernacular through the writing of various authors, like the widely read mathematician Matila Ghyka. Christian Kerslake reminds us that throughout the 1930s, 1940s, and 1950s, Ghyka's massively successful books popularized the notion that there existed a spectrum of organic and nonorganic rhythms in the cosmos, all of which are distinctive responses to, and emergences of, what Bergson called the *élan vital*, the vital force of Life. Ghyka's work dipped into the realm of esoteric thought and proposed a theory of proportionality—the geometry of spatial and temporal rhythms—that purported to unlock the key (a single golden number, *phi*) that governed the durational vibrations, the rhythms, and "cycles of instinct and respiration in living forms."[45]

We see the vitalistic approach in Gilles Deleuze's isolated commentary on cinematic rhythm in *Cinéma* (1983, 1985). It was Abel Gance's "superimpressions," for instance, sometimes sixteen images, all moving, superimposed over one another, that created a rhythm that presented to "the soul the idea of a whole as the feeling of measurelessness," of an expanse of life whose durations conflict and intersect, "a whole which changes and is Spirit (a great spiritual helix)."[46] Vitalism also informed the theories of one Jean-Pierre Chartier. Though largely forgotten today, Chartier was a major force in postwar film culture. Dudley Andrew writes that after majoring in philosophy at the Sorbonne, Chartier formed an exclusive film society with André Bazin during the Occupation (before joining the resistance), succeeded Bazin as the director of cultural services at the IDHEC, the national film school, and founded the Catholic weekly *Radio-cinéma-télévision* in 1950 (where Bazin published several important pieces and he wrote criticism under the pseudonym Jean-Louis Tallenay).[47] He also collaborated with Roger Leenhardt on two major post-Liberation documentaries (*La renaissance de la*

France, 1946, and *Départ pour l'Allemagne*, 1946). Perhaps more so than Deleuze, Chartier was a figure well positioned to inject the philosophy of vitalism into the auteur's craft practices.

In 1946, Chartier penned a five-part theoretical essay, "Art et réalité au cinéma," for the *Bulletin de l'IDHEC*. Part IV, "Rythme cinématographique et réalisme de la durée," argued that rhythm in film is altogether different from rhythm in music.[48] The ear, he contended, citing Bergson, is sensitive to subtle consistencies and changes in the length of tones and can thus intuit real vibrations in duration directly from musical meter. To argue that cinema achieved musical meter simply by regulating the length of shots is to return to what was for Chartier a naïve musical analogy of the kind he saw in the writings of Germaine Dulac. Unlike Dulac, Chartier put forth a theory of rhythm that acknowledged that cinema depended on "the durational relations . . . between scenes of life"—what the camera records from real durations. Rhythm therefore cannot be located in a film's cutting alone, in the form of a rigorous metric of shot durations (measured in seconds). Instead, he argued, we must incorporate into our theory of cinematic rhythm a Bergsonian psychology of differentiated intensive moments. Cinematic rhythm consisted of those vibrations in the viewer's attention that result from the coordination of shot changes with moments when the viewer's attention flags—that is, rhythm was generated when cutting efficiently moved the viewer through moments when attention was no longer seized by a gesture, word, or movement in a scene. Rhythm relied on cutting to sustain the stimulated engagement of viewers in a well-regulated flow of moments of intensive magnitude. More importantly, to sustain the viewer's immersion in a film's vibratory durations, these durations (and the editing that carries us through them) will correspond to "the usual prehension [grasping] of duration" in our real lives. Cinematic rhythm consisted not of abstract time, metrics, or the oscillation and pulsation of differentiated cues but of the more organic crests and troughs in the waves of everyday attention. "The camera permits the mechanical reproduction of real movements," but for a film to be a work of art, it "constructs a world" not through the use of mechanistic or clock time (what Henri Bergson called *l'étendu*) but by creating a rhythmic illusion of reality conceived as "la durée" (the time of active living).

In Chartier we see a drive to dissociate rhythm from rationalized order. In subsequent decades, other more prominent thinkers (who can only briefly be mentioned here) followed suit and promoted the breakdown of metrics, of values of proportionality and harmony, in notions of rhythm. Rhythm soon consistently pointed to realms beyond the verbal, the measurable, the cerebral. In *La révolution du langage poétique* (1974), Julia Kristeva reinvented rhythm as a disorderly feminine space, anterior to the sign, presymbolic.[49] Influenced by the philosophy of Gaston Bachelard, Henri Lefebvre viewed rhythm not as an object but a form of analysis—the decades-long, post-Fraissian effort to render rhythm as an exclusively virtual phenomenon was now complete. Rhythman-alysis, the namesake of his 1992 book, is "capable of listening to a house, a town as one listens to a symphony, an opera," and takes its bearings not just by study-ing the body but viewing the body as a primary orienting tool to understanding rhythm.[50] Furthermore, Gilles Deleuze, in his 1994 study of the painter Francis Bacon, proposed that rhythm is a direct sensorial impression, one that bypasses the cerebral.[51]

* * *

Film scholars like Philip Watts have argued that postwar film culture was a mod-ernist one that revived the classical Apollonian aesthetic criteria of simplicity, order, and symmetry.[52] By demonstrating that film culture participated in the creative extension of "rhythm," I have not only claimed that as musical, pan-aesthetic, and vitalistic notions of rhythm proliferated in the intellectual scene, the vernacular of film culture evolved with them but suggested that the more fluid notions of rhythm developed in film culture perhaps highlight, for us, a point where the Apollonian began to shade into the Dionysian, where classical modernist culture became mannerist. Technical control and ordered grace in the realm of editing and plot were also being replaced by a passion (expressed by Chartier) for variable notions of rhythmic time that responded to the durations of lived experience. Rhythm was being reconceived as something more intuitive for the filmmaker who, it was thought, ought to now distrust the idea of clock-work art and use style to dig up the deeper roots of time-based emotion and sub-rational, embodied intensity through a less rule-governed technical ambition. As we will now see, this rhythmic drift was pertinent to Bresson, who absorbed strict musical, panaesthetic, and vitalistic distinctions into his aesthetic theories and craft. But he did more than that. His experiments eventually revealed the artistic promise of his culture's increasingly Dionysian sensibility.

Bresson's Response: Le cinématographe

That is what I will eventually claim of Bresson's craft—that, over time, it skewed toward rhythms of a Dionysian sort (nonmetric, intuitively composed, embod-ied, and therefore nonmusical in the strict sense). But let's first determine what can be gleaned from his public remarks on the matter—from his vernacular of rhythm. It isn't necessary to prove that Bresson knew the work of these specific theorists and critics to demonstrate that the distinctions that animated their writings were alive in his thinking through of the limitations of mainstream cin-ema and his alternative to it, *le cinématographe* (writing in motion). His language alone reveals it. He eventually became taken with filmmaking problems that mixed what we can now call, for simplicity's sake, Dumesnilian with vitalistic concerns, admittedly in a residual form of his own preference.

As we saw in the previous chapter, Bresson considered himself a theorist but did not devise an *a priori* aesthetic system in isolation from film practice. By the late 1950s, Bresson had decided to dispense with the accepted label of *metteur-en-scène*, or "one who puts in the scene,"[53] to describe his role as a film-maker and turned to a title with a "rhythmic" and Apollonian flavor: *metteur-en-ordre*, or "one who puts in order."[54] He simply did not see any relationship between his craft and that of the theater director. While a popular term among his peers in the industry and, to be sure, among cinephiles writing for *Cahiers du cinéma*, *mise-en-scène* was for Bresson derived from theater and associated film directing with the act of staging and shooting actors on a set.[55] Bresson's art pointed in a different direction. *Mise-en-ordre* suggested an inventive process constrained by the need to place elements in just the right eloquent sequence or by the discovery of the appropriate position for individual parts in the carefully composed and harmonious temporal whole. In 1955, he boldly proclaimed to the filmmakers in training at the IDHEC that *mise-en-scène* "is not an art."[56] Music, however, was a legitimately creative medium, for it did more than simply copy reality or record a performance for posterity. If stripped of theatrical artifice, a film's images could take on the value of musical notes, which acquire their expressive force through juxtaposition: "I flatten, to the point where my image appears limp and lifeless, but when you put another one next to it, all of a sudden it takes on life. There must be transformation, and that's the only way to make cinema an art."[57] Sound and voice can also take on a musical quality. To insert the work of the actor into this transformative process, he worked with actors to give them "the pitch of the text, but not just the pitch, the speed, the rhythm: the *Tata ta*." The arts of the director and the actor thus became coordinated "just as a violin is in tune with a piano."[58] Furthermore, as he explained in a 1959 interview, during a production, "I do not direct anything. I take reality, pieces of reality, that I then put together in a certain order," using them to create rhythm, which "comes from precision."[59]

If he often relied on musical analogies, Bresson also believed that rhythm was the fundamental transformative power of art itself—a panaesthetic impulse. "In order for this system (which is the system of all art forms) to bear fruit," it was necessary for the filmmaker to overcome the camera's ability to reproduce the world before it: "For me, realism is not an end, but a means."[60]

The basic idea here is not entirely "Bressonian." The notion that pared-down shooting, staging, and acting were a means to achieving rhythmic configurations was also expressed by Roger Leenhardt, for instance, in a seminal 1936 essay, where cinema's capacity to avoid artifice was presented as a preparatory phase in the creation of a film's rhythm.[61] What is unique is that Bresson's sustained interest in, and exploration of, cinematic rhythm led to some of the most sophisticated, practice-based thinking about rhythm ever produced in film culture.

By the time his book *Notes sur le cinématographe* was published in 1975, Bresson had discovered that, through specific stylistic strategies, cinema could be transformed into a distinctive rhythmic form, *le cinématographe*, that liberated film practice from its subservience to representation as such—from its inherited codes of beauty, composition, and meaning—and accessed something purer, more directly bodily and experiential, a phenomenological flow of preverbal experience modeled on life as lived. Speaking with craft experience well beyond even that of filmmaker-theorists like Jean Mitry, who concluded, as we have seen, that narrative films could only achieve pseudorhythms that organized semantically rich signs, Bresson argued that fragmentation, among other strategies, could be employed to strip formal elements of constrictive meanings (in the Fraissian-Mitrian sense):

> ON FRAGMENTATION.
> This is indispensable if one does not want to fall into REPRESENTA-TION. See beings and things in their separate parts. Render them independent in order to give them new dependence.[62]

Le cinématographe, as he envisioned it, promised to be nonrepresentational in the sense that it "wrote" in visual sensations, in fragmented or isolated cues whose relative abstraction overwhelmed the viewer's ability to pin down any meaning in them: "See your film as a combination of lines and of volumes in movement apart from what it represents and signifies."[63] In panaesthetic terms, *le cinématographe* created its own equivalent to the musical note. Like a note, an image or sound need not carry a settled meaning in order to be substantive or have presence in the viewer's experience. This presence—this emergence to perception that fragments undergo—came from inserting these bits of time and space into rhythms (their "new dependence"):

> *Rhythms.*
>
> The omnipotence of rhythms.
>
> Nothing is durable but what is caught up in rhythms. Bend content to form and sense to rhythms.[64]

This new medium wrote directly in sound cues as well:

> *Rhythmic value of a noise.*
>
> Noise of a door opening and shutting, noise of footsteps, etc., for the sake of rhythm.[65]

Bresson's rhythmic fragments not only aspired to the noncerebral—to leave direct sensorial impressions on the viewer (*pace* Deleuze)—but to access the durations of life as lived (*pace* Chartier). *Notes sur le cinématographe* decried "the crude real recorded as is by the camera,"[66] so, like Chartier, Bresson denied that mechanical reproduction of real people and their movements alone created art or could capture the durational rhythms of life. "By choosing moments of action he has reproduced and by setting in order the shots thus obtained," Chartier wrote, "the director [*réalisateur*] does the work of an artist, for he constructs a certain temporal progression, he creates *la durée*."[67] Bresson had adapted this idea for his own purposes: "CINEMA seeks *immediate* and *definitive* expression through mimicry, gestures, intonations of voice,"[68] but "life cannot be rendered by photographic recopying of life."[69]

"The true is not encrusted in the living persons and real objects you use," he concluded. "It is an air of truth that their images take on when you set them together in a certain order. Vice versa, the air of truth their images take on when you set them together in a certain order confers on these persons and objects a reality."[70] "Placed in a certain order and projected onto a screen"—given a rhythm, in other words—the "living persons and real objects" he used "come to life again like flowers in water."[71]

Intermittently and thoughtfully musical, panaesthetic, and vitalistic, Bresson's writings about this rhythmic alternative to cinematic representation, *le cinématographe*, contributed to the creative extension underway in contemporary thought. But Bresson was above all an artist. The full range of his contributions to this cultural reinvention of "rhythm" is best appreciated through a detailed consideration of his films.

Plot Rhythms

Let us take one feature of Bresson's *cinématographe*—subject matter given form, sensation given rhythm. Both tasks are presented in *Notes sur le cinématographe* as aspects of rhythm's "omnipotence" in his film practice and entail shaping a film's subject to an organizational structure, and the viewer's sensorial impressions to the rhythms this structure depends upon. How did Bresson achieve this in practice and further push the bounds of film rhythm?

Bresson's affiliation with Objectif 49, a movement committed to the new avant-garde of postwar narrative filmmaking, meant that he sided with major critical voices like André Bazin in decrying the nonnarrative avant-garde of the 1920s for ignoring the popular narrative in favor of elitist nonnarrative experiments. Nevertheless, Bresson sometimes sounded nostalgic for this earlier era, when the market didn't require vanguard filmmakers to tell stories or employ actors. In 1963, he told Georges Sadoul, "I would give all the films in the world (and my films, too) for what I am looking for: little more than ten consecutive minutes of pure *cinématographe*, of something that comes alive solely from the beat of the images, and not because of facial expressions of actors."[72] Perhaps as a result of this combination of market and personal interests, Bresson split his craft between broader and looser plot rhythms and "purer," more precise editing rhythms that were sustained for brief periods of screen time. In this, too, Bresson was not alone. In his widely read essay on realism and rhythm alluded to earlier, fellow Objectif 49 auteur Roger Leenhardt observed that filmmakers can create both macrolevel rhythmic structures that unify an entire film ("découpage rhythms") and scene-length rhythmic flourishes ("montage rhythms").[73] Perceiving the problem of rhythm as one of both global plot structure and local clusters of sounds and images, Bresson worked through categories of thought available to other vanguard auteurs.

However, Bresson developed these different levels of rhythm in such a systematic way that, in my view, he deserves to be recognized as the single most important rhythmic filmmaker of midcentury France. In terms of plot rhythms, Bresson consistently explored the duration and oscillation of scenes, a panaesthetic approach of the kind *Télécine* critics observed in some skillfully made popular genre films like *La vérité sur bébé Donge*.

This is not to deny that other organizational principles play a role in Bresson's plots. For example, his adaptation of the Arthurian legend, *Lancelot du lac* (1974), experiments with some popular or mainstream principles by adapting the act structure scholars associate with classical Hollywood for new purposes. As Kristin Thompson has shown, the average film relies on an economical four-act paradigm—four movements in the protagonist's effort to achieve his or her goal, each separated by a turning point. *Lancelot du lac*'s hybrid storytelling approach combines acts that rely upon tight goal-oriented plotting with distinctly "unclassical" elements like mysterious turning points between acts where causal motivation is left unclear, thus inviting viewer speculation about the possibility of divine influence on the protagonist's life (a theme germane to the plot).

To illustrate, let's consider the film's formal arrangement. We begin with three precredit sequences (00:00–04:27), the last of which is a short scene showing an old woman predicting the death of he whose horse's steps can be heard (she is referring to Lancelot, the film's protagonist, who at this point is lost in Escalot). After the credits, the film is structured in terms of five acts.

Act 1 (06:13–25:40). In this act (the exposition), Lancelot, one of the Knights of the Round Table, returns to Camelot defeated, without having recovered the Holy Grail. He pleads with his love, Queen Guenièvre, to release him of his vow to her. King Arthur disbands the Round Table but believes that the miracle they require in order to find a sense of purpose again will come from Lancelot. Gauvain, another knight, goes to Arthur's side and pleads for a goal.

The goal now is to pray, the king replies. Lancelot tries to make amends with his enemy, Mordred, but fails. At the end of the act comes a mysterious turning point: Lancelot attends church to pray and asks for deliverance from his temptation for the queen. The causal relationship between his prayer and the goal-oriented action in Act 2 is never explained.

Act 2 (25:40–40:20). In the first scene of this act (the complicating action), two knights from Escalot arrive to invite the remaining Knights of the Round Table to a tournament. They have a fortnight to prepare (thus, a goal). Organized through "classic" intrigue, this act develops anticipation for the tournament in Act 3. The Lancelot plot now focuses on two obstacles that stand in the way of his goal: Mordred aims to kill him before the tournament, and Geneviève pleads with him to remain with her. Following her plea, Lancelot backs out of the tournament, but in another turning point mysterious in terms of causality, he suddenly decides to join the contest.

Act 3 (40:20–52:25). Now comes the development. On the day of the tournament, Lancelot appears in disguise. His goal now is to defeat his opponents. After doing so, he takes leave, and Arthur and his Knights debate whether it was Lancelot under the mask. One of the Knights reveals that he left the tip of his spear in Lancelot's abdomen. In a short scene with Geneviève, we are given a more conventional turning point (it raises a question the next act will answer): she wants to solve the Lancelot mystery.

Act 4 (52:25–1:03:19). The second half of the development is defined by a single objective: find Lancelot. Gauvain announces that two knights will search for him. Many declare him dead and believe that Geneviève will have to choose a new knight to protect her. But she is confident that Lancelot is still alive. The knights come upon the old woman from Escalot (the same from the precredit sequence). She has no news of his whereabouts. But she returns to her home where she tends to the injured Lancelot. Although she admonishes him that it would be foolish to do so, he feels tempted to return. In yet another mysterious turning point, Lancelot, believing that something is calling him, departs for Camelot.

Act 5 (1:03:20–1:20:14). In the film's climax, Lancelot is determined to resolve the conflict with Mordred, a goal that organizes the act. Geneviève asks him to avoid bloodshed. Lancelot learns of Mordred's plot to kill Arthur and orders his men to their horses to save their king. At the end of a highly elliptical confrontation between Lancelot, Mordred, and their men, Lancelot, fatally injured, staggers to a pile of bodies, utters Geneviève's name and collapses. His body goes limp.

Similar structures of narrative causality and goal-oriented characterization organize the plots of Bresson films from the 1940s (*Les dames du bois de Boulogne* follows Hélène's goal to extract revenge on her former lover, Jean), 1950s (*Un condamné à mort* recounts the POW Fontaine's effort to escape a Nazi prison), and 1960s (*Une femme douce* tells the story of the nameless pawnbroker's desire to understand his wife's suicide). Other films, like *Mouchette* (1967), are storytelling hybrids in a manner far more radical than *Lancelot du lac*. The plot is structured to oscillate between acts of "classic" intrigue with goal-oriented characters—in Act 3 (27:28–59:51), Mouchette becomes embroiled in the game-keeper Mathieu's confrontation with Arsène for stealing Louisa, the bartender, away from him—and acts that rely on thematically linked episodes alone—Act 2 (11:59–27:28) focuses on the theme of Mouchette's social and familial predicament and oscillates between scenes that show her elation and confident pride and scenes of her humiliation.

Alongside his explorations of character-oriented structuring principles, Bresson experiments with plot rhythms by repeating and varying certain themes, images, sounds, and plot situations, creating tight temporal (narrative) experiences. He accomplishes this in at least three ways: through recurring stylistic motifs (what I call the temporality of motivic patterning), oscillation or pendulum structures (the temporality of remembrance), and episodic structures (the temporality of ritual):

The Temporality of Motivic Patterning

On one level, Bresson's films create rhythms of plot by inserting the basic building blocks of film narrative—visual and aural cues—into motifs of repetition that allow these cues to emerge to perception as structures partially drained of plot significance, as patterns in their own right. These motifs run the course of the entire film and serve to imbue his narratives with the sensation of formal control, of compositional harmony, oscillation, and, periodically, subtle visual and acoustic modulation. Charles O'Brien points out that *Les dames du bois de Boulogne*, for instance, is a "rich resource of examples of the musical treatment of ambient sound," notably the noise of car horns, which is composed of a "post-synchronized repetition of the same two prerecorded sounds: first, a single bleat, and then a lower-pitch two-note honk."[74] Noël Burch observes that "while seemingly continuing to assign conventional meaning to dissolves," Bresson uses them "as a structuring element, as both a rhythmic and a plastic entity."[75] Brian Price traces the development of complementary, conflicting, and mixed hues in Bresson's first color film, *Une femme douce*. By "using color to represent the vacillations in, and ceaselessness of, the pawnbroker's thoughts," the film's pulsating color schemes reinforce the plot's temporal organization, establishing the salient beats in a narrative filtered entirely through the protagonist's thoughts.[76] Kristin Thompson argues that *Lancelot du lac* creates patterns that exist semi-independently from narrative motivations, using sounds (clinking armor, horse whinnies, bird calls) and visual motifs (various tents that decorate the settings, the abstract color designs that adorn the knights' saddles) "parametrically" by "introduc[ing] a device or pattern, then var[ying] it, often without regard to the causal logic" of the narrative action.[77]

Bresson also imbues his final film, *L'argent*, with rhythmic-temporal motivic structure through color design. The film utilizes variations on a red-yellow-blue primary triad to give the images a harmonious commonality that structures our experience of the plot and, in the penultimate murder scene, a sense of modulation when the triad is intensified and dispersed in time, each color dominant in three separate shots distributed throughout the film's climax. These effects give the film a subtle sense of temporal and emotional progression. In the first act (00:00–14:27), when the bourgeois adolescents Norbert and Martial arrive at a photography store to spend a fake bank note, a panning shot associates them with a particularly opulent, saturated iteration of the triad. Situated in the foreground, their attire is blue, while bright blue, yellow, and red-orange accents are spread across the busy Parisian intersection depicted in the background. The actors become elements in a compositional arrangement that ensures balance in the frame—foreground and background planes contain equally strong points of chromatic interest. This color scheme becomes a unifying motif in time when we are introduced to the film's protagonist, Yvon, a worker whose life is ruined by the fake note. In an over-the-shoulder shot showing him pumping oil into a nozzle, we see a more modest version of the triad, a scheme of pale yellows (the background wall), red-oranges (his gloves), and muted blue-greens (his jumpsuit). By the film's final act (57:02–1:20:42), Yvon is desperate and alone after serving time in prison for bank robbery. A gray-haired woman invites him to stay in the barn of her *banlieue* home. The triad does not completely disappear from the evenly lit, largely desaturated hues of this modest setting. Instead, it is used more sparingly and in the final moment of conflict "pops"—suddenly modulates in intensity for the purposes of graphic emphasis. Blue conspicuously dominates the image as Yvon awakens on the day he murders the woman and her family. That night, as he breaks into their home and makes his way through the kitchen, the golden light from a handheld lantern overwhelms the frame. Then, after Yvon swings an axe and kills the woman, crimson splashes on the wall at her bedside. The triad, now distributed as isolated dominants (blue followed by yellow, then red), imbue the final shot with a visceral, disturbing quality; the subtle modulating intensities of the waves and flows of primary color, serving to balance, unify, and lend a sense of order to individual shots in the film, instantaneously collapse as the image turns blood red. One might argue that Bresson's chromatic *mise-en-ordre* experiments with Robert Bataille's idea of a sudden rhythmic spike in a film's visual and narrative interest.

The Temporality of Remembrance

These isolated motifs often find context in plots organized in patterns of oscillation or pendulum swings. Some Bresson films cue us to attend to their fluctuations between simply drawn movements, spaces, and plotlines. Early critics found the tendency of his plots to swing back to familiar settings and situations somewhat perplexing. Almost dumbfounded, Luc Estang writes in his 1945 review of *Les dames du bois de Boulogne* that "one has never had the idea of overusing elevators and stairways to such an extent!"[78] Later critics began to see in these patterns the elements of a style; Manny Farber on *Une femme douce*: "The film is a geometric ballet of doors opening and closing, people exiting and entering, of objects or people moving into and out of range of the stationary camera." Scholars like David Bordwell have elaborated on this point. For Bordwell, *Pickpocket*, the sparse story of Michel, who becomes estranged from his mother and friends as he sinks into professional thievery, relies on shifts between Michel coming and going from his apartment ("Another director would vary our views of this locale far more," Bordwell speculates) and the virtuosic displays of subtle and innovative movement in the film's pickpocketing sequences: "The pickpocketing scenes gather their excitement from such nuances of handling as the fact that now the shots no longer hold on empty frames—a 'minimal' means of picking up pace. If the film did not break its cyclical repetition of set units with the more unpredictable and comparatively spectacular pickpocket scenes, it would be closer to the monodic construction of Bresson's later *Procès de Jeanne d'Arc*."[79] As sparse as cinematic storytelling gets, *Le procès de Jeanne d'Arc*'s plot follows a single solo line—the words exchanged during Joan's trial with only a handful of sequences showing spaces beyond the tribunal. As we will see, its rhythms are more local and stem from coordinating the tempos of line delivery and cutting.

There are deeper implications to the oscillating movements of the Bresson plot. Four of his thirteen feature films rely on subjective storytelling, on plots whose events are told from the protagonist's point of view (*Journal d'un curé de campagne*, which we discussed in chapter 3, but also *Un condamné à mort, Pickpocket*, and *Une femme douce*). Characters are granted authority to tell the story as they perceive it. In terms of rhythm, then, narrative form becomes determined by the embodied dynamics of remembrance.

If midcentury psychologists like Fraisse and film theorists like Mitry developed theories about rhythm's role in creating new memories,[80] Bresson's *cinématographe* explored memory's role in creating new rhythms. The screenplays of these four films rely on the inner world of memory images, which his characters experience through intersecting rhythms of past and present. In this, his art lends credence to an observation made by poet Paul Valéry, who wrote in 1914 that rhythm was an experience of simultaneity that collapses the distinction between linear moments in time: "In rhythm, the successive possesses certain properties of the simultaneous."[81] Bresson's insight also bears resemblance to cultural critic Walter Benjamin's theory of involuntary memories as "constellations of past and present," an idea formulated while reading Marcel Proust's *À la recherche du temps perdu*.[82]

The oscillating rhythms of remembrance in *Une femme douce* in particular grant the plot's movements back and forth between familiar and unfamiliar spaces and actions a dimension of simultaneity. Such was Bresson's intention. He balked at the suggestion, often repeated in reviews of the film, that he structured the narrative as a series of flashbacks. As he remarks to Charles Thomas Samuels, this is to ignore the life rhythms captured in his film: "I want to understand death, and I hate flashbacks. There are no flashbacks in the film: it is all the live husband now confronting his dead wife. Walking around the corpse, he says, 'I had only desired her body,' and there it is: dead. People saw the film as a series of flashbacks, but it is all life in the face of death."[83] He constructed the film as an alternation structure that moves rather briskly between a present life shaped by events that flash up from the past and a past seen through the eyes of a husband recollecting the life he shared with his dead wife. The past and the present, life and death are imbricated in one another—simultaneous in the act of remembrance.

Seen in this light, the film becomes one long experiment in the intuitive rhythms of oscillation. The narrative swings between short sequences set in the past and the present. Brian Price's observation that the husband's thoughts are ceaseless is astute; rhythmically, the film's narration almost feels unsettled, granting us access to his embodied impressions. After the opening suicide scene where we see the wife's shawl falling from their apartment balcony to the street below, we begin Act 1 (1:20–9:30). The husband is shown (in the present) pacing about, reflecting as his wife's corpse lies before him on his bed. At the end of this sequence, the camera tilts down to a circular object (a wash basin) and we cut to the next scene, which begins with a graphic match (a similar high-angle shot, this time a close-up of the palm of the husband's hand holding another circular object, a wedding ring). Set in the husband's pawnshop, the scene shows the young woman who becomes his wife entering with an item to sell. Thus begins the oscillation between sequences of the husband recollecting and sequences set in the past (and their first dealings when she pawns personal items to survive)—an A/B/A pattern. We also perceive patterns embedded within this pattern. At roughly even intervals, lasting ten, fifteen, or twenty seconds apiece, the film organizes our experience through recurring devices. In the first scene from the past, rhythmic tilts downward dominate the perceptual experience; the first comes at 2:57, then at 3:13, 3:32, and 3:50. When we swing back to the present (at 5:18), the tilting rhythms of the camera begin to organize the bedroom scenes as well. We begin with high-angle shot of the bed knob and tilt up at 5:26, and then moments later (5:35) Bresson provides another shot that tilts down toward the same bed knob. Just thirty seconds after we moved back to the present, we cut to a sequence in the past (5:47), and then back to the present (8:57) for another short scene to round out the act. These short interludes capture the husband's recollective state: the reasons for her suicide have little to do with their initial encounters when, as the husband states at the end of the act, "She was delighted with me." The plot need not linger.

We only return to the present approximately seven minutes later. But the film's rhythmic structure hardly breaks down. Act 2 (9:30–16:13) organizes the past through a very different rhythm, albeit one that builds on the recollective themes set in motion in Act 1. The husband's story now becomes a very classical one with predictable beats as he recounts the events leading up to their marriage through three-part scenes, each lasting approximately two to four minutes apiece (like the scenes in the past in Act 1) and composed of a beginning, middle, and end. The first three-part scene (9:30–11:26) recounts his marriage proposal (first part: he picks her up in his car; second part: they sit at the zoo of the Jardin des Plantes and he proposes to her; third part: she walks away, and he joins her next to the monkey cage [she is resistant to the idea of marriage]). In the second scene (11:27–12:41), he drops her off, and when she gets out of the car she tells him not to follow her home (part 1); he gets out and followers her (part 2); and in the stairwell to her apartment, he persuades her to leave this squalid abode and marry him (part 3). In the final three-part sequence (12:42–16:13), they sign the marriage certificate; they dine; and they enjoy an intimate evening in his apartment, where the wife's momentary elation is expressed through sprightly movements and the cacophony of car racing on TV.

The classical three-beat scene rhythms of Act 2—perhaps representing the husband's somewhat trite understanding of the progression of love (boy meets girl, boy nearly loses girl, boy regains girl)—are anomalous. The pendulum movements between past and present (A/B/A) return with force in Act 3 (16:13–41:48), where we witness the initial inklings of conflict in their marriage, and the tempo quickens—his search for answers leads to an unsettling rhythm. In a voice-over that appears in a short 45-second sequence set in the past, the husband confesses that he not only wishes to suffocate her youthful enthusiasm but to broaden her outlook, for until then, practical matters like finances mattered little to her. The narration begins to swing. In sequence 2 (set in the present, held for 14 seconds), the husband asks, "Why did we take to silence?" In sequence 3 (the past, 3 minutes, 29 seconds), he interrupts the exchange of glances between his wife and a male spectator at the movies. In sequence 4 (the present, 27 seconds), the husband speculates about what she wanted from life. In sequence 5 (the past, 32 seconds), the husband confesses in a voice-over that he was succumbing to jealousy. In sequence 6 (the present, 21 seconds), he describes her passion for books and records. In sequence 7 (the past, 1 minute, 16 seconds), the wife, listening to a record, suggests an outing to the natural history museum and leafs through an art catalogue of female nudes. In a very fragmentary sequence 8 (also in the past, 2 minutes 11 seconds), they visit the Louvre and then ride in his car to the country, where she picks flowers and looks at lovers in another car embracing. She throws her flowers away and returns to the car, where the husband gazes at her body, and after driving away, they nearly cause an accident but laugh off the incident. And in sequence 9 (the present, 14 seconds), the husband explains in a voice-over that they started to have problems when, while working at the shop, she paid more than necessary for pawned items. The rhythms here remain almost Valéryan; sound bridges (like snippets of music or the husband's voice-overs) and "hooks" (story elements evoked in one sequence that "hook into" the very next, like the records that connect sequences 6 and 7) suggest that these past and present events are temporally fluid, that they exist on a plane of simultaneity in the husband's psyche.

Act 3 continues on this way, as do Acts 4 and Act 5 (1:02:20–1:28:15), when, after her illness, the husband attempts to restore normalcy and his dominance, but she ultimately leaps from their balcony in the film's final scene (symmetrical, the film begins and ends with her act of suicide).

In *Une femme douce*, Bresson's *cinématographe* uses a flow of story fragments to capture the temporality of recollective imagination. The chain of memory images that overwhelm the husband as he mourns her loss, particularly given that this mourning is so ripe and suffused with guilt, is not a comforting one. The images seem to pilot themselves. His grief draws him away from the present moment; the succession of events transpiring now is interrupted by fragments of recollections that stir anxiety and blur the clear line that usually divides the present from the past tense of experience. And Bresson accomplishes this through the simplest of solutions: he fragments his plot into sequences in the present that reliably and predictably show the repetition of a few basic movements, like the husband circling his dead wife in the bed—images that have very little significance on their own—and sequences set in the past showing a richer variety of spaces and activities in isolated vignettes, like visiting museums. These plot fragments are then organized into a structure that gives them new rhythmic/temporal functions. Through controlled but deliberately not metrically timed intervals—relatively short sequences in the present intercut with relatively long sequences in the past—the film organizes our experience into an oscillating "beat" that allow us to feel alongside the protagonist the unruly durations of grief-stricken memory.

The Temporality of Ritual

If Bresson investigates the temporalities of remembrance in his first-person (subjective) narratives, his third-person (objective) stories at times rely on the temporalities of ritual. Ritual, like episodic memory, organizes experience through repetition. One of the foundational discoveries of midcentury French anthropology is that rituals are repeated sets of action that societies exchange, along with currencies, gifts, entertainments, feasts, and courtesies. In his classic *Essai sur le don* (1950), Marcel Mauss famously argued that, as a vital part of social life, from religion to politics to economics, rituals are consistently circulated and encourage circulation (of goods, be they material or conceptual), sweeping individuals into cycles of repetitive behavior.[84] Rituals reveal different ways of organizing time and space. The tribes Mauss studied, "these expeditions across the sea, these precious things and objects for use, these types of food and festivals, these services rendered of all kinds, ritual and sexual, these men and women,—were caught up in a circle, following around this circle a regular movement in time and space."[85] Ritual structures everyday life.

In some of Bresson's plots, we become aware of rhythm—of theme and variation and oscillation structures—through the patterns of ritual his characters experience. In chapter 1, we saw how *Les affaires publiques* is essentially a succession of variations on the theme of ceremonial rituals typically performed by a head of state (in this case, a farcical one). *Quatre nuits d'un rêveur*—whose title announces the film's four-part design—locks its protagonist's life into a rotating cycle of familiar situations. On four successive days, the young, lonely artist Jacques wakes in his sparse loft, listens to a recording of his voice recounting a romantic fantasy tale of love, lays a brushstroke on a vast white canvas, goes to the Pont-Neuf at night to console Marthe, a lovelorn, young woman, and has his conversations with Marthe interrupted by street performers singing love songs or playing the blues guitar. *Au hasard Balthazar* has a more complex, polyphonic plot that combines the principles of these two films to explore the rituals of a rural milieu caught between modernity and tradition. Bresson states that he worked with two intersecting temporal structures in the film—one cyclical, the other successive—both composed of archetypal rituals: "*Au hasard Balthazar* . . . is . . . two lines converging. . . . The first line: we discover in the life of a donkey the same stages as we find in the life of a man; childhood and its tender caresses, the age of maturity where for both man and donkey there is labor, talent and genius a little later, and finally the mystical period that precedes death. The other line is this: the donkey passed from owner to owner, who each represents a vice. And he suffers from it and dies from it."[86] Traditional religious rites (baptisms, processions, the last rites) and methods of transportation (the donkey Balthazar) clash with both the rituals of modern commerce and goods (like the sale and acquisition of Balthazar and the ridicule Marie faces from other teenagers because of her family's modest material possessions) and with the pursuance of vices that represent the waning of time-tested beliefs (like the lust that propels the film's adolescents into conflict with the old-fashioned sexual mores of their elders). Yet more rituals are tied in: the abuse (another vice) of Balthazar at the hands of various townsfolk and, perhaps most importantly

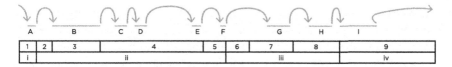

Fig. 5.1. Plot rhythms in *Au hasard Balthazar* (Bresson, 1966).

from a rhythmic standpoint, the ritual of reuniting as Balthazar's tortuous journey from owner to owner repeatedly returns him to the one character who consistently shows him tenderness, Marie. Rituals prove fundamental to the film's temporal *mise-en-ordre*.

I would argue that three, not two, narrative threads weave their way through *Au hasard Balthazar*. Figure 5.1 demonstrates how these sequences of ritual coexist in the film's one-hour-and-thirty-five-minute running time. A first line (i-iv) represents the four phases of the donkey's life where he experiences the archetypal rituals of spirituality, vice and of the rural marketplace. With (i) youth (1:51–6:04) comes a first trauma as he is taken from his mother. He is then baptized and consoled by the gentle caresses of children. Then come (ii) the typical experiences of animal labor (6:04–50:07), in which a mature Balthazar is trained, whipped, equipped with shoes, forced to pull a cart filled with dirt, and drag a plow, a chopped tree, and a bushel of hay. He eventually escapes and is reunited with Marie's destitute family, where he is used for transport (the town bully Gérard mocks them for it). He is sold to the town baker and becomes Gérard's means for making bread deliveries (the teenager repeatedly kicks and whacks him to urge him on). Driven to the point of exhaustion and nearly euthanized, Balthazar is saved by the town drunk, Arnold, who takes him on the road to carry his possessions. Booze-sodden, Arnold batters him more, but Balthazar flees. Next is (iii) talent and genius (50:07–1:17:19), where Balthazar is taken in by a circus and trained to perform mathematical tricks before awestruck audiences. Arnold reacquires him, but dies after a drunken binge. A greedy miller purchases Balthazar and whips him incessantly as he pumps *eau de source* for sale. This new master denies Balthazar basic sustenance, but he survives by drinking water collected from rainfall. Finally comes (iv) the mysticism of old age (1:17:19–1:35:22), as Balthazar is returned to Marie's family in the last of the film's economic transactions. After Marie runs away and her father dies, Marie's mother protects the old donkey from further labor and abuse and hails him a saint, and he walks in a religious procession.

Bresson subdivides these archetypal phases of life according to the situations Balthazar experiences with each new owner (1–9)—the second thread. As Balthazar is acquired, sold, purchased, and resold, he witnesses in succession the rituals of vice. James Quandt suggests that this thread appropriates a biblical structure:

"Passed from cruel master to cruel master, Balthazar traverses the Stations of the Cross, beaten, whipped, slapped, burned, mocked and, in the concluding crucifixion, shot and abandoned to bleed to death, the hillside on which he slowly perishes a modern-day Golgotha."[87] If in the end, as Quandt quite rightly points out, Bresson was not a religious allegorist,[88] he did conceive of Balthazar's owners as symbols (in Bresson's words) of "pride, greed, the need to inflict suffering, lust."[89] Jacques's family (1) (1:51–6:04) rips a young Balthazar from his mother (theft). A farmer (2) (6:04–9:57) initiates him to suffering. Now with Marie and her family (3) (9:57–23:03), Balthazar is served jealous kicks and knees from Gérard after Marie showed the donkey affection by adorning him with a crown of flowers. At the service of Gérard and the baker (4) (23:03–44:41), Balthazar is further exposed to the violence of male adolescence, as Gérard lights his tail aflame, and he witnesses lust as Gérard seduces Marie. Balthazar's next owner, Arnold (5) (44:01–50:07), succumbs to gluttony (alcoholism), and the fair (6) (50:07–54:50) introduces Balthazar to the suffering of other captive animals; he exchanges suggestive glances with a caged tiger, polar bear, monkey, and elephant. Returned to Arnold (7) (54:50–1:05:19), he is present for yet another display of gluttony when his owner rapidly spends a surprise inheritance, and for the capriciousness of lust as Gérard rejects Marie for another girl. Now comes greed: the miller (8) (1:05:19–1:16:19) rations Balthazar's food when he senses that the donkey has little life remaining, while Gérard abducts him from Marie's family (9) (1:16:19–1:35:22) to carry contraband across the border (which leads to Balthazar being fatally wounded by the gunfire of border police).

If this stream of vices organizes the film through an internal theme and variation structure, *Au hasard Balthazar* acquires an oscillating pulse through a third narrative line marked by the ritual of reuniting (A–I). As Balthazar moves through the cycle of life, he is exchanged among masters, but he also follows an itinerary that consistently—by chance, it would seem (the "hasard" of the film's title?)—swings him back toward Marie and her family. Around the middle of the film, the intervals that pull him away eventually become longer, while the periods where he reunites with Marie and her family get shorter—we alternate between relatively long and short durations. At end of a long stretch in Marie's care (3) (9:57–23:03), she begins to neglect Balthazar, which leads to his sale to the baker (4). Swapped between the baker, the alcoholic Arnold (5), the fair (6), and Arnold again (7), Balthazar drifts further from Marie. When they first reunite after his sale, she greets him with a gentle caress (C) (27:22–31:24); but she keeps her distance from Gérard and Balthazar when they arrive at her home after Gérard had taken her virginity (D) (32:01–33:10). Roughly ten minutes of screen time pass before a brief montage sequence shows Balthazar witnessing the sexual encounters between Gérard and Marie in an abandoned house as the seasons change (E) (42:18–43:46). Balthazar then swings away from Marie for five minutes of screen time, and we register just how far he has strayed from her when he swings back for a brief chance encounter not with her but with her father as he exits a city courthouse (F) (48:40–49:11).

The oscillations of plot that create the ritual reuniting of Balthazar and Marie (and her family) are central to the film's emotion structure. Increasingly severe rituals of trauma shape Marie's experience. Her father, a schoolteacher, tends to land owned by Jacques's family. At first, she experiences youthful bliss. As youngsters, with Balthazar at their side, Jacques and Marie pledge their love to one another. But Jacques's family moves away. When Marie enters adolescence, Gérard ridicules her and she becomes ashamed of her family's modest means. Balthazar is sold off against her will. Her family falls into destitution when her father decides—out of a "pride for his suffering," in Marie's words—to fight charges that he is embezzling from Jacques's father. Marie falls in love with the teenage boy, Gérard, who previously teased her and took her virginity. Rumors spread of her promiscuity, and her mother confronts her about the shame she is bringing to her family. Gérard rejects her at a dance, and she gives her body to the miserly miller, to whom she confesses that she no longer feels, loves. Gérard and his thuggish entourage then humiliate—strip and beat—her. The ritual of reuniting Marie with Balthazar serves at least two affective functions in this context. Their interactions become more and more estranged. Balthazar is almost part of the scenery when Marie barters her body to the miller in exchange for food and shelter (H) (1:09:04–1:16:18), and there is a single shot of her preparing to comb Balthazar when he finds himself back in her orbit and her parents' care (I) (1:17:17–1:24:02), but the moment is but a brief fragment (1:17:43–1:17:54), and we never actually see her caring for him. As these events transpire, we are reminded of the affection she once showed Balthazar and feel the extent to which her life's traumas have come to define her. Rhythmic, but hardly clockwork, their ritual reuniting soon reminds us of a *waning* ritual—that of the forms of affection—the gentle caresses, the crown of flowers—she once lavished upon him. And yet, seeing Balthazar and Marie back together here and there also raises the hope, as fleeting as the episodes themselves, that by caring for this ill-treated animal, Marie will regain the tenderness she has lost and perhaps share in his dignity—a dignity she so desperately seeks (and her mother so desperately wishes to restore) but which her adolescent folly, her father's aloofness, and the townsfolk's depravity continually deny her.

Editing Rhythms

These arrangements and temporalities of plot—stylistic motifs that arrange the perceptual textures of entire films and narratives organized through the patterns of memory and ritual—are but one facet of Bresson's contribution to the creative extension of rhythm. He also embedded local rhythms within these macrolevel structures and created strikingly distinctive pulsations of image and sound for brief periods of screen time. Like René Clair's scene-length rhythms in the early 1930s, his short flourishes of sound-and-image editing pushed cinematic rhythm to its Apollonian limits, creating an art of measured intervals and simple, controlled oscillations and durations. But it is also in these editing flourishes that we can truly appreciate Bresson's response to the Dionysian rhythms—more intuitive, elaborate, embodied durational forms—his culture increasingly embraced. And yet, how he responded to his culture was hardly culturally determined. He devised unique solutions.

Pacing a Scene: The Countess's Renunciation in Journal d'un curé de campagne

Initially, local montage or editing rhythms were a means for Bresson to solve the problem of pacing. No filmmaker committed to rhythm wanted to be charged with lingering; his scenes needed to follow a discernible beat or pulse.

We learned in chapter 3 that Bresson viewed *Journal d'un curé de campagne* as a challenge in faithful adaptation. Faced with the difficulty of remaining true to the Bernanos novel, Bresson seems to have felt that certain episodes needed to be presented in their entirety. Such is the case for one of the most iconic scenes in all of Bresson, the renunciation or medallion scene (42:06–52:39). In the English translation of the novel, the scene where the priest has an initially rather tense exchange with one of his parishioners, the countess, and eventually convinces her to renounce herself to God, unfolds over the course of 23 uninterrupted pages (of a 253-page text). Bresson cuts many lines from the scene, especially the longer speeches, like a page-long section where the priest scrutinizes the notions of Hell popular among laymen.[90] He instead retains the punchy back-and-forth of Bernanos's dialogue. When the countess selfishly suggests that her daughter Chantal's shame at her husband's infidelity is of no more consequence than her own, the priest replies: "Madame . . . be careful!" She snaps back: "Careful of whom, of what? You, I suppose." Transcribing these short lines word-for-word, Bresson retains the skeletal structure of the scene and keeps things moving along.

These adaptation choices leave Bresson with a ten-minute-thirty-second-long conversation scene, which as we now know, is remarkably long for a filmmaker whose scenes tended to be as short as thirty seconds and no longer than four minutes. Even with pithier snippets of dialogue, the sequence might appear as one large jumble of words—like the scene of a stage play where the "feel" and meaning of the exchange come from the lines and acting rather than from the auteur's cinematographic *mise-en-ordre*.

Critical of the theatrical, Bresson reinterprets the dramatic conversation as a challenge in rhythmic design and devises a subtle solution. He inserts into the conversation patterned breaks that create an oscillation effect as we shift at controlled intervals (accented by a repeated element of style, a sound cue) between segments of quick bursts of dialogue and segments where there are noticeably no words at all—none of which are in the novel. In short, the scene takes on the character of a performance not of the actors but of the auteur regulating the pacing of these oscillations.

With these breaks, the scene unfolds in seven distinct segments of increasing then decreasing durations. Each segment is interrupted by a moment of silence on the dialogue track and the sound of an offscreen rake, a prop whose appearance onscreen is strategically delayed until the final segment:

Segment 1 (shot 186; 16 sec.). The priest enters the grounds of the countess's *château*.

Transition: offscreen raking sound over a dissolve.

Segment 2 (shots 187–188; 63 sec.). In the countess's sitting room, the two characters discuss Chantal, whom he fears will commit suicide. The countess rises and walks over to a window to shut it.

Transition: offscreen raking sound during a break in the conversation.

Segment 3 (shots 189–195; 65 sec.). The countess resigns her and her daughter to the continued infidelities of the count. After conceding the failure of the intervention, the priest makes his way to the door.

Transition: offscreen raking sound during another break.

Segment 4 (shots 196–206; 107 sec.). The priest confronts her for casting Chantal out her home: "God will break you." But she no longer fears Him, for she has had to endure the loss of her son.

Transition: offscreen raking sound during another break.

Segment 5 (shots 207–210; 110 sec.). The priest reminds the countess that she risks losing God's love, and demands that she resign herself to Him.

Transition: the offscreen raking sound overlaps with dialogue (the priest tells her that she is face-to-face with God) and continues during a break in the conversation.

Segment 6 (shots 211–221; 159 sec.). Spent, the countess gazes at a medallion containing a photograph of her dead son. "What must I say to Him?" she asks. "Thy Kingdom comes," he replies. She prays.

Transition: the offscreen raking sound overlaps with dialogue (the countess repeats his prayer) and continues during a break in the conversation.

Segment 7 (shots 222–231; 113 sec.). Chantal eavesdrops from just outside the window. The source of the sound is revealed: a gardener raking pebbles outside in shot 223. The countess, feeling that her life has been turned topsy-turvy, casts the medallion into a fireplace, but the priest recovers it and reassures her with a blessing.

The ascending/descending pattern of the intervals between the offscreen sound effect (and the absence of dialogue it accents)—from roughly 60-second to 110-second to 160-second and back to 110-second periods—supported by other elements of style like stillness and motion of the actors and relatively close and distant framings, mark the countess's abandonment of her distant attitude toward her daughter and the Almighty as a series of six movements clearly (if subtly) delineated in time. The success of Bresson's experiment here is precarious for Fraissian-Mitrean reasons. In narrative cinema, elements of film form carry semantic or symbolic value. Too intrusive a cue—like the weighty sounds of a church bell—would have imposed constricting symbolic meanings on the viewing experience and disrupted its organic rhythms. But somewhat abstract (the sound has no prior associations, either in the film or culturally), delicately mixed at a lower pitch and volume than the voices, and inserted into the breaks between the phases of the countess's renunciation, the raking sound becomes the means through which Bresson discovers not the symbolic themes but the rhythms of Bernanos's scene. In other words, the sound rewards attention as evidence of authorial control—a Dumesnilian pleasure favored by a culture that evaluated but also felt films through the formal structures innovated by their auteur. In fact, for some, solutions like this marked a change in Bresson's approach to affect and form. André Bazin famously remarked that if *Les dames du bois de Boulogne* "could not touch us without us, if not understanding its method, at least feeling its method and grasping its structure," *Journal d'un curé de campagne*'s "aesthetic system" "speaks more to our hearts than to our minds."[91] Perhaps the genius of *Journal d'un curé de campagne*'s craft ultimately rests somewhere in between, not in choosing the heart ("warm" internal or spiritual feeling) over the mind ("cold" formal structure), but in creating forms that are delicately embedded in the tender movements of the spirit.

Speaking Tempo: The Second Trial Scene in Le procès de Jeanne d'arc

After *Journal d'un curé de campagne*, Bresson tended to avoid lengthy dramatic scenes of this kind. He preferred to chop his narratives up into smaller units of plot—they were better suited to his discovery of new rhythmic forms. But he returned to the problem of sustained conversation and its tempo with *Le procès de Jeanne d'arc*. Now the technical problem was much more pronounced because, as we saw earlier, this film consisted of a single narrative line, like Francis Seyrig's monophonic drum roll over the film's opening credits and final shot. Rhythm no longer came from a plot structure that oscillated between past and present or various narrative threads, but had to be discovered in a linear string of conversation scenes. He told *Cahiers du cinéma*, "Every new film poses new problems, completely different problems from those posed in earlier films. My first problem [for *Le procès de Jeanne d'arc*] was that of a film consisting entirely of questions and answers. . . . I gave them rhythm. The uniqueness of this film is that the rhythm of speech drove the rhythm of the images."[92] So persuaded of the "musical" quality of his solutions that he released the dialogue track as an LP record.[93]

Each of the film's trial sequences is a rhythmic experiment unto itself. Let us take as an example the second of these, which lasts just over three minutes of screen time (5:20–8:31). If we exclude the last four shots, which contain no dialogue among the principal characters and show Jeanne leaving the courtroom, the sequence is composed of 36 shots (shots 11 through 46 in the film) and has an average of 3.63 words per second and 18 words per shot (650 words in total)—rates comparable to those calculated by Lea Jacobs in her analysis of the maestro of fast-paced dialogue, Howard Hawks.[94] The image track relies on a simple shot/reverse shot editing scheme as we cut from Jeanne to her interrogator Bishop Cauchon and, on occasion, to another judge, Jeanne's counsel Isambart, a monk, and stenographers recording the exchange. Three solutions establish the sequence's beat. First, early in the exchange, Bresson allows line delivery to dictate the pace of the cutting. Shots are permitted just one short sentence or question—a one-line-per-shot tempo. Shots 14, 15, 16, and 17 follow a beat one could tap one's foot to. The speaking rate (3.5 words/sec.), the brevity of the lines, the coordination of the cutting with line delivery (the average shot length is 2 seconds), and the avoidance of dialogue overlap between shots (which, in other parts of the sequence, blunt the effect of the cut on our perception of the oscillation between characters) create a rhythmic pulsation as Jeanne defiantly questions the need to pledge a second oath of truth:

> Shot 14. 2 sec. Jeanne: "Faut-il jurer deux fois en justice?" (Must I swear twice before the court?) (3.5 words/sec.) /cut/
>   Shot 15. 2 sec. Cauchon: "Voulez-vous jurer simplement et absolument?" (Will you swear simply and absolutely?) (3 words/sec.) /cut/
>   Shot 16. 1 sec. Jeanne: "Vous pouvez bien vous en passer." (You don't need it.) (6 words/sec.) /cut/
>   Shot 17: 3 sec. Cauchon: "Nous vous requerons de jurer de dire la vérité." (We require you to swear to tell the truth.) (3 words/sec.)

In the words of critic and screenwriter Philippe Arnaud, "the alternating beat between [shots of the different] seats in the courtroom . . . becomes a rhythmic indicator [*curseur*], a scansion that marks the continuity of this confrontation with a brief syncopation."[95] A few moments later, in shots 22 through 25, the underlying principle shifts slightly; the pace of line delivery now bends to the rhythms of the image track. The cutting continues to flow at 2–3 seconds per shot, and to maintain this editing rhythm, the shots that contain more dialogue utilize faster delivery. In shot 24, the actor playing Cauchon poses a ten-word question delivered at an amazing rate of 6.67 words/second (the shot is held for approximately 1.5 sec.)— a sudden burst of speed that prevents the line and the shot from feeling any longer than those surrounding it (the line: "Par le conseil de qui avez-vous pris l'habille d'homme?" [On whose advice did you dress as a man?]). Then, when the pace of the cutting slows and Jeanne is left to respond to a question in a longer-held take, the visual stimulus of nodding downward on the part of the actress picks up the beat—that is, mimics the pace of the cutting elsewhere in the sequence. In shot 28, held for 31 seconds, she nods every 3 seconds, always between her lines of dialogue. This pendulous pattern of looking down and falling silent, then up to speak endures until the last three nods in the shot, which are separated by 4- to 5-second intervals—she nods at 6:27, 6:30, 6:33, 6:37, 6:40, and 6:45. Finally, Bresson slightly disrupts these rhythms—in fact, renders these sustained rhythms more salient—through silent intervals between a question and an answer. The strategic interruption of these coordinated visual and aural rhythms creates a shock—a sudden moment of tense anticipation. In shot 37, Cauchon asks: "Croyez-vous être dans la grâce de Dieu ?" (Do you believe you are in God's grace?) This is followed by one of the few shots in the sequence with no dialogue—a one-second shot of the hands of the court stenographers recording the question. These interruptions reveal how dominant the 2- to 3-second pulse—of complete lines, edits, or glances downward—remains throughout the scene.

Flirtatious Beats: The Bumper Car Sequence in Mouchette

We noted earlier that *Au hasard Balthazar*'s rhythms rely on an oscillating plot structure—a reuniting of two of the film's protagonists—to suggest the possibility of a life free of the traumas they experience. *Mouchette* accomplishes a similar shift in affective tone through a short, isolated flourish. One of the most commented upon passages in Bresson's oeuvre, the bumper car sequence (21:03–23:30), while brief, is quite resonant. Keith Reader writes that it is the protagonist's "one true moment of pleasure. She whirls around at the wheel of her car, gleefully colliding with others and smiling flirtatiously with a young man, in a scene with no equivalent in the novel, whose fleeting celebration of the joy of movement evokes the motor cycle ride in *Journal*."[96] Once again, Bresson alters a Bernanos source text, this time adding an original sequence whose sensuality finds form through rhythm.

Rhythm now emerges from the impact of bodies. If the rhythms of sound (the rake) in *Journal d'un curé de campagne*'s renunciation scene were disembodied, elegant, unassuming, the raking sound's source ambiguous, and its purpose fairly formal, then sound and image editing in this sequence from *Mouchette* is intimately linked to the main line of action and creates a rhythm that is relatively hot (at least, for a Bresson film), expressive, and erotically charged. Mouchette, like Marie from *Au hasard Balthazar*, is subjected to numerous rituals of humiliation and violence. Act 2 (11:59–27:08) is organized thematically, introducing the viewer to the variety of public traumas the young girl experiences, which compound those of the private space of her poor home, where her mother lies dying and Mouchette must care for her baby brother. When she arrives at school at the beginning of the act, we see immediately that she experiences something different than the innocent glee of her classmates—Bresson contrasts their pace of movement. While the other children flock into school with energy and enthusiasm, she walks alone, slowly, dragging her feet, made heavier by the grown-up shoes she awkwardly fills. In class, her teacher violently pushes her to the front of the room when she refuses to sing a patriotic tune about hope. Humiliated before her classmates, her head is forced close to the ivories of a piano, and when she fails to strike the right note, everyone glares and laughs at her as tears begin to flow down her cheeks. Her life has its own music, as we will see—blunter, inelegant, and less socially sanctioned.

After class, she throws mud at the dresses, satchels, and hair of the other girls, as if trying to make them look as soiled as hers, and they respond by exposing their posteriors to her—by "mooning" her—while, moments later, we witness more childhood pantomimes as two boys call her over and one "flashes" his genitalia. Adults react in ritualistic ways as well. Later in the same act, when Mouchette splashes in a puddle of mud before church, her father, repeating the gesture of the teacher, shoves her aggressively for her insolence. But the tone of the film shifts, at least momentarily, when she attends the local fair.

For reasons never explained, a woman holding a toddler gives Mouchette a chit for the bumper cars—perhaps an act of charitable kindness but certainly a mysterious plot twist of the kind that structures *Lancelot du lac*. Mouchette climbs into a car, begins to spin about, and a few moments pass before she is bumped and the collision lets out a metallic thud (1) (21:36). We hear it again when she is bumped 3.9 seconds later (2), then 4.4 seconds (3) after that. A pattern of relatively even but slightly ascending intervals controls the temporal structure of the sound editing. (That this was Bresson's intention is clear from the fact that between (2) and (3) Mouchette is nudged by another car, but no sound accents the impact.) Some 4.6 seconds pass, and the front of Mouchette's car slams into that of a smartly dressed young man (4). For the first time in the sequence, a collision results in an exchange of glances—Mouchette stares offscreen right at him and in a reverse-angle shot he returns the look, simpering slightly. A new acoustic rhythm begins to organize the action. Now for much of the sequence, Bresson doesn't simply organize the impacts through evenly measured intervals. He pairs them off: a relatively long interval will be followed by coupled sounds—bump, bump! After their exchange of glances, Mouchette and the boy drift from one another, and six seconds pass before we hear a bump as he is hit by a stranger (5); after 2.1 seconds, two strangers collide (6); then a longer interval of 5.9 seconds passes and the collision comes as Mouchette veers around for another strike on the young man, but he is nudged by yet another stranger (7); a shorter interval of 1.6 seconds elapses as the young man returns the favor on the stranger (8); the young man rocks another car offscreen 5.9 seconds later (9). The intervals between the metallic thuds (4–9) are astonishingly measured (figure 5.2).

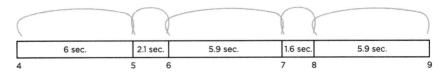

Fig. 5.2. Sound editing rhythms in the bumper car sequence of *Mouchette* (Bresson, 1967).

As the sequence progresses, these coupled sound cues begin to express the budding flirtations between Mouchette and the young man. After another 4.1 seconds, he bumps the back of Mouchette's car. She glances at him with a full grin, and he flirtatiously reciprocates. Just over 6 seconds afterward, she slams another car, and then two cars hit behind her 0.7 seconds after that. The young man once again catches her off guard with an aggressive bump from behind 7 seconds later. And then two descending intervals: 4.6 seconds pass and two strangers hit; 2.9 seconds tick away and Mouchette's and the young man's cars smash nose to nose. Another shot/reverse shot: they share smiles, showing more teeth and more affection. The intervals become shorter, but the coupling of bumps remains: 7 seconds, Mouchette bumps him; 1.8 seconds, two strangers bump; 2.7 seconds, two more strangers; 2.1 seconds, a stranger bumps Mouchette; 4.6 seconds, the young man bumps Mouchette from the rear; 1.3 seconds, two strangers; 3 seconds, Mouchette and the young man; 0.8 seconds later, the impact sends Mouchette into the car behind her; 4.7 seconds, two strangers; 2 seconds, the young man hits Mouchette from behind again, and they continue exchanging evermore brilliant smiles; and so forth.

Though it would be trite to do so, it is tempting to read this pulsation of collisions as the lub-dub of their young hearts, the most elemental of rhythmically paired sounds. The sequence's staccato cues do give a rising sense of heat, of bodily eros, but the sensation is precognitive; the collisions do not materialize as an analogy. We aren't given space to extrapolate the symbolic implications. We become embroiled in the nervous excitement. The experience is ludic, and spatial logic collapses. In one shot, their front bumpers slam into one another. In the very next one, Mouchette suddenly finds herself in the position to catch him from behind. Sonic consistency is overridden by the demands of the rhythm of flirtatious play, too. Some cars collide but the sound effect is suppressed to maintain the "bump-bumps" that shape our sense of time. In parts of the sequence, longer and longer gaps are paired with shorter and shorter ones. The longer intervals stretch from 3 to 5 to 10 seconds, while the shorter ones simultaneously shrink from 4.5 to 3 to 1. The collisions gain force with increasingly forte bursts. By matching this intensifying temporal and acoustic experience with inserts of their glowing visages, Bresson creates a visceral sense of mounting elated pleasure—a brief taste of it, at any rate, in a film about the tragic life of a character who will be scolded by her father for this frivolous display and ultimately, after enduring more traumas, commits suicide. But the sequence's youthful energy, its rhythm, remains with us as a glimpse of a life this young girl might have lived.

The Alienating Rhythms of Modern Life: The Public Transportation Scene in Le diable, probablement

If *Mouchette*'s editing rhythms are more embodied than those of *Journal d'un curé de campagne*, it is by virtue of their depiction of the temporalities of affect and physical encounter. The brute sounds of collision emerge in the rhythmic *cinématographe* as the intensifying expression of youthful desire. But the rhythms of *Mouchette*, while embodied, remain fairly musical in their dependence on a relatively controlled metric and the principle of oscillation between long and short intervals. *Le cinématographe* organizes these bodies into a preconceived, abstract structure—paired beats.

Editing rhythms in the films we've examined thus far stem from an Apollonian impulse. A single rhythmic line—composed of a recurring rake, 2- to 3-second intervals between line deliveries and cuts, the thuds of bumper cars—lends order and harmony to the sequence. But in Bresson's most conceptually and formally complex display of scene-length rhythmic design the depiction of bodily movement and tempo is more organic—metric control and unity through a single formal structure or stylistic motif break down. In the sequence to which I refer, from *Le diable, probablement*, Bresson takes on the problem of temporalities of the body where order cannot be sustained, where the vibrations of experience intensify to the point of creating unpredictable beats, disorderly irruptions, and repetition patterns so dense that they overwhelm the viewer's ability to assimilate them.

With *Le diable, probablement* Bresson turns toward the Dionysian or mannerist rhythms suggested in Jean-Pierre Chartier's vitalistic theories—toward a rhythm that moves closer to the eccentricities of life. The principles of musical composition that have governed his editing rhythms until now (repetition and variation, oscillation, periodicity) are placed at the service of new durational forms derived from lived experience. Localized forms of musical order are made to serve a governing impression of vitalistic disorder.

That Bresson would concern himself with disorderly life rhythms in *Le diable, probablement* perhaps should come as no surprise; he wrote the film's original script as a personal form of direct commentary on the feeling of disillusionment and aimlessness among young people in the post–May'68 moment. In May 1968, waves upon waves of French student and worker protests sought, through sit-ins, occupations, marches, and violent uprisings, to challenge the capitalist base of French society, expand worker's rights, and overthrow the regime of President Charles de Gaulle. Major auteurs joined the effort with increasingly radical storytelling forms.[97] Brian Price argues quite convincingly that *Une femme douce*'s color design and locations were expressions of solidarity on Bresson's part.[98] Bresson now felt compelled to address the aftermath of this near-revolution: "It's the first time I felt the need to express in the most direct way possible my own revolt against what is going on around me."[99] This "direct way" took thematic and rhythmic form.

From a certain standpoint, the film builds on previous experiments with plot rhythm. *Le diable, probablement* has an episodic-ritualistic structure, following the string of at times futile encounters and conversations of the disillusioned *soixante-huitard* Charles (Antoine Monnier). In search of a purpose—not unlike the Knights of *Lancelot du lac*—he attends an anarchist rally, debates environmental politics, joins with hippies singing on the bank of the Seine, and has his problems diagnosed by a psychoanalyst. He does all of this while continually exchanging his thoughts about the purpose of life and, somewhat ironically it sometimes seems, the most efficient ways to commit suicide.

However, the film's commentary on the seeming futility of post–May'68 radical causes comes through most forcefully in its editing rhythms, especially during the scene of public transportation where passengers contemplate the "hidden forces" that govern their existence (shots 415–439; 49:53–51:54). Like the sequences showing the husband circling his dead wife in *Une femme douce*, editing on some level seems to impose a unity on the sequence by cutting back to the protagonist, Charles, and his friend Michel as they are seated on a bus. These young intellectuals strike up a political conversation that workers around them eventually join. However, if the swinging movements of *Une femme douce*'s plot are relatively fluid—past and present merge with one another in the character's experience—the oscillations away from the protagonists in the bus sequence are more disruptive. The camera almost wanders away from them, and the viewing experience becomes distracted, here and there tempting shapelessness. The intervals that draw attention away from the conversation form variable clusters of at times somewhat abstract visual and acoustic stimuli. They draw us into the fragmentary impressions that constitute the flow of ordinary experience aboard the bus. Strategically, no single cluster of stimuli carries the sequence's rhythm. Instead of experiencing rhythm through a thin thread of familiar, reassuring elements, the viewer is given a dense weave of forms alienating in their digressive, abstract quality. Diverting us from the protagonist's conversation (ostensibly the narrative core of the scene) and overwhelming it in the process, the bus sequence implicates us in a swirl of impressionistic rhythms, leaving us with an unclassical sequence that tests our ability to discern its center—the truly dominant formal thread around which the sequence's subordinate forms are organized. Each disruptive cluster holds our attention briefly—becomes its own decentralized center—before ceding to the next cluster in unpredictable ways.

Initially, even the conversation between Charles and Michel seems to have no direction. In shot 416, Charles, seated on the bus, abruptly asserts, perhaps in reference to the lecture they heard in the previous scene about the effects of nuclear power and warfare: "What's amazing is that to reassure people you simply have to deny the facts."

"What facts? We are entirely supernatural. Nothing is visible," Michel retorts. "You're unbelievable," Charles shakes his head. Interrupting this fragment of conversation, a male passenger enters the shot from offscreen right and crosses leftward in front of Charles and Michel. The sound of his footsteps is heard, calling attention to his movements. We digress into the first rhythmic cluster.

In the first cluster (shots 417–426; 30 sec.), rhythms are created through repetition and variation—the experience is organized through rich color accents, movements of truncated figures across the frame, sound cues (footsteps, tickets being punched), and attention-grabbing objects (mirrors). However, the patterns are densely woven—at times, difficult to discern. In a 1-second shot, the same passenger (still moving leftward) presses a stop-request button. The soundtrack has been pared down to the man's footsteps. A 2-second insert: an *arrêt demandé* (stop requested) sign lights up with red lettering. In a 2.5-second shot, we see the bus driver, with his back to the camera, truncated by the frame. He reaches leftward to a panel dotted with red lights and presses a button. Another 2-second insert fragments the space: a strikingly abstract composition reveals the mirror above the rear exit of the bus. The door opens. For another 2.5 seconds, three passengers are shown walking rightward down the center aisle of the bus; we hear the taps of their footsteps. We see and hear passengers moving leftward now, exiting the door (4.5 sec.). As they do so, a peculiar repetitive sound appears from offscreen. The next shot (4.5 sec.) confirms its source: several figures shown from the chest down, fragmented, move leftward, pause, and validate their bus tickets—thump-thump. We might pick up on the fact that the insertion point on the validation machine has saturated red contours. With a steady flow of footsteps on the soundtrack, we see three passengers pass in front of the camera and hear two tickets punched at relatively even intervals. In the next shot (2 sec.), two passengers—again, truncated—walk rightward. A 1-second close-up: the bus driver releases the button. Cut to a 5.5-second shot: the bus's forward doors now—next to a bright red fire extinguisher—close. We no longer hear footsteps, and the bus drives off as the motor roars.

The plot event here is a simple, linear one (passengers getting off the bus), but these unusual visual and aural patterns, interwoven in unpredictable ways—odd camera angles that distract us with a point of perceptual fixation, headless bodies moving in something resembling a pattern (right-left-left-right), a tantalizing saturated-color motif that stands out against the otherwise neutral scheme of the bus but really doesn't lead anywhere, mechanically repeated gestures and movements that seem cyclical rather than linear (each accompanied by a simplified sonic profile)—amazingly render these basic actions somewhat opaque, distant, and frustrate efforts to set them to a regular "beat."

The second cluster (shots 427–434; 30 sec.) shifts emphasis and offers rhythmic digressions within—that cut through—snippets of conversation. Slightly off-balance, we don't see it coming: we suddenly cut back to Charles and Michel. By now, their conversation has moved on. Charles asserts: "Governments are short-sighted." A male passenger sitting in the seat in front of them pivots and replies: "Don't accuse governments. At the moment, no one, no government in the world can boast that it's governing." He turns back around: "It's the masses who determine events." Now the seat covers are red, picking up on the first cluster's color motif, but the pattern somehow seems less potent in cluster two. "Obscure forces whose laws are completely beyond our ability to know them," he continues, in a statement that might describe the viewer's experience of the sequence itself. The second half of this line leads into a visual digression: for 8 seconds we hold on a new abstract shot of a mirror, this time with the camera pointing outside the bus driver's window. The shot's ambiguous status diverts our attention its way—do these mirror shots capture his point of view? In the mirror and the background of the shot, cars zoom by in multiple directions. The rhythms of an image track invested in the temporality and directionality of traffic now begin to compete for attention with the rhythms of disembodied speech—short, unexpected one-line bursts. A female passenger intervenes: "It's true that something is driving us against our will." A third passenger, male, replies: "You have to keep moving along, moving along." A fourth male passenger, now shown on the image track, interjects: "And we do move along with it." But after this brief coordination of sound and image—speech is embodied once again—we oscillate back to the abstract shot of the mirror and its reflections of traffic (for 3.5 sec. now), and a fifth male passenger, unseen, asks: "Who is it that is making a mockery of humanity?" Several more cars drive toward screen left, including a bright red one. A passenger asks: "Yes, who is leading us by the nose?" The camera is now positioned in front of the passenger who earlier claimed power for the masses. "The devil, probably," he answers. In shot 434, Charles nudges Michel with his elbow in a gesture of approval.

Why shoot a conversation scene this way? The final cluster (shots 435–439; 43 sec.), equally unpredictable in terms of rhythm, begins to provide answers. In the first shot, we are surprised to find that the bus driver is now torqued, looking at the passengers behind him. He suddenly pivots to look out the windshield at the road ahead. A close-up shows him slamming on the brake pedal. Tires screech offscreen. The screeching stops as we hear the offscreen sound of the bus smacking a vehicle, presumably an oncoming one—sounds of metal slamming against metal, and glass shattering across the pavement, occupy the soundtrack. As this happens, the camera fluctuates, and the passengers are thrown forward from the force of the impact. We return to the shot of the bus driver pushing a button to open the forward doors of the bus. The driver leaves his seat, pauses at the center of the frame to remove his wallet from his back pocket, and exits the bus. The disorder of a traffic accident produces order of a fresh sort: a few seconds after the driver leaves the frame, a high-pitched car horn is heard offscreen (horn A). A slightly lower-pitched horn (horn B) follows twice. Horn A is heard again, then horn B—an A/BB/A/B oscillation, which is followed by a pattern of longer and shorter sequences of honks—ta-tatatata-ta-tatatata-ta—and so on.

The vitalistic rhythms of Bresson's *cinématographe*—multiform, often disruptive, conflicted, shifting randomly from metrically measured to looser patterns of experience—evoke one form of alienation experienced by the working class. This unharmonious yet intertwined medley of rhythms begins with a conversation between Charles and Michel about the dispiriting lies of those in power. The rituals of mass transit interrupt their exchange. A stop is requested, workers-cum-passengers move, their marching feet tap the floor, and like well-trained citizens they validate their tickets in an orderly manner. But other motifs rupture these orderly patterns somewhat. Recurring colors and complex compositions (using reflective surfaces), themes that exist semi-independently from these rituals, structure the experience, too—elicit our attention, which is now divided. When the conversation resumes between the two characters, other passengers chime in, raising the hopes of a proletarian awakening, but the exchange lacks intimate fluidity. Some voices are disembodied, and those speakers who are pictured occupy seats turned away from each another so that fellow passengers remain faceless. We cut away to other distracting rhythms—patterns of movement and color in the surrounding traffic. The driver, whose point of view is suggested in the mirror shots, is perhaps at this stage picking up bits of the conversation. But the conversation does not build to a harmonious crescendo; participants are not shown turning toward one another, standing and gathering in a show of conviction and solidarity. Instead, staging and editing keep the passengers separate, their voices isolated. The conversation doesn't lead anywhere. As a member of the proletariat, the driver becomes curious about the intellectualizing of his philosophically inclined passengers, awaiting insights into the deeper forces at play in society. Michel first expresses (perhaps ironically) his sense that the external world feels unreal to him ("Nothing is visible."), passengers ponder the invisible force guiding them, and some feel that this force should not be opposed, while others are perturbed that citizens like themselves simply "go with the flow." One passenger offers that the devil is to blame, which I gather we are to take as a rather reductive rationalization. Modern life, in short, isolates and ritualizes the worker's activities even outside the workplace. A bus is paradoxically a space where the proletariat gathers and a space where the rhythms of bodily experience prove to be inimical to the efforts of workers to coordinate in support of progressive causes. Their politicized exchange is cut short by ritualistic protocols and, for the driver, the rhythms of *his* workplace. His attention, like ours, becomes split, and the bus crashes. Other workers—in their cars outside the bus—don't greet the driver with a demonstration of proletarian solidarity, but, rather, with an impatient chorus of horn blasts, given a patterned "beat." They make music with their horns, but these same circumstances undermine their efforts to speak as a single voice in political life. The disorderly, unpredictable rhythms of modernity—in this case, of mass transit—secure the perpetuation of the status quo, thwart the potential for revolution "from below."

* * *

We know next to nothing about Bresson's working relationship with editors.[100] Perhaps with time, evidence will begin to mount, and a new layer of language and thought—that of the editing suite—will impose itself on our accounts of Bresson's plot and editing rhythms. Until then, our story of the editing and plot structures of his finished films remains one of engagement with a culture's ideas as they filtered into the realm of film practice through various well-positioned theorists, filmmakers, and critics. The culturally specific twists and turns in the French concept of rhythm provide a map for the development of Bresson's rhythmic alternative to mainstream cinematic storytelling, a form more preoccupied with the staging of actors than with the creation of harmonious (and sometimes unharmonious) temporal experiences.

Perhaps the most serious filmmaker of the midcentury rhythmic drift, Bresson absorbed the flexibility of his culture's vernacular language and extended "rhythm" even further. No Bresson rhythmic solution was the same: rhythm materialized as loose, unifying motifs; the oscillations of subjective experience; the theme-and-variation patterns of ritual behavior; authorial pacing devices; the pulsations and interruptions of speech patterns; the erotic, metrically measured beats of sound cues; and a series of unwieldy, shifting patterns that shed light on the life experiences that undermine radical politics. His films served up a rich palette of temporal experiences—a creative extension of "rhythm" expressed in the language, the vernacular, of *le cinématographe*.

Bresson came to believe that rhythm was more than an essential feature of cinema and art. It was the creative principle that dynamizes a new art of writing in motion—a radical medium that promised to liberate cinema from the systems of representation and meaning-making and the craft practices of an industry far too constrained by theatrical influences. But he did not invent this new art out of whole cloth. Bresson had a shared repertory of cultural resources to work from. Evolving notions about rhythm and widely appreciated developments in philosophy, aesthetics, psychology, and other intellectual spheres were being translated into the terms of film practice, theory, and reception (with which he was surely familiar) precisely at the moment he was engineering visual, aural, and narrative solutions that encouraged a more flexible, intuitive appreciation of rhythm than that of the metronomic metrician's tick-tock.

Notes

1. Robert Bresson, *Notes on the Cinematographer*, trans. Jonathan Griffin (Copenhagen: Green Integer, 1997), 68.
2. Georges-Michel Coissac, *Les coulisses du cinéma* (Paris: Les éditions pittoresques, 1929), 69.
3. David Bordwell, "The Musical Analogy," *Yale French Studies* 60 (1980): 145; for a detailed study of the period's styles, see Richard Abel, *French Cinema: The First Wave, 1915–1929* (Princeton: Princeton University Press, 1984), 279–526.
4. For an examination of the avant-garde of the early sound era, see Charles O'Brien, *Cinema's Conversion to Sound: Technology and Film Style in France and the U.S.* (Bloomington: Indiana University Press, 2005). See also Lea Jacobs, *Film Rhythm After Sound: Technology, Music, and Performance* (Berkeley: University of California Press, 2015).
5. Laurent Guido, *L'âge du rythme: Cinéma, musicalité et culture du corps dans les théories françaises des années 1910–1930* (Lausanne: Payot, 2007), 83.
6. Henri Meschonnic, *Critique du rythme: Anthropologie historique du langage* (Paris: Verdier, 1982).
7. Henri Meschonnic, "The Rhythm Party Manifesto" (trans. David Nowell-Smith), *Thinking Verse* 1 (2011): 165.
8. For a useful discussion of this, see Elizabeth Lindley and Laura McMahon, "Introduction," in *Rhythm: Essays in French Literature, Thought and Culture* (Bern: Peter Lang, 2008), 11–15.
9. Julia Kristeva, *La révolution du langage poétique: L'avant-garde à la fin du XIXe siècle, Lautréamont et Mallarmé* (Paris: Seuil, 1974), 23–29; Henri Lefebvre, *Élément du rythmanalyse: Introduction à la connaissance des rythmes* (Paris: Syllepse, 1992); and Gilles Deleuze, *Francis Bacon: Logique de la sensation* (Paris: Éditions de la Différence, 1994), 31.
10. Numerous postwar texts refer to silent-era theory about rhythm: René Clair, "Rythme," in *Intelligence du cinématographe*, ed. Marcel L'Herbier (Paris: Éditions Corréa, 1946), 291–293; Pierre Leprohon, *Les mille et un métiers du cinéma* (Paris: Jacques Melot, 1947), 62–63; Robert Bataille, *Le savoir filmer* (Paris: A. Taffin-Lefort, 1944), 95, 96, 101; Léopold Survage, "Le rythme coloré, *La revue du cinéma* 11 (March 1948): 51–52; Guido Aristarco, "Théories sur le cinéma," *La revue du cinéma* 18 (October 1948): 34.
11. Jean Cocteau, "Montage, style et écriture" (1952), in *L'art du cinéma*, ed. Pierre L'herminier (Paris: Seghers, 1960), 231.
12. Jacques B. Brunius, "La surface mitoyenne de l'objectif et du subjectif" (1954), in *L'art du cinéma*, ed. Pierre L'herminier (Paris: Seghers, 1960), 332.
13. Jean Renoir, "Il s'agit de raconter une histoire" (1959), in *L'art du cinéma*, ed. Pierre L'herminier (Paris: Seghers, 1960), 184.
14. Éric Rohmer, "Poésie et révélation" (1955), in *L'art du cinéma*, ed. Pierre L'herminier (Paris: Seghers, 1960), 583.
15. Cited in Alison Smith, *Agnès Varda* (Manchester: Manchester University Press, 1998), 14, n.3; the translation is the author's.

16. Jean-Luc Godard, *Jean-Luc Godard sur Jean-Luc Godard* (Paris: Cahiers du cinéma/ Éditions de l'étoile, 1985), 461.

17. Ibid., 461–462.

18. To cite two prominent examples: René Dumesnil, *Le rythme musical, essai historique et critique* (Paris: La Colombe, 1949), 9; Jean Mitry, *The Aesthetics and Psychology of the Cinema*, trans. Christopher King (Bloomington: Indiana University Press, 1997), 104.

19. Martin Lefebvre, "L'aventure filmologique: Documents et jalons d'une histoire institutionelle," *Cinémas* 19.2–3 (2009): 65. Fraisse was a student of Albert Michotte, who conducted numerous studies of the body's motor rhythms throughout the 1930s; see Guido, *L'âge du rythme*, 86.

20. Paul Fraisse, *Les structures rythmiques* (Louvain, Belgium: Publications universitaires de Louvain, 1956); see also Paul Fraisse, *La psychologie du temps* (Vendôme: Presses universitaires de France, 1957).

21. Paul Fraisse, *Psychologie du rythme* (Vendôme: Presses universitaires de France, 1974), 15–16.

22. Ibid., 120.

23. Mitry, *Aesthetics and Psychology of the Cinema*, 271.

24. Ibid., 271–272.

25. Ibid.

26. Aside from the 1949 edition of *Le rythme musical* cited above (note 18), René Dumesnil published "Sur le rythme musical," *Mercure de France*, (November 16, 1919), 231–254; *Le rythme musical, essai historique et critique* (Paris: Mercure de France, 1921); and "Musique et cinéma," *Mercure de France*, October 15, 1933, 454–458.

27. Dumesnil, *Le rythme musical*, 20.

28. Ibid., 22–23.

29. Matila Ghyka, *Essai sur le rythme* (Paris, Gallimard, 1938); Matila Ghyka, *Essai sur le rythme*, 11th ed. (Paris: Gallimard, 1952).

30. Jeannine Marroncle, Analysis of *La vérité sur bébé Donge*, *Téléciné* 32–33 (1952).

31. Ibid.

32. Janick Arbois, Analysis of *Journal d'un curé de campagne*, *Téléciné* 25 (1951).

33. Ibid.

34. Ibid. Bresson originally stated this in "Définition de la mise-en-scène," *La technique cinématographique* 139 (January 1954): 4.

35. Robert Bataille, *Grammaire cinégraphique* (Paris: Taffin-Lefort, 1947).

36. Bataille, *Le savoir filmer*, 94–101.

37. Ibid., 99.

38. Jacques Queval, "Three French Histories of Film," *Hollywood Quarterly* 3.4 (Summer 1948): 454–456.

39. Ibid., 455.

40. Jean Keim, *Un nouvel art: Le cinéma sonore* (Paris: Albin Michel, 1947), 97–98.

41. Ibid., 99–100.

42. Pierre Schaeffer, "L'élément non visuel au cinéma," in *La revue du cinéma, anthologie* (Paris: Gallimard, 1992), 475–6.

43. These critics and theorists were acting as middlemen between the world of aesthetics and the world of filmmakers, drawing on the period's major aestheticians and philosophers. For instance, Keim, *Un nouvel art*, 93, relies on the theories of Pius Servien; Schaeffer, "L'élément non visuel au cinéma," 475, cites Henri Bergson on the rhythms of humor; and Mitry, *Aesthetics and Psychology of the Cinema*, 107–108, draws on Dumesnil and Matila Ghyka.

44. Michael Temple, "Big Rhythm and the Power of Metamorphosis: Some Models and Precursors for *Histoire(s) du cinema*," in *The Cinema Alone: Essays on the Work of Jean-Luc Godard, 1985–2000*, ed. Michael Temple and James S. Williams (Amsterdam: Amsterdam University Press, 2000), 89. See Elie Faure, *Histoire de l'art: L'esprit des formes* (Paris: Les éditions G. Crès, 1927), 1–81.

45. Christian Kerslake, *Immanence and the Vertigo of Philosophy: From Kant to Deleuze* (Edinburgh: Edinburgh University Press, 2009), 237.

46. Gilles Deleuze, *Cinema 1: The Movement-Image*, trans. Hugh Tomlinson and Barbara Habberjam (Minneapolis: University of Minnesota Press, 2003), 48.

47. Dudley Andrew, *André Bazin* (New York: Columbia University Press, 1990), 53, 56, 84, 165–166, 167.

48. Jean-Pierre Chartier, "Art et réalité au cinema, IV: Rythme cinématographique et réalisme de la durée," *Bulletin de l'IDHEC* 4 (1946): 5.

49. Kristeva, *La révolution du langage poétique*, 23–29.

50. Lefebvre, *Elément du rythmanalyse*, 35. This translation comes from Henri Lefebvre, *Rhythmanalysis: Space, Time and Everyday Life*, trans. Stuart Elden and Gerald Moore (New York: Continuum, 2007), xii.

51. Deleuze, *Francis Bacon*, 31.

52. Philip Watts, "Jacques Rivette's Classical Illusion," *Contemporary French and Francophone Studies* 9.3 (September 2005): 291.

53. Bresson even attempted to cleanse *mise-en-scène* of its theatrical inflection in "Définition de la mise-en-scène," 33.

54. "Entretien avec Robert Bresson," *L'express*, December 23, 1959, 39. See also *Pour le plaisir*, "Un metteur en order: Robert Bresson," first broadcast on May 11, 1966, dir. Roger Stéphane, *Au hasard Balthazar* Criterion DVD. The earliest reference to *mise-en-ordre* available to me is in Marcello-Fabri, "Un art spécifique" (1939), in *L'art du cinéma*, ed. Pierre Lherminier (Paris: Éditions Seghers, 1960), 83.

55. See David Bordwell, *On the History of Film Style* (Cambridge, MA: Harvard University Press, 1997), 78, for a discussion of how *Cahiers du cinéma* critics viewed mise-en-scène as "a criterion of value." For a recent account of mise-en-scène, its origins and ambiguities, see Adrian Martin, *Mise en Scène and Film Style: From Classical Hollywood to New Media Art* (New York: Palgrave Macmillan, 2014), 1–20, 43–73.

56. Robert Bresson, "'Une mise-en-scène n'est pas un art:' Robert Bresson rencontre les étudiants de l'Institut des hautes études cinématographiques (décembre 1955)," *Cahiers du cinéma: Hommage Robert Bresson* (February 2000): 6–7.

57. Ibid.

58. Ibid., 9.

59. "Entretien avec Robert Bresson," 39.

60. "Entretien avec Robert Bresson," *Unifrance film* (December 1957): 2.

61. Roger Leenhardt, "Le rythme cinématographique," in *Chronique du cinéma* (Paris: Éditions Cahiers du cinéma, 1986), 40–43.

62. Bresson, *Notes on the Cinematographer*, 93.

63. Ibid., 90.

64. Ibid., 68; original emphasis.

65. Ibid., 52; original emphasis.

66. Ibid., 78–79.

67. Chartier, "Rhythme cinématographique et réalisme de la durée," 5.

68. Bresson, *Notes on the Cinematographer*, 46; original emphasis.

69. Ibid., 77.

70. Ibid., 80–81.

71. Ibid., 23. For an insightful analysis of this aphorism, see Jonathan Hourigan, "On Two Deaths and Three Births: The Cinematography of Robert Bresson," *Stills* I (Autumn 1981): 27–38.

72. Georges Sadoul, "Robert Bresson à Georges Sadoul: 'Si l'on veut que passé le courant électrique, il faut dénuder les fils . . . ,'" *Les lettres françaises*, March 7, 1963, 1.

73. Leenhardt, "Le rythme cinématographique," 42, n. 1.

74. Charles O'Brien, "Stylistic Description as Historical Method: French Films of the German Occupation," *Style* 32.3 (Fall 1998): 438.

75. Noël Burch, *Theory of Film Practice*, trans. Helen Lane (Princeton, NJ: Princeton University Press, 1981), 42.

76. Brian Price, *Neither God Nor Master: Robert Bresson and Radical Politics* (Minneapolis: University of Minnesota Press, 2011), 115–122.

77. Kristin Thompson, *Breaking the Glass Armor: Neoformalist Film Analysis* (Princeton, NJ: Princeton University Press, 1988), 300–304.

78. Luc Estang, Review *of Les dames du bois de Boulogne*, *Les étoiles* (October 2, 1945).

79. David Bordwell, *Narration in the Fiction Film* (Madison: University of Wisconsin Press, 1985), 303, 305.

80. Fraisse performed clinical studies about the relationship between the rhythmic patterning of words and numbers and our ability to memorize them; Paul Fraisse, "Études sur la mémoire immédiate, II: Le reproduction des formes rythmiques," *L'année psychologique* 43–44 (1942): 103–143. Moreover, Jean Mitry believed that rhythm depended on activating a type of recollection he described as the "persistence of image (auditory and visual)," an "effect of consciousness" similar to retinal persistence; Mitry, *Aesthetics and Psychology of the Cinema*, 104.

81. Cited in Robert Pickering, 'Tes pas . . . procèdent': Melos, marche, méditations dans les promenades de Rousseau et de Valéry," in *Paul Valéry: Musique, Mystique, Mathématique*, ed. Paul Gifford and Brian Stimpson (Lille: Presses universitaires de Lille, 1993), 108.

82. John McCole, *Walter Benjamin and the Antinomies of Tradition* (Ithaca, NY: Cornell University Press, 1993), 264.

83. Charles Thomas Samuels, "Robert Bresson," in *Encountering Directors* (New York: Capricorn Books, 1972), 74.

84. Marcel Mauss, *The Gift: The Form and Reason for Exchange in Archaic Societies* (New York: Routledge, 2002), 100.

85. Ibid., 28–9.

86. *Pour le plaisir*, "Un metteur en order: Robert Bresson."

87. James Quandt, "'All Things Conceal a Mystery': The Hidden God in Robert Bresson's *Au hasard Balthazar* and *Le Diable probablement*," in *Robert Bresson (Revised)*, ed. James Quandt (Toronto: TIFF, 2011), 494.

88. Ibid., 495.

89. *Pour le plaisir*, "Un metteur en order: Robert Bresson."

90. Georges Bernanos, *Diary of a Country Priest*, trans. Pamela Morris (London: Fontana Books, 1965), 139–140.

91. André Bazin, "*Diary of a Country Priest* and the Robert Bresson Style," in *What is Cinema?*, trans. Timothy Barnard (Montréal: Caboose, 2009), 141.

92. Yves Kovacs, "Entretien avec Robert Bresson," *Cahiers du cinéma* 140 (February 1962): 5.

93. Robert Bresson, *Le procès de Jeanne d'arc: D'après le film de Robert Bresson*, Disques Adès TS 30 LA 544, 1963, LP record.

94. Some characters in Hawks's *Scarface* (1932) speak at a rate of 5.3 to 6.6 words per second, while other Hawks films contain scenes that vary from 2.9 to 4.9 words per second; see Jacobs, *Film Rhythm After Sound*, 187, 203.

95. Philippe Arnaud, *Robert Bresson* (Paris: Cahiers du cinéma, 1986), 103.

96. Keith Reader, *Robert Bresson* (Manchester: Manchester University Press, 2000), 93.

97. Godard joined the Dziga Vertov group and codirected such Brechtian films as *Tout va bien* (1972). Popular genre cinema became more politicized as well; see Alison Smith, *French Cinema of the 1970s: The Echoes of May* (Manchester: Manchester University Press, 2005), 35–73.

98. For an overview of this period, see Brian Price, "*Une Femme douce* and the Spectrum of Revolt: Bresson's Transition to Color in the Aftermath of May'68," *Framework* 43.1 (Spring 2002): 131–133.

99. Jacques Fieschi, "Entretiens: Robert Bresson," *Cinématographe* 29 (July–August 1977): 28.

100. The one exception is Philippe Arnaud, Interview with Jean-François Naudon, in *Robert Bresson* (Paris: Cahiers du cinéma, 1986), 156–157, where the editor of *L'argent* describes Bresson's unique sound editing process and amazingly keen ear.

Afterword

LIKE MANY POSTWAR intellectuals, Father Paul Doncoeur became fascinated by the fact that cinema was swiftly becoming a serious form of cultural expression. A religious expert, he advised Walter Wanger on his 1948 adaptation of the Joan of Arc story, starring Ingrid Bergman, and in 1951 tried his hand at film criticism, writing a review of *Journal d'un curé de campagne* (1951) for the Jesuit weekly *Études religieuses*, for which he served as editor. He was intrigued not only by the film's faithfulness to Catholic doctrine but with Robert Bresson's unusual relationship with the Parisian film-going public, especially given the interest the long-awaited adaptation had stirred among cinephiles. "I do not think that it was Robert Bresson's intention to mobilize for his film the powers of publicity or the favoritism of critics," he began. "'A film,' [Bresson] likes to say, 'finds its own aims. Nothing can compensate for failures that belong to it and it alone.'"[1] From Doncoeur's perspective, the candid assertion that a film's successes and failures owed little to critical reception revealed just why Bresson ought to be considered apart from an industry obsessed with publicity—something that Doncoeur would have observed firsthand while working in Hollywood.

What Doncoeur found intriguing was that Bresson's distinctive sense of responsibility toward his work and eschewal of the forms of critical attention often sought within the industry, far from serving to separate the director from his surroundings, became the basis for his unique bond with postwar film culture—with cinephiles in particular:

> It is precisely this honesty [about publicity and critical favoritism] that initiates the whole game. . . . It is unlikely that a sympathetic audience, restive to displays of skill and cleverness, does not recognize a measure of good taste here [in Bresson]; and that the respect it [the audience] receives for its intelligence is not then returned in kind to the worker [Bresson]. The one and the other grow due to the severity of the game, and, dare I say, of the battle.[2]

Though brief, Doncoeur's analysis was a remarkably astute and even prescient one. As critics and scholars of film and media might today, he was attempting to map the cultural practices and values that linked two spheres sometimes thought to be separate—namely, those of auteur filmmaking and of reception culture. Bresson and his admirers were not crudely seeking favor with one another; however, their distinct performances nonetheless initiated a cultural exchange whose rewards consisted of the acknowledgement of intelligence and good taste and mutual displays of respect. This exchange, in turn, promoted each other's growth and aligned auteur and cinephile in the "battle" that united them, presumably against a commercial industry whose values and methods they set out to challenge.

This book has sought to elaborate and nuance Doncoeur's intuition about Bresson's relationship with film culture. I have argued that if we view Bresson as a social actor rather than a recluse, as a figure attuned to the cultures that shaped vanguard film style and storytelling in midcentury France rather than one whose sources of inspiration were far removed from the auteur's immediate circles of support, we would begin to see his aesthetics and his place in film history in a new light. A "cinematic" Bresson, I predicted, would emerge.

As we have discovered, the circle of support pertinent to this cinematic Bresson is not limited to the cinephilic community. We were compelled to map a much larger configuration of relationships. Throughout his almost sixty-year artistic career, Bresson participated in an evolving cultural market, in a site of exchange where ideas and cultural practices were "traded" among independent-minded artists, filmmakers, intellectuals, and filmgoers. I elected to highlight six intimately related aspects of Bresson's performance in this context—his artistic partnerships, institution-building, alliances, and competition with others; his lexical and conceptual synchrony with the paradigmatic discourses of this alternative culture; and the positive forms of reciprocity that resulted from these patterns of engagement. Through an exploration of these activities, I have attempted to promote a new understanding of Bresson's artistic style and the materials and forms that went into its invention.

In particular, I focused on the market as a configuration of practices and discourses where strategic partnerships (with cinephiles, but also Surrealist patrons, mentors, and others) became perceived as essential to the auteur's survival and development, where alternative institutions were imagined and put in place to nurture and protect the auteur's connection with the public, and specific aesthetic ideas and ideals were privileged through the common languages vanguard artists and communities of viewers refined and circulated around the medium of cinema. Rediscovering how Bresson performed within the cultural market—one that evolved from a declining interwar avant-garde into a thriving postwar cinephilia that attempted to launch an avant-garde of its own—has revealed the degree to which his art was of a piece with the market's core preoccupations. Faithful adaptation, first-person narration, realism, and rhythm—these were central areas of stylistic and narrative experimentation for any vanguard filmmaker and guided Bresson's ambition to revolutionize the medium, a goal he set for himself as he completed his first film in 1934. The *style bressonien* wasn't a creation of the market, but his artistic solutions certainly complemented it.

The aim here, then, has been to revive a version of Bresson that has largely been neglected by commentators. Drawing on Michel Foucault's notion of the author function,[3] I would claim that, until now, Robert Bresson has served two broad functions in film history:

1. *The solitary genius.* Filmmakers from far-flung regions of the globe, from Mani Kaul to Aki Kaurismäki, from Michael Haneke to Carlos Reygadas, have looked to Bresson as a master, the innovator of an aesthetic without precedent, and the model filmmaker whose entirely unique alternative to mainstream styles and forms makes him the very embodiment of the independent spirit in an art often treated as a mere commodity. This version of Bresson has become an aspect of a strategic discourse prevalent among independent-minded auteurs and cinephiles worldwide seeking to preserve the possibility of an untainted, personal form of cinematic expression.

2. *The maverick with "external" sources of inspiration.* Bresson has long been celebrated among fellow auteurs and cinephiles for drawing on sources from literary, philosophical, fine arts, and other spheres of thought and creativity never before explored in the realm of film style and storytelling. Through these, he was able to imbue cinema with a moral, theoretical, and affective profundity, with a truth and authenticity that elevated the medium to the status of poetry, music, painting, or theory.

These versions of Bresson will continue to benefit and provoke film culture in numerous ways—artistically, intellectually, and even spiritually. But because they have dominated discussions about Bresson for decades, critics and scholars have tended to overlook the third function the auteur played throughout his career:

3. *The visionary within a film-cultural market.* Bresson, as I have shown, drew creative strength from alternative cinematic discourses. He opposed commercial norms through the inventive appropriation and revision of cinematic-aesthetic ideas that, by way of culturally contingent processes, were transforming how artists and their supporters viewed the medium. Elevated by a culture of intellectuals, theorists, tastemakers, and artists who were intrigued by the possibilities of an alternative to spectacle cinema, Bresson's art transformed some of these possibilities into reality, through the artistic briefs—the creative challenges—he worked on in his films and recast as the foundation for his new rhythmic medium, *le cinématographe.*

This Bresson differs markedly from the others, first, by explicitly challenging the isolation myth. If we examine the role he played throughout film-cultural history and consider the implications of his ties to patrons and publicity artists, cinematographers and cinephiles, we learn of a Bresson whose effort to revolutionize the medium was not undertaken alone—he was scarcely the staunch individualist of legend—but in the context of several loosely connected networks of historical actors, each one projecting its own alternative practices and visions for the future of noncommercial cinema. Whether it was the loose Aurenche-Chanel-Surrealist network of the interwar period, or the postwar networks of Objectif 49 and *Cahiers du cinéma*, Bresson consistently found himself drawn to, and taken in by, groups of artists and critics, producers and theater owners, who all worked to create conditions that allowed auteurs like himself to thrive within the film industry. In no way an isolated figure, Bresson was instead an ambitious visionary whose style developed within both the structures and cultures of the industry and the discourses and practices of several intellectual/artistic networks seeking to reimagine cinema as a legitimately artistic, rather than purely commercial, form.

Second, the third version of Bresson helps us to *explain* the isolation myth—one might even say, explain it away. Until now, the culture Bresson and his art belonged to has largely been ignored by commentators. Why this is so is not difficult to understand. The two major contexts I have described as central to the alternative cultural market that Bresson responded to—the interwar avant-garde of publicity filmmakers, photographers, and Surrealist mentors and patrons, and the postwar avant-garde of the ciné-club Objectif 49—were relatively fleeting (each lasted just a few years) and have tended to be overlooked in standard histories. The auteur critic cannot be expected to read the origins and development of the auteur through historical contexts he did not know existed. By recovering these lost episodes from Bresson's career, we are now in a position to derive from them an understanding of the cultural sources of his style and to conclude that the isolation myth thrived for so long because of the very inaccessibility of these aspects of his personal and professional history.

Finally, this third Bresson differs from the previous two in the fundamental questions it raises about cinephilic writing. If we accept that Bresson was part of a cultural marketplace, a participant in a midcentury culture that circulated new cinematic ideas and practices, how are we now to express our admiration for the auteur? What does it now mean to write admiringly about his work? Do the "demystifying" aspects of the cultural-market approach not undercut everything we held dear about Bresson's role in film history?

It is fair to claim that I have been arguing against the idea of admiration through mystification. The Bresson commentator need not accept the Bresson mystery at face value, limit his or her discussions of his creativity to vague notions of personal vision and inspiration, or insist in the face of mounting evidence and new methodologies like the cultural-market paradigm that we know far too little about Bresson to draw even tentative conclusions about the development of his style. None of these mystifying tendencies is essential to writing admiringly of his films.

Nevertheless, it would be altogether unwarranted to assert that I have undercut admiration for him as an auteur *tout court*. I have simply endeavored to express my admiration in a new way. This book has modeled a style of analytical writing informed by a deep passion for film-cultural history. It has proposed that the cinephile critic wishing to deepen his or her admiration for Bresson and his work take on the role of *historical excavator*. The critic informed by history, Walter Benjamin has written, is a *bricoleur*, digging through the debris of history and patching together items left behind not, as Jo Labanyi has written, in order to "possess" the past but in order to be "possessed by" or become personally engaged in it.[4] The cultural-market critic seeks just that, taking up with tenacious enthusiasm old facts about Bresson long thought to be irrelevant, adding to these new traces of a past that becomes more vivid and complex with each passing day, and attempting to stitch together a set of suggestive historical connections between microlevel artistic decision-making and macrolevel cultural discourses and trends in order to return to the films with fresh eyes. In the years it has taken me to complete this book, I have never tired of this task, for the more I found myself drawn *away* from Bresson's canonical masterpieces (the thirteen feature films) and the more I was "possessed" with the minutia of history—Bresson's cultural ties, the dominant theoretical and critical discourses of his time, his evolving language acts, and all the subtle ways he appropriated from, nurtured, and provoked the market—the more I felt myself drawn *toward* the canonical films with a renewed enthusiasm for their rich textures and finer delights, and the more I felt compelled to understand the original culture that they addressed.

Over time, I came to realize that this way of approaching auteur cinema—as a critical-historical excavator digging up the traces of this "third Bresson"—was more than an analytic method or distinct form of cinephilia. At certain historical junctures, the role of critical excavator can carry a special urgency. To put the point bluntly, if Bresson admirers do not act, traces of his history may very soon be lost.

Apart from situating Bresson in the interwar and postwar avant-gardes, this study has positioned his cinematographers, set designers, and even makeup artists as part of the midcentury culture of exchange as well. I have relied upon their firsthand accounts to both relocate his creative decision-making in its proper production contexts and understand his craft in light of their unique skills and acquired creative habits. Their stories about his methods proved critical to my reinterpretation of Bresson's art. The effect of Bresson's cinema, as I see it, is precisely equivalent to the historically situated craft of its maker(s).

A renewed effort must be made to unearth collaborator testimony of this sort, before those in possession of further historical traces are no longer with us, or their personal effects—letters and notes exchanged with Bresson—are tragically and uselessly discarded. Imagine for a moment what we could learn from an interview with Jean Chiabaut, Bresson's camera operator for much of his career, or from Pierre Lhomme, the cinematographer on *Quatre nuits d'un rêveur*. What kind of discoveries would future scholars make if the estate of the film editor Raymond Lamy were to grant access to his correspondence with the director and his production notes for *Un condamné à mort s'est échappé, Pickpocket, Au hasard Balthazar, Mouchette*, and *Une femme douce*? These are but a few of the tasks before the cinephilic excavator. A coordinated effort on the part of Bresson admirers to record these and other personal histories would surely lead to new insights about the creative problems and challenges confronted by the Bresson style.

Of course, the most urgent question facing historically minded Bresson admirers today is the state of *his* personal archive. Unfortunately, at the moment these words are being written, no one but his estate can confirm the archive's status—how extensive it is, what condition it is in, and whether it will ever be made available to the public. This has left many scholars and archivists, myself included, deeply concerned about its future. If for some reason his version of history were lost, the thousands of questions we have about his career, the origins of his unique aesthetic sensibility, and the film cultures he participated in would effectively become unanswerable.

Perhaps this study, and others like it, will convince the estate that admiration for his films is cultivated, not diminished, if the sides of Bresson's professional and cultural life that have fallen into shadow are permitted to reemerge in the brilliant light of history.

Notes

1. Paul Doncoeur, "Le '*Journal d'un curé de campagne*' à l'écran," *Études religieuses* 286 (January–March 1951): 385.
2. Ibid.
3. Michel Foucault, "What is an Author?" in *The Foucault Reader*, ed. Paul Rabinow (New York, Pantheon Books), 101–120.
4. Jo Labanyi, "The Politics of the Everyday and the Eternity of Ruins: Two Women Photographers in Republican Spain," in *Cultural Encounters: European Travel Writing in the 1930s*, ed. Charles Burdett and Derek Duncan (New York: Berghahn Books, 2002), 87–88.

Selected Bibliography

Archives

Academy Film Archive, Fairbanks Center for Motion Picture Study, Beverly Hills, California: George Cukor Collection.
Bibliothèque du film, Paris: Fonds Crédit National, Fonds Pierre Charbonnier.
Dean Gallery, Scottish National Gallery of Modern Art, Edinburgh, Scotland: Roland Penrose Archive.

Books and Articles

Abdelmoumen, Smihi. "Entretien avec Robert Bresson." *Image et son* 215 (January 1968): 68–71.
Abel, Richard. *French Cinema: The First Wave, 1915–1929.* Princeton, NJ: Princeton University Press, 1984.
———, ed. *French Film Theory and Criticism, Volume I: 1907–1929.* Princeton, NJ: Princeton University Press, 1988.
———, ed. *French Film Theory and Criticism, Volume II: 1929–1939.* Princeton, NJ: Princeton University Press, 1988.
"Adorable créatures." *Téléciné* 35 (1953).
Agel, Henri. *Esthétique du cinéma.* Paris: Presses universitaires de France, 1966.
Agel, Henri, Jean-Pierre Barrot, and Jacques Doniol-Valcroze, ed. *Sept ans de cinéma français.* Paris: Éditions du cerf, 1953.
Ajame, Pierre. "Le cinéma selon Bresson." *Nouvelles littéraires,* May 26, 1966, 1, 13.
Albera, François. *L'avant-garde au cinéma.* Paris: Armand Colin Cinéma, 2005.
Alceste. "Daquineries." *Je suis partout,* April 30, 1943, 7.
Alpers, Svetlana. *Rembrandt's Enterprise: The Studio and the Market.* Chicago: University of Chicago Press, 1988.
Alpers, Svetlana and Michael Baxandall. *Tiepolo and the Pictorial Intelligence.* New Haven, CT: Yale University Press, 1994.
Andrew, Dudley. *André Bazin* [1978]. New York: Columbia University Press, 1990.
———. "Desperation and Meditation: Bresson's *Diary of a Country Priest* (1951)." In *Modern European Filmmakers and the Art of Adaptation,* edited by Andrew Horton and Joan Magretta, 20–37. New York: Frederick Ungar, 1981.
Annales de la Société d'Agriculture: Histoire naturelle et arts utiles de Lyon, quatrième serie, tome deuxième. Paris: Librairie de la société géologique de France, 1870.
Apart, André. "La technique du film en couleur." *La revue du cinéma* 8 (Fall 1947): 79–80.
———. "La technique du film en couleur (fin)." *La revue du cinéma* 9 (January 1948): 78–80.
Arbois, Janick. Analysis of *Journal d'un curé de campagne. Téléciné* 25 (1951).

Argus. "Le secrèt de Polichinelle." *Radio-cinéma-télévision*, March 19, 1950, 4.

Aristarco, Guido. "Théories sur le cinéma." *La revue du cinéma* 18 (October 1948): 32–41.

Arnaud, Philippe. *Robert Bresson*. Paris: Éditions Cahiers du cinéma, 1986.

Association des amis de l'orgue. *Jean-Jacques Grunenwald*. Special Issue of *L'orgue: Cahiers et mémoires* 36 (September 1986).

Astre, Georges-Albert, ed. *Cinéma et roman*. Special Issue of *La revue des lettres modernes* 36–38 (Summer 1958).

Astruc, Alexandre. "Naissance d'une nouvelle avant-garde: La caméra-stylo." In *Du stylo à la caméra . . . et de la caméra au stylo: Écrits (1942–1984)*, 324–328. Paris: L'Archipel, 1992.

Audinet, Pierre. "'Le procès de Jehanne [*sic*] d'Arc' se tourne à huis clos." *Nouvelles littéraires*, October 5, 1961, 9.

Aurenche, Jean. *La suite à l'écran: Entretiens*. Lyon: Institut Lumière/ Actes Sud, 1993.

Aurenche, Jean, and Pierre Bost. "*Jeanne d'Arc* (extraits d'un scénario original)." *La revue du cinéma* 8 (Fall 1947): 3–24.

Auriol, Jean-George. "Faires des films (I): Les origines de la mise en scène." *La revue du cinéma* 1 (October 1946): 7–23.

———. "Petit vocabulaire du cinéma." *La revue du cinéma* 1 (October 1946): 79–80.

———. "Faire des films II: D'abord, les écrire." *La revue du cinéma* 2 (November 1946): 37–53.

———. "Petit vocabulaire du cinéma." *La revue du cinéma* 2 (November 1946): 78–80.

———. "Faire des films III: Avec de la technique et du génie." *La revue du cinéma* 3 (December 1946): 45–50.

———. "Faire des films IV: Pour qui?" *La revue du cinéma* 4 (January 1947): 4–15.

———. "Faire des films V: Avec qui?" *La revue du cinéma* 6 (Spring 1947): 28–41.

———. "Faire des films VI: Comment?" *La revue du cinéma* 7 (Summer 1947): 19–26.

Ayfre, Amédée. "L'univers de Robert Bresson." *Télécine* 70–71 (November–December 1957).

———. "Le moraliste, l'esthète et le professeur devant le cinéma, ou le sens de la culture cinématographique." *Télécine* 90 (July–August 1960).

Baby, Yvonne. "Du fer qui fait du bruit." *Le monde*, September 26, 1974, 15.

Balsom, Erika. "'One Single Mystery of Persons and Objects': The Erotics of Fragmentation in *Au hasard Balthazar*." *Canadian Journal of Film Studies* 19.1 (Spring 2010): 20–40.

Barkan, Raymond. "En faisant voire la vérité, le cinéma travaillera pour la paix . . ." (Interview with Louis Daquin). *Les lettres françaises*, August 26, 1948, 1.

Barrot, Olivier. *L'écran français: Histoire d'un journal et d'un époque, 1943–1953*. Paris: Les éditeurs français réunis, 1979.

Barsacq, Léon. *Le décor du film*. Paris: Éditions Seghers, 1970.

Barthes, Roland. "The Death of the Author." In *Theories of Authorship*, edited by John Caughie, 208–213. London: British Film Institute, 1981.

———. "Les anges du péché." In *Oeuvres complètes, tome I*, edited by Éric Marty, 37–39. Paris: Éditions du seuil, 1993.

Bataille, Robert. *Le savoir filmer*. Paris: Taffin-Lefort, 1944.

———. *Grammaire cinégraphique*. Paris: Taffin-Lefort, 1947.

Baxandall, Michael. *Painting and Experience in Fifteenth Century Italy: A Primer in the Social History of Pictorial Style*. Oxford: Oxford University Press, 1972.

——. *The Limewood Sculptors of Renaissance Germany.* New Haven, CT: Yale University Press, 1980.

——. "Art, Society and the Bouguer Principle." *Representations* 12 (Autumn 1985): 32–43.

——. *Patterns of Intention: On the Historical Explanation of Pictures.* New Haven, CT: Yale University Press, 1985.

Bazin, André. "Défense de l'avant-garde." *L'écran français*, December 21, 1948, 1.

——. "Le Festival du Film Maudit s'est terminé cette nuit." *Parisien libéré*, August 6, 1949, 2.

——. "À la recherché d'une nouvelle avant-garde." In *Almanach du théâtre et du cinéma*, 146–152. Paris: Éditions de Flore, 1950.

——. "De la forme et du fond, ou la 'crise' du cinéma." In *Almanach du théâtre et du cinéma*, 171–177. Paris: Éditions du Flore, 1951.

——. "La difficile définition de la qualité." *Radio-télévision-cinéma*, April 8, 1951, 6.

——. "Le *Journal d'un curé de campagne* et la stylistique de Robert Bresson." *Cahiers du cinéma* 3 (June 1951): 7–21.

——. "L'avant-garde nouvelle." *Cahiers du cinéma* 10 (March 1952): 16–17.

——. "De la carolinisation de la France." *Esprit* 22 (1954): 298–304.

——. "*Un condamné à mort s'est échappé.*" *France observateur*, November 15, 1956, 22–23.

——. "De la politique des auteurs." *Cahiers du cinéma* 70 (April 1957): 2–11.

——. *What is Cinema?* Translated by Hugh Gray. Berkeley: University of California Press, 1971.

——. *Jean Renoir.* Translated by W. W. Halsey II and William H. Simon, edited by François Truffaut. New York: Simon and Schuster, 1973.

——. *Le cinéma de l'occupation et de la résistance.* Paris: Union générale éditions, 1975.

——. "On the *politique des auteurs.*" In *Cahiers du cinéma: The 1950s: Neo-Realism, Hollywood, the New Wave*, ed. Jim Hillier, 248–259. Cambridge, MA: Harvard University Press, 1985.

——. *Bazin At Work: Major Essays & Reviews from the Forties & Fifties.* Edited by Bert Cardullo. New York: Routledge, 1997.

——. *What is Cinema?* Translated by Timothy Barnard. Montréal: Caboose, 2009.

Becker, Howard S. *Art Worlds.* Berkeley: University of California Press, 1982.

Becker, Jacques. "Hommage à Bresson." *L'écran français*, October 17, 1945, 3.

Béguin, Albert. "Bernanos au cinéma." *Esprit* (January 1951): 248–252.

——. "L'adaptation du 'Journal d'un curé de campagne.'" *Glanes: Cahiers de l'amitié franco-néerlandaise* 18 (May–June 1951): 24–28.

Bernanos, Georges. *Diary of a Country Priest.* Translated by Pamela Morris. London: Fontana Books, 1965.

——. *Correspondences inédites, tome II (1934–1948).* Edited by Albert Béguin. Paris: Librairie Plon, 1971.

Beylie, Claude, ed. *Une histoire du cinéma français.* Paris: Larousse, 2000.

Billard, Pierre. *Le mystère de René Clair.* Paris: Plon, 1998.

Bloch-Delahaie, Pierre. "Encourageons la qualité: Un aspect important de la Défense du cinéma français." *L'écran français*, October 16, 1950, 6, 23.

Bordwell, David. "The Musical Analogy," *Yale French Studies* 60 (1980): 141–156.

———. *Narration in the Fiction Film.* Madison: University of Wisconsin Press, 1985.

———. *Ozu and the Poetics of Cinema.* Princeton, NJ: Princeton University Press, 1988.

———. *On the History of Film Style.* Cambridge, MA: Harvard University Press, 1997.

———. "Sound of Silence." *Artforum International* (April 2000): 123.

Bordwell, David, Kristin Thompson, and Janet Staiger. *The Classical Hollywood Cinema: Film Style and Mode of Production to 1960.* New York: Columbia University Press, 1985.

Bordwell, David, and Kristin Thompson. "Functions of Film Sound: *A Man Escaped.*" In *Film Art: An Introduction,* 5th ed., 341–349. New York: McGraw-Hill, 1997.

Boullet, Jean. "La nouvelle avant-garde." *Saint-cinéma-des-prés* 2 (1950): 1.

Bourcier, Noël. "L'ascèse radieuse d'Emmanuel Sougez." *Photographie magazine* 49 (1993): 69–70.

Bourgeois, Jacques. "À quoi sert donc la critique?" *La revue du cinéma* 4 (January 1947): 72–74.

Boussinot, Roger. "*Journal d'un curé de campagne*: Un film qui suscitera peu de vocations." *L'écran français,* February 14, 1951, 8.

Bradby, David. *Le théâtre français contemporain, 1940–1980.* Lille: Presses universitaires de Lille, 1990.

Brandon, Thomas J. "A Trio of Footnotes on L'Affaire 'Priest:' Distributor's Opinion." *New York Times,* May 9, 1954, X3.

Bresson, Mylène, ed. *Bresson par Bresson.* Paris: Flammarion, 2013.

Bresson, Robert. "The Best Films of Our Life (suite et fin)." *Cahiers du cinéma* 12 (May 1952), 71.

———. "Définition de la mise-en-scène." *La technique cinématographique* 139 (January 1954): 33.

———. "Propos de Robert Bresson (sténographie d'une conférence de presse)." *Cahiers du cinéma* 75 (October 1957): 3–9.

———. "Témoignages." *Cahiers du cinéma* 91 (January 1959): 28–35.

———. *Le procès de Jeanne d'Arc: Film.* Paris: R. Juillard, 1962.

———. "J'ai voulu que Jeanne d'Arc soit un personnage d'aujourd'hui: Propos recueillis par Michel Capdenac." *Les lettres françaises,* May 24, 1962, 12.

———. *Notes sur le cinématographe.* Paris: Gallimard, 1975.

———. "Rhythm Comes from Within." In *Rediscovering French Film,* edited by Mary Lea Bandy, 155. New York: Museum of Modern Art, 1983.

———. *Notes on the Cinematographer.* Translated by Jonathan Griffin. Copenhagen: Green Integer, 1997.

———. "'Une mise-en-scène n'est pas un art:' Robert Bresson rencontre les étudiants de l'Institution des hautes études cinématographiques (décembre 1955)." *Cahiers du cinéma: Hommage Robert Bresson* (February 2000): 4–9.

"Bresson Talks About His First Color Film." *Cinema Canada* (January–February 1969): 3.

Briot, René. *Robert Bresson.* Paris: Éditions du cerf, 1957.

Bruckberger, Raymond-Léopold. *Tu finiras sur l'échafaud: Mémoires.* Paris: Flammarion, 1978.

Bruno, Edoardo. "L'évolution de De Santis." *Positif* 5 (December 1952): 19.

Burch, Noël. *Theory of Film Practice.* Translated by Helen Lane. Princeton, NJ: Princeton University Press, 1981.

Burke, Seán. *The Death and Return of the Author: Criticism and Subjectivity in Barthes, Foucault and Derrida*. Edinburgh: Edinburgh University Press, 1998.

Burnett, Colin. "Inside Bresson's *L'Argent*: An Interview with Crew-Member Jonathan Hourigan." *Offscreen*, August 31, 2004, http://www.horschamp.qc.ca/new _offscreen/ hourigan_interview.html (August 2004).

———. "Muting the Image: Lighting and Photo-Chemical Techniques of Bresson's Cinematographers." *Studies in French Cinema* 6.3 (2006): 219–230.

———. "A New Look at the Concept of Style in Film: The Origins and Development of the Problem-Solution Model." *New Review of Film and Television Studies* 6.3 (August 2008): 127–149.

———. "Under the Auspices of Simplicity: Roger Leenhardt's New Realism and the Aesthetic History of Objectif 49." *Film History* 27.2 (2015): 33–75.

Camus, Albert, and Jean Grenier. *Correspondence, 1932–1960*. Translated by Jan F. Rigaud. Lincoln: University of Nebraska Press, 2003.

Camus, Albert, and René Char. *Correspondence, 1946–1959*. Paris: Gallimard, 2007.

Carroll, Noel. *On Criticism*. New York: Routledge, 2009.

Cassarini, Maria Carla. *Ignazio di Loyola di Robert Bresson: Cronaca di un film mai nato*. Special Issue of *Ciemme: Ricerca e informazione sulla comunicazione di massa* 152–153 (September 2006).

Cawkwell, Tim. *The Filmgoer's Guide to God*. London: Darton, Longman and Todd, 2004.

Centre nationale du cinéma et de l'image animé. *45 ans d'avances sur recettes*. Paris: CNC, 2004.

Chanel, Coco. *Bijoux de diamants*. Paris: L'imprimerie Draeger, 1932.

Chardère, Bernard. "À propos de Bresson . . . I: Un art de suggestion, des visages à l'âme." *Positif* 3 (July–August 1952), 1–56.

———. "À propos de Bresson II: Les rouages de la réalité." *Positif* 4 (November 1952): 43–48.

Charensol, Georges. *Renaissance du cinéma français*. Paris: Éditions du sagittaire, 1946.

———. *D'une rive à l'autre*. Paris: Mercure de France, 1973.

Chartier, Jean-Pierre. "Art et réalité au cinéma, IV: Rythme cinématographique." *Bulletin de l'I.D.H.E.C.* 4 (1946): 5.

———. "Les 'films à la première personne' et l'illusion de réalité au cinéma." *La revue du cinéma* 4 (January 1, 1947): 32–41.

Chartier, Jean-Pierre, and François Desplanques. *Derrière l'écran: Initiation au cinéma*. Paris: Éditions Spes, 1950.

Chion, Michel. *Un art sonore, le cinéma: Histoire, esthétique, poétique*. Paris: Éditions Cahiers du cinéma, 2003.

Clerc, Henri. "Plus de bricolage au cinéma." *Pour vous*, July 19, 1934, 6.

———. "La lumière." *La revue du cinéma* 14 (June 1948): 71–72.

Cocteau, Jean. *Le coq et l'arlequin: Notes autour de la musique*. Paris: Éditions de la sirène, 1918.

———. *Cock and Harlequin: Notes Concerning Music*. Translated by Rollo H. Meyers. London: The Egoist Press, 1921.

Coissac, Georges-Michel. *Les coulisses du cinéma*. Paris: Les éditions pittoresques, 1929.

Collet, Jean. Analysis of *Le blé en herbe*. *Téléciné* 42 (August 1954).

"Conversation avec Robert Bresson." *Opéra*, February 14, 1951, 7.

Crafton, Donald. *The Talkies: American Cinema's Transition to Sound, 1926–1931.* Berkeley: University of California Press, 1997.

Creton, Laurent. *Cinéma et marché.* Paris: Armand Colin/ Masson, 1997.

———. *Histoire économique du cinéma français: Production et financement, 1940–1959.* Paris: Éditions CNRS, 2004.

Crisp, Colin. *The Classic French Cinema: 1930–60.* Bloomington: Indiana University Press, 1993.

Crowther, Bosley. "The Screen in Review: French Film, 'Diary of a Country Priest,' Opens." *New York Times*, April 6, 1954, sec. 2, 1.

———. "On Editing Imports: French Film Man Vexed at a Usual Practice." *New York Times*, May 2, 1954, sec. 2, 35.

Cunneen, Joseph. *Robert Bresson: A Spiritual Style in Film.* New York: Continuum, 2003.

Curran, Beth Kathryn. *Touching God: The Novels of Georges Bernanos in the Films of Robert Bresson.* Bern: Peter Lang, 2006.

Dalio. *Mes années folles.* Paris: Éditions Jean-Claude Lattès, 1976.

Daix, Didier. "Les films nouveaux: *C'était un musicien.*" *Pour vous*, May 3, 1934, 6.

Daquin, Louis. "Remarques déplacées. . . ," *L'écran français*, March 8, 1949, 3.

Dauman, Anatole. *Souvenir-écran.* Paris: Éditions du Centre Pompidou, 1989.

De Baecque, Antoine. *Les cahiers du cinéma: Histoire d'une revue, tome I: À l'assaut du cinéma, 1951–1959.* Paris: Éditions Cahiers du cinéma, 1991.

———. "Contre la qualité française: Autour de l'article de François Truffaut." *Cinémathèque* 4 (Fall 1993): 44–67.

———. *La cinéphilie: Invention d'un regard, histoire d'une culture, 1944–1968.* Paris: Librairie Arthème Fayard, 2003.

De Baecque, Antoine, and Serge Toubiana. *Truffaut: A Biography.* Translated by Catherine Temerson. Berkeley: University of California Press, 1999.

De Baroncelli, Jean. "'Lancelot du lac,' de Robert Bresson." *Le monde*, September 26, 1974, 15.

Debrix, Jean R. "Bilan 1950." *Glanes: Cahiers de l'amitié franco-néerlandaise* 18 (May–June 1951): 8–13.

De Gouvion Saint-Cyr, Agnès, Jean-Claude Lemagny, and Alain Sayag. *Art or Nature: Twentieth Century French Photography.* London: Trefoil Publications, 1988.

De la Varende, Jean. "Cinémagrée." *Glanes: Cahiers de l'amitié franco-néerlandaise* 18 (May–June 1951): 19–23.

De la Torre Giménez, Estrella. "Les essais cinématographiques de René Magritte." *Mélusine* 24, Special Issue on "Le cinéma des surréalists" (2004): 125–135.

Deleuze, Gilles. *Cinema 1: The Movement-Image.* Translated by Hugh Tomlinson and Barbara Habberjam. Minneapolis: University of Minnesota Press, 2003.

———. *Francis Bacon: Logique de la sensation.* Paris: Éditions de la Différence, 1994.

Denoyelle, Françoise. "Photographie et publicité, les promesses d'un art nouveau (1919–1939)." In *La photographie publicitaire en France: De Man Ray à Jean-Paul Goude*, 9–25. Paris: Les arts décoratifs, 2006.

Devigny, André. *Un condamné à mort.* Paris: Gallimard, 1956.

"Dictionnaire des mots retrouvés du cinéma." *Positif* 3.22 (March 1957): 33–34.

Dixon, Wheeler Winston. *The Early Film Criticism of François Truffaut*. Bloomington: Indiana University Press, 1993.

Doncoeur, Paul. "Le *'Journal d'un curé de campagne'* à l'écran." *Études religieuses* 286 (January–March 1951): 384–388.

Doniol-Valcroze, Jacques. "Le triomphe d'une bonne intention: *Citizen Kane*." *La revue du cinéma* 1 (October 1946): 68–69.

———. "Naissance du véritable ciné-oeil." *La revue du cinéma* 4 (January 1, 1947): 25–29.

———. "Les yeux ouverts," *Gazette du cinéma* 5 (November 1950): 3.

———. "Problèmes et prospects du cinéma français." *Cahiers du cinéma* 41 (December 1954): 48–51.

Donkin, Hazel. *Surrealism, Photography and the Periodical Press: An Investigation into the Use of Photography in Surrealist Publications (1924–1969)*. PhD Diss., University of Northumbria at Newcastle, 2009.

Dorléac, Laurent Bertrand. *The Art of the Defeat: France, 1940–1944*. Translated by Jane Marie Todd. Los Angeles: The Getty Research Institute, 2008.

Douchet, Jean. "Pour moi le cinéma est mouvement intérieur." *Gazette du cinéma* 2 (June 1950): 1.

———. "Bresson on Location." *Sequence* 13 (1951): 6–8.

Dumesnil, René. "Sur le rythme musical," *Mercure de France*, November 16, 1919, 231–254.

———. *Le rythme musical, essai historique et critique* [1921]. Paris: La Colombe, 1949.

———. "Musique et cinéma," *Mercure de France*, October 15, 1933, 454–458.

D'Yvoire, Jean. "Feu d'humanisme." *Téléciné* 42 (August 1954).

———. "Si Versailles m'eut été mieux conté." *Téléciné* 42 (August 1954).

"Éditorial (à propos d'une avant-garde nouvelle)." *La revue du cinéma* 7 (Summer 1947): 3–11.

Editors. "À la recherché d'une avant-garde." *L'âge du cinéma* 1 (March 1951): 2.

Editors. "Réalismes." *Positif* 5 (December 1952): 1.

Ehrenstein, David. "Bresson et Cukor, Histoire d'un correspondence." Translated by Michelle Herpe-Voslinsky. *Positif* 430 (December 1996): 103.

———. "Pretty Young Thing." *Film Comment* 45.6 (November–December 2009): 50–53.

Ehrlich, Evelyn. *Cinema of Paradox: French Filmmaking Under the German Occupation*. New York: Columbia University Press, 1985.

"En deux mots." *Radio-cinéma-télévision*, January 29, 1950, 6.

"Entretien avec Robert Bresson." *L'express*, (December 23, 1959), 38–39.

"Entretien avec Robert Bresson." *Unifrance film* 45 December 1957: 1–3.

Erlanger, Philippe. "La recherche de la qualité: Cannes 1946." *La revue du cinéma* 1 (October 1946): 76–77.

Estang, Luc. Review of *Les dames du bois de Boulogne*. *Les étoiles*, (October 2, 1945).

Estève, Michel, ed. *Jeanne d'Arc à l'écran*. Special Issue of *La revue des lettres modernes* 71–73, 1962.

———. *Robert Bresson*. Paris: Éditions Seghers, 1962.

———. *Robert Bresson: La passion de la cinématographe*. Paris: Éditions Albatros, 1983.

Farber, Manny. "New York Film Festival, 1969." In *Negative Space: Manny Farber on the Movies*, 241–245. New York: Praeger, 1971.

Fargue, Léon-Paul. "Salut à la publicité." *Arts et métiers graphiques* 45 (February 15, 1935): 5–7.

Faure, Elies. *Histoire de l'art: L'esprit des formes.* Paris: Les éditions G. Crès, 1927.

Festival du film maudit Catalogue. Paris: Éditions Mazarine, 1949.

Fieschi, Jacques. "Entretiens: Robert Bresson." *Cinématographe* 29 (July–August 1977): 28–30.

F.L.E.C.C. "L'enseignement scolaire du 7e art." *Téléciné* 90 (July–August 1960).

Flot, Yonnick. Interview with Albina du Boisrouvray. In *Les producteurs: Les risques d'un métier*, 27–39. Paris: Hatier, 1986.

Ford, Charles. "Pour Christian-Jaque, virtuose de la caméra, cinéma est synonyme de mouvement." *Radio-cinéma-télévision*, June 25, 1950, 8.

Fortin, Olivier. "Les élites culturelles et la diffusion du cinéma italien en France de 1945 aux années 1970." *Rives méditerranéennes* 32–33 (2009): 153–170. http://rives.revues.org/2960 (December 22, 2010).

Foucault, Michel. "What is an Author?" In *The Foucault Reader*, edited by Paul Rabinow, 101–120. New York, Pantheon Books, 1984.

Fraisse, Paul. "Études sur la mémoire immédiate, II: Le reproduction des formes rythmiques." *L'année psychologique* 43–44 (1942): 103–143.

———. *Les structures rhythmiques.* Louvain, Belgium: Publications universitaires de Louvain, 1956.

———. *La psychologie du temps.* Vendôme: Presses universitaires de France, 1957.

———. *Psychologie du rhythme.* Vendôme: Presses universitaires de France, 1974.

Frank, Nino. "Un art indompté?" *Pour vous*, June 21, 1934, 2.

Gabaston, Pierre. *Pickpocket de Robert Bresson.* Crisnée, Belgium: Yellow Now, 1990.

Gargiani, Roberto. *Paris: Architektur Zwischen Purismus Und Beaux-Arts, 1919–1939.* Wiesbaden, Germany: Vieweg+Teubner Verlag, 1992.

Garrigou-Lagrange, Madeleine. Analysis of *Procès de Jeanne d'Arc.* *Téléciné* 12 (October 1963).

Gastaut, Amélie. *Le film d'animation publicitaire en France, 1912–2007.* Paris: Chalet pointu, 2007.

Gauteur, Claude, ed. *Théâtre et cinéma: L'acteur.* Special Issue of *Études cinématographiques* 14–15 (Spring 1962).

Gendron, Bernard. *Between Montmartre and the Mudd Club: Popular Music and the Avant-Garde.* Chicago: University of Chicago Press, 2002.

Gerard, Lillian. "A Trio of Footnotes on L'Affaire 'Priest:' Letter to the Editor." *New York Times*, May 9, 1954, X3.

Gerstner, David, and Janet Staiger, ed. *Authorship and Film.* New York: Routledge, 2003.

George, G.-L. "Un jeune premier: Paul Bernard." *Pour vous*, May 24, 1934, 7, 14.

Ghyka, Matila. *Essai sur le rythme.* Paris: Gallimard, 1938.

———. *Essai sur le rythme*, 11th ed. Paris, Gallimard, 1952.

Gidel, Heny. *Coco Chanel: Biographie.* Paris: Flammarion, 2000.

Gili, Jean-Antoine, and Francesco Rosi. *Cinéma et pouvoir.* Paris: Le Cerf, 1977.

Gilson, Paul. "'Les Affaires publiques:' Film d'actualités imaginaires." *Pour vous*, August 30, 1934, 11.

Gimello-Mesplomb, Frédéric. "Le prix de la qualité: L'état et le cinéma français (1960–1965)." *Politix* 61 (2003): 95–122.

———. "The Economy of 1950s Popular French Cinema." *Studies in French Cinema* 6.2 (2006): 141–150.

———. *Objectif 49: Cocteau et la nouvelle avant-garde*. Paris: Séguier, 2014.

Giraudoux, Jean. *Le film de Béthanie*. Paris: Gallimard, 1944.

Godard, Jean-Luc. "Dictionary of French Filmmakers." In *Godard on Godard*, translated and edited by Tom Milne, 47–48. New York: Da Capo Press, 1972.

———. *Jean-Luc Godard sur Jean-Luc Godard*. Paris: Cahiers du cinéma/Éditions de l'étoile, 1985.

Gombrich, Ernst. "The Logic of Vanity Fair." In *The Philosophy of Karl Popper*, edited by Paul A. Schlipp, 925–957. La Salle, IL: Open Court, 1974.

———. "Michelangelo's Last Paintings." In *Reflections on the History of Art*, ed. Richard Woodfield, 81–90. Berkeley: University of California Press, 1987.

Gourmelen, Armand. "Le 'Festival du Film Maudit' et le 'Rendez-Vous de Biarritz' (Biarritz, 1949 et 1950)." *1895* 29 (December 1999): 105–126.

Gray, Jonathan, and Derek Johnson, ed. *A Companion to Media Authorship*. Malden, MA: Wiley-Blackwell, 2013.

Green, Julien. "En travaillant avec Robert Bresson." *Cahiers du cinéma* 50 (August–September 1955): 18–23.

Grodal, Torben, Bente Larsen, and Iben Thorving Laursen, ed. *Visual Authorship: Creativity and Intentionality in Media*. Copenhagen: Museum Tusculanum Press, 2005.

Guido, Laurent. *L'âge du rythme: Cinéma, musicalité et culture du corps dans les théories françaises des années 1910–1930*. Lausanne: Payot, 2007.

Guitry, Sacha. "Les anges du péché." In *Le cinéma et moi*, 91. Paris: Éditions Ramsay, 1977.

Guth, Paul. *Autour des dames du bois de Boulogne*. Paris: Juillard, 1945.

Hammond, Paul. *L'âge d'or*. London: British Film Institute, 1997.

Hanlon, Lindley. "The 'Seen' and the 'Said:' Bresson's *Une femme douce* (1969)." In *Modern European Filmmakers and the Art of Adaptation*, edited by Andrew Horton and Joan Magretta, 158–172. New York: Frederick Ungar, 1981.

———. *Fragments: Bresson's Film Style*. Toronto: Associated University Presses, 1986.

Hayette des Fontaines, André. "Une réponse à Marcel L'Herbier." *Combat*, February 14, 1955.

Hayman, Ronald. "Robert Bresson in Conversation with Ronald Hayman." *Transatlantic Review* 46–47 (Summer 1972), http://www.mastersofcinema.org /bresson/ Words/Trans AtlanticReview.html (April 12, 2008).

Hayward, Susan. *French Costume Drama of the 1950s: Fashioning Politics in Film*. Bristol: Intellect, 2010.

Herubel, Michel. "Robert Bresson au travail." *Le figaro littéraire*, May 19, 1963, 21.

Hourigan, Jonathan. "On Two Deaths and Three Births: The Cinematography of Robert Bresson." *Stills* 3 (Autumn 1981): 27–38.

Hommage à Georges Bernanos et débat sur le film "Journal d'un curé de campagne." Paris: Centre catholique des intellectuels français, 1951.

Huisman, Georges. "À propos de quatre films récents." *Glanes: Cahiers de l'amitié franco-néerlandaise* 18 (May–June 1951): 14–18.

Jackson, Jeffrey H. *Making Jazz French: Music and Modern Life in Interwar Paris*. Durham, NC: Duke University Press, 2003.

Jacob, Guy. "Température du néo-réalisme." *Positif* 5 (December 1952): 14–18.
Jacobs, Lea. *Film Rhythm After Sound: Technology, Music, and Performance.* Berkeley: University of California Press, 2015.
Jahier, Valéry. "Le cinéma et l'argent." *Esprit* 25 (October 1, 1934): 89–107.
———. "*Angèle.*" *Esprit* 27 (December 1, 1934): 499–501.
Janne, Henriette. "À Épinay Cette Semaine . . ." *Ciné-Magazine*, July 26, 1934.
Jay, Martin. "Modernism and the Specter of Psychologism." *Modernism/Modernity* 3.2 (1996): 93–111.
Jeancolas, Jean-Pierre, Jean-Jacques Meusy, and Vincent Pinel. *L'auteur du film: Description d'un combat.* Lyon: Institut Lumières/Actes Sud, 1996.
Johnson, Paul. *The Intellectuals.* New York: Harper & Row, 1988.
Jones, Kent. *L'Argent.* London: British Film Institute, 2000.
———. "Robert Bresson." In *The Films of Robert Bresson*, ed. Bert Cardullo, 1–3. London: Anthem Press, 2009.
———. "Bresson." *Senses of Cinema* 7, June 2000, http://archive.sensesofcinema.com /contents/cteq/00/7/bresson.html (January 2010).
Jurt, Joseph. *La réception de la littérature par la critique journalistique: Lectures de Bernanos, 1926–1936.* Paris: Éditions Jean-Michel Place, 1980.
Keating, Patrick. *Hollywood Lighting from the Silent Era to Film Noir.* New York: Columbia University Press, 2010.
Keim, Jean. *Un nouvel art: Le cinéma sonore.* Paris: Éditions Albin Michel, 1947.
Kerslake, Christian. *Immanence and the Vertigo of Philosophy: From Kant to Deleuze.* Edinburgh: Edinburgh University Press, 2009.
Key, Margaret. *Truth from a Lie: Documentary, Detection, and Reflexivity in Abe Kobo's Realist Project.* Plymouth, UK: Lexington Books, 2011.
Kovács, András Bálint. *Screening Modernism: European Art Cinema, 1950–1980.* Chicago: University of Chicago Press, 2007.
Kovacs, Yves. "Entretien avec Robert Bresson." *Cahiers du cinéma* 140 (February 1963): 4–10.
Kristeva, Julia. *La révolution du langage poétique: L'avant-garde à la fin du XIXe siècle, Lautréamont et Mallarmé.* Paris, Seuil, 1974.
Kyrou, Ado. "Le cinéma n'a pas besoin de dieu." *L'âge du cinéma* 1 (March 1951): 25–26.
Labanyi, Jo. "The Politics of the Everyday and the Eternity of Ruins: Two Women Photographers in Republican Spain." In *Cultural Encounters: European Travel Writing in the 1930s*, ed. Charles Burdett and Derek Duncan, 85–104. New York: Berghahn Books, 2002.
Laboratoire de recherche historique Rhône-Alpes/Institut des sciences de l'homme. "Institutions: Thomas et Gibbs." *Système d'information: patrons et patronat français, XIXe-XXe siècles*, http://sippaf.ish-lyon.cnrs.fr/Database/Institutions _fr.php?ID=IN000007539 (September 29, 2009).
Lacombe, Alain, and François Procile. *Les musiques du cinéma français.* Paris: Bordas, 1995.
Langdale, Allan. "Interview with Michael Baxandall, February 3rd, 1994, Berkeley, California." *Journal of Art Historiography* 1 (December 2009): 1–31.
Langlois, Henri. "L'avant-garde d'hier et d'aujourd'hui." *La revue du cinéma* 11 (March 1948): 43–50.

Larcher, Jérôme. *"Ce que l'on voit dans la caméra: Entretien avec Emmanuel Machuel."* *Cahiers du cinéma: Hommage Robert Bresson* (February 2000): 15–17.

Latil-Le Dantec, Mireille. *"L'argent."* *Cinématographe* 90 (June 1983): 8–12.

Latour, Bruno. *Reassembling the Social: An Introduction to Actor-Network-Theory.* Oxford: Oxford University Press, 2005.

Leenhardt, Roger. "À propos des films burlesques." *Esprit* 27 (December 1, 1934): 494–499.

———. *Les yeux ouverts: Entretiens avec Jacques Lacouture.* Paris: Éditions du seuil, 1979.

———. *Chroniques du cinéma.* Paris: Éditions Cahiers du cinéma, 1986.

Lefebvre, Henri. *Élément du rythmanalyse: Introduction à la connaissance des rythmes.* Paris: Syllepse, 1992.

———. *Rhythmanalysis: Space, Time and Everyday Life.* Translated by Stuart Elden and Gerald Moore. New York: Continuum, 2007.

Lefebvre, Martin. "L'aventure filmologique: Documents et jalons d'une histoire institutionelle." *Cinémas: Revue d'études cinématographiques* 19.2–3 (Spring 2009): 59–93.

Leglise, Paul. *Histoire de la politique du cinéma français, tome I: Le cinéma et la IIIe république.* Paris: Librairie générale de droit et de jurisprudence, 1970.

Lelong, Michel. *Les dominicaines des prisons (Béthanie).* Paris: Éditions du cerf, 1938.

"Léonce-Henry Burel." *Cinéma 77* 221 (May 1977): 125–126.

Leprohon, Pierre. *Les mille et un métiers du cinéma.* Paris: Éditions Jacques Melot, 1947.

———. "Dans un château d'Artois, d'après l'œuvre de Bernanos, Robert Bresson tourne Le Journal . . ." *Radio-cinéma-télévision,* April 9, 1950, 8.

Leterrier, François. "Philosophe de métier, vedette de fortune." *Le nef* (December 1956): 47–48.

———. "Robert Bresson l'insaisissable." *Cahiers du cinéma* 66 (December 1966): 34–36.

L'Herbier, Marcel, ed. *Intelligence du cinématographe.* Paris: Éditions Corréa, 1946.

———. "Chéri-Bibi contre la princesse de Clèves." *Combat,* February 14, 1955.

Lherminier, Pierre, ed. *L'art du cinéma.* Paris: Éditions Seghers, 1960.

Lhote, Jean-Marie. "À propos de . . . *Si Versailles m'était conté.*" *Téléciné* 42 (August 1954).

Lindeperg, Sylvie. *Les écrans de l'ombre: La seconde guerre mondiale dans le cinéma français (1944–1969).* Paris: Éditions CNRS, 1997.

Lindley, Elizabeth, and Laura McMahon, ed. *Rhythm: Essays in French Literature, Thought and Culture.* Bern: Peter Lang, 2008.

Lo Duca, Joseph-Marie. "Septième art, dixième muse." *La revue du cinéma* 3 (December 1946): 39–44.

Mac Orlan, Pierre. "Graphisme." *Arts et métiers graphiques* 11 (May 15, 1929): 645–653.

Magny, Claude-Édmonde. *L'âge du roman américain.* Paris: Éditions du seuil, 1948.

Malraux, André. "Préface." In *S.O.S. Indochine,* by Andreé Viollis, vii-xi. Paris: Gallimard, 1935.

Marchaudiau, Jean-Noël. *L'illustration 1843–1944: Vie et mort d'un journal.* Toulouse: Éditions Privat, 1987.

Marion, Denis, ed. *Le cinéma par ceux qui le font.* Paris: Librairie Arthème Fayard, 1949.

———. "Les adaptations." In *Almanach du théâtre et du cinéma,* edited by Jean Cocteau, 132–137. Paris: Éditions du Flore, 1949.

Marroncle, Jeannine. Analysis of *La vérité sur bébé Donge*. *Téléciné* 32–33 (1952).

Marroncle, Jeannine, and G. Marroncle. Analysis of *Le cas du docteur Laurent*. *Téléciné* 66 (June 1957).

Martin, Adrian. *Mise en Scène and Film Style: From Classical Hollywood to New Media Art*. New York: Palgrave Macmillan, 2014.

Martin, Marcel. *Le langage cinématographique*. Paris: Éditions du cerf, 1962.

———. "Rencontre, à propos de l'évolution esthétique de l'image, avec Philippe Agostini." *Cinéma pratique* 147 (August–September 1976): 146–149.

Mary, Philippe. *La nouvelle vague et le cinéma d'auteur: Socio-analyse d'une révolution artistique*. Paris: Éditions du seuil, 2006.

Matthews, Herbert. "Paris Views New Films and Theatres." *New York Times*, January, 15, 1933, X4.

Mauriac, Claude. "Le premier film de la vie intérieure: *Journal d'un curé de campagne*." *Le figaro littéraire*, February 10, 1951, 15.

———. "Le nouveau Bresson." *Le figaro littéraire*, November 17, 1956, 14.

———. *Petite littérature du cinéma*. Paris: Éditions du cerf, 1957.

Mauss, Marcel. *The Gift: The Form and Reason for Exchange in Archaic Societies*. Translated by W. D. Halls. London: Routledge, 1990.

McCole, John. *Walter Benjamin and the Antinomies of Tradition*. Ithaca, NY: Cornell University Press, 1993.

Mellers, Wilfrid. "Jean Wiener Redivivus." *Tempo* 170 (September 1989): 24–29.

Meschonnic, Henri. *Critique du rythme: Anthropologie historique du langage*. Paris: Verdier, 1982.

———. "The Rhythm Party Manifesto" (translated by David Nowell-Smith). *Thinking Verse* 1 (2011): 161–173.

Metz, Christian. *Language and Cinema*. Translated by Donna Jean Umiker-Sebeok. The Hague: Mouton & Co. N.V., 1974.

Michaels, Lloyd. *Terrence Malick*. Urbana: University of Illinois Press, 2009.

Millan, Juan Antonio Perez. *Pasqualino de Santis: El esplendor en la penumbra*. Valladolid: Semana internacional de cine, 1993.

Mitry, Jean. "Le montage: Naissance historique." *Technicien du film* 22 (November 1956): 4.

———. "Le montage: Les différentes conceptions du montage selon Eisenstein." *Technicien du film* 26 (March 1957): 12–13.

———. *Esthétique et psychologie du cinéma, tome I: Les structures*. Paris: Éditions universitaires, 1963.

———. *Esthétique et psychologie du cinéma, tome II: Les formes*. Paris: Éditions universitaires, 1965.

———. *The Aesthetics and Psychology of the Cinema*. Translated by Christopher King. Bloomington: Indiana University Press, 1997.

Monod, Roland. "En travaillant avec Robert Bresson." *Cahiers du cinéma* 64 (November 1956): 16–20.

Montbrun, Daniel. Analysis of *Les sorcières de Salem*. *Téléciné* 66 (June 1957).

Moreau, Jean-Guy. "Allô Bresson? J'ai un petit prêtre pour toi." *Radio-cinéma-télévision*, February 11, 1951.

Morgan, Daniel. "Rethinking Bazin: Ontology and Realist Aesthetics." *Critical Inquiry* 32.3 (Spring 2006): 443–481.

Mortier, Michel. Analysis of *Mouchette*. *Téléciné* 134 (August–September 1967).

Moussinac, Léon. *L'âge ingrat du cinéma*. Paris: Éditions du sagittaire, 1946.

Neupert, Richard. *A History of French New Wave Cinema* [2002]. 2nd ed. Madison: University of Wisconsin Press, 2007.

Noel, J.-P. Analysis of *Nous sommes tous des assassins*. *Téléciné* 35 (1953).

O'Brien, Charles. "Stylistic Description as Historical Method: French Films of the German Occupation." *Style* 32.3 (Fall 1998): 429–451.

———. *Cinema's Conversion to Sound: Film Style and Technology in France and the U.S.* Bloomington: Indiana University Press, 2005.

O'Neill, Rosemary. *Art and Visual Culture on the French Riviera, 1956–1971: The École de Nice*. Burlington, VT: Ashgate, 2012.

Ostrowska, Dorota. *Reading the French New Wave: Critics, Writers and Art Cinema in France*. New York: Wallflower Press, 2008.

Palmer, Tim. *Brutal Intimacy: Analyzing Contemporary French Cinema*. Middletown, CT: Wesleyan University Press, 2011.

Pechel, Irving. "La création doit être l'ouvrage seul." *La revue du cinéma* 2 (November 1946): 54–61.

Pélégri, Jean. "Robert Bresson ou la fascination." *Les lettres françaises*, December 31, 1959, 1, 4.

Pena, José. Analysis of *Au hasard Balthazar*. *Téléciné* 133 (February–March 1967).

Penrose, Antony. *Roland Penrose: The Friendly Surrealist*. London: Prestel, 2001.

Penrose, Roland. *Scrap Book, 1900–1981*. London: Thames and Hudson, 1981.

Photographie 1932. Special Issue of *Arts et métiers graphiques* (August 25, 1932).

Pickering, Robert. "'Tes pas . . . procèdent': Melos, marche, méditations dans les promenades de Rousseau et de Valéry." In *Paul Valéry: Musique, Mystique, Mathématique*, ed. Paul Gifford and Brian Stimpson, 95–112. Lille: Presses universitaires de Lille, 1993.

Piéron, Henri. *La sensation, guide de vie*. Paris: Gallimard, 1945.

Piette, Alain and Bert Cardullo. *The Crommelynck Mystery: The Life and Work of a Belgian Playwright*. Selinsgrove, PA: Susquehanna University Press; London: Associated University Presses, 1997.

Pillard, Thomas. "Cinéphilie populaire et usages sociaux du cinéma dans les années 1950: Le courrier des lecteurs du *Film complèt* (1949–1958)." *Studies in French Cinema* 15.1 (2015): 69–87.

Pinel, Vincent. *Le réalisateur de films face à son interprète*. Paris: Institut des hautes études cinématographiques, 1961.

———. *Introduction au ciné-club: Histoire, théorie et pratique du ciné-club en France*. Paris: Éditions ouvrières, 1964.

———. "*Les Affaires publiques*: Interview de Robert Bresson." In *Le cinématographe de Robert Bresson*, 97. Tokyo: Tokyo International Foundation for Promotion of Screen Image Culture, 1999.

Pipolo, Tony. "Fire and Ice: The Films of Robert Bresson." *Cineaste* 31.2 (Spring 2006): 22–27.

———. *Robert Bresson: A Passion for Film*. New York: Oxford University Press, 2010.

Plot, Bernadette. *Un manifeste pour le cinéma: Les normes culturelles en question dans la première Revue du cinéma*. Paris: L'Harmattan, 1996.

Poiré, Alain. *200 films au soleil*. Paris: Édition Ramsay, 1988.

Powel, Pete and Gretchen. *New York, 1929*. Paris: Black Sun Press, 1930.

Prédal, René. "Les grands opérateurs: Léonce Henri Burel." *Cinéma 72* 168 (July–August 1972): 107–113.

———. "Léonce H. Burel." *Cinéma 74* 189 (July–August 1974): 104–108.

———. *80 ans de cinéma français: Nice et le 7ième art.* Nice: Éditions Serre, 1980.

———. *Robert Bresson: L'aventure intérieure.* Special Issue of *L'avant-scène cinéma* 408–409 (1992).

Prédal, René., and L. H. Burel. *Souvenirs de L.H. Burel.* Paris: Avant-scène, 1975.

"The Press: Where is the Tra-La-Lo?" *Time,* February 9, 1948, http://www.time.com/time/magazine/article/0,9171,856016,00.html (December 2009).

Price, Brian. "*Une Femme douce* and the Spectrum of Revolt: Bresson's Transition to Color in the Aftermath of May '68." *Framework* 43.1 (Spring 2002): 127–160.

———. "The End of Transcendence, the Mourning of Crime: Bresson's Hands." *Studies in French Cinema* 2.3 (2002): 127–135.

———. *Neither God Nor Master: Robert Bresson.* Minneapolis: University of Minnesota Press, 2011.

Problèmes économiques du cinéma européen. Special Issue of *Téléciné* 32–33 (1952).

Provoyeur, Jean-Louis. *Le cinéma de Robert Bresson: De l'effet réel à l'effet de sublime.* Paris: L'Harmattan, 2003.

Quandt, James, ed. *Robert Bresson.* Toronto: Cinematheque Ontario, 1998.

———, ed. *Robert Bresson (Revised).* Toronto: TIFF, 2012.

"Quelques statistiques." *Cahiers du cinéma* 71 (May 1957): 78–84.

"Qu'est-ce que la 'Défense du cinéma français'?" *L'écran français,* October 23, 1950, 11–14.

Queval, Jacques. "Three French Histories of Film." *Hollywood Quarterly* 3.4 (Summer 1948): 454–456.

Queval, Jean. "Dialogue avec Robert Bresson." *L'écran français,* November 12, 1946, 12.

———. "Au temps du muet le cinéma russe a inventé le film social." *Radio-cinéma-télévision,* June 4, 1950, 9.

———. "Le cinéma contre la société." *Glanes: Cahiers hollandaise du mercure de France* 29 (May–June 1953): 25–38.

———. Analysis of *Portes de lilas. Téléciné* 70–71 (November/December 1957).

Rajewsky, Irina O. "Intermediality, Intertextuality, and Remediation: A Literary Perspective on Intermediality. " *Intermédialités* 6 (Autumn 2005): 43–64.

Ramirez, Francis, and Christian Rolot. "Fautes exemplaire: Marcel Pagnol." *Cinémathèque* 16 (1999): 69–79.

Rancière, Jacques. *Film Fables.* Translated by Emiliano Battista. New York: Berg, 2006.

Reader, Keith. *Robert Bresson.* Manchester: Manchester University Press, 2000.

Reed, Muriel. "Robert Bresson, le janséniste du cinéma." *Réalités* 143 (1957): 80–87.

Régent, Roger. *Cinéma de France* (Paris: Bellefaye, 1948).

———. "Notes et remarques sur le cinéma français en 1951." *Glanes: Cahiers de l'amitié franco-néerlandaise* 18 (May–June 1951): 33–39.

Remond, Claude. "Les ciné-clubs en France." *Glanes: Cahiers de l'amitié franco-néerlandaise* 18 (May–June 1951): 40–47.

Revault D'Allonnes, Fabrice. *La lumière au cinéma.* Paris: Éditions Cahiers du cinéma, 1991.

Rhodes, John David. *Stupendous Miserable City, Pasolini's Rome.* Minneapolis: University of Minnesota Press, 2007.

Riding, Alan. "Robert Bresson, Film Director, Dies at 98." *New York Times,* December 22, 1999, C27.

Rifkin, Adrian, ed. *About Michael Baxandall*. Malden, MA: Blackwell Publishers, 1999.

Robbins, Bruce, ed. *Intellectuals: Aesthetics, Politics and Academics*. Minneapolis: University of Minnesota Press, 1990.

Rosenbaum, Jonathan. "Robert Bresson's *Affaires Publiques*," *JonathanRosenbaum.net* (18 July 1999), http://www.jonathanrosenbaum.net/1999/07/robert-bressons -affaires-publiques-tk/ (July 29, 2015).

———. "Defending Bresson." *Chicago Reader*, April 1, 2004, http://www.chicagoreader .com/chicago/defending-bresson/Content?oid=915048 (January 23, 2010).

———. Review of Tony Pipolo's *Robert Bresson: A Passion for Film*. *Cineaste* 35.3 (Summer 2010): 59–60.

Roque, Georges. "The Surrealist (Sub-)Version of Advertising." In *Surreal Things: Surrealism and Design*, edited by Ghislaine Wood, 161–175. London: V&A Publications, 2007.

Roy, Jean. *Le groupe des Six*. Paris: Seuil, 1994.

Roy, Jules. "J'ai vu Robert Bresson tourner au Fort Montluc." *Le figaro littéraire*, July 14, 1956, 7.

Sadoul, Georges. "Le néo-réalisme américain?" *Les lettres françaises*, September 30, 1948.

———. "Une nouvelle avant-garde," *Les lettres françaises*, May 19, 1949.

———. "Néo-réalisme américain: *La dernière rafale*." *Les lettres françaises*, August 18, 1949.

———. "Naturalisme descriptif." *Les lettres françaises*, October 13, 1949.

———. *Histoire de l'art du cinéma*. Paris: Flammarion, 1949.

———. "Quelques aspects du cinéma soviétique." *Positif* 5 (December 1952): 2–10.

———. "Délit et châtiment." *Les lettres françaises*, December 24, 1959, 7.

———. "Bresson, au sommet de son art." *Les lettres françaises*, May 24, 1962, 10.

———. "Le langage du film: Cinéaste, mot français créé le 27 mai 1921." *Les lettres françaises*, February 28, 1963, 8.

———. "Robert Bresson à Georges Sadoul: 'Si l'on veut que passe le courant électrique, il faut dénuder les fils . . .'" *Les lettres françaises*, March 7, 1963, 1, 9.

Salachas, Gilbert. "Notes brèves sur quelques films: *Monsieur Ripois*." *Téléciné* 42 (August 1954).

———. "Notes brèves sur quelques films: *Touchez pas au grisbi*." *Téléciné* 42 (August 1954).

———. Analysis of *Celui qui doit mourir*. *Téléciné* 66 (June 1957).

———. "Remarques sur la fiche de Jean Queval." *Téléciné* 70–71 (November–December 1957).

Salachas, Gilbert, and Jean Collet. "Les quatorze films du festival vénitien 1956." *Téléciné* 60 (October 1956).

Salt, Barry. *Film Style and Technology: History and Analysis*. 2nd ed. London: Starword, 1992.

Samuels, Charles Thomas. "Robert Bresson." In *Encountering Directors*, 57–76. New York: G. P. Putnam & Sons, 1972.

Sarris, Andrew. *American Cinema: Directors and Directions, 1929–1968*. New York: E. P. Dutton & Co., 1968.

Sartre, Jean-Paul. "François Mauriac and Freedom." In *Literary and Philosophical Essays*, translated by Annette Michelson, 7–25. New York: Collier Books, 1962.

——. *The Writings of Jean-Paul Sartre*, edited by Michel Contant and Michel Rybalka and translated by Richard C. McCleary. Evanston, IL: Northwestern University Press, 1974.

——. *"Citizen Kane"* (translated by Dana Polan). *Post Script: Essays in Film and the Humanities* 7.1 (Fall 1987): 60–65.

Schaeffer, Pierre. "L'élément non visual au cinéma I." *La revue du cinéma* 1 (October 1946): 45–48.

——. "L'élément non visual au cinéma II: Conception de la musique." *La revue du cinéma* 2 (November 1946): 62–65.

——. "L'élément non visual au cinéma III: Psychologie du rapport vision-audition." *La revue du cinéma* 3 (December 1946): 51–54.

——. "L'élément non visual au cinéma." In *La revue du cinéma, anthologie.* 459–477. Paris: Gallimard, 1992.

Schrader, Paul. *Transcendental Style in Film: Ozu, Bresson, Dreyer.* New York: Da Capo Press, 1972.

Schwartz, Vanessa. *It's So French! Hollywood, Paris, and the Making of Cosmopolitan Film Culture.* Chicago: University of Chicago Press, 2007.

Segond, Joseph. "Rythme inhérent au film." *Revue internationale de filmologie* 2 (September–October 1947): 159–160.

Sellier, Geneviève. *Masculine Singular: French New Wave Cinema.* Translated by Kristin Ross. Durham, NC: Duke University Press, 2008.

——. "Éditorial: Le cinéma populaire et ses usages dans la France d'après-guerre." *Studies in French Cinema* 15.1 (2015): 1–10.

Sémolué, Jean. *Bresson.* Paris: Éditions universitaires, 1959.

——. Analysis of *Quatre nuits d'un rêveur. Téléciné* 173 (October-November 1971).

——. Analysis of *Lancelot du lac. Téléciné* 191–192 (September-October 1974).

——. *Bresson ou l'acte pur des métamorphoses.* Paris: Flammarion, 1993.

Servien, Pius. *Les rythmes comme introduction physique à l'esthétique.* Paris: Bibliothèque de la revue des cours et conférences, 1930.

"Six personnages en quête d'auteurs: Débat sur le cinéma français." *Cahiers du cinéma* 71 (May 1957): 17–29, 90.

Sloan, Jane. *Robert Bresson: A Guide to Sources and References.* Boston: G. K. Hall & Co., 1983.

Smith, Alison. *Agnès Varda.* Manchester: Manchester University Press, 1998.

——. *French Cinema of the 1970s: The Echoes of May.* Manchester: Manchester University Press, 2005.

Solanas, Fernando and Octavio Gettino. "Towards a Third Cinema." In *Movies and Methods: An Anthology*, vol. 1, ed. Bill Nichols, 44–63. Berkeley: University of California Press, 1976.

Sontag, Susan. "Spiritual Style in the Films of Robert Bresson." In *Against Interpretation*, 177–195. Toronto: Doubleday, 1990.

Souriau, Étienne, ed. *L'univers filmique.* Paris: Flammarion, 1953.

Spaak, Charles. "Introduction: Le cinéma français." *Glanes: Cahiers de l'amitié franco-néerlandaise* 18 (May–June 1951): 5–7.

Survage, Léopold. "Le rythme coloré." *La revue du cinéma* 11 (March 1948): 51–52.

Tacchella, Jean-Charles. "When Jean Cocteau Was President of a Cine-Club: Objectif 49 and the Festival of *Film maudit*." In *Cocteau*, ed. Dominique Païni, 84–87. (London: Paul Holberton, 2003).

Tanner, Jeremy. "Michael Baxandall and the Sociological Interpretation of Art." *Cultural Sociology* 4.2 (July 2010): 231–256.

Taufour, Bernard, Robert Claude, and Victor Bachy. *Panoramique sur le 7e art*. Paris: Éditions universitaires, 1959.

Temple, Michael. "Big Rhythm and the Power of Metamorphosis: Some Models and Precursors for *Histoire(s) du cinema*." In *The Cinema Alone: Essays on the Work of Jean-Luc Godard, 1985–2000*, ed. Michael Temple and James S. Williams, 77–95. Amsterdam: Amsterdam University Press, 2000.

Temple, Michael, and Michael Witt, ed. *The French Cinema Book*. London: British Film Institute, 2004.

Thompson, Kristin. *Breaking the Glass Armor: Neoformalist Film Analysis*. Princeton, NJ: Princeton University Press, 1988.

Thuillier, Pierre. Analysis of *Patrouille de choc*. *Téléciné* 69 (October 1957).

Timmory, François. "Le débat Sadoul-Bazin-plus-public, sur 'l'avant-garde au cinéma,' est devenu 'La bataille de la forme et du fond.'" *L'écran français*, March 15, 1949, 2.

Todd, Olivier. *Camus: A Life*. Translated by Benjamin Ivry. New York: Knopf, 1997.

Toland, Gregg. "L'opérateur de prise de vue." *La revue du cinéma* 4 (January 1, 1947): 16–24.

Tomlinson, Doug. "Performance in the Films of Robert Bresson: The Aesthetics of Denial." In *More Than a Method: Trends and Traditions in Contemporary Film Performance*, edited by Cynthia Baron, Diane Carson and Frank P. Tomasulo, 71–93. Detroit: Wayne State University Press, 2004.

Tournès, Ludovic. *New Orleans sur Seine: Histoire de jazz en France*. Paris: Fayard, 1999.

Tremois, Claude-Marie. Analysis of *Deus sous de violettes*. *Téléciné* 29 (1952).

———. Analysis of *Le voyage en Amérique*. *Téléciné* 32–33 (1952).

———. Analysis of *Gervaise*. *Téléciné* 60 (October 1956).

Truffaut, François. No title. *Elle* 264 (December 18, 1950): 12.

———. "Une crise d'ambition du cinéma français," *Arts*, March 30, 1955, 5.

———. "*Un Condamné à s'est échappé*: Le plus beau film de Bresson." *Arts*, November 15, 1956, 3.

———. "Une certain tendance du cinéma français." *Cahiers du cinéma* 31 (January 1954): 15–29.

———. "Clouzot au travail, ou la règne de la terreur." *Cahiers du cinéma* 77 (December 1957): 18–22.

———. *The Films of My Life*. New York: Simon & Schuster, 1985.

Tual, Denise. *Le temps dévoré*. Paris: Fayard, 1980.

———. *Au coeur du temps*. Paris: Carrère, 1987.

Tylski, Alexandre. "*Entretien avec Emmanuel Machuel*." *Cadrage: La revue du cinéma internationale*, April–May 2003, http://www.cadrage.net/entretiens/machuel /emmanuel .html (November 2004).

Ulf-Møller, Jens. *Hollywood's Film Wars with France: Film-Trade Diplomacy and the Emergence of the French Film Quota Policy*. London: Frank Cass, 2003.

Van Steerthem, Angie. "Jean Cocteau collaborateur de Jean Delannoy pour *La princesse de Clèves*." In *Le revue lettres modernes: Jean Cocteau 5 (Les adaptations)*, edited by Serge Linares, 111–129. Caen: Lettres modernes Minard, 2008.

Vincendeau, Ginette. *The Companion to French Cinema*. London: British Film Institute, 1996.

Vinneuil, François. "Giraudoux au couvent." *Je suis partout*, July 9, 1943, 7.

Vivet, Jean-Pierre. "Le présent et l'avenir du cinéma français I: Claude Autant-Lara, Jean Grémillon." *La revue du cinéma* 6 (Spring 1947): 58–63.

Von Kreustbruck, Vera. "Interview with Tilda Swinton: 'I am Probably a Woman.'" *The Wip* (March 20, 2009), http://thewip.net/2009/03/20/interview-with-actress-tilda-swinton-i-am-probably-a-woman/ (August 20, 2015).

Walter, H. "A Trio of Footnotes on L'Affaire 'Priest:' Pro M. Bresson." *New York Times*, May 9, 1954, X3.

Watkins, Ray. "Robert Bresson's Modernist Canvas: The Gesture Toward Painting in *Au hasard Balthazar*." *Cinema Journal* 51.2 (Winter 2012): 1–25.

Watts, Philip. "Jacques Rivette's Classical Illusion." *Contemporary French and Francophone Studies* 9.3 (September 2005): 291–299.

Wexman, Virginia Wright, ed. *Film and Authorship*. New Brunswick, NJ: Rutgers University Press, 2003.

Wiazemski, Anne. *Jeune fille*. Paris, Gallimard, 2007.

Wiener, Jean. *Allegro appassionato*. Paris: Belfond, 1978.

Williams, Alan. *Republic of Images: A History of French Filmmaking*. Cambridge, MA: Harvard University Press, 1992.

Williams, James S. *Jean Cocteau*. Manchester: Manchester University Press, 2006.

Wimsatt, W. K., and Monroe Beardsley. "The Intentional Fallacy." In *The Verbal Icon: Studies in the Meaning of Poetry*, 2–18. London: Methuen, 1970.

Wolff, Geoffrey. *Black Sun: The Brief Transit and Violent Eclipse of Harry Crosby*. New York: New York Review Books, 2003.

Wolff, Janet. *The Social Production of Art*. New York: New York University Press, 1981.

Wollen, Peter. *Signs and Meaning in the Cinema*. Bloomington: Indiana University Press, 1969.

Index

Note: Page numbers followed by f indicate a figure.

COLIN BURNETT is Assistant Professor of Film and Media Studies at Washington University in Saint Louis. He has published articles in *Film History*, *Transnational Cinema(s)*, *Studies in French Cinema*, *The Journal of American Studies*, and *New Review of Film and Television Studies*, and written essays for *Robert Bresson (Revised)*, *The Routledge Encyclopedia of Film Theory*, *Directory of World Cinema: France*, *A Companion to Media Authorship*, and *Arnheim for Film and Media Studies*. He is currently at work on a second book, titled *Serial Bonds: The Multimedia Life of 007*.

CPSIA information can be obtained
at www.ICGtesting.com
Printed in the USA
LVOW04s1052180117
521378LV00017B/195/P